A
RELIGIOUS
HISTORY
OF
AMERICA

AUTHOR OF

Historical Atlas of Religion in America

❖ ❖ ❖ ❖ ❖ ❖ ❖ ❖ ❖

A
RELIGIOUS
HISTORY
OF
AMERICA

BY
Edwin Scott Gaustad

HARPER & ROW, PUBLISHERS
NEW YORK, EVANSTON, SAN FRANCISCO, LONDON

❖ ❖ ❖ ❖ ❖ ❖ ❖ ❖ ❖

For

SUE, SCOTT & PEG

First Harper & Row paperback edition published in 1974.

LIBRARY OF CONGRESS CATALOG CARD NUMBER: 66-11488

ISBN: 0-06-063093-0

Contents

PART IV   THIS NATION UNDER GOD: AT WORSHIP

List of Quotations

PART III

PART IV

PART V

Acknowledgments

The courtesy of the publishers listed below is gratefully acknowledged; each has kindly granted permission to use materials under its copyright.

ASSOCIATION PRESS
Robert M. Brown et al., *Vietnam: Crisis of Conscience* (1967).

CHRISTIAN CENTURY
April 13, 1960, quoting Martin Luther King.
August 26, 1964, quoting sixteen rabbis.

CHRISTIANITY AND CRISIS
January 24, 1955, quoting Reinhold Niebuhr.
March 31, 1969, quoting Alan Paton.

COLUMBIA UNIVERSITY PRESS
T. F. Hamlin (ed.), *Form and Function in Twentieth Century Architecture* (1952), quoting Max Abramovitz and Maurice Lavanoux.

DOUBLEDAY & COMPANY, INC.
Neil McCluskey, *Catholic Viewpoint on Education* (rev. 1962).
Herman Wouk, *This Is My God* (1959) [with HAROLD MATSON COMPANY, INC.].

FARRAR, STRAUS & GIROUX
Abraham Heschel, *Man Is Not Alone* (1951).
Abraham Heschel, *God Is In Search of Man* (1955).

HARVARD UNIVERSITY PRESS
Nathan Pusey, *The Age of the Scholar* (1963).

MACMILLAN COMPANY
H. E. Fosdick, *Modern Use of the Bible* (1925).
O. E. Winslow, *Meetinghouse Hill 1631–1783* (1952).
Gustave Weigel, *Faith and Understanding in America* (1959).
Gustave Weigel, *The Modern God* (1963).

MCGRAW-HILL BOOK COMPANY
J. K. Shear (ed.), *Religious Buildings for Today* (1957), quoting Otto Spaeth.
Christ-Janer and Foley (eds.), *Modern Church Architecture* (1962), quoting Paul Tillich and Maurice Lavanoux.

NATIONAL CATHOLIC WELFARE CONFERENCE
Providentissimus Deus (1893).
Quadragesimo Anno (1931).
Divino Afflante Spiritu (1943).
Pacem in Terris (1963).
Opening Address, Session 2, Vatican II (1963).

NEW YORK TIMES
    April 2, 1969, column by James Reston.
PRENTICE-HALL, INC.
    Norman Vincent Peale, *The Power of Positive Thinking* (1952).
PRINCETON UNIVERSITY PRESS
    Smith and Jamison (eds.), *The Shaping of American Religion* (1961),
    quoting H. Richard Niebuhr.
RANDOM HOUSE, INC.
    William Faulkner, *The Bear* (1942).
    J. William Fulbright, *The Crippled Giant* (1972).
CHARLES SCRIBNER'S SONS
    Reinhold Niebuhr, *Children of Light and Children of Darkness* (1944).
SIMON AND SCHUSTER, INC.
    Edward R. Murrow (ed.), *This I Believe*, Vols. I and II (1952, 1954),
    quoting William O. Douglas, Edith Hamilton, and Clarence Randall.
TIME, INC.
    Life Magazine, January 8, 1965, quoting Henry Roth.
VIKING PRESS, INC.
    Arthur Miller, *After the Fall*, special preface in *Saturday Evening Post*,
    February 1, 1964.
WESTMINSTER PRESS
    Armstrong, Loetscher, and Anderson (eds.), *Presbyterian Enterprise* (1956),
    quoting David McClure.
WESTMINSTER THEOLOGICAL SEMINARY
    J. G. Machen, *Christian Faith in a Modern World* (1936).
WORLD PUBLISHING COMPANY
    Reinhold Niebuhr, *Leaves from the Notebooks of a Tamed Cynic* (1929).
    Reinhold Niebuhr, *Essays in Applied Christianity* (1959).

List of Illustrations

CHAPTER 17

CHAPTER 18

CHAPTER 19

Preface

SINCE THE PURPOSE OF THIS BOOK is to describe the role of religion in American life, national history more than denominational history is pursued. Instead of the rise and progress of ecclesiastical bodies or the decline and fall of archaic forms, America's own development guides the story: the discovery and settlement of a continent, the birth and growth of a nation, the aim and aspiration of a people.

Like all histories, this one proceeds from a point of view. Among its assumptions are these: (1) in the heritage of America religion's role has always been significant and has often been crucial; (2) examination of that role is as vital and legitimate as is the study of any other aspect of America's past; (3) religious history, while admittedly complex and controversial, cannot be ignored without doing violence to the integrity of the American experience; and (4) controversy and variety enrich rather than impoverish both democracy and the educative process.

Of course, good history—religious or any other kind—must strive for fairness and balance. In searching the records of the past, the historian hears many voices: strident voices, persuasive voices, conflicting and partisan voices, anguished voices. Rather than filter all these through the author's single voice, it seemed preferable to permit the reader to hear many voices too. The temper and testimony of earlier witnesses is therefore presented so that all of us may more readily enter into a mood or a manner that may differ from our own.

In the writing of this book, assistance has come from many sources and in many forms. The writer of history, above all others, can hardly be unaware of his debt to the pilgrims and pioneers of previous scholarship. He also recognizes, with increasing uneasiness, his inability to repay or even adequately to acknowledge that debt. But gratitude must be expressed at least to the Library of Congress for its generous provision of research facilities, to the American Council of Learned Societies for a grant-in-aid, to the University of Redlands (California) for a year of sabbatical leave, to Nelson R. Burr for careful and informed bibliographical assistance, to numerous colleagues in the area of America's religious history for encouragement and direction, and to my wife for sufferance without stint.

E. S. G.

Preface to 1974 Edition

IN THE DECADE THAT HAS PASSED since the writing for the earlier edition was first begun, much has happened both to the American nation and to religion. With respect to the former, a mood of ebullient "New Frontier-ness" has given way to a darker and more skeptical mood regarding the country's role both at home and abroad. Public protest and social divisiveness have often appeared to typify the times as national destiny has, at the very least, become less manifest.

With respect to religion, Vatican II has come and gone, leaving in its wake a great ecclesiastical institution less sure of its destiny or less agreed on the best earthly road toward that destiny. In this same decade, the ecumenical thrust has also come and—almost—gone. Fascination with the Orient, the occult, and the religious commune have come and not yet gone. Theology, having lost its Heschels, Murrays, Niebuhrs, and Tillichs, has not yet rallied around a unifying standard bearer. And church attendance, as well as growth in church membership, appears to have lost a momentum that had been sustained for well over a hundred years.

In the course of a mere decade, then, a rather different America is spoken to by a rather different church. Yet it does not seem possible to discard the assumptions of the earlier preface, even if the mood might be more optative than declarative. Or perhaps the interrogative is best of all—as, for example, in the formulation of James Reston (see p. 348): "If religion was so important in the building of the Republic, how could it be irrelevant to the maintenance of the Republic?"

E.S.G.

PART I

Age of Exploration

1 ❖ The Admiral and the Church

W HEN ONE CROSSES a horizon never before traversed, he not only sees a new world, he creates one. This was the incomparable achievement of those who sailed west from Palos and Bristol, St. Malo and Amsterdam; of those who waded onto Florida's sands or paddled through the Mississippi's mud; of those who coursed the St. Lawrence or the Hudson; of those who faced the Algonquin and the Iroquois; of those whose great exploration was their final adventure. Among all those engaged in this courageous quest, one stands foremost: Christopher Columbus, Admiral of the Ocean Sea.

In America we are told every proposal for action must first be referred to a committee—with the frequent result that no action whatever occurs. But this, as we shall see, is not exclusively an American trait.

Christopher Columbus, native of Genoa, wanted to go east by sailing west. He wished to find a new route to India, one that did not follow the medieval pattern of hugging a coastline until ultimately the goal was reached. He wanted to strike out daringly across an uncharted ocean, an ocean of unknown and therefore infinite size. Having been turned down by Portugal (because she preferred to hug the African coastline, following it to the end, if it had an end), Columbus left Lisbon in 1485 for the port of Palos in the southwestern corner of Spain. By May of the next year he was granted an audience with Isabella, the Catholic Queen. He made his plea; it was referred to a committee, a committee of the Church.

For centuries churchmen had debated the question of the antipodes: that is, of lands on the other side of the earth. Did such lands exist? If so, were they inhabited? And if inhabited, were they of the same creation? Did they share in Adam's fall and in Christ's redemption? Did Christ appear to them as he had to the "middle of the earth"—the Mediterranean world? If not, then what must the Church do? But if the missionary cannot reach the antipodes, what hope is there of salvation? Perhaps God in his wisdom has taken care of this by seeing that the antipodes are not populated until such time as Christian missionaries can get there. And so the arguments went, back and forth, modifying and shifting, until one day the matter would be no longer a question of debate but an event of discovery.

In the fifth century, St. Augustine, Bishop of Hippo, questioned the existence of men on the other side of the earth (*City of God,* XVI : 9).

> But as to the fable that there are Antipodes, that is to say, men on the opposite side of the earth, where the sun rises when it sets to us, men who walk with their feet opposite ours, that is on no ground credible. And, indeed, it is not affirmed that this has been learned by historical knowledge, but by scientific conjecture, on the ground that the earth is suspended within the concavity of the sky, and that it has as much room on the one side of it as the other; hence they say that the part which is beneath must also be inhabited . . . Although it be supposed or scientifically demonstrated that the world is of a round or spherical form, yet it does not follow that the other side of the earth is bare of water; nor even, though it be bare, does it immediately follow that it is peopled . . . it is too absurd to say that some men might have taken ship and traversed the whole wide ocean, and crossed from this side of the world to the other, and that thus even the inhabitants of that distant region are descended from one man.

In all the haggling about the antipodes, the question of the world's being round or flat was not at issue. One of the persisting myths of American history is that Columbus had to convince everybody, especially churchmen, that the earth was not flat. This is simply not the case. In the fifteenth century the question was not whether the earth was round, but how big around? Was its circumference 20,000 miles (Columbus), 180,000 miles (Ptolemy), or 400,000 miles (Aristotle)? Obviously the answer to this question was of extreme significance in considering a voyage across that trackless ocean sea.

But was the earth a sphere? Yes. Cartographers drew it so (see Fig. 2); astronomers reckoned it so; mariners intended to prove it so. It is true that in the sixth century a geographer with the burdening name of Cosmas Indicopleustes wrote a book designed to show (1) that the earth was flat and (2) that Jerusalem was its exact geographic center (see Fig. 3). But his *Christian Topography* was regarded as an obsolete curiosity even in his own time, without demonstrable influence on any later scholarship.

Columbus' proposal to sail into the unknown West raised again the question of the antipodes, raised it with a new urgency now that a decision must be made. It was only natural in fifteenth-century Spain that the queen would turn to the Church for an answer, since the Church was then the custodian of intellectual endeavor, not of theology alone, but of all learning. The ablest astronomers, cartographers, historians, and anthropologists were trained by the Church and often were pastors and teachers within the Church.

We left Christopher Columbus in a committee meeting—at least his proposal was left there. But knowing the leisurely way of committees, there

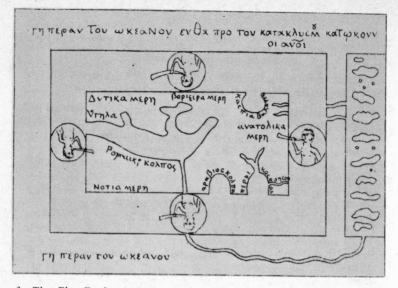

3. *The Flat Earth of Cosmos Indicopleustes* • *This early medieval map portraying "the limits of the world" shows the Mediterranean as, quite literally, the "middle of the earth."*

is no need to hurry. Father Talavera's committee first met in the summer of 1486; some four or five years later, it submitted a report. After years of distraught and anxious waiting, Columbus was crushed by the negative result. His proposal, the committee stated, was impossible, vain, weak, and worthy of rejection. Why? The reasons were these: (1) such a voyage would take at least three years; (2) the western ocean might be without limit; (3) even if Columbus reached the antipodes, he could not get back; (4) it was quite possible that there was no land on the other side anyway, especially since St. Augustine so believed; and (5) because these lands have not been known before, it is most unlikely—this long after the Creation—that they can be discovered now. This last contention is, of course, always the perfect argument against ever doing anything for the first time.

Columbus waited another half year after the report was issued to see if the queen would call him. But no messenger came. Shaking the dust from his boots, the Genoese sailor vowed to go to France and give King Charles VIII the opportunity to back such an expedition. At this citical juncture a friendly ecclesiastic intervened: Juan Pérez. Believing in Columbus' mission and having some influence with the queen, this Franciscan friar persuaded Columbus to wait so that one more try might be made. His timely intervention brought another interview with Isabella and the appointment of yet another committee. The decision, again, was negative.

But with a difference! This time the learned men believed the feat *might be* possible; however, the State found the cost too high, the demands of

EXPLORERS SEARCH FOR A WAY TO THE EAST

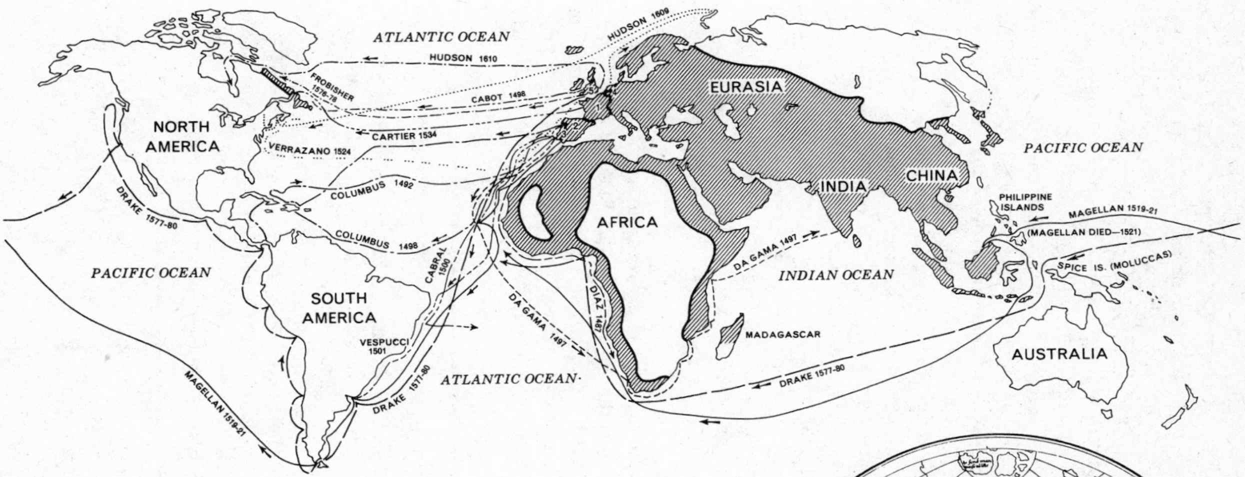

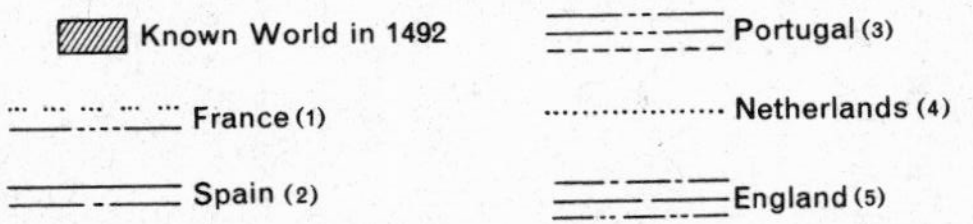

Known World in 1492

France (1)

Spain (2)

Portugal (3)

Netherlands (4)

England (5)

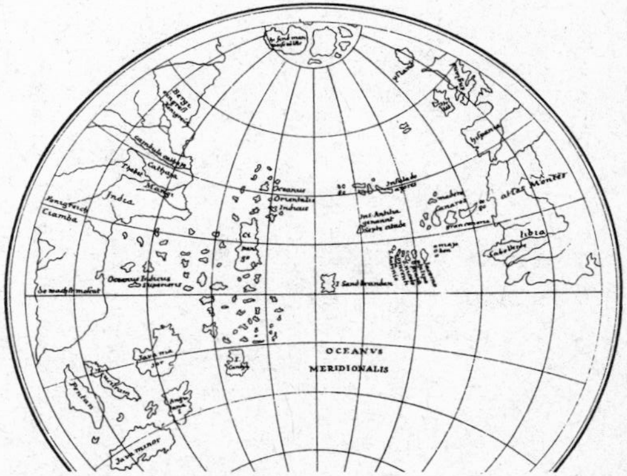

1. *Explorers of the New World*

2. *Martin Behaim Globe, 1492 • This globe made in the year of Columbus' discovery shows England and Spain in the east separated from India in the west by only a few small islands.*

Columbus too ambitious. His last ray of hope extinguished, Columbus left the queen's court. Riding his mule down the dreary road, Columbus, worn and discouraged, had gone about four miles when a messenger overtook him. He was to return, the queen had changed her mind.

Or rather she had it changed by the persuasive argument of the general treasurer. The risks, he said, were small, while the possible rewards were great. The treasurer convinced Isabella that the expedition "could prove of so great service to God and the exaltation of his Church, not to speak of very great increase and glory for her realms and crown" that to decline the offer would be "a grave reproach to her." The decision was made: Spain would authorize and support the epic venture of this ruddy-faced, red-haired, forty-year-old, tall, blue-eyed Italian dreamer.

After three months of negotiating the details, Columbus received his commission on April 30, 1492. "Whereas you, Cristóbal Colón, are setting forth by our command . . . to discover and acquire certain islands and mainlands in the ocean sea . . . it is our will and pleasure that you . . . shall discover and acquire, and shall be our Admiral and Viceroy and Governor therein, and shall be empowered henceforward to call and entitle yourself Don Cristóbal Colón . . . and enjoy the offices of Admiral of the Ocean Sea."

For three months the Admiral-to-be made ready to sail. On August 3, 1492, with ninety men aboard, the *Nina*, *Pinta* and *Santa Maria* weighed anchor, turned from the known waters of Palos to the unknown waters of the setting sun. Seventy days and nights later, Columbus and his men knelt on an island of the Bahamas; Columbus named it Holy Savior: San Salvador.

This entry appears in the log book of Columbus' first voyage, 1492.

> Sunday, September 23rd. Sailed N. W. and N. W. by N. and at times W. nearly twenty-two leagues. Saw a turtle dove, a pelican, a river bird, and other white fowl;—weeds in abundance with crabs among them. The sea being smooth and tranquil, the sailors murmured, saying that they had got into smooth water, where it would never blow to carry them back to Spain; but afterward the sea rose without wind, which astonished them. The admiral says on this occasion "The rising of the sea was very favorable to me, as it happened formerly to Moses when he led the Jews from Egypt."

No priests accompanied Columbus on his first voyage, the primary reason being that this was a voyage of discovery only. On Columbus's later trips, however, priests in large numbers journeyed with him. In the absence of an official ministry during the first voyage, Columbus took quite seriously his religious duties, both public and private. Vespers were conducted on each of the ships shortly after sunset. Prayers were offered, the creed recited, and the old Benedictine chant, *Salve Regina,* sung. On San Salvador, Columbus immediately made overtures to those Indians who gathered to stare in amazement and disbelief. "In order that we might win good friendship, because I knew that they were a people who could better be freed and converted to our Holy Faith by love than by force, I gave to some of them red caps and to some glass beads, which they hung on their necks, and many other things of slight value, in which they took much pleasure."

His private religious life, testified to in the Journals as well as in the writing of contemporaries, left no doubt as to the sincerity of his devotion. A regular communicant, given to daily prayer, well acquainted with biblical writing, Columbus was sustained by faith in a God who was greater than even the Ocean Sea.

In 1493, Columbus, "Admiral of the Fleet of the Ocean," addressed this letter to Gabriel Sanchez, Spain's General Treasurer.

. . . these great and marvelous results are not to be attributed to any merit of mine, but to the holy Christian faith, and to the piety and religion of our Sovereigns; for that which the unaided intellect of man could not compass, the spirit of God has granted to human exertions, for God is wont to hear the prayers of his servants who love his precepts even to the performance of apparent impossibilities. Therefore let the king and queen, our princes and their most happy kingdoms, and all the other provinces of Christendom, render thanks to our Lord and Savior Jesus Christ, who has granted us so great a victory and such prosperity. Let processions be made, and sacred feasts be held, and the temples be adorned with festive boughs—Let Christ rejoice on earth, as he rejoices in heaven in the prospect of the salvation of the souls of so many nations hitherto lost. Let us also rejoice, as well on account of the exaltation of our faith, as on account of the increase of our temporal prosperity of which not only Spain, but all Christendom will be partakers.

Such are the events which I have briefly described. Farewell.

The Admiral and the Church, invisibly and indissolubly bound to each other and to a common mission, reached out to "men who walk with their feet opposite ours." Now the question about the antipodes was new—yet old, old as Isaiah: "Whom shall I send and who will go for me?"

2 ❖ From the Halls of Montezuma

EXPLORATION OF THE NEW WORLD proceeded from a wide variety of personal motives: profit, privilege, curiosity, adventure, love of gold, love of God. National or public motives, motives of church and state, also prompted men. These usually lay somewhere in the realm of self-interest—an economy to be saved, an ideology to be proclaimed. The competitiveness among nations and religions could be enlightened and genteel; it was more often short-sighted and coarse. A good and sufficient public motive for entering the race to the New World was simply to get there first.

Competition developed early between Portugal and Spain. Both were seafaring nations; both stood at the gateway to the Atlantic; both enjoyed papal sanction and support. And, following Columbus's success, both laid claim to the new lands. Portugal in the fifteenth century had discovered or rediscovered the Canaries, the Cape Verdes, and the Azores, thus placing her nearer to those new territories than any other European power. Spain's claims rested, of course, on the voyage of Columbus. How much or how many of the other islands of the Atlantic (islands were all that Columbus had seen by 1493) were properly Portugal's, how many Spain's?

The nearest thing to an international arbiter or world court in the fifteenth century was the Holy See: the Church at Rome. Spain's Ferdinand and Isabella appealed, therefore, to Pope Alexander VI to settle the matter. In response the Pope "drew" the famous line of demarcation, west of which Spain should have sovereignty. The line proved unsatisfactory to

---

The papal decree, setting the line of demarcation between Spanish and Portuguese territories, was issued by Alexander VI in 1493.

We . . . by the authority of Almighty God conferred upon us in blessed Peter and of the vicarship of Jesus Christ, which we hold on earth . . . give, grant, and assign to you and your heirs and successors, kings of Castile and Leon, forever, together with all their dominions, cities, camps, places, and villages, and all rights, jurisdictions, and appurtenances, all islands and mainlands found and to be found, discovered and to be discovered toward the west and the south, no matter whether the said mainlands and islands

8

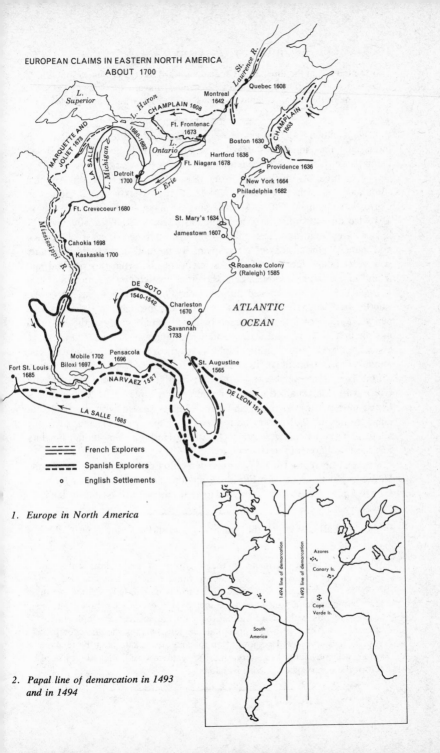

EUROPEAN CLAIMS IN EASTERN NORTH AMERICA
ABOUT 1700

L. Superior

L. Huron

CHAMPLAIN 1608

1680-1682

MARQUETTE AND JOLIET 1673

LA SALLE

L. Michigan

L. Ontario

Ft. Frontenac 1673

Ft. Niagara 1678

Detroit 1700

L. Erie

Mississippi R.

Ft. Crevecoeur 1680

Cahokia 1698

Kaskaskia 1700

St. Lawrence R.

Montreal 1642

Quebec 1608

CHAMPLAIN 1603

Boston 1630

Hartford 1636

Providence 1636

New York 1664

Philadelphia 1682

St. Mary's 1634

Jamestown 1607

Roanoke Colony (Raleigh) 1585

DE SOTO 1540-1542

Charleston 1670

Savannah 1733

ATLANTIC OCEAN

Mobile 1702

Pensacola 1696

Biloxi 1697

Fort St. Louis 1685

NARVAEZ 1527

LA SALLE 1685

St. Augustine 1565

DE LEON 1513

≡≡≡≡ French Explorers

▬▬▬ Spanish Explorers

○ English Settlements

1. Europe in North America

1494 line of demarcation

1493 line of demarcation

Azores

Canary Is.

Cape Verde Is.

South America

*2. Papal line of demarcation in 1493
and in 1494*

are found . . . in the direction of India or toward any other quarter, the line to be distant one hundred leagues [263 miles] toward the west and south from any of the islands commonly known as the Azores and Cape Verde.

Portugal, and in 1494 it was moved farther west, with the result that it intersected the "hump" of Brazil (see Fig. 2). This accounts for Brazil being the only Portuguese-speaking nation in South America.

The elimination of Portugal from most of North and South America stimulated Spanish penetration. In 1511 twenty-six-year-old Hernando Cortes left Spain for Cuba. After serving as mayor of Santiago, Cortes in 1518 led an expedition into the mainland to the west. With 508 men, 16 horses, 4 cannon, and 2 chaplains Cortes began the conquest of Mexico and launched the history of New Spain. By the end of 1519 Mexico City and Montezuma, the king of the Aztecs, were his. From this position and from Cuba as well explorers and missionaries entered North America.

Even before Cortes moved into Mexico, Ponce de Leon, sailing out of Puerto Rico in 1513, made his way northwest through the Bahamas to a peninsula north of Cuba. Impressed by the flowered beauty of the land and having first seen it on Easter Sunday (in Spanish *Pascua Florida*), he named the new land Florida. Eight years passed before Ponce de Leon attempted a settlement. In 1521 he wrote to Charles V of Spain: "I return to that island [not yet known to be part of a great continent]; if it please God's will, being enabled to carry a number of people . . . that the name of Christ may be praised there, and your Majesty served with the fruit that land produced." Temporary houses and a chapel were erected, probably about halfway up the west coast (Charlotte Harbor). But Indian hostility forced the collapse of this early effort.

In the same year (1521), Vásquez de Ayllón discovered and named the St. Johns River in northern Florida. Obtaining a patent or charter from the king in 1523, Ayllón also attempted to settle the wild, if beautiful, land. In

---

Emperor Charles V issued this patent for Florida to Vásquez de Ayllón on June 12, 1523.

Whereas our principal intent in the discovery of new lands is that the inhabitants and natives thereof, who are without the light or knowledge of faith, may be brought to understand the truths of our holy Catholic faith, that they may come to a knowledge thereof and become Christians and be saved, and this is the chief motive that you are to bear and hold in this affair, and to this end it is proper that religious persons should accompany you, by these presents I empower you to carry to the said land the religious whom you may judge necessary, and the vestments and other things needful for the observance of divine worship.

1526 he sailed as far north as Chesapeake Bay, where log and brush structures, including a chapel, were erected. Adversity again struck. Ayllón died; the winter brought bitter weather; Indians attacked; and among the Spanish, mutiny broke out. By spring this settlement, somewhere in Virginia, was abandoned.

Even greater tragedy accompanied an expedition led by Pánfilo de Narváez. Arriving at the west coast of Florida in 1527 quite by accident— he was trying to make the port of Havana—Narváez determined to explore the country for possible settlement. His five ships were unloaded and then vaguely directed to stay near the coast. Ships and the six hundred settlers (including five Franciscan monks and some secular priests)[1] never found each other. The country and the natives being inhospitable, the Spaniards had to leave by whatever means at hand. Of the whole company, only four persons are known to have survived. One of those four was Cabeza de Vaca.

When Cabeza de Vaca arrived in Mexico City nine years later, he had incredible tales to tell. While he failed to describe bountiful deposits of gold and silver, the imagination of his Spanish listeners supplied all that was missing. Stories of gold from Peru and legends of "seven cities" to the north spurred lusty adventurers on, notably Hernando de Soto and Vásquez de Coronado (see Fig. 3).

Of somewhat greater consequence to the religious history of America were the travels of Father Mark (Fray Marcos) of Nice. This Franciscan friar, directed in 1539 by Spain's viceroy (Mendoza) to explore the interior, set out to determine if any large towns suitable for a mission existed north of Mexico. Traveling on foot Father Mark made his way from Mexico City to upper Arizona and New Mexico. He erected a "small and slender" cross near the Zuñi pueblo at Cibola and claimed all that he had traversed for the viceroy and the king of Spain. He then returned to Mexico City, having walked about three thousand miles.

Father Mark promised all Indians he met that they were no longer to be enslaved by the conquistadors. And there lay a critical problem, not only between Spaniard and Indian but between Spaniard and Spaniard, between church and state. The white man's brutality in the Caribbean Islands, his exploitation, his lust, and his greed shocked the spiritual fathers, notably Bartholomew Las Casas. When accounts of atrocity began to filter back to the Old World, the Church demanded that Spanish procedures conform to Christian principles. In 1516 Las Casas, the first Christian priest ordained in the New World, accepted the title of Defender of the Indians. Charged

---

[1] Roman Catholic clergy may be members of a monastic community (e.g., Dominicans, belonging to the Order of Preachers; Jesuits, belonging to the Society of Jesus; Franciscans, members of the Friars Minor, or Humble Brethren), or they may serve chiefly in the activities of parish or diocese. The former are sometimes called "the religious," the latter "the seculars."

3. *De Soto Landing at Tampa Bay*

to look after the interests of the natives, the earnest priest gave himself wholly to the mighty challenge. Eloquence and devotion, however, were not enough. Las Casas sadly announced what the Indians easily saw: the Christians' real god was gold. In 1537 Pope Paul III forthrightly proclaimed the only honorable course to follow with the subdued natives. But strong resistance from the Spanish crown virtually nullified the force of this humane pronouncement.

Pope Paul III in *Sublimis Deus* (1537) set a standard of humanitarianism seldom attained in North America.

> We . . . consider . . . that the Indians are truly men and that they are not only capable of understanding the Catholic Faith but, according to our information, they desire exceedingly to receive it. Desiring to provide ample remedy for . . . evils, we define and declare . . . the said Indians and all other people who may later be discovered by Christians, are by no means to be deprived of their liberty or the possession of their property; even though they be outside the faith of Jesus Christ; and that they may and should, freely and legitimately, enjoy their liberty and the possession of their property; nor should they in any way be enslaved; should the contrary, it shall be null and of no effect.

As a result of Father Mark's report, Coronado, with a sizeable military force and three Franciscans, left Mexico in 1540 for Cibola and fabled cities beyond. Though he traveled east as far as central Kansas, Coronado found neither turquoise mansions nor gilded palaces. After two years of fruitless wandering, he returned to Mexico, leaving behind the Franciscans who desired to begin their mission in mid-continent. One of the friars, Juan de Padilla (joined by a Portuguese, a Negro, and two Indians), resolved to work with the people at Quivira. No sooner had he set himself to this task when he was murdered by the Indians. His companions barely escaped to tell the story of America's first recorded martyrdom. The fate of the other two Franciscans was never learned.

Florida continued to allure. As a site both for missions and for settlement it promised much. But for the next one hundred years, those promises were like the siren's call that dashed brave men to their death. In 1549 an able Dominican father, Louis Cancer, fresh from successes among Indians of Central America, determined to press his Christian mission into Florida. He and other Dominican priests set foot on the coastline near Tampa Bay in 1549; before the day was over, all were slain by Indians, Father Cancer dying in full view of those aboard the ship from which he had debarked.

Tensions between Protestants and Catholics, so prominent in nineteenth century America, found little ground for battle in earlier centuries. Yet as early as 1565 conflict came to Florida's soil. French Protestants, called Huguenots, fled their hostile homeland for the New World. Sailing into St. Johns River in 1564, these refugees created a fort (Carolina) near its mouth.

But more than two generations earlier Spain had discovered, named, and claimed title to Florida. In the name of the Spanish crown, therefore, Pedro Menéndez de Avilés left Spain in 1565 to retake unlawfully settled land. The French fled, and Spain stayed to erect the first permanent settlement in North America: St. Augustine. The garrison was so named because Menéndez reached Florida's coast on August 28 (1565)—the feast day of St. Augustine. From that small, struggling settlement Spanish missions fanned out to the north, the west, and even to the south.

With the heady success of defeating the French behind him and with the impressive title of governor of Florida upon him, Menéndez determined to move north to the Carolinas and the Chesapeake, then west as far as the Gulf of Mexico. Members of the Society of Jesus—the Jesuits—arrived to assist the Dominicans and those parish priests already in Florida. In 1569, missionaries moved northward into Georgia (at Guale or Amelia Island) and into South Carolina (Orista, near Port Royal). But within a year, success was so meagre and Indian resistance so great that the missions were closed.

Later in that year, 1570, a leading Jesuit, Father Segura, resolved to go personally into the Chesapeake area, taking several other Jesuits with him. The black-robed fathers began their work in September; in February the Indians they sought to help turned against them, and once more American soil, somewhere near the Rappahannock, received martyrs' blood. One month later Francis Borgia, the Jesuit General, dismayed at the cost in lives and disheartened by pathetically modest results, recalled all Jesuits from the Florida missions.

General of the Jesuits, Francis Borgia, in 1571, reluctantly informed Governor Menéndez of the necessity of withdrawing the Jesuits from the Chesapeake Bay area.

> Since it is evident, in our long experience in Florida, that we could count, so to say, with fingers of our hand those who during this long period have been converted, and even they have turned back to darkness, and since, moreover, there is in this Society . . . such a small personnel for the many enterprises which the Society has assumed; it is evident that for a time until God our Lord, little by little, stirs those pagans in the capacity of their souls, that not only is it not fitting to keep the Society in that land, but it must not be done.

In 1577, the Franciscans once more took up the work abandoned by the Jesuits, but again Indian insurrections in the New World and adverse political decisions in the Old seriously impaired their labors. Yet by the middle of the seventeenth century, the Franciscans in Florida had introduced some twenty-six thousand Indians to Christianity. Before that century was over, however, the Florida mission felt the pressure of English colonization in the Carolinas. Some Indians, being pushed southward and westward, harassed Florida. Other Indians in or near Florida aligned themselves with the English. Still others played one force against the other. With English colonization growing and Spanish power waning, Florida's Franciscan missions steadily declined from the end of the seventeenth century on. The final blow came in 1763 when, by the Peace of Paris, Spain ceded Florida to England.

Franciscans labored with most lasting success in the American southwest. The Order of Humble Brethren, charged with the salvation of natives in New Mexico, Texas, Arizona, and California, carried on the witness begun by Fathers Mark and Juan de Padilla. The royal city of Santa Fe (Holy Faith), established around 1610, became the principal site in which and from which missionary efforts were made. Before 1630 a church was raised and nineteen Franciscan priests, assisted by two lay brothers, served in New Mexico. By Florida standards the success of the enterprise was phenomenal, with estimates of the number of converts at mid-seventeenth century running as high as one hundred thousand.

Yet all was not well. While Indians helped construct pueblo missions, they simultaneously plotted revolt. Friction between the Spanish secular and spiritual authorities in New Mexico, costly in its own right, further encouraged the Indians to resist and rebel. In 1680 the devastating blow came. Led by an Indian medicine man named Popé, natives all around Santa Fe attacked, burned, destroyed and killed. Those Spaniards who could, fled; others remained to fight or to die. Nearly four hundred fell, including many Franciscans.

A dozen years later a military expedition led by Diego José de Vargas recaptured Santa Fe. And in 1693 the Franciscans returned to their rebellious people, to begin all over the rebuilding of missions and of men. This time the culture of New Mexico absorbed not only the flavor of Christianity but also the unmistakable fragrance of Spain.

Shortly before the reconquest of Santa Fe, Spanish Catholicism found its way into both Texas and Arizona. In 1690 two Franciscan missions arose

---

Father Damien Massanet in 1690 reported the first permanent mission established in Texas: San Francisco de los Texas.

The next morning I went out . . . a little way, and found a delightful spot close to the brook, fine woods, with plum trees like those in Spain. And soon afterwards, on the same day, they began to fell trees and cart wood, and within three days we had a roomy dwelling and a church wherein to say Mass with all propriety—we set in front of the church a very high cross of carved wood. . . .

When the church and the dwelling intended for the priests had been finished they carried into these buildings all that was to be left for the priests, and on the morning of the first of June . . . we consecrated the church and celebrated Mass, after which the *Te Deum Laudamus* was sung in thanksgiving, the soldiers firing a royal salute. The church and village were dedicated to Our Holy Father St. Francis. . . .

---

in the eastern woods of Texas, along the Neches River. A series of such missions, thus begun, continued spawning to the end of the eighteenth century. One of these, founded in 1744, achieved a special fame in Texas' fight for independence: the Alamo (see Fig. 5).

In Arizona the name of a Jesuit, Father Eusebio Kiño, stands like a Joshua tree on the desert landscape. Kiño, almost as much geographer as preacher, traveled throughout northern Mexico (Sonora) and southern Arizona. In the 1690's he mapped rivers, founded towns, pacified Indians, learned languages, built chapels, taught farming—all the while spending most of his time on horseback! In 1697 he founded his largest and best-known mission, San Xavier del Bac, famed today for its restored beauty (see Figs. 6 and 7). When Kiño died in 1711, Catholic efforts declined in Arizona but were later greatly revived by Franciscans in California (see below, pp. 161 f.).

Franciscans, Dominicans, Jesuits and other clergy from Spain raised a Christian cross wherever a Spanish flag unfurled. Missions planted at the edges of savagery occasionally succumbed, but more often survived to

4. St. Augustine, "East Florida," 1848 • Though by 1848 St. Augustine had been a part of the United States for almost a generation, the Spanish flavor is still evident.

6. Mission San Xavier del Bac (detail) • This fresco in the nave pendentive reveals no medieval Gothic angel but one of more recent Arizona variety.

5. San Antonio de Valero Mission: The Alamo • San Antonio's first mission was established in 1718, but the cornerstone of the present building was laid in 1744. In 1793, the Alamo was closed as a mission.

7. Mission San Xavier del Bac • Originally founded by the Jesuit Kino, this mission was later taken over by the Franciscans. The present building was erected between 1783 and 1797.

change the face and future of the land. Missionaries caught in the complex of national ambitions sometimes surrendered to political demands; more frequently, true to the spirit of Las Casas, they lessened brutality and widened charity. From the Atlantic to the Pacific and in deserts where no waters flowed, American culture bore enduring brands of Spanish life and thought. When much later America's settlers moved across eastern mountains onto western plains, they met and merged with a civilization transported in Spanish ships, with a faith transmitted in Spanish hearts.

3 ❖ Fish, Fur, and Faith

NEWFOUNDLAND'S FISHING BANKS first drew France's attention to the New World. Brave Breton fishermen crossed the stormy Atlantic to net as great a catch as their tiny vessels could safely carry back. Then in 1534 Jacques Cartier sailed from St.-Malo with sixty men and two small ships past Newfoundland into the Gulf of St. Lawrence. For more than two hundred years thereafter other Frenchmen explored and defended, colonized and evangelized the region which Cartier first penetrated and described.

Early in the seventeenth century Samuel de Champlain took up where Cartier left off, exploring New England's coast as well as the New York water which bears his name. Pushing west all the way to the Great Lakes, Champlain prompted further exploration. And this in turn led to a growing trade in furs as well as a hopeful probe of faith (see Fig. 1).

Accompanying Champlain, the sieur de Monts attempted the first French colonization off the coast of Maine. On an island which he named Sainte Croix (Holy Cross) New England's first Catholic chapel was erected in July 1604. De Monts was Protestant, but France's colonial policy required that only Catholic priests serve as missionaries to the New World. De Monts's colony failed, however; a later Jesuit effort in Maine likewise collapsed when some Virginians, led by Samuel Argall, attacked the small settlement, scattering priests and people.

In 1608 Champlain established the most significant of the early French settlements: Quebec. Here many Frenchmen came to barter and build; others came to preach and die. Spiritual direction derived first from Franciscans (the Recollets) but they, awed by the magnitude of the mission opportunities among the Indians, soon sought help from France's stronger order, the Society of Jesus.

With the sturdy rock of Quebec as their base, Jesuits made their way up the St. Lawrence River, past the present site of Montreal, into the region of the Great Lakes. They labored both on land later to be called Canadian and on soil someday to be designated American. They preached to Indians friendly to France, to Indians favorable to England, and to Indians hostile to both. But all was done under a commission that knew no political borders, that accepted no boundaries of region or race.[1]

Father Jean de Brébeuf in 1625 began his work among the Indians, notably the Hurons. Joining with a Huron band for a five-months hunting trip in the dead of Canada's winter, Brébeuf learned of Indian wiles and ways as he, at the same time, proved his mettle and might. Later he lived with the Hurons, mastering their language, enduring their diet, and slowly winning their confidence. But at the end of two years he had won not a single adult convert. When in 1629 New France fell before English power, Brébeuf along with all other French missionaries or traders returned to their native land.

The political reversal, however, was brief. And in 1633, when Samuel de Champlain was permitted to sail for Canada once more, Jean de Brébeuf was by his side. Again in Quebec, Brébeuf, joined by other newly arrived missionaries, resumed the work begun eight years before. By August 1634

Jean de Brébeuf, S. J., gave detailed and delicate instructions to newly arrived Jesuit missionaries (1637).

You must have sincere affection for the Savages—looking upon them as ransomed by the blood of the Son of God, and as our brethren with whom we are to pass the rest of our lives.

EUROPEAN POSSESSIONS
IN NORTH AMERICA, 1750

1. European Possessions in North America

[1] Students of Indian culture often group the diverse tribes of the North American continent according to language families. On this basis two major "families" occupied the northeastern quarter of the United States: the Algonquin and the Iroquois. The Iroquois, or "Five Nations" (Mohawks, Oneidas, Onondagas, Cayugas, and Senecas), were concentrated in central New York. The Algonquin family, represented by a large number of independent tribes, could be found on all sides of the Iroquois pocket in New York. Linguistic relationships, however, did not imply military alliance or political kinship. Indeed, the Hurons, among whom the French Jesuits labored so long, were virtually destroyed by their linguistic kin, the Iroquois confederation of New York.

To conciliate the Savages, you must be careful never to make them wait for you in embarking.

You must provide yourself with a tinder box or with a burning mirror, or with both, to furnish them fire in the daytime to light their pipes and in the evening when they have to encamp; these little services win their hearts.

You should try to eat their sagamite or salmagundi in the way they prepare it, although it may be dirty, half-cooked, and very tasteless. As to the other numerous things which may be unpleasant, they must be endured for the love of God, without saying anything or appearing to notice them.

Father Brébeuf managed to make his way back among the Hurons, comforting the sick, instructing the young, and—soon—baptizing the penitent.

Throughout the 1630's and into the next decade Brébeuf continued to labor in the upper Great Lakes region. Occasionally returning to Quebec for succor or supplies (and once to have a broken collarbone properly set), the earnest priest was ever eager to get back to his flock. In 1648 Iroquois hostility increased sharply. Near the end of that year a band of Senecas attacked three hundred Huron men and women (most of whom were converts) and killed or carried into captivity the entire group. Brébeuf and others, recognizing the threat to the Huron nation, ordered stockades built and defensive weapons carefully stored. In March 1649 the Iroquois destroyed the mission at St. Ignace, several hundred Hurons being massacred. Though three survivors rushed to warn Brébeuf and a fellow priest, the savages quickly arrived and Brébeuf was captured. On him the Iroquois could let all their vengeance fall: he was a prisoner of war; he was a Frenchman; he was the enemy of their god, Areskoui, and a friend to their enemy, the Hurons. Certainly Jean de Brébeuf expected no mercy, and certainly he received none. The slow, deliberately drawn out, agonizing torture defies description. After four unbelievable hours the furious frenzy was over. Brébeuf, who had counseled his fellow Jesuits to have "sincere affection for the Savages," had demonstrated the sincerity—more, the sublimity—of his own.

Thirteen years before that heroic death, Father Isaac Jogues arrived in Quebec seeking to bolster the faltering mission effort among the Hurons. After a nine-hundred-mile journey, by birchbark canoe where possible and by foot where not, the young Jesuit and his colleagues arrived at their destination about one hundred miles north of Lake Ontario. Hardly had his ministry begun when an epidemic broke out, striking Indian and Frenchmen alike. For weeks Jogues himself hung between life and death.

By a primitive logic (not altogether outgrown in the modern world) the Hurons reasoned that since the plague arrived after priests had come, the priests were naturally responsible for this unnatural distress. As Huron chiefs deliberated the proper time and the proper means for putting the missionaries to death, the Jesuits, fully aware of the deliberations, continued their faithful ministry to the sick and the dying. The threat passed, the fevers subsided, and Jogues recovered. The center of the Jesuit work soon moved to Sainte Marie (southern end of Georgian Bay) where the Black Robes built a significant mission.

Some time later, in 1641, the Chippewas invited Jogues to establish a mission in their midst. In the peninsula between Lake Michigan and Lake Superior he founded Sault Sainte Marie, ultimately to become a major settlement. Though eager to press westward where no white man had yet been, to preach to the Illinois, to the Sioux, and to other tribes, Jogues remained near Georgian Bay and the mission at Sainte Marie. Here for a time the work thrived and conversions increased.

In June 1642 Jogues accompanied a group of Hurons back to Quebec to secure needed supplies. The journey, already made hazardous by rapids, waterfalls, hunger, and sheer physical exhaustion, now posed even greater threats: Iroquois were raiding along the route. After thirty-five anxious days Jogues and his party reached Quebec. In late July, supplies aboard, the return trip began. One day out of Three Rivers (the first stop) a band of Mohawks ambushed the canoeing party, and Jogues, along with many others, was taken captive. Driven, tortured, and abused, the prisoners dragged themselves along Lakes Champlain and George all the way to the Mohawk River in New York. His body mutilated and diseased, his spirit somehow unbroken, Jogues managed to survive a year of barbarous captivity.

Isaac Jogues describes his captivity among the Mohawks (1642).

> Amid these dreads and alarms, these recurring deaths, while every day I die, or rather live a life harder to bear than death, there passed two months. During these two months, I made no effort to study the Iroquois tongue; for why should I learn it, since I believed I was about to die at any moment? The village was a prison to me. I avoided being seen. I loved the quiet, lonely places, in the solitude of which I begged God that He should not disdain to speak to His servant, that He should give me strength in the midst of these fearful trials.

In May 1643 the sinewy priest, under heavy Mohawk guard, visited the Dutch settlement at the present site of Albany, some forty miles east of his tribal prison. There fellow Europeans tried to secure his release, if possible without incurring the warring wrath of the Indians. Impressed by this merciful effort, Jogues was even more deeply touched by the action of Albany's Dutch Reformed pastor, John Megapolensis. This Protestant minister returned to Jogues his lost breviary,[2] the book having been rescued

---

[2] The breviary (related to the word "brief") contains those prayers and portions of scripture recited by the priest in his daily worship.

from a Mohawk Indian trying to barter with it. This charitable act greatly moved Jogues, who had seen so little charity in eleven months of fearful deprivation.

After only a few days among the Dutch Jogues was returned to the Mohawk village. In the summer his first opportunity for escape came. The Dutch offered to help him get on a ship bound for Europe. After a deliberate weighing of the matter, Jogues decided to accept their offer. Fear of Iroquois reprisal caused the Dutch to hold the long-suffering missionary in or near Fort Orange (Albany) until late September. Finally he sailed down the Hudson to Manhattan, being the first Catholic priest to set foot there. Early in November 1643 he embarked for France, where royalty and hierarchy paid a proper homage.

But his story did not end here. Isaac Jogues still yearned for that mission field where laborers were so few and needs were so great. His wish to return granted, the Jesuit Father found himself once more in Quebec in June 1644. There he learned that the Iroquois and Algonquins were locked in ferocious battle. The French resolved to send a peace envoy to the Mohawks, and Jogues was clearly the man for the task. In the summer of 1646 he led a peace mission into New York and returned safely to Quebec. In the fall of that year, at the request of the Hurons, he again journeyed toward the Mohawk River in quest of peace. But this time the Mohawks, ever ready to blame the French for all their ills, were in a sullen and belligerent mood. A band of young warriors intercepted Jogues and his companion and brought them to the village, where they were beaten, slashed, and clubbed. All this Jogues had endured before and was prepared to endure again. But on the evening of October 18, 1646, torture, abuse, and degradation came to an end as a Mohawk axe granted him the release of death. His voice was stilled, but his message was not.

That message other Jesuits carried into Maine, where a mision among the Abenaki, an Algonquin tribe, continued well into the eighteenth century. Following the collapse of the Huron mission, some Jesuits even worked among the greatest enemies of Huronia: the Iroquois. This mission in New York, near the present city of Syracuse, came to a sudden end, however, when by the terms of the Treaty of Utrecht (1713) France yielded her claims to Iroquois territory.

Labors in the great Mississippi Valley left a more lasting imprint on American life. In 1669 a Jesuit named Jacques Marquette arrived in Wisconsin. Father Marquette's fame rests principally on his 1673 exploration (with Louis Jolliet) of the upper Mississippi River (see Fig. 4). Indeed, this single venture virtually obscured Marquette's later efforts among the several tribes of Wisconsin and Illinois. Speaking at least six Indian languages and eager to meet new tribes to the south, Marquette was an ideal choice for Jolliet. Hoping to find that elusive route to the great western sea, the explorers drifted down the widening, silt-laden river far enough to

2. *National Shrine of the North American Martyrs* • *In Auriesville, New York, this shrine marks the place where Isaac Jogues and two other early missionaries met their death.*

3. *Old Cathedral of St. Francis Xavier* • *This church in Vincennes, Indiana, and its predecessors served French traders and settlers from the beginning of the eighteenth century.*

4. *Marquette and Jolliet entering the Upper Mississippi River*

know that it flowed not into the Pacific but into the Gulf of Mexico. In four months the expedition was over. France now had a claim to the vast heartland of North America from the Gulf of St. Lawrence to the Gulf of Mexico. And France's Church now had a vast new mission field before it.

Later Robert La Salle, accompanied by the Franciscan Recollet, Louis Hennepin, explored the eastern end of Lake Erie. In 1678 they came upon Niagara Falls, and Hennepin published for Europeans the first, if not the most reliable, account of this western wonder. While exploring the Upper Mississippi, Hennepin was captured by a band of Sioux. Taking advantage of this captivity of several months duration, he became the first Christian missionary to the Dakota Territory. In 1682 La Salle completed the exploration of the Mississippi River all the way to the broad delta, thereby proving its navigability from the Illinois River to the Gulf of Mexico.

While Marquette had sought to establish a mission in Illinois as early as 1674, no Jesuit missionary labored in the lower Mississippi Valley until the eighteenth century. (One of the causes for this delay was a trifle embarrassing: when approaching the Mississippi by way of the Gulf of Mexico, French navigators had trouble finding the mouth of the river.) Early in 1700, however, the first Jesuit to arrive via the Gulf sailed into Biloxi, Mississippi. Father Paul Du Ru saw before him a mission field without limit and a task without end. Confronted by that bane of all missionaries to the native Americans, the vast diversity and appalling difficulty of Indian languages, Du Ru exclaimed, "If one would want to ask God for a miracle in their favor, it would be the gift of tongues."

In 1702, Mobile was founded, becoming the oldest French colonial town on the Gulf Coast (Biloxi being only a fort). And in 1718 New Orleans, destined to be the capital of Louisiana and the major center for mission enterprises, was established. For two decades or more the missionary effort languished, chiefly because of disagreements between the managing Company of the Indies and the priests. In 1726 Father de Beaubois, superior of the Jesuit mission, concluded an agreement with the Company that renewed growth and enhanced effectiveness.

Other Catholic clergy found their way to Louisiana—Capuchins, Carmelites, Recollets, as well as secular priests from the seminary in Quebec. One order of nuns, the Ursulines, rendered particularly outstanding service both in New Orleans and Quebec. Ursuline sisters conducted schools, organized and operated hospitals, and cared for orphans. Their work in New Orleans, begun in August 1727, resulted in the first religious institute for women in the United States (see Fig. 5).

For almost half a century, however, the major burden of missionary effort all along the Mississippi was borne by the Society of Jesus. Among the Indians, among the French, and among the slaves on the plantations the Black Robes labored. Missions began to the Yazoos in 1726, and to the Arkansas, the Choctaws, and the Alibamons in 1727.

ÉLÉVATION DE LA FAÇADE DU QUAY DU BATIMENT DES R. URSELINES

5. *Ursuline Convent in New Orleans* • The plans shown here are of the first convent, completed in 1734. Soon falling into decay, the original building was replaced by the present structure.

6. *Ursuline Convent Today*

Two events, unrelated except in time, brought an end not only to French mission efforts here but also to France's hopes in all of North America. In 1763 France suppressed the Society of Jesus.[3] This startling reversal of Jesuit fortune cut the major artery of France's missionary supply to America. Jesuit property was sold, seized, or transferred to the Capuchins, and the priests themselves sought the first available passage out of New France and away from the New World.

The other event of 1763, the Peace of Paris, marked the end of the French and Indian War, the last of a series of hostilities between France and England. By the terms of this Peace, France ceded to England all her territories east of the Mississippi (except New Orleans, which went to Spain) and to Spain all of its claims west of that great river. After 1763 a few priests, some scattered Indians, and a modest number of French settlers struggled to keep their faith alive in North America. But only a single generation later, in the wake of the French Revolution, clerical reinforcements began to arrive in abundance. By then, however, a new nation had been born, a nation not French, not Spanish, not English, but American.

[3] France's suppression was seconded by the Pope in 1773, when he abolished the order. This precipitate action arose from a host of European resentments and jealousies. Some regarded the order as an economic competitor, some as a political threat, and others as a theological variant. In 1814, by papal edict, the Society of Jesus was restored.

4 ❖ Hakluyt and Purchas

WHILE ENGLAND HESITATED, Spain marched and France explored. To many an impatient Englishman of the sixteenth century it seemed that England's sun was being eclipsed by the brilliant daring of other nations. And if patriotism were not a sufficient goad to colonial activity, perhaps Protestant piety was. That piety, of course, often included a large measure of fear and suspicion regarding the advances made by Catholic France and by Catholic Spain.

To be sure, England had not been completely dormant. John Cabot sailed for Henry VII at the close of the fifteenth century. John and later his son, Sebastian, explored Newfoundland and portions of the American coast, confident they were seeing the northeastern portion of Asia and that the Pacific was just across a mountain or up a river. Their ventures resulted, however, in neither great voyages of exploration nor serious attempts at settlement. But they did give England a quasi-legal claim in the New World, especially to the northern portions far removed from Spain's adventures (see Fig. 1).

The notorious Francis Drake, knighted by Queen Elizabeth in 1581, also explored when exploration did not interfere with his piracy. As English and Spanish hostility grew, Drake became a major maritime nuisance to the ships from the Spanish Main. He wrecked many a Spaniard's fortune, lined many an Englishman's pocket, and took the view, with surprising seriousness, that his efforts were a kind of Protestant crusade. Like Columbus before him, Drake enforced regular religious services aboard his ships—ships that carried Bibles, prayer books, and Foxe's *Book of Martyrs*.[1] A blow against the fortunes of Spain was a blow for the faith of England, and in 1588 came the boldest blow of all: England's defeat of the Spanish Armada.

Leading clergymen, too, struck blows for the faith of England. Their motives, like those of explorer and adventurer, could also be mixed. As Sir

---

[1] Foxe's famous *Book* offered elaborate and blood-chilling accounts of Protestant sufferings, particularly under England's Catholic Queen Mary (1553–1558). This volume, enjoying quick and continuing popularity, kept religious animosities alive for generations of Englishmen.

Walter Raleigh well wrote, "Men have traveled, as they have lived, for religion, for wealth, for knowledge, for pleasure, for power and the overthrow of rivals." The motive which Raleigh put first, however, is fully evident in the promotion of Britain's entire colonial enterprise. Sermons were preached by the hundreds, tracts and broadsides printed by the thousands, all pointing to the opportunities for England's Protestantism.

Religion, in the eyes of England's clergymen, could be advanced more through the creation of colonial towns than by the building of mission posts. When the planting of "true, Protestant Christianity" seemed possible, colonial enthusiasts insisted on the actual settlement of English families. This basic position shaped all British policy and changed all American history.

For the expansion of England and the progress of Protestantism, two British clergymen merit highest credit: Richard Hakluyt and Samuel Purchas. A graduate of Christ Church, Oxford, Hakluyt maintained a dual loyalty to geography and religion. It was not an unreasonable combination, for cartography and the art of navigation were essential to the spread of the gospel. And if it were to be the right gospel, the "true and sincere religion," in Hakluyt's words, then it must be England, not Spain, who would carry it.

Most systematically, persuasively, and exhaustively Hakluyt argued the allied causes of Protestantism and England. Working closely with Raleigh, he composed *A Discourse of Western Planting* and presented it to Queen

---

In *A Discourse of Western Planting* (1584), Richard Hakluyt calls on England to colonize in order to evangelize.

It remains to be thoroughly weighed and considered by what means and by whom this most godly and Christian work may be performed of enlarging the glorious gospel of Christ, and reducing [leading] of infinite multitudes of these simple people that are in error into the right and perfect way of their salvation. The blessed apostle Paul, converter of the Gentiles, Romans 10, writes in this manner: "Whosoever shall call on the name of the Lord shall be saved. But how shall they call on him in whom they have not believed? and how shall they believe in him of whom they have not heard? and how shall they hear without a preacher? and how shall they preach except they be sent?" Then it is necessary, for the salvation of those poor people who have sat so long in darkness and in the shadow of death, that preachers should be sent unto them. But by whom should these preachers be sent? By them no doubt who have taken upon them the protection and defense of the Christian faith. Now the Kings and Queens of England have the name of Defenders of the Faith. By which title I think they are not only charged to maintain and patronize the faith of Christ, but also to enlarge and advance the same.

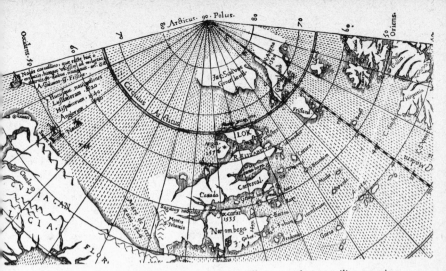

1. *Lok's Map, 1582* • *This early map clearly illustrates the prevailing conviction that a "northwest passage" to the East existed. See just above the 60° parallel.*

Elizabeth in 1584. Here he pleaded for what became England's distinctive approach: settlements, not outposts. If the nation's energies be devoted to genuine colonization, he argued, then conversion of the heathen could go forward more surely and at less tragic cost. Missionaries could learn the language and customs of the Indians, then discreetly and diplomatically "distill into their purged minds the sweet and lively liquor of the gospel." Otherwise, the English cleric wrote, "for preachers to come unto them rashly without some such preparation for their safety, it were nothing else but to run to their apparent and certain destruction; as it happened unto those Spanish friars that, before any planting, without strength and company, landed in Florida where they were miserably massacred by the savages."

So England should plant colonies in the New World. But did not Spain hold title to North America, a title granted by Pope Alexander VI and confirmed by formal treaty? Nonsense, said Hakluyt, for "no Pope had any lawful authority to give any such dominion at all." To prove this, he appealed to scripture, to history, to the voyages of John Cabot, and to common sense. Most of his argument would strike modern readers as curiously dated, but then as now possession was nine tenths of a valid claim. And possession was precisely what Hakluyt urged. "This enterprise may stay the Spanish King from flowing over all the face of that vast [land] of America, if we seat and plant there in time, in time I say. . . ."

Watching French and Spanish explorations convinced Hakluyt that not much time remained. Aware of what Englishmen had done and hopeful about what England could do, he goaded the nation by describing the heroic adventurers of the British past. Hakluyt dramatized and popularized these exploits, rescuing the accounts that "lay so dispersed, scattered and hidden in several hucksters hands, that I now wonder at myself, to see how I was able to endure the delays, curiosity and backwardness of many from whom I was to receive my originals." All were edited to form the basis of the most widely read of all Hakluyt's works, *The Principall Navigations, Voiages, Traffics, And Discoveries Of The English Nation, made by Sea or over Land,* first published as one volume in 1589, then enlarged to three volumes in 1598–1600.

This multivolume collection of wondrous derring-do, usually called simply *The Principal Navigations,* became England's epic. It inspired the country. It stirred the heart. If so much had been done so grandly in the past, how then could England continue to sit in its "sluggish security"? In his letter of dedication Hakluyt told of his consternation as he heard other nations "miraculously extolled for their discoveries and noble enterprises by sea," while England was either "ignominiously reported, or exceedingly condemned." After feasting on the delights of Hakluyt's volumes, Englishmen agreed that sluggish security was not enough.

Of Hakluyt's contemporaries the half-brothers Sir Humphrey Gilbert and Sir Walter Raleigh were no sluggards. These two, with Hakluyt's constant encouragement, stirred England not only to dream but to plan and to dare. Gilbert's long-delayed expedition to Newfoundland in 1583 unfortunately displayed more bold ambition than careful execution. Only one of the five ships completed the voyage as planned, and Gilbert himself was lost at sea.

Hakluyt and Raleigh nonetheless remained enthusiastic. Gilbert's expiring patent was promptly transferred to his half-brother, and the very next

2. *John White's "Arrival of Englishmen in Virginia"*

year Raleigh backed an expedition to North Carolina and Virginia. His two ships returned to England late in 1584 to report a land full of deer, rabbits, and fowl; waters alive with fish; soil "the most plentiful, sweet, fruitful and wholesome of the whole world"; and Indians who were a "kind and loving people." This extravagant report, by Arthur Barlowe, was only the first of a series that advertised the delights of Virginia and, on occasion, tragically misled prospective colonists.

Actual settlement began the following year. Seven ships, commanded by Sir Richard Grenville and Sir Ralph Lane, left 108 settlers on Roanoke Island in August 1585. But when Francis Drake drifted by the following June, he found the weary colonists ready to accept passage home. Among other difficulties, the Indians had proved to be less than kind and loving. Two of the settlers, Thomas Hariot and John White, carried back detailed reports maintaining that a colony, rightly managed and advantageously situated, could survive and even prosper.

The religion that Englishmen found in Virginia is briefly described by Thomas Hariot (in Hakluyt's *Principal Navigations*, 1589). See Fig. 3.

> Some religion they have already, which although it be far from truth, yet being as it is, there is hope it may be the sooner and easier reformed.
>
> They believe that there are many Gods, which they call Mantoac, but of different sorts and degrees, only one chief and great God, which hath been from all eternity. Who, as they affirm, when he purposed to make the world, made first other gods of a principal order, to be as means and instruments to be used in the creation and government to follow; and after the sun, moon and stars, as petty gods, and the instruments of the other order more principal.

Thus encouraged, Raleigh sent three small ships from Plymouth for Roanoke Island on May 8, 1587. The 150 settlers, this time including women and children, debarked on Roanoke Island, and there on August 13 America's first English Protestant service was held. Five days later another novel event took place: Governor John White's wife gave birth to the first English baby born in North America—Virginia Dare. Shortly after, White reluctantly returned to England to insure the dispatch of urgently needed supplies. Incredibly it took him four years to get back, war between Spain and England being the principal cause of delay. When he did return, he searched for but found no trace of family or friends. And the "lost colony" of Roanoke has not since yielded its secret to later, if less tortured, searchers.

As the Roanoke colony was being drawn toward its unknown fate, Hakluyt called attention to the courageous settlements attempted by French Protestants in Florida. He participated in the formation of the East

3. *Worship of the Virginia Indians • The illustration is taken from a water-color by John White who is also the author of the descriptive text.*

4. *Arts and Crafts among the Virginia Indians • Again both text and drawing are by John White.*

India Company, encouraged Martin Pring's voyages to New England, led in creating the Virginia Company, and became a charter member of the Northwest Passage Company. Until his death in 1616 the indefatigable Hakluyt—author, editor, geographer, and preacher—gave his whole heart to that "most godly and Christian work . . . of enlarging the glorious gospel of Christ."

Hakluyt's Elisha was Samuel Purchas, a fellow clergyman of the Church of England. While not as acute as Hakluyt, Purchas popularized even more successfully the cause of English expansion. His two major efforts were *Purchas His Pilgrimage*, published in 1613, three years before Hakluyt's death, and *Hakluytus Posthumus* (1625), which carried on the grand tradition of *The Principal Navigations*.

To a twentieth-century reader the writings of Purchas appear untidy. Religion gets mixed up with politics, anthropology is bedded with economics, and history with revelation. But the principal point is that all these things were in fact mixed in the minds and lives of Europeans in this age of exploration. Those interested in England's colonies, for any cause, could relish in Purchas an enthusiastic endorsement of the colonies for every cause: military defense, mercantile profits, national honor, population growth, scientific discovery, and—not at all an afterthought—the greater glory of God.

The title page describes *Purchas His Pilgrimage* as "a Theologicall and Geographical Historie of Asia, Africa, and America, with the Ilands Adiacent." This was quite an undertaking—even in the days of universal history! But it was precisely this universality, at a time when Europe stood on the brink of a new age, that held so great an appeal. Moreover, to encompass the history of all the world, where better to begin than with "that soul of the world: RELIGION"? Here Samuel Purchas himself began, hoping that those many parts of the world now "in their withered and fouler hue of passed, worn-out rites, or present irreligious religions, not washed with the purer streams of sacred baptism," may yet turn from error to truth.

Purchas His Pilgrimage (1614) is introduced by a sentiment that flavors not only this large work but much of sixteenth century thought as well.

ON THE LEARNED PREACHER'S PILGRIMAGE

The Body of this Book is HISTORY
Clad in quaint garments of GEOGRAPHY
Adorn'd with Jewels of CHRONOLOGY
Fetch't from the Treasure of ANTIQUITY
The better part thereof, THEOLOGY
Soul of the World: Religious PIETY
Adds life to all, and gives ETERNITY.

Looking over the world from his Olympus, Purchas saw how little of it was Christian. And looking over Christianity he was dismayed by the "infinite" number of "sects and superstitions." (The Reformation was less than a century old when he wrote.) Then, surveying England he found chiefly profanity, ingratitude, sedition, "the beastly sin of drunkenness, that biting sin of usury, that devilish sin of swaggering. . . . These are payments we return unto the Lord, instead of prayers for, and loyalty to his majesty: peaceableness and charity to each other; modesty and sobriety in ourselves."

His was a sermon to be sure, a sermon out of place in a history of the world—unless the point of the history was to change the future of that world. "To the glory of God, and good of my Country" was more than a phrase in his note to the reader; it was the same duality which had inspired Hakluyt and was in the seventeenth century to inspire thousands upon thousands of his countrymen.

When Purchas died in 1626, the message of English expansion had been preached long enough. Action now replaced hesitation. Earlier Purchas had noted that while he held in high esteem the English liturgy, he was not overly fond of the English lethargy. He, with Hakluyt and a score of others, had overcome that lethargy. Before long preachers on the American side of the Atlantic echoed the urgent tones of *A Discourse of Western Planting* and *Purchas His Pilgrimage*. Only this time instead of shouting "Go!" they cried "Come!"

PART II

Age of Colonization

5 ✤ "Almighty God Hath Opened the Gate":

VIRGINIA

W HEN SAMUEL PURCHAS DIED in 1626, Europe's Reformation was
already a century old. In that hundred years, often brutal and
bloody, churches and nations had passed through schism and storm. After
Luther nailed his ninety-five academic propositions to the door of Wittenberg's village church in 1517, passions and parties soon erupted everywhere. Before long the propositions ceased to be academic.

Lutheranism spread across the provinces of Germany, especially in the
north. Lutheran preachers made their way, with effect, into Denmark,
Sweden, Norway, and Finland. And the question quickly arose: which land
is Catholic, which Lutheran? But this question was no sooner asked than it
was found too simple. Some land was neither Catholic nor Lutheran, but
was called Calvinist or Reformed, then another called Anabaptist, another
Socinian, another Anglican. Would the splintering of Europe never end?

During the reign of King Henry VIII (1509–1547) England, by a series
of Parliamentary acts, severed its ecclesiastical ties with Rome. But this
marked only the beginning, not the end, of the broiling turbulence that
rocked the British Isles for generations. When Henry died, the kingdom
first veered sharply toward Protestantism under Edward VI (1547–1553),
then sharply toward Catholicism under Mary I (1553–1558). In the long
reign of Elizabeth I (1558–1603), a measure of stability returned as the
Church of England steered its cautious *via media*—a middle course between the Catholicism of Rome and the Protestantism of Calvin or Luther.

This Elizabethan settlement, however, failed to please all. Notably the
Puritans, seeking to move England's Church toward a more clear-cut Protestantism, grew restive. Under Elizabeth's successor, James I (1603–
1625), some of the Puritans, despairing of a thorough reform in Anglicanism, withdrew to form their own churches. Others opposed the episcopal
polity of the established Church, that is, they did not accept a church
government based on the spiritual authority of bishops. Of these some
asserted that each individual church was the seat of authority; thus their
polity or government was congregational. Others held that elders, or
presbyters, elected to boards or synods, should control the church; their
government, then, was presbyterian.

In the seventeenth century all dissenters or nonconformists (that is, those who refused to conform to the Church of England and its Book of Common Prayer) came under increasingly heavy attack. Under Charles I (1625–1649), Archbishop William Laud oppressed dissenters with special severity. As a result, thousands conformed; other thousands left England's restricted isle for free latitudes in the New World. After Charles was beheaded in 1649, Oliver Cromwell ruled. The pressures of persecution waning, numerous new sects arose. In addition to Baptists, Presbyterians, and Independents (or Congregationalists) already on the scene before Cromwell, other groups—some short-lived, some visionary and radical—vied for the loyalties of Englishmen. Of these the most significant was the Society of Friends, or Quakers.

With the restoration of the monarchy under Charles II (1660–1685), the demands for conformity returned. Reacting against the Puritans, English authorities imposed stern penalties upon all who refused to give "unfeigned assent and consent" to the liturgy and law of the National Church. While Charles died a Catholic, he prudently refrained from pressing his own convictions upon the people. When James II (1685–1688) determined to turn the whole country toward Catholicism, however, resentment and resistance broke loose. The "Glorious Revolution" of 1688, led by William of Orange, moved against James who fled to France. Early the next year William and Mary became joint sovereigns of England, and on May 24, 1689, the Toleration Act became law for England and its colonies. While the Act did not grant full religious freedom and was particularly restrictive against Catholics, it did recognize that society could survive even where diversity in religion prevailed.

For England the Reformation was therefore no mere political shift, no sly Parliamentary maneuver. None escaped the tremors of sectarian rumblings, none remained aloof to the religious options and critical choices. Religion was a daily diet, and faith the key to how one lived—and where. For without faith the daring scheme of colonization was neither thinkable nor endurable. Like Abraham, Englishmen bound for the New World sustained themselves with the assurance that God led. From them God would raise a new people and a new realm. Englishmen undertook their grand pilgrimage to Virginia, John Rolfe observed, as "a peculiar people, marked and chosen by the finger of God, to possess it, for undoubtedly He is with us."

On April 10, 1606, King James I chartered two companies to support settlements in the New World. One, the London Company, exercised dominion over land between the thirty-fourth and forty-first degrees of latitude, with control a hundred miles out to sea and a hundred miles inland. The other, the Plymouth Company, received a similar grant farther north. Eight months later, January 1, 1607, the London Company expedition sailed, sighting the Virginia coast on April 26th. Three days later a

The Royal Charter of Virginia, dated April 10, 1606, reveals the religious motivation.

We greatly commending, and graciously accepting of, their desires for the furtherance of so noble a work, which may, by the providence of Almighty God, hereafter tend to the glory of his divine Majesty, in propagating of Christian religion to such people, as yet live in darkness and miserable ignorance of the true knowledge and worship of God, and may in time bring the infidels and savages, living in those parts, to human civility, and to a settled and quiet government: Do by these our letters patents, graciously accept of and agree to, their humble and well intended desires.

cross was erected on Cape Henry. The first town, built about fifty miles up the James River received the name of the colonists' king, which was appropriate. Even more appropriate was naming the rector of the New World's first English parish: the honorary title went to Richard Hakluyt.

Terrors and tragedies filled these early years at Jamestown. Of little more than a hundred settlers in May, half were dead by September. Indians attacked even before the fort was finished. And when it was completed, fire broke out, utterly destroying it along with several houses, the church, and Chaplain Robert Hunt's entire library. Food rotted, rats invaded, supplies disappeared. Sickness, always on the heels of famine, spread. The settlers did not need to read their Bibles to know the Four Horsemen of the Apocalypse, but they read to endure.[1] More supplies and more settlers were followed by more tribulations. In the winter of 1609–1610 a particularly severe "starving time" reduced the Jamestown colony from some five hundred to a mere sixty "most miserable and poor creatures." But, adds Captain John Smith, God "would not it should be unplanted," and little by little the colony's feeble fortune improved. A dozen years after the first planting, reasonable men began to believe that Virginia might survive.

The second church, built in 1611 at the newly organized town of Henrico, was led by Alexander Whitaker, able pastor and propagandist. Combining both functions, he preached a sermon, "Good News from Virginia," which soon found its way back to England, where in published form it won wide attention. Whitaker also performed the celebrated marriage of Englishman John Rolfe and Indian maiden Pocahontas, a marriage which Rolfe defended more on religious than on romantic grounds (see Fig. 1).

[1] The Four Horsemen are described in Rev. 6:1–7. The white horse, symbolizing conquest and invasion, is followed by the red horse, whose rider takes "peace from the earth." The black horse, representing famine, is third; finally comes the pale horse, whose "rider's name was Death."

1. *Baptism of Pocahontas* • *This famous painting hangs in the Capitol rotunda, Washington, D. C.*

2. GOOD NEWS FROM VIRGINIA, *1613* • *In the spirit of Richard Hakluyt, Alexander Whitaker carried on the propaganda drive for the New World.*

3. SUSAN CONSTANT *at Jamestown* • *This replica of the largest of the three ships arriving in Virginia in 1607 is now docked at a restored Jamestown.*

In a letter in 1614 to Thomas Dale, John Rolfe reveals a mixture of motives in his plea to marry Pocahontas.

> Let therefore this my well advised protestation, which here I make between God and my own conscience . . . condemn me herein if my chiefest interest and purpose be not, to strive with all my power of body and mind, in the undertaking of so mighty a matter, no way led (so far forth as man's weakness may permit) with the unbridled desire of carnall affection: but for the good of this plantation, for the honor of our country, for the glory of God, for my own salvation, and for the converting to the True Knowledge of God and Jesus Christ, an unbelieving creature, namely Pocahontas. To whom my heart and best thoughts are, and have a long time been entangled, and enthralled in so intricate a labyrinth, that I was even awearied to unwind myself thereout. But almighty God, who never faileth his that truly invoke his holy name hath opened the gate, and led me by the hand that I might plainly see and discern the safe paths wherein to tread.

For many reasons the Church in Virginia found itself incapable of duplicating the Church left behind. First, parishes were not neat parcels of land centering on the village green. They were measured in miles, not blocks; and while thick with trees, they were thin with people. Thus a parish of vast size might nonetheless find the support of a ministry most difficult. The minister having two or three such parishes could not offer regular services or be on hand for all christenings, weddings, and funerals. And if by chance he was in the right place at the right time, the planters considered their own houses more sacred than the church. First funerals, then weddings, and even baptisms became sacraments of the home more than of the church. Dotting the landscape, the family cemetery also became a familiar sight. In the southern colonies, therefore, the churches, though growing in number, often maintained themselves on the edge, not in the center, of life—and death.

Not only was the parish church far removed and difficult to reach, but clergy were scarce. In its early years Virginia offered little to potential pastors but personal hardship and hostile country. Laws strengthened the position of the minister and determined his income. But since he was paid in a fixed amount of tobacco or corn, fluctuations on the market undermined a stable salary. By mid-century Governor William Berkeley instructed every congregation that had a minister to "build for him a convenient Parsonage House." Two hundred acres of "glebe land" (that is, land owned by the church but used for farming, grazing, or the like) were also set aside "as near his Parsonage House as may be," with the parishoners and their servants obliged to work the land for three years. Yet these provisions availed little. A dozen years later, 1662, Roger Green bitterly complained of a clerical shortage so severe that settlers "see their families disordered, their children untaught, the public worship and service of the great God they own neglected—neglected upon that very day which they here call the Lords Day."

If enticing clergymen over from England was difficult, encouraging young Virginians to enter the ministry was almost impossible. No theological training was available in the southern colonies until near the end of the century. Harvard College, founded in 1636, was available but unthinkable, since it did not carefully conform to the Church of England. Theology students from Virginia, therefore, had to make two costly, dangerous trips across the Atlantic, spend several years in England away from home and friends, and then return to a parish that gave no assurance of support.

A third shackle that hobbled the Church in Virginia was ministerial quality. Since the New World had so many problems, often only those in Europe with even greater problems fled the awful known for the awful unknown. As early as 1632 the Virginia Assembly found it advisable to decree: "Ministers shall not give themselves to excess in drinking, or riot, spending their time idly by day or night, playing at dice, cards, or any other unlawful game; but they shall . . . occupy themselves with some honest study or exercise, always doing the things which shall appertain to honesty, and endeavor to profit the church of God, always having in mind that they ought to excel all others in purity of life, and should be examples to the people to live well and Christianly." But John Hammond, in 1656, was not impressed by what he saw. "Virginia savoring not handsomely in England," he wrote, it got those who could wear black coats, "babble in a pulpit, roar in a tavern, exact from their parishioners, and rather by their dissoluteness destroy than feed their flocks." Yet this picture, overdrawn even for the 1650's, perceptibly changed during the remainder of the seventeenth century. In the eighteenth the Anglican clergy discharged with great diligence their task of teaching the people "to live well and Christianly."

As the laity had troubles with the clergy, so the clergy had its problems with the laity. Unsure and uneven church discipline constituted a fourth obstacle to religious progress in Virginia. Virginia had no bishop. No ecclesiastical courts met as in England to examine orthodoxy or enforce discipline. This left power principally to the congregation and especially to those men elected to the vestry. Thus while Virginia's church was technically episcopal (ruled by bishops), it was in fact more nearly congregational (ruled by the vestrymen). The rector consequently was sometimes at the mercy of an unsympathetic vestry; the vestry was sometimes under the spell of an unworthy ministry.

Despite these handicaps, as the colony grew, so the churches also grew. There were twenty parishes in Virginia by 1650 and twice that number by the turn of the century. By 1750 nearly one hundred parishes had been established. When the American Revolution broke out, however, Anglicanism lost favor and following to the rapidly growing forces of dissent.

For the Church of England, while enjoying an official status in Virginia,

4. *Bruton Parish Church, Williamsburg* • *Completed in 1715, Bruton Parish numbered George Washington, Thomas Jefferson, and Patrick Henry among its worshippers.*

did not maintain a religious monopoly. Even before the middle of the seventeenth century Puritans in Nansemond County (across the river from Jamestown) appealed to Massachusetts for ministers. Governor Berkeley, however, discouraged such action and discouraged even their remaining in Virginia. Tentative efforts by Quakers in the 1660's to settle in the colony met vigorous resistance. Soon new laws made Quaker life in Virginia unpleasant and Quaker growth impossible.

After England's Toleration Act (1689) Virginia's restrictive walls against the nonconformists began to crumble. In the eighteenth century Presbyterians, Baptists, and later Methodists made deep inroads. Part of the growth of the dissenting or nonconforming churches resulted directly from new immigration. In the 1690's, for example, many French Protestants, fleeing their native land after the revocation of the Edict of Nantes[2] in 1685, came to Virginia. In 1713 a small group of German refugees found similar welcome in the colony. But a larger growth of dissent stemmed from overland migration. From New England and the Middle Colonies, Baptists and Presbyterians came in force down the back country's valleys, so much so that Anglicans felt themselves threatened. One Anglican, Charles Woodmason, complained that dissenters "if they could not suppress, they would cramp the progress of the liturgy and the Church Established."

[2] The Edict of Nantes, issued in 1598 by King Henry IV of France, granted to that country's Protestants (Huguenots) freedom of worship in certain specified areas. It also permitted Huguenots to hold public office and exempted their children from Catholic training.

5. *St. Luke's Church, near Smithfield* • *America's oldest existing church established by Englishmen, St. Luke's dates from around 1632. It stands today as the only remaining example in America of seventeenth century buttressed Gothic.*

6. *St. Luke's Church (interior)* • *The sounding board over the pulpit served to amplify the voice of the minister. (The stained glass windows are late nineteenth century.)*

A wave of intense religious excitement known as the Great Awakening also stimulated religious growth. The prime mover in this furor was a youthful English preacher named George Whitefield. Although an Anglican, Whitefield wore denominational labels lightly. So lightly, in fact, that he antagonized his own church as often as he won great followings among the others. Whitefield's first visit to Virginia near the end of 1739 was followed by two others, in 1746 and 1754–1755. In each case eager and expectant crowds awaited him. "Many have come," Whitefield noted in his Journal, "forty or fifty miles, and a spirit of conviction and consolation seemed to go through the assemblies." In Virginia as elsewhere, he joyfully perceived that "rich and poor flock to hear the everlasting Gospel."

The powerful ministrations of Presbyterian Samuel Davies left a more enduring print on Virginia history. Coming into the colony in 1747 from Pennsylvania, Davies first functioned, like Whitefield, as an itinerant or traveling evangelist. The next year, however, he settled in Hanover County as pastor of the Presbyterian Church there. So vigorous was Davies' widespread evangelizing that the acting governor grew fearful. But the Board of Trade in London, hoping to insure the colony's economic growth, advised the governor: "A toleration and free exercise of religion is so valuable a branch of true liberty and so essential to the improving and enriching a trading nation, it should ever be held sacred to his Majesty's Colonies. We must therefore earnestly recommend to your care that nothing be done which can in the least affect that great point." Davies therefore continued to preach, inviting other Presbyterians into the colony to assist him in the work. Determined that the gospel reach all classes and all conditions, he was particularly concerned about the Negro in Virginia. And in the Revolutionary Period his dedication to liberty stirred patriot hearts.

Samuel Davies, as indicated in his letter to Philip Doddridge (October 2, 1750), pressed with vigor the mission effort among Negro slaves.

> I have also comfortable hope that Ethiopia will soon stretch out her hands unto God for a considerable number of Negroes have not only been proselyted to Christianity and baptized but seem to be the genuine seed of Abraham by faith. . . . I have baptized about 40 of them in a year and a half, 7 or 8 of whom are admitted into full communion and partake of the Lord's Supper. I have also sundry catechumens who, I hope, will be added to the church after further instruction.

Baptists entered Virginia in the first half of the eighteenth century, but their great thrust came in the second half. In 1754 Shubal Stearns, formerly a Congregationalist of New England, migrated to Virginia with some of his followers. Though soon moving on to North Carolina, Stearns continued to encourage the growth of Baptists, whose theology drew deeply from Calvin. With the wide use of evangelistic techniques developed in the Awakening, Stearns-style preachers, often without formal education and always without civil support, won followers in great numbers. As congregations grew, opposition solidified. Between 1768 and 1776 Virginia jailed more than forty Baptist preachers, usually on the charge of disturbing the peace. But persecution provided excellent advertising. By the time of the Revolution more than fifty Baptist congregations had been organized. When that war ended, Baptists joined Presbyterians in battle not for mere toleration but for full liberty.

The founding of a college signals a high point in Virginia's religious history. In 1689 the bishop of London appointed James Blair as his representative, or "commissary," in Virginia. Fully aware of the urgent need for a proper ministry in Virginia, Commissary Blair struggled to create a college for Church of England men. Early in 1691 Blair petitioned the legislature for sanction and support, then opened up a private subscription list for merchants and planters. Before the year was over, he left for England to raise additional funds and to obtain a charter.

From England, Blair wrote Virginia's governor of the elaborate preparations for his audience with King William. "I kneeled down and said these words, 'Please your majesty here is an humble supplication from the Government of Virginia for your majesty's charter to erect a free school and college for the education of their youth,' and so I delivered it into their [the council's] hand. He answered, 'Sir, I am glad that that colony is upon so good a design and I will promote it to the best of my power.' " More than a year passed before the simple conversation could become legal fact, but on February 8, 1693, the Royal College of William & Mary received its charter. The chosen site having been renamed Williamsburg, construction of the main building—planned by England's famous Christopher Wren—soon began (see Fig. 7). Blair became the college's first president, a post he retained for fifty years. The Southern colonies' only college (and America's second) thus started on its somewhat unsteady path toward pious education in "good letters and manners."

England's royal sovereigns, William and Mary, in 1693 granted the charter to the college that bears their name.

Forasmuch as our well-beloved and faithful subjects, constituting the General Assembly of our colony of Virginia, have had it in their minds, and have proposed to themselves, to the end that the Church of Virginia may be furnished with a seminary of ministers of the gospel, and that the youth may be piously educated in good letters and manners, and that the Christian faith may be propagated amongst the Western Indians, to the glory of Almighty God: to make, found, and establish a certain place of universal study, or perpetual College of Divinity, Philosophy, Languages, and other good Arts and Sciences. . . .

We . . . have granted and give leave [to the founders that they] may have power to erect, found, and establish a certain place of universal study . . . within the bounds of the aforesaid colony, to continue for all time coming.

By the time that Yorktown's bloody battle ended, those bitter years of Jamestown's starvation and distress seemed far away. The planting was secure. God, as John Rolfe had written, "hath opened the gate." And having opened the gate, he sustained those who by faith walked through. In this way all "might plainly see and discern the safe paths wherein to tread."

7. *Wren Building, College of William and Mary • The college's original building, the design for which is ascribed to London's Sir Christopher Wren, was first built in 1695–1702, and was rebuilt after a fire in 1705.*

6 ❖ "One Small Candle
May Light a Thousand":

PURITAN NEW ENGLAND

WHEN IN 1620 the pilgrims sailed out of Holland for England, thence
to the New World, their pastor, John Robinson, offered this assurance: "the Lord hath more truth and light yet to break forth out of his holy
Word." Making the pilgrimage across the Atlantic to New England, they
clung to that promise. God's great plan for this world was not yet complete
nor even fully unfolded. To become a part of His continuing revelation, to
be sent by Him on an errand into the wilderness, to be used by Him in the
fashioning of a pure church—such was to find one's true calling, one's
vocation in this vain and fleeting life.

What were these pilgrims doing in Holland? Like other Puritans, the
members of Robinson's congregation contended that England's established
Church had not completed its reformation. The Church was not yet pure,
not in membership, not in worship, not in its government. Unlike some
others, however, the pilgrims in Holland had given up trying to reform the
Church of England from within. Having broken away, having become
Separatist, they fled England to escape the heavy penalties of the law.
First to Amsterdam, then in 1608 to Leyden they hurried, leaving friends
and fortune behind.

They could not stay in England because they were now Separatists. They
could not stay in Holland because they were still Englishmen—Englishmen
desiring a more vital part in broadening and deepening their country's
reformation. The religion of England should be in example to all the world
of what true reformation meant. If in Holland Englishmen were subject to
foreign law, and if in England they were subject to false law, where then
did hope lie? The answer came: it lay across the ocean, in land under
England's claim but hardly under England's control. Thus in 1620 a pur-
poseful minority of Robinson's church left their pastor, their fellows, and
"that goodly and pleasant city" of Leyden. But, wrote William Bradford,
"they knew they were pilgrims, and looked not much on those things but
lift up their eyes to the heavens, their dearest country, and quieted their
spirits."

The ship sailing from Leyden, the Speedwell, joined another vessel in
southern England, the Mayflower; the two then sailed west. Three hundred

miles out to sea the leaky Speedwell had to turn back; the Mayflower returned to Plymouth, taking on as many additional passengers as possible. With 102 colonists aboard, the Mayflower set out alone on September 6, 1620; sixty-six days and four deaths later, landfall was made off Cape Cod (see Fig. 1).

Authorized to settle in Virginia, the settlers to their dismay found themselves off New England. With supplies short and winter near, continuing the voyage down the coast seemed out of the question. Without laws and without authorization, the settlers decided to draw up a compact or covenant—patterned after the voluntary church covenant. This Mayflower Compact, intended only as a temporary expedient, guided the small Plymouth Colony for many years. Under its canopy, seeds of social order were sown.

In December the site of Plymouth was chosen, and the grand mission began. The odds against the colonists were enormous—so much so that William Bradford, governor of Plymouth Plantation for thirty years, wavered as he reckoned them. "What could now sustain them but the Spirit

---

In his account *Of Plymouth Plantation* William Bradford voices a firm faith (November 1620).

Being thus passed the vast ocean, and a sea of troubles before in their preparation, they have now no friends to welcome them nor inns to enter-

1. *Embarkation of the Pilgrims from Holland* • *This often reproduced painting hangs in the nation's Capitol*

tain or refresh their weatherbeaten bodies; no houses or much less towns to repair to, to seek for succor. . . . [Indians] were readier to fill their sides full of arrows than otherwise. And for the season, it was winter . . . subject to cruel and fierce storms, dangerous to travel to known places, much more to search an unknown coast. Besides, what could they see but a hideous and desolate wilderness, full of wild beasts and wild men . . . What could now sustain them but the Spirit of God and His grace? May not and ought not the children of these fathers rightly say: "Our fathers were Englishmen which came over this great ocean, and were ready to perish in this wilderness, but they cried unto the Lord, and He heard their voice and looked on their adversity."

---

of God and His grace?" Even that, during the hard winter months, seemed to falter or fail. By spring about one-half of the settlers had died. Of the twenty-six heads of families only twelve survived, and of eighteen married women only three lived to see the winter snows melt away. With the coming of spring "the mortality began to cease amongst them," Bradford wrote, "and the sick and lame recovered apace." This put new life into them, he added, "though they had borne their sad affliction with as much patience and contentedness as I think any people could do. But it was the Lord which upheld them. . . ."

The ravaged colony began to plant, to fish, to hunt, to cut and saw. The Indian Squanto, "a special instrument of God for their good," showed them how to cultivate and fertilize the corn. Timber was abundant, and a measure of trade could begin. By the fall of 1621 Pilgrims and Indians shared in New England's first thanksgiving, not a ritual of indulgence but a hymn to survival. In two more years life was reasonably secure and famine forgotten.

Growth in Plymouth was never phenomenal. By 1630 the population rose to about three hundred, and by the middle of the century it was still less than one thousand. The surge in settlers came farther to the north, under the charter of the Massachusetts Bay Company. In the 1630's, the decade of "The Great Migration," first hundreds then thousands fled the growing religious oppression in England. America attracted while Archbishop Laud repelled, the result being that population in and around Boston increased swiftly. By 1642 some sixteen thousand settlers had found refuge there.

These colonists were also Puritans, but, unlike their Plymouth fellows, they had not taken that final dread step of separation or schism. For them the Church of England, though given to folly and prone to sin, remained nonetheless their church. It was their dear mother, from whom they had received new birth and tender nursing. Yet it was wrong in certain stated particulars. What to do? One could try to reform or change it, which indeed the Puritan party had for generations been attempting to do. But authorities were inflexible, unyielding. The obvious alternative, then, was to leave it, forsake it, abandon it. But this was to be an ungrateful son and a rude schismatic. Was there a third alternative? Normally, no. Either conform, or die; either conform, or shatter the church of God. But now in the early decades of the seventeenth century another alternative did appear. Emigrate. Go as a son of England and England's Church to a new land, three thousand miles from England's archbishops and England's jails. There create a true Church of England, a Church purified, a Church reformed, a Church redeemed and redeeming.

The attempt thus to create a new church, all the while not separating from the old one, was sincere if impossible. The new creation became a new denomination: Congregationalism. Each local church ruled itself, joining with other churches only for friendly counsel, admonition, and fellowship. Before long New England's Puritans, separatist and nonseparatist alike, all gathered under the banner of Congregationalism.

Congregationalists of New England did not regard themselves as different in fundamental doctrine. The prominent Boston divine John Cotton enumerated the real distinctions: (1) rule exercised by the bishops and conformity demanded by law are burdens too great to bear; (2) the use of the Book of Common Prayer violates the Second Commandment's prohibition against manmade images; (3) the local congregation is the highest earthly ecclesiastical authority; (4) only those who give evidence of conversion in their lives and conversation are eligible for church membership; (5) the church is formed by means of a voluntary covenant among the believers.

Out of these distinctions a "New England way" emerged. Both Connecticut and Massachusetts (and later New Hampshire) sought to maintain and enforce that "way" by all appropriate means. These colonies intended to prove that the Bible could be the rule of life, that a church could faithfully reproduce the New Testament model, that a society could both reflect and execute the will of God. All theory and practice pointed to this end.

It is easy to scoff at the Puritans who came to America for religious liberty and then denied that liberty to others. But Puritans came for their own liberty, not all men's liberty. They came to conduct a delicate, deliberate experiment in perfect obedience and proper worship. True, such an experiment might—indeed, should—redound to the benefit of all mankind. But none should be allowed to tamper with the laboratory—at least not until the mold had been safely set. In failing to extend liberty to everyone the Puritans may well have been quite wrong—but they deceived no one.

To "preserve the churches in unity and verity" demanded not only unceasing vigilance but more. Pilgrims along the New England way sought to realize their grand vision by conversion, legislation, education, and, most of all, endurance.

CONVERSION

Visible saints, only those consciously redeemed by the saving grace of God, constituted the proper subjects of church membership. In other words, the church covenant presumed a prior contract: the covenant of grace. In Puritan theology all communion between God and man rested fundamentally on this covenant; herein God acknowledged and accepted those foreordained to receive His grace. The covenant bound God to man and man to God in a union eternally sure. Men or women so bound should stand before their peers, demonstrating "their knowledge in the principles of religion, and of their experience in the ways of grace, and of their godly conversations among men."

The Puritan church was therefore a withdrawn, restricted, exclusive fellowship. All who sought admission did so voluntarily, but not all who volunteered got in. Examination of life and thought was rigid and frequent; those falling short in either behavior or belief could be excluded from the fellowship. Thus the New England way rested on the notion of a regenerate church membership—each one responsible in personal loyalty to the corporate ideal. The covenant of the first church organized in the Massachusetts Bay Colony, Salem ("gathered" in 1629), is a simple, single sentence: "We covenant with the Lord and one with another; and do bind ourselves in the presence of God to walk together in all his ways, according as he is pleased to reveal himself unto us in his blessed word of truth."

New England's church government is illustrated in the covenant used in Charlestown-Boston beginning in 1630.

In the name of our Lord Jesus Christ, and in obedience to His holy will and divine ordinance.

We whose names are hereunder written, being by His most wise and good Providence brought together into this part of America in the Bay of Massachusetts, and desirous to unite ourselves into one congregation or church, under the Lord Jesus Christ our Head, in such sort as becometh all those whom He hath redeemed and sanctified to Himself, do hereby solemnly and religiously (as in His most holy presence) promise and bind ourselves to walk in all our ways according to the rule of the Gospel, and in all sincere conformity to His holy ordinances, and in mutual love and respect each to other, so near as God shall give us grace.

By nurture in the home, by instruction in the school, and by exhortation in the church the signs of visible sainthood were promoted and praised. The first formal statement of faith adopted in New England, the Cambridge Platform (1648), emphasized that conversion preceded church membership. "The doors of the churches of Christ upon earth, do not by God's appointment stand so wide open, that all sorts of people good or bad, may freely enter therein at their pleasure." Persons seeking admission must be "examined and tried first" to see that they possess, above all else, "repentence from sin and faith in Jesus Christ." Ordinarily potential members made "a personal and public confession," detailing "God's manner of working upon the soul." Such public avowal was deemed "lawful, expedient, and useful, in sundry respects, and upon sundry grounds."

The conviction that the church is used by God for announcing His divine grace is conspicuously evident in the life of John Eliot. Arriving in Boston in 1631, Eliot was called as pastor to Roxbury the following year. From 1632 to the end of his life, some fifty-seven years later, he continued in this pastoral care. Along with Richard Mather, father of Increase and grandfather of Cotton, John Eliot helped prepare the first book printed in the English colonies, *The Whole Booke of Psalmes Faithfully Translated into English Metre* (Cambridge, 1640). Eliot's greatest fame, however, rests neither on his long and faithful pastorate nor on his work with the Bay Psalm Book. Rather posterity best recalls his patient, protracted mission to the Indians. God "put into my heart," he wrote, "a compassion for their poor souls and a desire to teach them to know Christ and to bring them into his kingdon." To learn the language—always the first and most demanding obstacle—Eliot brought into his home a young Indian servant who had some knowledge of English. With his assistance Eliot soon began translations of the Lord's Prayer and the Ten Commandments. By 1646 he was ready to preach in the Algonquin tongue. The report of his successes, *The Day-Breaking, if not the Sun-Rising of the Gospell with the Indians in New-England* (London, 1647), brought swift and generous response from England. The earliest English foreign mission enterprise, the Society for the Propagation of the Gospel in New England formed in 1649, was one result. Directed primarily toward the Indian, this society assured support to Eliot and others in this notable venture.

Convinced that piety leaned on learning, Eliot gave the Indians their first literature. To do this he had to invent a written language and to find new words to convey biblical concepts. The next step was to teach the Indians how to read these strange-looking symbols. To achieve this end Eliot in 1654 published a brief catechism for the Indians. All this careful preparation looked to one great end: the Indians reading their own Bible in their own language. By 1663 the work was done, as Eliot's ambitious and justly famous Indian Bible came forth.

These earnest efforts did not diminish Indian apprehension about the white man's growing population and power. Indian lands were invaded, Indian rights were ignored. While in a few places cooperation and amity occurred, hostility and mutual fear more often prevailed. Racial and cultural tensions violently erupted in 1675–1676. A devastating Indian attack, King Philips's War, took hundreds of lives, ransacked and ruined

3. *Meetinghouse in Litchfield, Connecticut • The colonial church sketched here was erected in 1762, torn down in 1827.*

2. *The Bay Psalm Book, 1640*

4. *Old Ship Meetinghouse, Hingham, Massachusetts • Ships carpenters cut and trimmed nearby oak trees to build this famous New England church in 1681.*

forty towns, and left memories so bitter that trust on both sides was permanently shaken. To the end of his life in 1690 Eliot nonetheless persisted in providing additional translations, hopeful that an infinite God might send down a peace beyond the understanding of finite men.

LEGISLATION

The Puritan, standing firmly in the tradition of John Calvin, indulged in no sentimental illusions about the nature of man. Man was a sinner, utopian society was a delusion. Perversity, cruelty, lust, war, death—with these the world abounded, and to these the Puritan was no stranger. New England from the very beginning, therefore, acknowledged the necessity for law, discipline, and control. So in addition to a church covenant and a covenant of grace a civil compact was provided.

The covenant between God and society encompassed both saints and sinners. Because New England was a commonwealth, all were equally subject to the active dominion of God. Because it was a Puritan commonwealth, the saints were in charge. The entire experiment in the wilderness rested on the premise that state and church would be one, not in their organization or in their immediate purposes but in their common recognition of the sovereignty and omniscience of God. New England was not "priest-ridden" in the sense that clergymen forced reluctant magistrates to do their bidding. The colony was "piety-driven," however, in the sense that basic religious motives propelled state no less than the church.

The colonies' charters together with the background of English common law formed the fundamental framework within which New England's laws were made. Beyond that, however, the eternal laws of the Bible guided civil and ecclesiastical societies alike. If biblical sanctions were not sufficiently detailed or explicit, then every effort should be made, said the Massachusetts General Court, to administer justice "as near the laws of God as they can." Governor John Winthrop saw no essential difference between the civil and the ecclesiastical covenant. Both were by mutual consent, both were agreements with God and therefore inviolate, both sought the larger public good as opposed to "all private respects."

While a union of church and state is not necessary, no opposition need arise between them. Church government, asserted the Cambridge Platform, neither weakens nor threatens civil government. Rather it strengthens the magistrates "and furthereth the people in yielding more hearty and conscionable obedience unto them." The two governments should "both stand together and flourish, the one being helpful unto the other, in their distinct and due administrations." Magistrates should recognize their duty to provide for "not only the quiet and peaceable life of the subject in matters of righteousness and honesty, but also in matters of godliness."

This was the ideal, and to help attain that ideal the Massachusetts Bay

Colony early decided that "no man shall be admitted to the freedom of this body politic, but such as are members of the churches within the limits of the same." But this was not "theocracy," John Cotton and others protested. Officers of state were not chosen by the church, nor did they govern by direction of the church, nor did the clerics make civil law. All the church did was to prepare "fit instruments both to rule and to choose rulers." Fit instruments demonstrated their fitness by consulting with "men of God . . . in all hard cases and matters of religion."

Enforcement of orthodoxy and preservation of religious uniformity became, therefore, a joint responsibility. The line between civil and ecclesiastical legislation frequently wavered as church synods made basic social policy and as magistrates restrained or punished "idolatry, blasphemy, heresy, venting corrupt and pernicious opinions . . . profanation of the Lord's day, disturbing the peaceable administration and exercise of the worship and holy things of God, and the like. . . ." The happy alliance was unhappily and unsuccessfully resisted by all those not of the "Congregational Way." But throughout the seventeenth century Puritan New England, especially Connecticut, maintained its religious uniformity with conspicuous success. Toleration came slowly, painfully, and bloodily.

EDUCATION

New England's intellectual leadership in the colonial period rested on a religious foundation. Where no bishops ruled and where Bibles must be read, education was a momentous concern. The proportion of university men was high among New England's early colonists, and every energy was bent to provide—so far as the primitive conditions would allow—comparable education for the young. When John Eliot argued in 1679 for schools in every village and town, his listeners acknowledged the force of his fervent plea: "Lord, for schools everywhere among us! That our schools may flourish! That every member of this assembly may go home and procure a good school to be encouraged in the town where he lives!"

If "mutual consent" were the basis of civil and religious compacts, then education of the consenters was essential. Neither the spiritual nor the temporal estate could long endure in that commonwealth which neglected learning. "It being one chief project of that old deluder, Satan, to keep men from the knowledge of the Scriptures," the General Court of the Bay Colony took steps in 1647 to see "that learning may not be buried in the graves of our forefathers in Church and Commonwealth." Every town of fifty householders was required to maintain a teacher of reading and writing, and towns of one hundred or more families were obliged to establish and support a grammar school. Connecticut soon followed with similar laws, and by 1671 all Puritan New England had a system of compulsory education.

Boston's first grammar or Latin school, still surviving today, began in 1636. But for a colony that dreaded "to leave an illiterate ministry to the churches, when our present ministers shall lie in the dust," grammar schools were not enough. The Southern colonies looked to the mother country for their clerical supply, but the New England colonies, in their provoking nonconformity, expected little assistance from that quarter. However meager the resources and audacious the project, Puritan New England must educate its own ministry. Thus wrote Thomas Shepard, pastor in Cambridge: "the Lord was pleased to direct the hearts of the magistrates . . . to think of erecting a School or College, and that speedily to be a nursery of knowledge in these deserts. . . ."

The founding of Harvard College in 1636 demonstrates the Puritan concern that the passions of the heart not overthrow the powers of the mind. Under the direction of its twenty-three-year-old governor, Henry Vane, the Massachusetts "Great and General Court" set aside £400 for the establishment of a college. Locating the college in Newtown (more appropriately renamed Cambridge), authorities admitted the first students in 1638. That same fall John Harvard, a young citizen of Charlestown, died and left to the College a legacy of almost £800 and all his library. This generous grant, as Cotton Mather wrote, laid "the most significant stone in the foundation." The Court returned the high favor by leaving the legacy of John Harvard's name to his adopted countrymen (see Fig. 5 and 6).

In 1646 Harvard College adopted "Rules and Precepts" for its students, the first four of which appear here.

1. When any Scholar is able to read Tully or such like classical author *ex tempore,* and make and speak true Latin in verse and prose . . . and decline perfectly the paradigms of nouns and verbs in the Greek tongue, then may he be admitted into the College, nor shall any claim admission before such qualifications.
2. Every one shall consider the main end of his life and studies to know God and Jesus Christ which is eternal life.
3. Seeing the Lord giveth wisdom, every one shall seriously by prayer in secret seek wisdom of him.
4. Every one shall so exercise himself in reading the Scriptures twice a day that they be ready to give an account of their proficiency therein, both in theoretical observations of language and logic, and in practical and spiritual truths. . . .

Harvard College, designed to prepare a literate ministry, was a liberal arts college, concerned, said the 1650 Charter, with "the advancement of all good literature, arts and sciences." Such broad learning was wholly appropriate in the midst of a people for whom theology crowned a pyramid of liberal education. The Puritans were not enemies of any learning: scien-

5. *The Yard, Harvard University* • *In the foreground, John Harvard watches over his school.*

6. *Massachusetts Hall, Harvard University* • *Still in regular use, Massachusetts Hall was erected in 1720.*

tific, literary, historical or theological. Well then, a voice is heard to ask, why were witches hanged at Salem?

The simplest explanation for Salem is found in the European world from which the Puritans emerged. The reality of witches and wizards was universally assumed, witchcraft being merely another wile of that old deluder Satan himself. Evil demons and unclean spirits had to be cast out or driven into the sea, as in the New Testament. Seventeen hundred years had brought about some refinements of the driving-into-the-sea method, but these benefited pigs more than people.

The intensity of New England's religious experiment, the urgency—almost the frenzy—with which Puritans sought success, made fertile soil for witchhunting. Increase Mather (1639–1723) and his son Cotton Mather (1663–1728) are popularly identified with Salem's 1692 outbreak of the heresy-sin-crime disease. While the Mathers did not produce the event, they and others did contribute to a climate of excited expectancy. These learned divines—and learned they indisputably were—found the study of "witchcrafts and possessions" relevant both to their scientific interests and to their religious responsibilities. While Cotton Mather's *Memorable Providences* (Boston, 1689) may well have contributed to the mounting fever in New England, just as surely Increase Mather's *Cases of Conscience* (Boston, 1693) discouraged the admission of more questionable forms of evidence and helped persuade the governor, Sir William Phips, to bring the trials to an end.

The outburst itself came in the spring of 1692. In Salem Village (now Danvers) "the Sovereign and Holy God was pleased to permit Satan and his Instruments to affright and afflict those poor mortals in such an astonishing and unusual manner." Led by the accusations of several young girls of the village, the witch-hunt ferreted out many a poor mortal, charging him or her with being the devil's own instrument. Before the feverish epidemic had passed, execution befell more than twenty persons duly declared to be witches. To be sure, hundreds and even thousands were burned, hanged, and drowned in Europe on similar charges and on even more questionable evidence. But that hardly brightens this dreary page of New England's history. What does brighten it somewhat was the public and private repentance that soon followed. Judge Samuel Sewall, member of the court that handed down the convictions, stood before his church in Boston in 1697 and acknowledged his "blame and shame . . . asking pardon of men, and especially desiring prayers that God, who has unlimited authority, would pardon that sin and all other his sins. . . ." The same year the Massachusetts General Court set apart a day for prayer and fasting, begging Divine pardon for "all the errors of His servants and people."

Massachusetts had its college; Connecticut sought hers. Puritans there longed for "a nearer and less expensive seat of learning" than that found in distant Cambridge. Harvard, moreover, failed to meet conservative Congregational needs, even in Massachusetts. Though the Mathers, Samuel Sewall, and others in the Bay Colony actively favored the founding of Yale, Connecticut's leading Congregational ministers actually established it. In October 1701 "An Act for Founding of a Collegiate School" provided that "within this His Majesty's Colony of Connecticut" a school be founded "and suitably endowed . . . for the educating and instructing of youth in good literature, arts, and sciences." Here, as in Cambridge, citizens desired "a succession of learned and orthodox men," but the education offered would prepare students "for public employment both in the Church and the Civil State." Originally established in Saybrook, the "Collegiate School" moved to New Haven in 1716.

Yale's trustees, on November 11, 1701, constituted the new college.

> Whereas it was the glorious public design of our blessed fathers in their removal from Europe into these parts of America both to plant and under the Divine blessing to propagate in this wilderness, the blessed reformed Protestant religion, in the purity of its order and worship, not only to their posterity, but also to the barbarous natives. . . .
>
> We their unworthy posterity lamenting our past neglects of this grand errand, and sensible of our equal obligations better to prosecute the same end, are desirous in our generation to be serviceable thereunto. Whereunto the liberal and religious education of suitable youth is under the blessing of God a chief and most probable expedient.

In January of 1718 Cotton Mather wrote to a wealthy Londoner (though a native of New England), Elihu Yale, suggesting that "if what is forming at New Haven might wear the name of Yale College, it would be

7. *Jonathan Edwards College, Yale University* • *Named after one of its most distinguished alumni (class of 1720), this college was completed in 1932.*

better than a name of sons and daughters." In fact, a proper gift might commemorate and perpetuate his name "much better than an Egyptian pyramid." As an Anglican Mr. Yale had some scruples about promoting "an academy of dissenters." But Jeremiah Dummer, the colony's agent in London, persuaded him "that the business of good men is to spread religion and learning among mankind without being too fondly attached to particular tenets, about which the world never was nor ever will be agreed." Besides, if the Church of England should be right, what "better way to make men sensible of it than by giving them good learning." Under the spell of such ingenious argument Elihu Yale came through with a generous gift, and the college came through with its enduring monument— better than a pyramid (see Fig. 7).

The founding of Harvard and Yale, together with the establishment of free common schools without number, does not exhaust the examples of New England's dedication to learning. But perhaps it is already clear that for the Puritan the path to piety was paved with masters, schools, colleges, and perfect "paradigms of nouns."

ENDURANCE

Informing the mind was one task; transforming the heart was quite another. Although "perserverance of the saints" was cardinal Calvinist doctrine, the saints seemed distressingly unable to endure. The high hopes and fervent faith of the fathers were repeatedly forsaken or compromised by the sons. All knew something was amiss when church membership was stretched to include more than the "visible saints." Churches admitted persons "not scandalous in life" instead of the redeemed who could relate "their experience in the ways of grace." So membership gradually became a matter of respectability more than of regeneration.

By 1679 the decline in zeal was sufficiently alarming to warrant calling a "Reforming Synod" to meet in Boston. A series of disasters, including King Philip's War, a major fire in Boston, the outbreak of smallpox, and the hostility of King James II, made repentance fashionable. Addressing itself to "the necessity of reformation," the Synod described in detail those evils which in its opinion "have provoked the Lord to bring his judgments on New England." The candid, cold self-examination produced a detailed indictment: (1) professing Christians failing to live up to their profession; (2) an excess of pride in spiritual matters and in dress; (3) neglect of the church and its ordinances; (4) profanity and irreverance; (5) sabbath-breaking; (6) decline in family devotions and discipline; (7) "sinful heats and hatreds," "uncharitable and unrighteous censures, back-bitings, hearing and telling tales"; (8) intemperance and drunkenness; (9) dishonesty; (10) "inordinate affection to the world"; (11) hardhearted continuing in sin; (12) lack of community concern; and (13) impenitence and unbelief.

It was a damning catalogue, and the path prescribed for correction was not easy.

The calls for repentance and reform continued into the eighteenth century, but with agonizingly meager results. Ministers each year warned of impending disaster in tones more mournful than the year before. But as orthodoxy further declined, "many and great impieties" arose. New England fell into a "time of extraordinary dullness in religion," to be roused therefrom in a Great Awakening.

The religious excitement of the 1740's moved the Puritan colonies, as it did the Southern and middle colonies, to a refreshed, enlivened, and sometimes embittered attention to religion. Here, as to the south, George Whitefield was a powerful catalyst. Coming from Charleston, South Carolina, to New England in September 1740, the bustling, driving Whitefield swept over New England in a six-week tour that left everyone except himself breathless. Those favoring Whitefield and his impassioned appeals concluded that he was the messenger of God. Thomas Prince of Boston reported joyfully that "great numbers in this town were so happily concerned about their souls, as we have never seen anything like it before, except at the time of the general earthquake." Others, however, such as Boston's Charles Chauncy, thought less of this one-man earthquake. "Wherever he went he generally moved the passions, especially of the younger people, and the females among them; the effect whereof was a great talk about religion. . . . But so far as I could judge upon the nicest observation, the town in general was not much mended in those things wherein a reformation was greatly needed."

When Whitefield left New England at the end of October 1740, resident pastors pursued the revival spirit. One of those pastors defended the Awakening against all who would defame or oppose it. Jonathan Edwards possessed the ablest theological and philosophical intellect in colonial America. Often known only as the preacher of "Sinners in the Hands of an Angry God," Edwards should be better known for his later, fuller work. From that starkly realistic sermon, delivered in Enfield, Connecticut, in 1741, Edwards proceeded to examine the whole question of conversion, of God moving among men, of men moved by the Spirit of God—indeed, the whole question of the nature of religion itself.

How can one distinguish revelation from delusion? How can one be sure what is of God, what of Satan? One can hardly judge on the basis of the emotional pitch or the noisy fervor, the fainting, the ranting, the namecalling. Yet neither can one throw out the emotions or "affections" as irrelevant to a genuine transformation. "For I am persuaded," Edwards wrote, "that there was never any considerable change wrought in the mind or conversation [life] of any person . . . that had not his affections moved." What then? Emotions may lead to excesses and delusions, but only through emotions can a hard heart, "like a stone, insensible, stupid, unmoved," be melted and reformed. How can one know which path he walks? By the fruits of the Spirit, Edwards answers. In his final great defense of the Awakening, *A Treatise Concerning Religious Affections,* the Northampton pastor proclaims that "the essence of all true religion lies in holy love." As one devotes himself, habitually, to this love and manifests the fruits of such love, he possesses "the whole of religion."

In a 1732 sermon, Jonathan Edwards distinguishes two ways of knowing God.

> There is a twofold understanding or knowledge of good that God has made the mind capable of. The first, that which is merely speculative and notional. . . . And the other is that which consists in the sense of the heart. . . . In the former is exercised merely the speculative faculty or the understanding. . . . In the latter the will, or inclination, or heart, is mainly concerned.
>
> Thus there is a difference between having an opinion that God is holy and gracious, and having a sense of . . . that holiness and grace. There is a difference between having a rational judgment that honey is sweet, and having a sense of its sweetness. A man may have the former that knows not how honey tastes; but a man cannot have the latter unless he has an idea of the taste of honey in his mind. . . . There is a wide difference between mere speculative rational judging anything to be excellent, and having a sense of its sweetness and beauty. The former rests only in the head . . . but the heart is concerned in the latter.

While the Great Awakening revived interest in religion, increased membership, and strengthened moral resolve, it also hastened the end of Congregationalism's monopoly in Puritan New England. Many broke away from the established churches, departing from a ministry regarded as too formal, graceless, and cold. As the "church-rending, unpeaceable, party spirit" grew, New England's churches fell into two camps, designated Old Lights (generally opposed to the Awakening) and New Lights (generally favorable to it). "Such distinguishing names of reproach," commented Edwards, "divide us into two armies, separated and drawn up in battle array, ready to fight one another."

In 1630 William Bradford, looking at the growing population around him, wrote: "Thus out of small beginnings greater things have been produced by His hand." Then he added prophetically: "As one small candle may light a thousand, so the light here kindled hath shone unto many, yea in some sort to our whole nation." If New England's light seemed in the colonial period to shine more brightly than most, the credit goes to town, meetinghouse, and school. Closely settled rather than scattered widely along rivers and valleys, New England's colonists could better maintain discipline, carry on tradition, and pursue the public good. The meetinghouse was not only the geographical center of the town, it was the focus of New England life. A place of general assembly, it was not the "church." For the church consisted of those gathered saints who had covenanted to walk together after the ways of the Lord. All the meetinghouse did was hold that small candle until it had lit a thousand.

A modern author, Ola E. Winslow, portrays the church as New England's centerpiece (*Meetinghouse Hill 1630–1783*).

On Sunday the town assembled here for preaching; on town meeting Monday essentially the same group met in the same place to vote "fence repairs," convenient "Horse Bridges," rings for swine, bounty on crows and wolf heads; to specify more trees for the "shade of cattle" or to vote penalties for those who "deaded" trees contrary to order; to grant one applicant "liberty to set his house upon a Knole," another "liberty" to move into town or depart; to elect chimney viewers, hogreaves, surveyors, constables or other officers, and to learn "the mind of the town" as to various other imperatives of their daily lives. . . . The drumbeat at any other time than the accustomed hour on Sunday morning was a signal to assemble here at once for some purpose that brooked no hesitation. All paths led to this spot of "rising ground"; all distances to other towns were measured from the front door. The meetinghouse was the center of life.

---

7 ❖ "A Full Liberty in Religious Concernments":

RHODE ISLAND

I N THE PRECEDING CHAPTER the term "Puritan New England" was used so that none would err by including Rhode Island. The Puritan never made that mistake. So completely did he disdain all that went on in and around Providence Plantations that one unskilled in geography might suppose that these plantations lay somewhere to the south of Spanish Florida. Devoutly the Puritans wished it were so.

But Rhode Island was tucked up under Plymouth and Massachusetts Bay Colonies and only a short way from New Haven. While easy to scorn, it was hard to ignore. The tight lid that Massachusetts and Connecticut kept on religious life required a safety valve: hence, the Colony of Rhode Island and Providence Plantations.

That colony's founding is intertwined with the early days of Massachusetts Bay, this connection and confusion embodied in the person of Roger Williams. Early in 1631 Williams debarked at Boston where he was happily received. For "godly ministers" (as Governor Winthrop called him) were few, and there was much to be done. Boston even offered Williams its pulpit, but he declined the generous invitation because, as he later wrote, "I durst not officiate to an unseparated people." The Puritans of Massachusetts Bay, as already noted, considered themselves still part of the Church of England—the truer and better part. Williams saw this unwillingness to break away from the national establishment as an improper compromise. "This middle walking," he wrote, is "no less than halting." New England's visible saints must separate "holy from unholy, penitent from impenitent, godly from ungodly."

Cherishing such convictions, Williams moved on to Salem, where the church planned to install him as its pastor. When the rebuffed Bostonians heard of this, they decided to "counsel" the Salem flock. Salem's offer was withdrawn, and Williams moved southward to the Plymouth pilgrims who noted nothing scandalous in separation. But in 1633 this disturbing dissenter was back in Salem as assistant pastor.

In his brief ministry there Roger Williams confirmed every suspicion that any puritan divine ever entertained. Having already attacked the church government, he now proceeded to attack the civil government, protesting that magistrates must not punish Sabbathbreakers or violators of any other religious requirement. Moreover, the New England government had no authority since it possessed no land. As no proper purchase had been made, Massachusetts still belonged to the Indians! King Charles could not have given it to the Puritans, because, dear friends, King Charles never owned it!

A more sweeping program of subversion could hardly be imagined. Clearly the limits of Puritan endurance had been reached. In 1634 the opposition gathered its evidence and the next year brought Williams to trial. The verdict surprised no one. "Whereas Mr. Roger Williams . . . hath broached and divulged diverse new and dangerous opinions against the authority of the magistrates and churches here . . . it is therefore ordered that the said Mr. Williams shall depart out of this jurisdiction."

In his *Ecclesiastical History of New England* (1702) Cotton Mather offers his unflattering appraisal of Roger Williams.

In the year 1654, a certain windmill in the Low Countries, whirling round with extraordinary violence, by reason of a violent storm then blowing—the stone at length by its rapid motion became so intensely hot as to fire the mill, from whence the flames, being dispersed by the high winds, did set a whole town on fire. But I can tell my reader that, about twenty years before this, there was a whole country in America like to be set on fire by the rapid motion of a windmill in the head of one particular man. Know, then, that about the year 1630 arrived here one Mr. Roger Williams, who being a preacher that had less light than fire in him hath by his own sad example preached unto us the danger of that evil which the apostle mentions in Romans 10 : 2, "They have a zeal, but act not according to knowledge."

The court granted Williams six weeks in which to leave, later extending his stay to spring. This leniency contained the stern proviso that all preaching and persuading by Williams must stop; he must not "go about to draw others to his opinions." But "others" calling on Williams and his family found his opinions freely expressed and wholly unchanged. Authorities quickly determined to send him to England immediately. When Williams heard of this plan, he left home "in the bitter winter season," making his way through the "howling wilderness" to the headwaters of Narragansett Bay. There he founded a settlement, naming it Providence "in a sense of God's merciful providence unto me in my distress." Williams's wife and two small children, along with friends from Salem, soon joined him there.

Promising freedom in religion, this new land (which Williams had been careful to purchase from the Indians) swiftly became a haven for dissenters, for the persecuted, the adventurers, the self-seekers. When in 1639 a few Baptists drifted into the colony, Williams decided to join them in founding America's first Baptist church. Williams probably found in "believer's baptism" (as opposed to infant baptism) something of his own concern for a voluntary choice in religion. Also, like Williams, Baptists suffered persecution, and against this "bloudy tenent" he and they made common cause. While affiliated with this denomination for only a brief time, Williams continued to influence the early Baptists (see Fig. 1).

John Clarke, founder of Newport, pastor and physician, joined Williams in colonial and denominational causes. Clarke too left Massachusetts Bay when he found himself in 1638 on the wrong side of an intense theological dispute. To Newport (actually the "island" part of Rhode Island) Clarke and other sympathizers came in March of that year; following Williams's example, they purchased the land from the surrounding Indians with beads, coats, and hoes. The new settlers agreed "in the presence of Jehovah" to "incorporate ourselves in a Body Politic, and as He shall help us, will submit our persons, lives and estates unto our Lord Jesus Christ, the King of Kings, the Lord of Lords. . . ."

Clarke's and Williams's separate settlements formed in 1647 a single colony to rule by "Democracy, or Popular Government." While land had been duly bought, royal recognition was still essential. Earlier, in 1643, Williams had secured a charter for Providence. But changes both in that colony and in England made securing another charter essential. In 1651 Williams and Clarke embarked for England. While Williams returned to America in 1654, Clarke labored for twelve long, desperate years to place the young colony on firm legal footing. Finally, July 8, 1663, the "English Colony of Rhode Island and Providence Plantations in New England, in America" received its royal charter. The rights there granted, rights to be enjoyed "forever hereafter," reflected the prophetic views of the two men most responsible for that document.

For in 1652 John Clarke had written that "this forcing of men in matters of conscience toward God to believe as others do, cannot stand with peace, liberty, prosperity and safety of a place, commonwealth or nation." And in that same year Roger Williams had written: "While heaven and earth last . . . no one tenent that either London, England, or the world doth harbor is so heretical, blasphemous, seditious, and dangerous to the corporal, to the spiritual, to the present, to the eternal good of all men as . . . the bloudy tenent of persecution for cause of conscience."

Religious liberty is guaranteed in Rhode Island's Royal Charter, obtained by John Clarke in 1663.

And whereas, in their humble address, they have freely declared that it is much on their hearts (if they may be permitted) to hold forth a lively experiment, that a most flourishing civil state may stand and best be maintained . . . with a full liberty in religious concernments; and that true piety rightly grounded upon gospel principles will give the best and greatest security to sovereignty, and will lay in the hearts of man the strongest obligations to true loyalty:

Now know ye, that we being willing to encourage the hopeful undertaking of our said loyal and loving subjects and to secure them in the free exercise and enjoyment of all their civil and religious rights . . . do hereby publish, grant, ordain and declare . . . that no person within the said colony at any time hereafter shall be any wise molested, punished, disquieted, or call[ed] in question, for any differences of opinion in matters of religion, and do not actually disturb the civil peace of our said colony; but that all and every person and persons may, from time to time, and at all times hereafter, freely and fully have and enjoy his and their own judgments and consciences. . . .

Because the doors of toleration were opened wide, Clarke's Baptists could not maintain a monopoly or even a preferred position. By 1676 an Anglican missionary referred to the Quakers as "the Grandees of the place," so powerful had they become in the colony's political and economic life. Despite pleas by neighboring colonies, Rhode Island steadily refused to "remove those Quakers that have been received, and for the future prohibit their coming among you." This request from the New England Confederacy was promptly rejected, Rhode Island's General Assembly asserting that "freedom of conscience we still prize as the greatest happiness that man can possess in this world."

Quaker growth and Quaker toleration did not mean that all Rhode Island citizens either agreed with Quakers or approved of them. Indeed, none other than Roger Williams himself, over seventy years of age, felt obliged to prove Quakers wrong in their religious opinions. When the Society's founder, George Fox, arrived in Newport in 1672, the time seemed ripe for a direct challenge. Williams, a "New England firebrand," as Fox called him, drew up fourteen propositions for debate. By the time all arrangements were made, Fox had left New England, but three other Quaker witnesses took his place. In August the debate took place. Neither side won, for neither listened to the other. And posterity has done little better, acknowledging only the quaintness of the record left behind: *George Fox Digged Out of his Burrowes* (Boston, 1676) and *A New England Firebrand Quenched* (London, 1678). To grant the Quakers religious liberty was one thing; to agree with them—well, that was quite another!

Quaker developments in Rhode Island are revealed in George Fox's *Journal* (1672).

And in Rhode Island we had ten glorious meetings together, one day after another with only one Seventh-day in between. . . . And all Friends were filled with the love of God, and the glory of the Lord shineth over all. And at Narragansett where almost all the country came to hear, in a justice's barn, there was another justice there, and they were all drawing up a paper to invite me to come again, for they were so taken with the truth. . . .

And at another place they, with an ancient justice, said that if they had money enough they would hire me. So I said then it was time for me to go away [when] they would not come to their own teacher. For that (viz., hiring) did and had spoiled them and many for not improving their own talents, for we brought every one to their own teacher.

Among those to enjoy that toleration, still so rare in the seventeenth century, were Jews who arrived at Newport, perhaps as early as 1658. Coming originally from the Iberian peninsula, these settlers later received Jewish immigrants from Central and Eastern Europe as well as from Portugal and Spain. Unable to build a synagogue for more than a hundred years, Newport's Jews held religious services in private homes or rented halls. Finally, in 1759 they broke ground, and four years later on December 2, 1763, they dedicated the finest of colonial synagogues. Touro Synagogue (named after the congregation's rabbi at the time), like the Puritan's meetinghouse, became a place of general civic assembly, especially following the devastation of the Revolutionary War. With few breaks in continuity, Touro continued to serve as the center for Jewish religious life in Newport from pre-Revolution days to the present. In 1946 the handsome structure became a national historic site (see Fig. 1).

Before the end of the seventeenth century Anglicanism penetrated into the "ungospellized Plantations," as Cotton Mather disdainfully called the Rhode Island colony. Huguenots, fleeing from France's oppression, joined with English churchmen in Newport to form Trinity Church in 1698. Supported in its struggling infancy by missionaries of the Society for the Propagation of the Gospel, the congregation managed by 1726 to erect "the most beautiful timber structure in America" (see Figs. 3 and 4). In 1733 England's visiting Bishop Berkeley gave the parish a pipe organ, and by the middle of the century Church of England parishes existed in Kingston, Warwick, Providence, and Westerly.

By then even Congregationalism, swallowing its pride, had added to the bright diversity in Rhode Island religion. In 1728 Boston's Old South Church sent Josiah Cotton as a "missionary" to Providence to organize a Puritan church. To that church Eleazar Wheelock, founder of Dartmouth College, came in the turbulent days of the Great Awakening. In 1741, preaching there "to a full assembly," Wheelock found "many scoffers present." And after exposing himself to the local Baptists, "a poor, bigoted, ignorant, prejudiced people," Wheelock could only exclaim, "O, what a burden dear Mr. Cotton has daily to bear."

First Baptist Church of America, Providence, Rhode Island • Founded by Roger Williams, this church built the meetinghouse shown above in 1774–5 "for the worship of Almighty God and also for holding commencement in." Brown University continues to use the meetinghouse for its annual commencement.

2. Touro Synagogue, Newport, Rhode Island • Home of Congregation of Jeshuat Israel since 1763, this beautiful colonial structure is America's oldest surviving synagogue. In 1946 it was named a national shrine.

3. Trinity Episcopal Church, Newport, Rhode Island • Built in 1726, this magnificent structure won the praise of many a visitor, including England's Bishop George Berkeley who was moved to present the congregation with an organ.

4. *Trinity Episcopal Church (interior)*

5. *University Hall, Brown University • Brown's original college edifice, built in 1770, served both as barracks and as hospital during the American Revolution; it is now a national historic landmark.*

Following the Awakening, Baptists rapidly increased in Rhode Island, as they did in Puritan New England. But the liberal climate of Rhode Island made it a logical choice for that denomination's first college. With support from Baptists in the middle colonies as well as in New England, the College of Rhode Island, later Brown, came into being in 1764. The third New England college, Brown followed its predecessors, Harvard and Yale, in regarding an education for the ministry as also an education qualifying all men "for discharging the offices of life with usefulness and reputation." Thus to Brown all pious and earnest "youth may freely resort for education in the vernacular and learned languages, and in the liberal arts and sciences" (see Fig. 5).

Brown University's Charter (1764) preserves religion but guards against sectarianism.

> And furthermore, it is hereby enacted and declared: That into this liberal and catholic institution shall never be admitted any religions tests: But on the contrary all the members hereof shall forever enjoy full, free, absolute and uninterrupted liberty of conscience: And that the places of Professors, Tutors and all other officers, the President alone excepted, shall be free and open for all denominations of Protestants: And that youth of all religious denominations shall and may be freely admitted to the equal advantages, emoluments, and honors of the College or University. . . . And that the sectarian differences of opinion shall not make any part of the public and classical instruction, although all religious controversies may be studied freely, examined and explained by the President, Professors and Tutors in a personal, separate and distinct manner to the youth of any or each denomination.

If the power of Puritan New England came from its settled towns and their central meetinghouses, the force of Rhode Island lay in its "lively experiment that a most flourishing civil state may stand and best be maintained . . . with a full liberty in religious concernments." Out of this small beginning, too, "greater things have been produced by His hand."

8 ❖ "The Gospel into a Fruitful Bosom":

MARYLAND

I N APRIL 1632 King Charles I granted to Cecil Calvert a charter for lands around the Chesapeake Bay. Eighteen months later Calvert, whose title of nobility was Lord Baltimore, dispatched two small ships for the shores of Maryland.

Lord Baltimore, the only Roman Catholic proprietor among America's colonists, recognized that England's Catholics needed a haven as much as England's Puritans. So Maryland, honoring both England's last Catholic queen and the Virgin Mother, came into being. Lord Baltimore, however, also recognized the virtue and value of religious toleration. From the very beginning, therefore, Maryland's gates opened to Protestant and Catholic alike.

Indeed, on those first two ships, the *Ark* and the *Dove,* both Protestants and Catholics sailed. Concerning the passengers the young Baltimore gave judicious but demanding instructions to his governor: "Be very careful to preserve unity and peace among all the passengers on shipboard and suffer no scandal nor offence to be given to any of the Protestants . . . cause all acts of Roman Catholic religion to be done as privately as may be . . . instruct all the Roman Catholics to be silent upon all occasions of discourse concerning matters of religion . . . treat Protestants with as much mildness and favor as justice will permit. And this to be observed at land as well as at sea."

In March 1634 the expedition arrived at the mouth of the Potomac River, then it made its way up the Chesapeake to St. Clement's [Blakiston] Island. On March 25 mass was first offered. Then, adds Andrew White, one of the three Jesuit fathers aboard, "bearing on our shoulders a huge cross, which we had hewn from a tree, we moved in procession to a spot selected . . . and erected it as a trophy to Christ our Savior; then humbly kneeling, we recited with deep emotion the Litany of the Holy Cross." The first Catholic chapel was erected soon after in St. Mary's, the original capital of the colony.

Father White attempted missionary work among the Indians, but their unyielding hostility made his recall to St. Mary's mandatory. Yet Jesuits missions among the Indians remained a major objective in and around

72

Maryland. As Father White noted: "It is much more prudence and charity to civilize and make them Christians than to kill, rob, and hunt them from place to place, as you would do a wolf."

Father Andrew White, S. J., in 1633 encouraged his fellow countrymen to colonize Maryland and there sow seeds of religion and piety.

The first and most important design . . . is not to think so much of planting fruits and trees in a land so fruitful, as of sowing the seeds of religion and piety. Surely a design worthy of Christians, worthy of angels, worthy of Angles [Englishmen]. The English nation, renowned for so many ancient victories, never undertook anything more noble or glorious than this. Behold the lands are white for the harvest, prepared for receiving the seed of the Gospel into a fruitful bosom. . . . Who then can doubt that by one such glorious work as this, many thousands of souls will be brought to Christ?

In that first decade of the 1630's missionaries also directed their efforts toward Protestants emigrating to Maryland. One report from the young colony declared that "among the Protestants, nearly all who have come from England in this year, 1638, and many others have been converted to the [Catholic] faith, together with four servants whom we purchased in Virginia. . . ." But soon the colony began to receive large numbers of Protestants from the surrounding areas who resisted conversion. A resulting alteration in religious complexion together with a changing political complexion in England meant for Maryland turbulent times ahead.

A rebellion promoted by William Claiborne in the 1640's wrested control from Baltimore's hands and caused the Jesuits to be expelled from Maryland. In 1646 legitimate authority was restored. Aware that much of his opposition came from Englishmen unsympathetic to the idea of a Catholic colony, Lord Baltimore deliberately invited Puritans to settle in Maryland. And in 1649 the colonial assembly passed a Toleration Act whose words echoed those of the farsighted and fair-minded Baltimore.

The 1649 Act decreed that "no persons professing to believe in Jesus Christ should be molested in respect of their religion, or in the free exercise thereof, or be compelled to the belief or exercise of any other religion, against their consent. . . ." While the law offered no sanctuary to the Jew, freedom for Judaism at this period of Maryland's history was an academic question. In all other respects the act outshone any feeble lights of liberty flickering in Europe or—except for Rhode Island—in the other colonies (see Fig. 1).

The next decade found the opportunistic Claiborne active once more. Possessing an ambiguous commission from Cromwell's government, this "pestilent enemy" in 1651 began to assert his authority, winning full control by 1655 after bitter bloodshed. Action of the new legislature regarding religion stood in marked contrast to the preceding ones. The new house granted a kind of religious liberty—a liberty that specifically excluded "popery or prelacy." Those attempting to continue in "the popish (commonly called Roman Catholic) religion" were "to be restrained from the exercise thereof," while Royalists as well as Catholics were barred from the legislative assembly.

The entire action, military and political, directly violated rights granted by the Crown to the colonial proprietor. Lord Baltimore, constantly defending his rights in England, never found enough calm to visit Maryland in person. If he was not wrestling authorities in London, he was battling officialdom in Maryland. Governor Josias Fendall, for example, not only usurped unlawful powers but also attempted to rid Maryland of newly arrived Quakers, those "vagabonds that have of late presumed to come into the country." Such persons he ordered "apprehended and whipped."

After a monarch was restored to the throne of England in 1660, comparative quiet settled once more upon the colony. When Cecil Calvert died in 1675, his son and at that time governor, Charles Calvert, succeeded to the proprietary title. Some then thought it time to improve the position of the Church of England. One Anglican rector complained that while Catholics had an adequate ministry and Quakers took care of their own, "some established support for a protestant ministry" was still missing. Because of this lack, he argued, Maryland's religion was more darkness than light: "The Lord's day is profaned; religion is despised, and all notorious vices are committed, so that it is become a Sodom of uncleanness, and a pest house of iniquity." While evil was never quite that triumphant, the good rector's report was a dramatic call for financial support of England's lagging church. When those fearful of irreligion joined with those fearful of "popish" religion, the door to Anglican establishment opened wide.

After England's "Glorious Revolution" of 1688 brought William and Mary to the throne, Maryland followed suit with its own "protestant revolution." In April 1689 an association formed "for the defence of the protestant religion, and for asserting the rights of King William and Queen Mary to that province [Maryland] and all the English dominions." Amid wild rumors of papal plots the association submitted a list of extravagant "grievances" to King William. As it was in the king's interest to have strong Protestant backing both at home and abroad, he turned from Charles Calvert in 1691 to establish a new royal government in the colony.

An assembly, convened in 1692, lost little time in making clear where its religious loyalties lay. An act "for the service of Almighty God, and the establishment of the Protestant religion" was quickly passed. Counties were divided into parishes; these were to appoint vestries; and vestrymen were to build churches if none then existed. The whole establishment was

1. *Maryland Toleration Act Monument* • *Erected in the original capital of Maryland, St. Mary's City, this modern sculpture by Hans Schuler commemorates the colony's 1649 "Act Concerning Religion."*

2. *Third Haven Meeting, Easton, Maryland* • *This Quaker meetinghouse, erected in 1682–84, is one of the oldest wooden houses of worship in the country. William Penn was among those who attended meeting here.*

3. *Methodism's First College* • *Cokesbury College, which no longer exists, was founded in Maryland because that was the first major stronghold of American Methodism.*

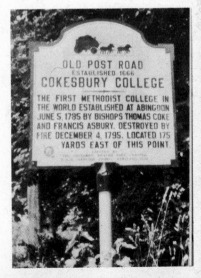

OLD POST ROAD
ESTABLISHED 1666
COKESBURY COLLEGE

THE FIRST METHODIST COLLEGE IN THE WORLD ESTABLISHED AT ABINGDON JUNE 5, 1795 BY BISHOPS THOMAS COKE AND FRANCIS ASBURY. DESTROYED BY FIRE DECEMBER 4, 1795. LOCATED 175 YARDS EAST OF THIS POINT.

to be supported by taxation (fifty pounds of tobacco per head), the taxes to be collected by the sheriff. While thirty-one parishes were thus created by law, neither sufficient clergy nor buildings existed to give substance to the law.

The task of implementing these ambitious legal provisions fell largely to Francis Nicholson, who became governor in 1694. He actively encouraged the building of churches and also imported eight additional Anglican clergymen. With an eye on newly founded William and Mary College he established a free primary school designed to feed into the Virginia college. Yet with Quaker and Roman Catholic resistance, with increasing Irish Catholic immigration, and with a rumor that Lord Baltimore was returning to royal favor, Anglicans felt little security. If they could not obtain a bishop (and that seemed out of the question), they then requested someone with authority that would "capacitate him to redress what is amiss, and supply what is wanting in the Church." This petition resulted in the appointment of Thomas Bray as commissary, that is, a representative of the bishop.

The energies and the attainments of this zealous missionary were enormous. Moreover, they were contagious. Bray's name is intimately linked with the names of two societies vital to the religious life of all colonial America: the Society for Promoting Christian Knowledge (S.P.C.K.) and the Society for the Propagation of the Gospel in Foreign Parts (S.P.G.). In the creation of both, Bray was the moving force.

Appointed commissary to Maryland in 1695, Thomas Bray delayed his departure for America until legal questions regarding establishment could be clarified. More than three years passed before Bray paid his first visit to the colony, but those years were not idly spent. A graduate of Oxford, Bray was a gifted student, pastor, and teacher. After his appointment by the bishop of London he determined to help colonial pastors be both students and teachers. As a minimum this meant providing books and establishing libraries in the colonies. He conceived of a corporation empowered to receive gifts and legacies; with the monies received, missionaries could be sent to and maintained in the plantations, catechetical schools could be set up, and libraries could be established. Bray was especially eager to help those that "shall most hazard their persons in attempting the conversion of the Negroes or native Indians."

With several influential backers the S.P.C.K. emerged in 1699. Agreeing to consult regularly on "how we may be able by due and lawful methods to promote Christian knowledge," the members immediately launched a program of vast vision. Much of that program, then and now, pertained to books. When in 1695 Thomas Bray set down his *Proposals for encouraging Learning and Religion in the Foreign Plantations,* what he had chiefly in mind were books. Thus the S.P.C.K. early entered the book business in an ambitious way—buying, printing, distributing, educating. The vigorous initiative of Bray's first society greatly enriched the whole cultural life of the colonies.

After Commissary Bray's first visit to Maryland in 1700, he returned to establish a second society, the S.P.G. Though he had been in America less than six months, this keen observer fully recognized the churches' difficult straits. Support for an adequate ministry was urgently required. To secure such, Bray proposed that a society be created to insure the place of the Church of England in "foreign parts" and, secondly, to proceed to the conversion of the Negro and the Indian. Again, with strong support from the archbishop of Canterbury as well as the bishop of London, Bray tasted the sweets of success. On June 16, 1701, King William granted the charter, and within two weeks the S.P.G. first met at Lambeth Palace, the archbishop presiding.

The Society for the Propagation of the Gospel received its charter in 1701 from King William III.

> Whereas We are credibly informed, That in many of our Plantations, Colonies and Factories beyond the seas, belonging to Our Kingdom of England, the Provision for ministers is very mean; and many others . . . are wholly destitute and unprovided of a maintenance for ministers and the public worship of God; and for lack of support and maintenance for such, many of our loving subjects do want the administration of God's Word and Sacraments, and seem abandoned to atheism and infidelity. . . .
>
> Know ye herefore, That We . . . do will, ordain, constitute, declare and grant [that the charter members and their successors] shall for ever hereafter be, and by virtue of these presents shall be one body politic and corporate, in deed and in name, by the name of, The Society for the Propagation of the Gospel in Foreign Parts.

By the time of Bray's death in 1730 the S.P.G. had won a sure place in England and was winning a sure place for England's church in the colonies. In that year David Humphreys, secretary of the S.P.G., published the first history of that lively organization, *An Historical Account of the Incorporated Society for the Propagation of the Gospel in Foreign Parts*. While properly proud of the Society's achievements in so short a time, Humphreys was not blind to its failures. Failure among the Indians was an old story, as old as the expedition of Ayllón. In ministering to the Negro the problems and perplexities were newer.

From the beginning, the Society ordered its missionaries to "use their best endeavors, at proper times to instruct the Negroes." Hundreds became converts, but thousands did not. "It must be confessed," wrote Humphreys, "what hath been done is as nothing, with regard to what a true Christian would hope to see effected." He then described those obstacles most seriously affecting the work among Negroes.

4. *Cathedral of the Assumption of the Blessed Virgin Mary, Baltimore • Designed by the best known American architect of his time, Benjamin Latrobe, this cathedral was built in a Classic style inspired by Rome's Pantheon.*

(1) Negroes do not have enough time for real instruction. Usually they have only Sunday off, when "the Minister of a Parish is fully employed in other duties." Also "many planters in order to free themselves from the trouble and charge of feeding and clothing their slaves allow them one day in a week to clear ground and plant it, to subsist themselves and families." In that event the Negro worked on Sunday, for his family "doth absolutely depend on this."

(2) Problems of space no less than of time impeded the effort. Plantations were so large and so far apart that "neither can a minister go to many families, if the Negroes were allowed time to attend him; nor can a proper number of them assemble together at one place, without considerable loss of time to their masters."

(3) Finally, "the greatest obstruction is [that] the masters themselves do not consider enough the obligation which lies upon them to have their slaves instructed." In dismay, the Secretary added: "Some have been so weak as to argue, the Negroes have no souls; others, that they grew worse by being taught and made Christians. I would not mention these if they were not popular arguments now, because they have no foundation in reason or truth." The English, like the French and the Spanish, found economic interest often at odds with religious intent. And if the S.P.G. failed to do all that it sought, the earnestness of its effort was—for the eighteenth century—something of a victory.

Maryland early offered a toleration that excluded none—not even the papist. All Englishmen, as a Maryland ordinance of 1639 declared, "shall have all their rights and liberties according to the Great Charter of England." But by an ironic twist Roman Catholic Englishmen at the end of that century found little sanctuary in their own Catholic colony. For some, Maryland provided fruitful soil, but for others the ground grew stony and hard.

Catholicism nonetheless remained stronger in Maryland than elsewhere among the colonies. And when the first Catholic bishop presided in America, he chose Baltimore as his episcopal see (see Fig. 4). Cecil Calvert would have approved.

9 ❖ "We Put the Power in the People":

MIDDLE COLONIES

NEW YORK, DELAWARE, NEW JERSEY, AND PENNSYLVANIA present a picture of striking diversity. Variety extended to the colonists' languages, their origins, and their religions. One heard Swedish spoken along the Delaware, Dutch on both banks of the Hudson, French near the East River, German on the Susquehanna, and English—after 1664— almost anywhere. Lutherans worshiped in Wilmington, Calvinists gathered in Albany, Quakers met in Burlington, Presbyterians preached in Newark, Anglicans evangelized Westchester, Jesuits heard confession in Philadelphia, and Jews in New York heard the Law of Moses. Together or separately, devout colonists built churches, established colleges, and strengthened economies. In all of youthful America, the middle colonies demonstrated most convincingly that out of diversity may come unity: *e pluribus unum.*

NEW YORK AND DELAWARE

Even before the end of the sixteenth century the Dutch entertained hopes of a West India Company. Such a company might (1) bring to Holland a share of the rumored riches of the New World, (2) open up a path to India itself, and (3) enable Holland to resist the growing menace of Spanish might. Though proposed as early as 1592, the company did not receive its charter until 1621. Two years later the West India Company occupied territory around the mouth of the Hudson River.

Ignoring the overlapping claims of Virginia and New England, Peter Minuit in 1626 made his celebrated $24.00 purchase of Manhattan Island from the Indians. Following this with other good bargains, Dutch merchants within a decade were becoming Dutch colonists. Down the Delaware at Fort Nassau (near Gloucester, New Jersey) and up the Hudson at Fort Orange (near Albany, New York) the Dutch settled before 1630.

While the company's charter contained no reference to religion, colonial promoters proposed that ministers be sent to instruct both the settlers and the Indians "in religion and learning." On April 7, 1628, the first Dutch minister, Jonas Michaëlius, arrived on Manhattan Island at the settlement called New Amsterdam. Despite the death of his wife soon after, Michaëlius resolved to remain among a "rather rough and unrestrained" people.

If he found his fifty communicants ("Walloons and Dutch") rather rough, Michaëlius found the Indians "entirely savage and wild." Michaëlius wrote home that all previous reports of the Indians as peaceable, lovable, and naturally religious were simply not so. They are as "uncivil and stupid as garden stakes," he asserted, and the very thought of attempting to convert them staggered him. "Now by what means are we to prepare this people for salvation, or to make a salutary breach among them?" Answering his own question, Pastor Michaëlius concluded that the adults were beyond hope; hence, all attention should be given to the children, who ought "to be separated from their parents, yea, from their whole nation."

In 1629 the Dutch Reformed Church was officially established in New Netherland (New York). While most understood this to exclude all other religious groups, the directors of the company followed a liberal policy, encouraging colonists of many faiths to settle there. When Michaëlius' three-year term of service to the company was over, he returned to Holland, quite ready to leave to others his ministry to rough colonists and savage natives.

The first entry in New Amsterdam's city records is the prayer of Pastor John Megapolensis at the opening of the court on February 6, 1653. A portion follows.

> Graciously incline our hearts, that we exercise the power which thou hast given us, to the general good of the community, and to the maintenance of the church, that we may be praised by them that do well, and a terror to evil-doers.
>
> Incline, also, the hearts of the subjects unto due obedience, so that through their respect and obedience our burdens may be made the lighter.
>
> Thou knowest, O Lord, that the wicked and ungodly do generally condemn and transgress thine ordinances; therefore clothe us with strength, courage, fortitude and promptness, that we may, with proper earnestness and zeal, be steadfast unto the death against all sinners and evil-doers.

However properly and legally constituted, the Dutch Reformed Church exerted little influence in the first generation. Rarely was more than a single minister present in the whole colony. It was no longer a question of quickly converting the Indians but of grimly holding on to the Dutch. Even here success was minimal. When Peter Stuyvesant took over as director general of the colony in 1647, he found the citizens of New Amsterdam "without discipline and approaching the savage state." The Dutch were crowded aside by other nationalities and faiths, some eighteen different languages being heard in New Netherland alone. If internal affairs were dismaying,

1. Hudson's HALF MOON • This is a replica of the ship that Hudson sailed up the river which bears his name, exploring it as far north as the present site of Albany.

2. Old Dutch Reformed Church, Albany • This structure was erected in 1715 on a church site dating back to 1651. In 1806, this building was razed.

3. Holy Trinity (Old Swedes) Church, Wilmington, Delaware • Swedish Lutherans erected this church in 1698; it became an Episcopal parish in 1791.

external affairs were demoralizing. The French bought furs from the Mohawks before traders at Albany could even make a bid. The English pushed into Dutch territory both in Connecticut and Long Island. Finally, to the south a small colony of Swedes seemed to be getting out of hand.

New Sweden, as the settlement along the Delaware River was called, began in 1638. In March of that year Peter Minuit, who had been relieved of his duties with the Dutch seven years earlier, sailed into Delaware Bay with two ships, *Kalmar Nyckel* and *Vogel Grip*. Near the present site of Wilmington he established Fort Christina, named after the eleven-year-old Swedish queen. But it was the Swedish king, Gustavus Adolphus, who long before had envisioned such a "planting" in the New World. The hero of European Protestantism in the seventeenth century, King Gustavus strongly backed the colonial enterprise. After his death in 1632 the venture languished for a time, but within six years Sweden's flag finally flew over American territory (see Fig. 3).

To a great extent an economic venture (beaver furs from the Indians, tobacco from the Virginians), the settlement on the Delaware was also a Swedish mission, and such it remained down to the Revolutionary War. The Church of Sweden, now Lutheran, served as religious overseer. A clergyman arrived with the second expedition in 1639 and another, John Campanius, in 1643. Though Campanius remained in New Sweden only five years, he, like John Eliot, seriously sought to evangelize the Indians. He learned their language and translated Martin Luther's *Catechism* into "American-Virginian." Printing of the catechism was unfortunately delayed until 1696, when King Charles XI sent five hundred copies from Stockholm to the Delaware Indians.

In his *Description of the Former and Present Condition of . . . New Sweden* (Stockholm, 1759) Israel Acrelius describes the difficulties in Delaware.

> The people waited, but no clergyman came. All the church service they now had [1692] was that an old man . . . sat and read [sermons on the gospels]. The young people were not very anxious to hear these things. The youth who came were fonder of riding races than of attending Divine service. There was no order, no reverence among the people. It was time for God to help them, for all human help had failed. Such have always been the ways of the Lord: to let all human counsel, wisdom, and greatness first come to naught, so that He may then accomplish great things by small and despised instrumentalities.

Like other colonies New Sweden was short of clergy. Even more serious, it was short of settlers. In the first fifteen years of its existence New Sweden never had more than two hundred permanent residents. When a new governor, John Rising, arrived in 1654, some three hundred new settlers accompanied him. Under the spell of this population explosion the Swedes took over a Dutch fort, Casimir, that had been deliberately built just south of Christina. In response to this affront Stuyvesant led seven armed vessels up the Delaware, forcing the surrender of Fort Christina. The Swedish flag came down; the Dutch flag flew in its stead.

Holland's national banner waved proudly but briefly; for in 1664 England asserted, or reasserted, her claim to all of New Netherland. Arguing that it was not a true Dutch colony but only a trading post, King Charles II granted to his brother, the duke of York, the necessary legal title. Four warships arrived in New Amsterdam harbor in August 1664, and the next month Stuyvesant surrendered. When New Netherland became New York, English possessions extended from Maine to the Carolinas.

Under this new control the Dutch feared loss of their ecclesiastical privileges and properties. England, however, permitted Holland's national church to remain in New York. The terms of surrender, the Dutch pastor reported to his ecclesiastical superiors in Amsterdam, "stipulate that our religious services and doctrines, together with the preachers, shall remain and continue unchanged." With these guarantees the Dutch Reformed Church exercised continuing influence in New York and neighboring New Jersey throughout the colonial period.

The year after the Dutch surrender, new laws encouraged the building of Anglican churches and the growth of an Anglican ministry. Yet such laws once more proved ineffective. When the new governor, Colonel Caleb Heathcote, arrived in the colony in 1692, he found it "the most rude and heathenish country I ever saw in my whole life." For a territory that pretended to be Christian, New York somehow managed to be without "the least marks or footsteps of Religion of any sort."

Under Heathcote's vigorous leadership land was purchased in New York City; in 1697 Trinity Church, the first Anglican church in the colony of New York, was chartered. A half century later more than sixty Anglican churches flourished in the middle colonies. A large measure of this growth may be traced to the Society for the Propagation of the Gospel. In 1702 John Bartow, the society's first missionary to New York, settled in Westchester County, where he labored for twenty-five years. A steady growth followed the arrival of other missionaries, whose ministries included the Negro slave and the hostile Indian.

By an Act passed October 21, 1706, New York's Legislature encouraged the conversion of slaves.

Whereas divers of her Majesty's good subjects, inhabitants of this Colony [New York] now are and have been willing that such Negro, Indian and Mulatto slaves who belong to them and desire the same, should be baptized, but are deterred and hindered therefrom by reason of a groundless opinion that hath spread itself in this Colony—that by the baptizing of such Negro, Indian, or Mulatto slaves they would become free and ought to be set at liberty. In order therefore to put an end to all such doubts and scruples. . . . Be it enacted by the Governor, Council, and Assembly . . . that the baptizing . . . shall not be any cause or reason for the setting them or any of them at liberty.

In New York the S.P.G.'s concern for an educated ministry found concrete expression. As early as 1702 the society assisted Trinity Church to obtain farm land for a college. Trinity Church secured "King's Farm," a parcel of about thirty-two acres; but for a half century little else was done. In 1746 the New York General Assembly authorized a public lottery "for the advancement of learning and toward the founding of a college." When time came to consider a site, the vestry of Trinity Church offered as much of King's Farm as would be necessary. Trustees were appointed (eleven of them from Trinity's vestry), the farm was accepted, a charter was applied for. In 1754 King George II granted a charter to "the College of the Province of New-York in the City of New-York in America." Called King's College, the school became Columbia College in 1784 and Columbia University in 1896.

A majority of Columbia trustees were Anglicans; by terms of the charter the president of the school was to be "forever hereafter" "a member of and in communion with the Church of England, as by law established." An able

---

The original charter of Columbia University (King's College), dated October 31, 1754, provided for daily services of worship.

> And we do further will, ordain, and direct that there shall be forever hereafter public morning and evening service constantly performed in the said College, morning and evening forever, by the President, Fellows, Professors, or Tutors of the said College, or one of them, according to the liturgy of the Church of England, as by law established; or such a collection of prayers out of the said liturgy, with a Collect peculiar for the said college, as shall be approved from time to time by the Governors of the said College. . . .

---

lawyer and Yale man, William Livingston, protested against this sectarianism in New York's college. Not only were Congregationalists, Presbyterians, and Dutch Reformed more numerous than Anglicans in New York, he noted, but we also have "Anabaptists, Lutherans, Quakers and a growing Church of Moravians, all equally zealous for their discriminating tenents." To give any one group the control of the college, he argued, would inevitably "kindle the jealousy of the rest, not only against the persuasion so preferred, but the College itself."

Granting of the charter seemed to spell defeat for Livingston, but that document also provided that no person was to be excluded from "equal liberty and advantage of education" because of his religious affiliation. New York's religious diversity steadily advanced, so that "equal liberty" made Anglican domination increasingly inappropriate. Columbia soon removed all vestiges of sectarian control that Livingston and others so feared.

Religious diversity could not be gainsaid, however much it was deplored by some. Congregationalists moved down from New England, Presbyterians moved in from Scotland and Ireland, Quakers moved out from wherever they were thrust. Lutheranism, which had a small beginning in New Netherland in 1649, swelled early in the eighteenth century, when German refugees from the Palatinate (in the central Rhineland of Germany) began arriving in New York.

Ravaged by war, harassed by petty princes, and utterly discouraged by a devastating winter in 1708–1709, several thousand Germans fled first to England and, with England's hurried help, thence to America. The first group of forty-one Germans, Protestants led by the Reverend Joshua Kocherthal, settled at Newburgh, New York, early in 1709. By that time thousands from the Palatinate, arriving in England, awaited some merciful asylum.

Ships bearing the Palatines to New York began arriving in June 1710; by fall most who survived a long, crowded, disease-ridden voyage set about building crude huts on either side of the Hudson and along the Schoharie and Mohawk Rivers. Here the impoverished settlers served England by becoming a bulwark against further French encroachment as well as by providing naval stores (tar, pitch, turpentine). And here Lutherans and German Reformed alike (and sometimes together) built their churches, called their clergy, imported their hymnals, memorized their catechisms, and in general prepared for the greater influx of Germans yet to come in the 1730's.

In the middle of the seventeenth century America's first Jewish colonists arrived in New Amsterdam. Their reception was cooler than expected. For these Jews, tolerated in Holland, anticipated no less in Holland's New World outpost. But Peter Stuyvesant, already badgered by Lutherans, Quakers, French Catholics, and Puritans, thought the arrival of twenty-three Jews in 1654 too much for even a man of godly patience to endure. The priority of the Dutch Reformed Church was rapidly becoming a farce.

Stuyvesant, therefore, sought "in a friendly way" to eject the newly arrived Jews. Protesting to the Dutch West India Company, the refugees received assurance that they "may travel and trade to and in New Netherland and live and remain there, provided that the poor among them shall not become a burden to the company or to the community." Though

Opposing the settlement of Jews, Peter Stuyvesant tried to persuade the Dutch West India Company to support his position. His letter is dated September 22, 1654.

> The Jews who have arrived would nearly all like to remain here, but learning that they (with their customary usury and deceitful trading with the Christians) were very repugnant to the inferior magistrates, as also to the people having the most affection for you; the Deaconry also fearing that owing to their present indigence they might become a charge in the coming winter, we have, for the benefit of this weak and newly developing place and the land in general, deemed it useful to require them in a friendly way to depart. . . .

Stuyvesant continued to erect every imaginable obstacle in their path, the Jews hung on. Augmented by other arrivals in March 1655, Jewish settlers held private religious services in their homes. In 1656 they purchased a cemetery, but not for many years did New York's Jews have any definite place for worship. And not until the next century, in 1729, did the Congregation Shearith Israel, erect its first synagogue.

In the seventeenth century all Europe feared the kind of religious mixing that seemed to be taking place willy-nilly in New York and Delaware. In the eighteenth century these anxieties only increased. And nothing in either New Jersey or Pennsylvania seemed likely to set them at rest.

NEW JERSEY

Before the English defeated the Dutch in 1664, Hollanders settled much of eastern New Jersey. In Bergen, Hoboken, and Weehawken the Dutch Reformed Church maintained modest strength throughout the remainder of the seventeenth century. In the next century, because of the Great Awakening and the vigorous preaching of Theodore Frelinghuysen, Dutch religious life prospered.

4. *Theodore Frelinghuysen • T h i s portrait hangs in the Library of Rutgers, the school which he helped create.*

Frelinghuysen, a native of Westphalia, was called to the church at Raritan, New Jersey, in 1719. He arrived early in 1720 and startled his congregation by the force and fervor of his sermons. Dutch churchmen, reportedly "very feeble in spiritual knowledge," held on to a formal orthodoxy and clung tenaciously to the Dutch language. All this Frelinghuysen sought to change—and that swiftly (see Fig. 4).

In his audacious drive for moral reform, for personal conviction of sin, for public penance, and for speedy condemnation of all "hypocrites, and dissemblers, and deceivers" this provocative preacher alienated many of his flock, even as he anticipated motifs of the Great Awakening. The anxious question "What must I do to be saved?" received disconcertingly different answers as churchman vied with fellow churchman. Thus when George Whitefield arrived in New Jersey in 1739, he found just that pitch of electric, even angry, excitement that insured large audiences and avid attention. Whitefield acknowledged Frelinghuysen's role in preparing the way: "He is a worthy soldier of Jesus Christ, and was the beginner of the great work which I trust the Lord is carrying on in these parts."

That "great work" likewise spread among New Jersey's Presbyterians, who had come into the colony in the late seventeenth century. The remarkable Tennent family furthered New Jersey's Presbyterianism most dramatically. William, Sr., who arrived in Philadelphia in 1718, contributed directly and powerfully to the preparation of a ministry both learned and zealous. After some years of educating young men in his own home in Pennsylvania, he built in 1735 a log cabin for this purpose. The "Log College" trained at least eighteen ministers whose services cut a wide swath in the middle colonies. Three of those eighteen were William's own sons: Gilbert, John, and William, Jr.

In 1726, New Brunswick Presbyterians called Gilbert Tennent to be their pastor. There the twenty-three-year-old Tennent and the thirty-four-year-old Frelinghuysen found common cause in seeking to reform both the doctrine and the ethics of dormant churches. Inspired by the fervor aroused among the Dutch Reformed, Tennent determined to do as much for Presbyterians. To church members who rested in a "presumptious security," sure that they were God's specially chosen, Tennent had words as harsh, as relentless, as devastating as Frelinghuysen's. His results were even greater. By 1729 sleepy sinners in New Brunswick and on Staten Island had been startled into fresh alertness. And before a decade had passed, Presbyterians throughout the middle colonies no longer nodded but were greatly awakened. In Freehold, for example, where John Tennent and William, Jr., labored, "the terror of God fell generally upon the inhabitants of this place, so that wickedness as ashamed in a great measure hid itself." New converts joined with revived members to revitalize the ministry and the church. But as in New England, opposition grew with equal speed, so that Presbyterianism found itself bitterly divided and torn.

In January 1707 the governor of New York, Lord Cornbury, issued the following warrant for the arrest of Presbyterian preachers Francis Makemie and John Hampton.

Warrant for Arrest

Whereas I am informed that one Makemie and one Hampton, two Presbyterian preachers who lately came to this city, have taken upon them to preach in a private house without having obtained my license for so doing . . . and being likewise informed that they are gone into Long Island with intent there to spread their pernicious doctrine and principles to the great disturbance of the Church by law established and of the Government of this Province: You are therefore hereby required and commanded to take into your custody the bodies of the said Makemie and Hampton, and them to bring with all convenient speed before me at Fort Anne in New York.

One of the converts of the Awakening in New England, David Brainerd, spent most of his brief ministry among the Indians of New Jersey. Though stricken with tuberculosis, he continued his service to those "beloved people" until the last months of his life. Then he moved into the home of Jonathan Edwards, there to be lovingly cared for by Jerusha, one of Edwards's daughters. Brainerd, not yet thirty, died in 1747. Fatally stricken herself, Jerusha, to whom he was engaged, died shortly thereafter in her eighteenth year. Brainerd's diary, used by Jonathan Edwards as the basis for a moving biography, inspired missions around the world.

Two weeks before his death, in the last entry written in his own hand, David Brainerd recorded these words in his *Diary*.

Friday, September 25 [1747]. This day I was unspeakably weak and little better than speechless all the day. However, I was able to write a little and felt comfortably in some part of the day. Oh, it refreshed my soul to think of former things, of desires to glorify God, of the pleasures of living to Him! Oh, my dear God, I am speedily coming to Thee, I hope. Oh come Lord Jesus, come quickly. Amen.

Those clergymen favorable to the revival, many of them Log College "alumni," recognized the need for a proper college offering a full course of instruction. In 1746 the College of New Jersey, later Princeton University,

The Charter for Princeton University (1746) assures "free and equal liberty."

Wherefore the said petitioners have also expressed their earnest desire that those of every religious denomination may have free and equal liberty and advantage of education in the said College notwithstanding any different sentiments in religion. We being willing to grant the reasonable requests and prayers of all our loving subjects, and to promote a liberal and learned education among them . . . do . . . will, ordain, grant and constitute that there be a College erected in our said Province of New Jersey for the education of youth in the learned languages and in the liberal arts and sciences.

---

received its charter, instruction being offered the following year in the home of its first president. Supported by Presbyterians both in America and in the British Isles, the college grew in significance and size, greatly aiding the causes of Presbyterianism and colonial nationalism. Princeton's president during the Revolution, John Witherspoon, was the only clergyman to sign the Declaration of Independence.

The Dutch in New Jersey also hoped for a college. Unlike the Presbyterians, however, the Dutch churches still acknowledged foreign ecclesiastical control. From Amsterdam came all major decisions; to Amsterdam went all doctrinal and ecclesiastical appeals. Frelinghuysen pleaded for both local control of the church and local training of that church's clergy. Because he died in 1748, he did not see either hope fulfilled. Both, however, were soon realized.

In 1766 Queen's College (Rutgers) received its charter. Like the other colonial colleges, Rutgers was founded "for the education of youth in the learned languages, liberal and useful arts and sciences, and especially in divinity, preparing them for the ministry and other good offices." In 1771 the college was located in New Brunswick, and instruction began shortly thereafter. The imminence of the American Revolution, however, made the early days of the school marginal and hazardous. Buildings burned, faculty

---

During the American Revolution, Rutgers University submitted the following notice to the New Jersey *Gazette* (January 1779).

The faculty of Queen's College take this method to inform the public that the business of said college is still carried on at the North Branch of Raritan, in the county of Somerset, where good accommodations for young gentlemen may be had in respectable families at as moderate prices as in any part of the State. This neighborhood is so far distant from headquarters that not any of the troops are stationed here, neither does the Army in the West interfere with the business of the college. The faculty also take the liberty to remind the public that the representatives of this State have enacted a law by which students at college are exempted from military duty.

---

moved or were missing, and the college itself shifted from place to place. In 1795 the school closed for more than a decade, but it revived in the nineteenth century to educate young citizens "for the ministry and other good offices."

In the western and southern segments of New Jersey religion again motivated colonization—this time by the Quakers. When the duke of York received New Netherland in 1664, portions of the land passed ultimately to William Penn and other prominent English Quakers. In 1675 Quakers established at Salem the first permanent English settlement in that part of New Jersey. In 1677 over two hundred persons, nearly all Quakers, sailed some fifty miles farther up the Delaware to establish the town of Burlington. These and later settlements came under the protection of the famous "Concessions and Agreements of the Proprietors, Freeholders and Inhabitants of West New Jersey." Describing this democratic constitution of 1676, Penn later wrote: "There we lay a foundation for after ages to understand their liberty as men and Christians, that they may not be brought in bondage but by their own consent, for we put the power in the people." By 1681 more than fourteen hundred Quakers had emigrated to Salem, Burlington, and the surrounding settlements.

Of all New Jersey's Quakers none is better known nor deserves to be than John Woolman. Born at Mount Holly, New Jersey, in 1720, Woolman provided powerful stimulus to antislavery sentiment. Slavery, firmly entrenched in New Jersey by the middle of the eighteenth century, existed among all religious groups, including the Quakers. From the year 1742 (when he was obliged to make out a bill of sale for a slave) until his death thirty years later Woolman was fired with the hope, even the duty, of abolishing slavery. To the Yearly Meeting gathered in Philadelphia in 1758

In his *Journal* for 1749 John Woolman reveals his growing anxieties over slavery.

Two things were remarkable to me in this journey [to the south]. First, in regard to my entertainment, when I ate, drank and lodged at free cost with people who lived in ease on the hard labor of their slaves, I felt uneasy. . . . Where the Masters bore a good share of the burden and lived frugally, so that their servants were well-provided for and their labor moderate, I felt more easy. But when they lived in a costly way, and laid heavy burdens their slaves, my exercise was often great, and I frequently had conversation with them, in private, concerning it.

Secondly, this trade of importing slaves from their native country being much encouraged amongst them, and the white people and their children so generally living without much labor was frequently the subject of my serious thoughts. And I saw in these Southern Provinces so many vices and corruptions, increased by this trade and this way of life, that it appeared to me as a gloom over the land. And though now many willingly run into it, yet in the future, the consequence will be grievous to posterity. . . .

---

he announced that the time for delay was passed; Quakers should immediately release their own slaves and seek prompt suspension of the slave trade. Otherwise "God may by terrible things in righteousness answer us in this matter."

PENNSYLVANIA

William Penn launched the greatest of Quaker colonization efforts in that area which today bears his name: Pennsylvania. In 1681 King Charles II, canceling a debt against the throne, presented Penn with a huge domain west of the Delaware River, between Maryland and New York. (Just exactly where became a matter of complex, lengthy dispute.) Penn seized this opportunity to conduct in the New World a "Holy Experiment." Pennsylvania was to be a model of what men of good will could do, especially when guided by the inner light of God's Spirit.

Less than a month after the charter was his, Penn published an account of the new province, encouraging worthy colonists to settle there. In the summer and fall of 1681 "First Purchasers," mostly well-to-do Quakers of southern England, bought more than three hundred thousand acres. In 1682 the city of Philadelphia, the most carefully planned of the major colonial towns, was laid out by Penn himself who arrived in October. By then a steady stream of English Quakers flowed into the area, soon overwhelming the earlier Dutch and Swedish residents.

William Penn, in *A Further Account of the Province of Pennsylvania* (1685), encourages prospective colonists to "count the cost."

> Now for you that think of going thither, I have this to say by way of caution: if a hair of our heads falls not to the ground without the Providence of God, remember, your removal is of greater moment. Wherefore have a due reverence and regard to his good Providence. Go clear in yourselves, and of all others. Be moderate in expectation, count on labor before a crop, and cost before gain; for such persons will best endure difficulties, if they come, and bear the success as well as find the comfort that usually follows such considerate undertakings.

Besides the generous tracts of land the guarantee of religious freedom also attracted. As a Quaker, Penn was no stranger to intolerance, ostracism, and imprisonment. During the reign of Charles II some fifteen thousand Quakers were confined to British jails, more than four hundred of them dying there. As early as 1670 Penn wrote in passionate defense of liberty in religion. In *The Great Case of Liberty of Conscience* he argued on all conceivable grounds—biblical, theological, prudential, rational, natural—that restraint, persecution, and force have no place in matters of

5. *Mennonite Church, Hinkleton, Pennsylvania*

6. *Old Lutheran Church, Philadelphia • Philadelphia's Lutheran Church and Fifth Street as both appeared around 1800.*

the spirit. God is dishonored, the Christian religion overthrown, reason violated, and government undone when force is used in religion. "Let no man," Penn admonished, "put too slight a value upon the lives, liberties and properties of so many thousand freeborn English families embarked in that one concern of liberty of conscience."

But Penn, like others before and after, found the fruits of liberty sometimes bitter. To many liberty meant license, a cheap evasion of responsibility rather than a costly assumption of that responsibility. Trusted deputies mismanaged their funds and abused their positions. Again and again Penn sought to stave off disasters brought on by those who mistook responsible freedom for moral anarchy. In a reflective, if not disillusioned mood Penn later wrote: "Liberty without obedience is confusion, and obedience without liberty is slavery."

While he worked hopefully for "a blessed government, and a virtuous, ingenious and industrious society," the Holy Experiment, as he envisioned it, seemed doomed. Quakers disputed with each other; civil authority grew tangled and corrupt; pacifism proved untenable under frontier conditions; and the "holy law within" was generally absent, even within his own family. Penn died in 1718, a broken and saddened man.

Yet the Holy Experiment did not fail; for in "Penn's woods" religious liberty received its fullest expression and its severest test. Persons of countless persuasions poured into Pennsylvania, weaving America's most richly colored tapestry of religious faith and practice.

In the 1730's the great wave of German immigration to America began. Lasting almost until the Revolutionary period, this massive movement threatened for a time to depopulate the Rhineland. By 1750 Pennsylvania looked like a German colony, as tens of thousands swarmed in and through the port of Philadelphia. Many of these Germans were Calvinist or Reformed, more were Lutheran, others Catholic, and still others (including segments from the German cantons of Switzerland) Mennonite.

Poverty and austere conditions encouraged Germans of differing churches to cooperate, even to unite, in religious worship. In Philadelphia, for example, Lutherans and Reformed shared the rent (£3 per annum) of "an old and dilapidated butcher's house" which they used for religious services. This arrangement continued until the Lutherans in 1744 grew prosperous enough to erect a church of their own. Elsewhere the two groups often cooperated in building a church, or in purchasing hymnals, or occasionally in calling a minister.

Lutheranism in Pennsylvania found in Heinrich Melchior Mühlenberg its ablest colonial leader. Coming to Philadelphia late in 1742, Mühlenberg gave new strength to a wavering community. He organized churches in Philadelphia and Trappe, saw a liturgy adopted in 1748, and the same year formed the first permanent Lutheran synod in America. Not confining his activities to Penn's colony, Mühlenberg journeyed to New York, New Jersey, Delaware, Maryland, South Carolina, and Georgia, and he corresponded with colonists he could not reach. Wherever he went, he preached (in German, Dutch, or English), settled congregational disputes, introduced Christian discipline, and helped secure books, medicine, money, schools, and churches. In short, he became "the Patriarch of the Lutheran Church in America."

In his *Journals* (1751) Heinrich Mühlenberg reveals singular capacities matched by great energies.

Now that the Dutch language has become easier for me, and since it seemed to me to be a pity to spend Sunday [in New York] for such a small group alone, I decided to conduct a brief English service or *Kinderlehre* on

Sunday evenings, though it is rather difficult during the week to meditate and write out three sermons in three different languages along with house catechizations and many other duties.

July 28. In this morning preached in Dutch; in the afternoon a German sermon. In the evening at seven o'clock lights were lit in the church . . . and many English Church people assembled. . . . Having only one copy of the English hymn book containing our hymns, I had to read each stanza separately and sing it for them. I soon observed that the English people did not know our tunes, so I selected familiar English melodies which fitted some of our Lutheran hymns. Then the whole congregation sang very pleasingly and inspiringly, for the English Church people here in New York know how to sing. . . .

———————————

Arriving in the midst of the Awakening, Mühlenberg carried this revival spirit to non-English-speaking congregations that otherwise would have been isolated from the movement. In his *Journals* he often wrote of "old Father [Gilbert] Tennent" to whose sermons he listened with profit. And George Whitefield, Mühlenberg reported, "filled Pennsylvania with the sound of the Gospel." On these foundations the vigorous and effective Lutheran patriarch built steadily until his death in 1787.

While Irish and English Catholics entered Pennsylvania in small numbers earlier, the German influx brought the first significant missionary aid to Catholics. The Jesuits, the only Roman Catholic order working in the English colonies, began their Pennsylvania mission in 1733 in Philadelphia. In 1741 two Jesuit missionaries from the Rhineland arrived to work among the German population. "Both men of much learning and unbounded zeal," in the words of the later Bishop John Carroll, Theodore Schneider and William Wappeler established mission stations at Goshenhoppen and Conewago. While the number of Catholics in Pennsylvania remained small, that colony was, after Maryland, the most fruitful soil for the growth of the Roman church. In 1750 Maryland had fifteen Catholic churches, Pennsylvania eleven, and all the other colonies together only four! None existed in either New England or the Southern colonies.

The earliest Germanic migration to Pennsylvania occurred under the leadership on Francis Daniel Pastorius in 1683. With Dutch and Swiss backgrounds, the Germantown community of Philadelphia followed no single religious form. Many of Mennonite background had been converted to Quakerism. Others retaining the older Continental faith were strengthened by additional Mennonite migrations in the eighteenth century. Pastorius, a Lutheran turned Quaker and convinced that "by the coercion of conscience nothing else than hypocrites and word-Christians are made," urged full freedom of conscience "so that each serves God according to his best understanding." Thus Germantown became the refuge for many small and sometimes short-lived sects of German origin.

In his *Autobiography* Benjamin Franklin describes Moravians in Pennsylvania.

[1755.] While at Bethlehem, I inquired a little into the practice of the Moravians; some of them had accompanied me, and all were very kind to me. I found they worked for a common stock, eat at common tables, and sleep in common dormitories. . . . I was at their church, where I was entertained with good music, the organ being accompanied with violins, hautboys [oboes], flutes, clarinets, etc. I understood that their sermons were not usually preached to mixed congregations of men, women, and children as is our common practice, but that they assembled sometimes the married men, at other times their wives, then the young men, the young women, and the little children, each division by itself.

The Mennonites themselves offered fascinating variety. Differing with each other on such matters as dress, military service, washing the feet of fellow believers, "shunning" the backsliding believer, intermarriage, missions, and education, the Mennonites have long provided the idly curious as well as the seriously concerned with abundant samples of "peculiarity." In the 1730's an Amish settlement arose in Berks County, Pennsylvania. Determined to resist the changing way of the world, the Amish sought to perpetuate the simple Swiss culture they or their grandparents had known. All aspects of life were to be simple and plain, not fancy or "proud." Amish worship services, held every two weeks, centered in the homes, for there were and are no Amish churches.

In 1719 German Baptist Brethren, or Dunkers, began settling in Germantown. Pietists and pacifists, they often aroused the ire of their neighbors. One of this group, Johann Conrad Beissel, withdrew in 1728 to form the German Seventh-Day Baptists. Within a few years a community established near Lancaster, "Ephrata Cloister," became the center of Beissel's effort and his enduring monument. Life was communal and severely ascetic. Men and women lived apart, each tending to that aspect of the economy to which he or she could best contribute. The community prospered and purchased a saw mill, an oil mill, a paper mill. In printing, in music, and in the art of illuminating manuscripts Ephrata reached great heights before its decline at the end of the eighteenth century.

Not all British migration into Pennsylvania was Quaker. Indeed, a heavy Scotch-Irish influx, largely Presbyterian, aided the colony's development. This large-scale invasion overwhelmed the meager resources of Presbyterian synods then in existence. Few clergy accompanied the thousands of immigrants, so that every available minister was pressed into service. By the end of the colonial period hundreds of churches had been established along the several western frontiers. In ministering so earnestly to these

Scotch-Irish, Presbyterianism in America became itself largely Scotch-Irish in the nineteenth century.

Pennsylvania promised both liberty and land—land that seemed to stretch infinitely west, land that opened freely into the backcountry of the south. The Scotch-Irish explored and exploited both the land and the liberty. They moved west to the Susquehanna River, paused, then moved west some more into the Cumberland Valley. By 1750 settlers had pushed their way into the valleys of the Juniata River and adjacent creeks. By a Proclamation of 1763 the British attempted to halt all colonial migration west of the Allegheny Mountains, but such effort was futile. The land was there, and it called. Soon Presbyterian ministers, such as David McClure, directed those congregations west of the Alleghenies.

David McClure, in his *Diary* for 1773, describes the "poor and enterprising people" who, moving west of the Alleghenies, make up the flock.

> In this journey we overtook several families removing from the old settlements in [Pennsylvania], and from Maryland and New Jersey, to the western country. Their patience and perseverance in poverty and fatigue were wonderful. They were not only patient but cheerful, and pleased themselves with the expectation of seeing happy days, beyond the mountains.
>
> I noticed, particularly, one family of about twelve in number. The man carried an axe and gun on his shoulders—the wife, the rim of a spinning wheel in one hand, and a loaf of bread in the other. Several little boys and girls, each with a bundle, according to their size. Two poor horses, each heavily loaded with . . . necessaries; on the top of the baggage of one was an infant rocked to sleep in a kind of wicker cage, lashed securely to the horse. . . . The above is a specimen of the greater part of the poor and enterprising people who leave their old habitations and connections, and go in quest of lands for themselves and their children, and with the hope of enjoyment of independence in their worldly circumstances, where land is good and cheap.

Pennsylvania also attracted settlers from Wales. Some of the Welsh were Presbyterian, some Anglican, others Baptist. The earliest Baptist churches in the colony, formed near the end of the seventeenth century, were largely Welsh. English immigrants and colonial migrants from the other colonies soon augmented the Welsh. By 1707 Baptists formed their first major interchurch alliance, the Philadelphia Association. This organization, serving all the Middle colonies and beyond, stood foremost in Baptist life and growth until after the Revolution.

With only two churches in all the Middle colonies (New York City and Philadelphia) before 1700, Anglicanism turned its missionary eyes toward Pennsylvania. After the founding of the Society for the Propagation of the

Gospel (1702) prospects improved, even though the clerical supply remained distressingly short. One weary S.P.G. itinerant, John Talbot, complained: "If I had known as much as I do now, that the Society were not able for their parts to send neither Bishop, Priest, nor Deacon, Lecturer nor Catechist, I would never have put the people in these parts to the charge and trouble of building churches; nay, now they must be stalls or stables for Quakers' horses when they come to market or meeting." However, the S.P.G. managed to keep churches from becoming stalls or stables; indeed, the society built even more houses of worship so that by 1750 Pennsylvania had nineteen Anglican churches.

Philadelphia also became a major center for Jews. While synagogue services in Philadelphia began only in mid-eighteenth century, by the end of the colonial period this Jewish community was the largest in America. Its social and economic status being relatively high, the Philadelphia community by 1761 obtained a Scroll of the Law (Torah) from New York. Ten years later these Jews had prayer books, vestments, and other essentials for proper worship. In 1782 the Cherry Street Synagogue was built; later (1822–1825) it was reconstructed in Egyptian style, Philadelphia's first example of this style of architecture.

So religiously diverse was Pennsylvania's population that its college, chartered in 1755, is the only colonial university that lacked clear or dominant support of a single denominational group. Yet even the University of Pennsylvania traces its lineage to the omnipresent George Whitefield, who in 1740 encouraged Philadelphia's citizens to build a charity school for boys and girls. The building, when erected, also served as a preaching platform for traveling ministers of any denomination. Benjamin Franklin, who in a famous passage pays tribute to Whitefield's power to

---

Franklin's *Autobiography* testifies to George Whitefield's effectiveness as a preacher.

[1739.] I happened soon after to attend one of his [Whitefield's] sermons, in the course of which I perceived he intended to finish with a collection, and I silently resolved he should get nothing from me. I had in my pocket a handful of copper money, three or four silver dollars, and five pistoles in gold. As he proceeded, I began to soften, and concluded to give the coppers. Another stroke of his oratory made me ashamed of that, and determined me to give the silver; and he finished so admirably that I emptied my pocket wholly into the collector's dish, gold and all.

---

raise money, encouraged all formal schooling. In 1749 he issued *Proposals Relating to the Education of Youth in Pennsylvania,* arousing wide support for education in Pennsylvania. In 1751 the "academy and Charitable School of Philadelphia" opened, offering instruction in Latin, English, and

7. *Statue of George Whitefield* • *The "great awakener" par excellence stands within the dormitory triangle of the University of Pennsylvania, the founding of which he fostered.*

mathematics. Launched by "a suitable sermon" on the text "ye shall know the truth," the school within four years added college instruction. The University of Pennsylvania was on its way.

Throughout the colonial period Pennsylvania by its chaos of cults scandalized some, gratified others. Could social order or good sense ever emerge from such a medley? Thomas Barton, S. P. G. missionary to Lancaster County, thought not. Finding only about five hundred Anglicans in the area, he glumly reported that "the rest are German Lutherans, Calvinists, Mennonites, New Born, Dunkers, Presbyterians, Seceders, New Lights, Covenanters, Mountain Men, Brownists, Independents, Papists, Quakers, Jews, etc. Amidst such a swarm of sectaries, all indulged and favored by the Government, it is no wonder that the national Church should be borne down." What remained a wonder was that society did not collapse, morality did not disappear, religious devotion did not cease. Even out of Barton's many sects, as out of America's many colonies, unity could and did come. And that, to all the world, was wonder indeed.

10 ❖ "An Excellent School to Learn Christ In":

CAROLINA AND GEORGIA

BETWEEN THE JAMES RIVER in Virginia and St. Johns River in Florida colonization came late. In 1670 Carolina's first permanent settlement appeared on the Ashley River: Charles-Town, or Charleston. The
charter granted seven years before by Charles II included all lands between
the thirty-first and the thirty-sixth parallels, from sea to sea. This vast
territory (not separated into North and South Carolina until the eighteenth
century) established close ties with the West Indies. To Charleston came
the overflow population, both white and Negro, from Barbados, Jamaica,
and other Caribbean islands. Emigrants also arrived from England, Ireland, France, and New England, bringing the population of the Charleston
area to about 16,000 (half slave) by the end of the seventeenth century.

Drawing settlers from such varied sources, Carolina presented religious
variety as well. Many French Protestants, following the revocation of the
Edict of Nantes in 1685, fled to Carolina shores. In 1692 almost one-third
of the colony's popular assembly were Huguenots. In Dorchester, Massachusetts, Congregationalists organized a church in 1695 "to go to South
Carolina to settle the gospel there." Typically the New Englanders first
formed a church, then sent colonists out—organization intact—"to set up
the ordinances of Jesus Christ there if the Lord carried them safely thither.
. . ." The church, duly established in Dorchester (South Carolina)—the
settlers brought even the town name with them, later (1754) moved to
Midway in Liberty County, Georgia (see Fig. 1).

The growth of "dissenters" antagonized the "churchmen" (Anglicans),
for Carolina was officially a Church of England preserve. With the election
of an Anglican governor in 1700 religious "broils" aggravated the seething
political unrest. Dissenters viewed Anglicans as apostles of persecution and
discord, interested only in privilege and preferment for themselves. Anglicans viewed dissenters as noisy interlopers, forgetful of colonial preroga-
tives and royal wishes.

The Quaker John Archdale, a former governor, tried to pour oil on
turbulent waters. Urging all in authority to give up their quarreling over
"poor trifles and barren opinions," he wrote in 1707: "It is stupendous to
consider how passionate and preposterous zeal not only veils but stupefies,

oftentimes, the rational powers." Reasonable men were to consider the qualification of a prospective settler *as settler,* not as debator or worshiper. "For cannot Dissenters kill wolves and bears as well as Churchmen? as also fell trees and clear ground for plantations, and be as capable of defending the same generally as well as the other?" If anyone really had doubts on these questions, Archdale suggested that Pennsylvania "can bear witness to what I write." If Carolina takes away freedom of conscience or deprives men of their liberty, he warned, it will draw no immigrants. Men "zealous for liberty and property . . . will by no persuasion be attracted to any part where their native rights are invaded, or who rather expect an enlargement thereof in a Wilderness Country than an abridgement thereof." It was a telling argument, heard again and again all along the Atlantic coast.

Archdale's oil failed to calm all water; for example, a vicious Indian attack in 1715 virtually reduced all but Charleston to ashes. But his spirit prevailed, and toleration increased. A major center of colonial Judaism arose in Charleston. The Society for the Propagation of the Gospel alleviated distress not only among the English but also among the French, the Germans, the Indians, the Negroes. The last needed special help, for the harsh slave code of Barbados was imported along with its victims. In 1712 one S.P.G. missionary, shocked at "the barbarous usage of the poor slaves," reported in dismay the severe tortures and practiced cruelties of the masters.

As settlements pushed up the rivers from Charleston and into the back-country, the S.P.G. actively and generously supported a parish ministry. Prayer books and Bibles were dispatched in quantity, clergy were given some financial security, schools were opened, and religion prospered. By 1759 the society found conditions in South Carolina encouraging enough to justify withdrawal to needier areas.

Neither North Carolina nor Georgia gave the society ground for much encouragement. North Carolina had no settlements until colonists began about 1653 to drift down from Virginia into the region around Albemarle Sound. Many of these were Quakers, their affiliation encouraged by George Fox's visit in 1672. By the beginning of the eighteenth century over four

---

George Fox, founder of the Quakers, preached to the southern Indians during his visit to America in 1672. The excerpt is from his *Journal.*

And now they say we are 1,000 miles from Boston—they that have travelled it; all of which we have travelled by land, and down bays, and over rivers, and creeks, and bogs, and wildernesses. . . . On the 29th day of the 9th month [November], I went among the Indians. Their young king and others of their chief men were very loving, and received what I said to

2. *St. Michael's Church, Charleston • Begun in 1752, this great Georgian church opened for Anglican worship in 1761. Exposed to British artillery in 1780, the church suffered the further indignity of having its bells stolen and shipped back to England.*

1. *Midway Congregational Church, Liberty, Georgia • Organized in 1754, the Midway Congregationalists lost their first log meetinghouse to the British in 1778. The present structure was built in 1792.*

3. *Beth Elohim Synagogue, Charleston • Charleston's Jewish community dates from the middle of the eighteenth century, but this Greek-revival tabernacle was not dedicated until 1843.*

them. And I showed them how that God made all things in six days, and made but one man and a woman, and how that God did drown the old world, because of their wickedness, and so along to Christ; and how he did die for all and for their sins, and did enlighten them. . . .

———————

thousand inhabited North Carolina, most of these persons having migrated from other colonies. S.P.G. missionaries promoting a worship of "decency and order" were appalled both by the character of the people they met and by the hostility of the country they traversed.

In 1704 John Blair, sent to that hostile country by the society, found few Anglicans and fewer churches. He discovered "four sorts of people" there, he reported. First, the Quakers; second those without religion, who would be Quakers except that they did not want to change their habits; third, "something like Presbyterians"; and, as an anticipated climax, "a fourth sort who are really zealous for the interest of the Church." These last are the "fewest in number, but the better sort."

But even among the better sort transportation was difficult and cooperation minimal. Blair's closest colleague was 120 miles away, he noted, so that just getting around to his own "parish" took him from ten to twelve weeks. He officiated only on the Sabbath, for "they won't spare time of another day," and "five miles is the furthest they will bring their children or willingly come themselves." Blair left shortly for London in disgust, only to have his ship captured by the French and to land in a French prison for several months.

Other missionaries sent from England in 1707 found their assignments no more reassuring. One, James Adams, reported despairingly shortly before his death in 1710: "Nothing but my true concern for so many poor souls, scattered abroad as sheep having no shepherd . . . could have prevailed upon me to stay in so barbarous and disorderly place as this now is, where I have undergone a world of trouble and misery both in body and mind." This unflattering judgment was so nearly unanimous that the society had difficulty recruiting volunteers. From 1700 to 1730 never more than two Anglican missionaries served in North Carolina, and at times there were none. For generations afterward North Carolina's bosom still seemed unfruitful.

Though the colonial assembly made legal provisions for Anglicanism as early as 1715, successful implementation of the law depended, as always, on the sentiment and sympathy of the people. And North Carolina's people seemed unwilling or unable to establish effectively the Church of England in their midst. Time after time clergymen acknowledged that salaries voted were never paid, parsonages promised were never built, churches begun were never finished. One clear-eyed clergyman observed that missionaries "must be planters too, if they have families, or starve." And another reported that his lodging was "an old tobacco house" where he was "exposed even in my bed, to the injuries and violence of bad weather."

Disillusionment of the ministry intensified disillusionment among the laity. As late as 1771 a society evangelist wrote that he "found the people of the Church of England disheartened and dispersed like sheep." Perhaps fruitfulness was meant for others. Both the Quakers and Presbyterians, of whom John Blair had despaired, made North Carolina a major center for proselytes and propaganda. And in the final decades of the eighteenth century Baptists found that "barbarous and disorderly place" congenial for careful cultivation and great growth.

Thomas Bray's formation of those two great Societies (one for promoting Christian knowledge, the other for propagating the gospel) molded much of the colonies' culture. In Georgia, the last of the English colonies to be founded, Bray's contribution was even more crucial. In the final decade of his life Bray received a substantial bequest to further his grand dreams for England's colonies in the New World. When he became seriously ill, he provided for the proper care of this trust by creating still another organization: "Dr. Bray's Associates." Formally commissioned in 1731 the associates were appointed as "Trustees for instructing the Negroes in the Chrisitan religion and establishing a charitable colony for the better maintenance of the poor of this kingdom, and for other good purposes."

Concern for the wretched conditions in English jails brought Bray into contact with General James Ogelthorpe, who shared that concern. Together they discussed establishing in America a colony for imprisoned debtors and impoverished unemployed. When to that humanitarian goal the expedient goal of resisting Spanish advances from Florida was added, their common hope came within grasp. A month after the incorporation of "Dr. Bray's Associates," Ogelthorpe petitioned King George II for a land grant south of Carolina. Two years later a charter was given, and about one hundred men, women, and children embarked for King George's colony.

In the early years of Georgia's settlement the principal concerns of Bray and Oglethorpe are clearly evident. Their sincere intent to instruct and convert the Negro is apparent in the charter's prohibition against slavery, a restriction removed in 1749. The "poor of this kingdom" were conspicuous among the colony's first settlers. And the "charitable colony" welcomed Lutherans fleeing persecution in Salzburg, Moravians leaving the protection of Saxony, Scottish Presbyterians escaping political and economic distress to build at Darien an outpost against the Spanish. Even Jews, though forbidden to come, arrived in 1733. Oglethorpe not only permitted them to stay but granted them land as well; soon synagogue services were heard in Savannah.

After the earliest settlements around Savannah other colonists moved up the river to Augusta and down the coast to St. Simon's Island. In 1735, faced with the need for additional clergymen, Oglethorpe invited two brothers from an Anglican family he knew back in England: John and Charles Wesley. On shipboard the Wesleys came to know and admire the Moravians also bound for Georgia. Arriving in Charleston in February 1736, John proceeded to Savannah, Charles to St. Simon's. Within four months, Charles, buffeted by constant opposition to his rigid ecclesiastical demands, gave up and returned home. John's stay in America was longer but no happier.

He too aroused opposition by demanding much of the Church of England members, as he likewise did of himself. When he refused communion

---

In his *Journal* entry for October 29 and 30, 1737, John Wesley describes his busy Sundays in Georgia.

> Saturday, 29th.
> Some of the French of Savannah were present at the prayers at Highgate. The next day I received a message from them all that . . . they hoped I would do the same to those of Savannah, where there were a large number who did not understand English.
> Sunday, 30th. I began to do so, and now I have full employment for that holy day. The first English prayers lasted from five to half-past six. The Italian . . . began at nine. The second service for the English (including the Sermon and Holy Communion) continued from half an hour past ten to half an hour past twelve. The French service began at one. At two I catechised the children. About three I began the English Service. After this was ended, I had the happiness of joining with as many as my largest room would hold in reading, prayer, and singing praise; and about six the service of the Moravians . . . began, at which I was glad to be present, not as a teacher, but a learner.

---

to a young lady to whom he had been engaged, her family sued at court. While the case was pending, Wesley abruptly left the colony on December 2, 1737, for Charleston, and then home. In his *Journal* he noted: "As soon as evening prayers were over, about eight o'clock, the tide then serving, I shook off the dust of my feet and left Georgia, after having preached the gospel there (not as I ought, but as I was able) one year and nearly nine months." John and Charles Wesley never returned to America. Yet their impact on that country has been such as to suggest that they never left. That impact, of course, came not in their capacity as missionaries for the Church of England but in their later role as founders of Methodism.

As John Wesley sailed into the English harbor, George Whitefield sailed out. Whitefield's many visits to Georgia aroused both hostility and adulation—in about equal amounts. In 1740 he started an orphanage near Savannah (Bethesda) which survives to the present. In South Carolina he incurred the enmity of Anglican authorities. Church of England cleric though he was, Whitefield took too casually the liturgy and discipline of his own communion. Though formally censured, Whitefield continued, unchanged and undisturbed in his itinerant ministry throughout the colonies.

George Whitefield tells in his *Journal* entry for August 28, 1738, of his departure from Georgia.

> Monday, August 28
> I think I never parted from a place with more regret; for America in my opinion is an excellent school to learn Christ in. And I have great hopes some good will come out of Savannah, because the longer I continued there the larger the congregations grew. And I scarce knew a night, though we had Divine Service twice a day, when the church house has not been full. A proof this, I hope, that God has yet spiritual and temporal blessings in store for them.

In 1758 the Georgia Assembly created eight parishes, recognized the doctrine and practice of the Church of England as the official religion, and stipulated a salary for the eight nonexistent clergymen. Like the 1715 law in North Carolina, this act had little force. Parishes lacked either a church or a ministry, and public interest remained low. There was, said the Anglican priest at Augusta in 1768, "a famine, not a famine of bread, nor a thirst for water, but of hearing the word of the Lord." At this time, a decade after the Assembly's impressive act, Anglican churches existed only in Augusta and Savannah. And the missionary in Savannah concluded that the colonists "seem in general to have but very little more knowledge of a Savior than the aboriginal natives." Echoing the plea of many other Anglicans throughout all the colonies, the Savannah clergyman urged that a resident bishop be sent to cure the Church's woes. But none came, and Georgia, like Carolina, proved more fruitful for others.

The Lutheran "Salzburgers," about two hundred in number in 1736, moved from their first site ("Old Ebenezer") to a more favorable Ebenezer, "Stone of Help," on the Savannah River. The community prospered remarkably. Indeed, during Georgia's trusteeship (1732–1753) these German-speaking Protestants constituted the largest single ethnic or religious segment of the colony's population. By the time of the Revolution, Ebenezer was a thriving town. Then in 1779 the British captured it. During a three-year occupation the Salzburgers' sturdy brick edifice, Jerusalem Church, became first a hospital for the British wounded, then a stable for the British cavalry (see Figs. 4 and 5).

The Moravians, or United Brethren, whom the Wesleys met coming to Georgia, were pacifists. Finding Oglethorpe's colony too much committed to the military resistance to Spain, the Moravians began leaving Georgia in 1737. They journeyed first to Pennsylvania, founding the towns of Nazareth and Bethlehem. Then in 1753, accepting an offer by Lord Grenville, they purchased a large tract of land in northwestern North Carolina which they named Wachovia. The first settlers arrived in November of that year: thirteen unmarried males, including a minister. These hardy souls set about to tame the wilderness, bringing the flavor of John Huss[1] and Saxony to Atlantic shores.

The early struggles of the Moravians in Salem, North Carolina, are described in their own *Memorabilia* (1766).

In the first months of the year, we were rejoiced and strengthened by the safe arrival of the first company of Brethren and Sisters coming to us direct from Europe by way of Charleston; and also by tender and important letters . . . which brought word that the Lord had directed them and us to proceed with the building of the town, Salem. Already on Jan. 6th, before we received these letters, we had faint heartedly made a small beginning there, but now in hope and faith we took up the work, and on Feb. 19th, a little household of eight Brethren was established there, in childlike trust that He would bless and prosper the work of their hands. This year, for lack of help only one house on the main street could be built and occupied, and two houses away from the street, which were necessary for the housekeeping of the Brethren and for the outside workmen employed. But for this small beginning we thank our Heavenly Father and He will help us further next year.

America, traditionally the melting pot, also proved a refuge for those who did not wish to melt away their distinctiveness in an American or any other pot. This priceless opportunity to preserve a peculiar heritage was greatest when land was cheap, population sparse, and mass conformity unheard of. All three conditions prevailed when the Moravians began to build. In 1766 Salem was started as the central town of Wachovia. Community cooperation and common ownership came under the direction of the church or congregation board. By the time of the American Revolution, Salem could boast of at least thirty homes, a community store, an impressive tavern, a "congregation house," a "single brethren's house," and even a fire department (see Figs. 6 and 7).

Excitement over the Stamp Act threatened this pacifist community for a

---

[1] John Huss, of Bohemia, burned at the stake for heresy in 1415, became a kind of patron saint for the Moravians. Widely persecuted themselves in the seventeenth century, the Moravians finally found a refuge in Saxony on the estate of a leading pietist, Count von Zinzendorf.

Salzburgische Emigranten.

Nichts, als das Evangelium
Vertreibt uns ins Exilium.
Verlassen wir das Vaterland,
So sind wir doch in Gottes Hand.

4. *The Georgia Salzburgers • Carrying their Bible and their Augsburg Confession, these Lutherans in 1732 fled Austria's persecution. The quatrain reads: "Nothing but the Gospel / Drives us into Exile. / Though we leave the Fatherland / We are still in God's hand."*

5. *Old Jerusalem Church, Ebenezer • This is Georgia's only colonial building in continuous use since its construction in 1767.*

6. *Community Store of Old Salem, North Carolina • This store, owned and operated by the Moravians, has been restored to its 1775 appearance.*

7. *Home Moravian Church, Old Salem • Consecrated in 1800, this church continues to serves the Moravians of the Winston-Salem area.*

time, but "the mighty arm of our Heavenly Father has been held over us, so that nothing has been demanded of us contrary to our conscience, but under His protection we have remained peaceful and undisturbed as the quiet people of the land." But throughout the Revolution itself the Moravians could not remain undisturbed. While communicant members declined to enlist in the army, many younger men and boys did so. All were heavily taxed, however, and all contributed abundantly to the supplies constantly required by the Continental Army. Though often overrun by the British and depleted by the patriots, Salem survived to become the major trading center in the western part of North Carolina. Because of the Moravians, Salem also became a major mission center, notably to the Cherokees in northern Georgia. The Moravians' "childlike trust that He would bless and prosper the work of their hands" seemed fully vindicated.

And so it did across America as the age of colonization drew to a close. However small the beginning, however keen the suffering, however dark the prospects, most colonists were—like the Moravians—willing to "thank our Heavenly Father and He will help us further next year." The next year He did, and the next, and the next. Soon economies were strong enough, principles bold enough, and men brash enough to cut the binding tie with England. Some colonists found sanction and support in an ancient biblical command: "Proclaim liberty throughout all the land unto all the inhabitants thereof." That verse, inscribed on a bell that hung briefly in Independence Hall, became a proclamation in 1776. And by 1783 the proclamation had become a deed.

8. *The Liberty Bell, Independence Hall, Philadelphia*

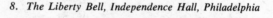

PART III

Age of Expansion

11 ❖ Liberty and Law

IN THE HISTORY OF MANKIND religion has often been the enemy, not the ally, of liberty. Some even see the rise of liberty as a progressive emancipation from religion. Whatever one's philosophy of history, the American scene discourages simple formulas for the complex affairs of men. The period of the American Revolution, in particular, shows the forces of religion moving sometimes in concert, sometimes in contradiction; crying in this quarter for force, in that for peace; here embracing liberty, there fearing it. The forces were not evenly matched, however, and through coalitions sometimes strange, often fortuitous, victory came for the friends of liberty.

LIBERTY WON

Even before the Declaration of Independence most colonies granted a measure of religious toleration and the right of worship. But the conditions under which these privileges might be enjoyed varied from place to place. The two churches enjoying legal sanction, Congregationalism in New England and Anglicanism elsewhere, failed to maintain their respective religious monopolies—despite sometimes frantic efforts to do so. Threatened by growing dissent, the Anglican and the Congregationalist jockeyed for favor and continued control. Soon, however, these intramural feuds yielded to larger, intercolonial fears.

In the arena of religious opinion two great anxieties haunted America's colonials. One was the fear of episcopacy (i.e., of the coming of Anglican bishops to American shores); the other, the fear of popery (i.e., of a foreign Roman Catholic power gaining control of the North American continent). Neither was a purely religious fear. In both instances it was the conjunction of civil and spiritual power, the confluence of church and state, that provoked grave concern. Legitimate political anxieties ignited the fire; religious suspicions and animosities fanned the flames.

First, with regard to episcopacy we have often noted in Part II the urgent requests, especially by the missionaries of the Society for the Propagation of the Gospel, that Anglican bishops be settled in the colonies.

These pleas were more than matched by an earnest determination that such prelates never come to America. Why? Because the spiritual overseers of the Church of England were always more than just that: they were wielders of great power in Parliament and out. About four-fifths of the American population at the time of the Revolution was of British background; and in their memories, sacred or seared, England's civil and ecclesiastical jurisdictions were wondrously or woefully mixed. Whether it was wonder or woe depended upon which church one called his own.

Congregationalists, Presbyterians, Baptists, and Quakers had in varying degrees a personal knowledge of "the bloudy tenent of persecution for cause of conscience." In the turbulence of seventeenth-century England thousands had been tossed about: jailed, exiled, or put to death. The merest possiblity of such power being imposed upon the dissenting churches raised immediate fears and resolute resistance.

But even among many Anglicans themselves, especially in the Southern colonies, enthusiasm for a resident bishop was weak or wholly absent. In Virginia, vestries who controlled their clergy were reluctant to yield that authority to bishops. And those clergy who hardly missed an overzealous overseer supported the status quo. Many recognized, moreover, that the arrival of bishops would destroy all hope of amiable relations with dissenters. In 1771 Virginia's House of Burgesses voted unanimously against "the expediency of an American Episcopate." Richard Bland, one of that body's members and himself an Anglican, noted that the colony's "whole ecclesiastical constitution . . . must be altered if a bishop is appointed in America." Obviously reluctant to surrender legislative powers to an appointed bishop, Bland also warned of the divisive effect such a move would have. "For let me tell you, a religious dispute is the most fierce and destructive of all others to the peace and happiness of government." Bland concluded with a sentiment typical of many Southern Anglicans: "I profess myself a sincere son of the established church, but I can embrace her doctrines without approving of her hierarchy. . . ."

As waters of political tension between the colonists and the mother country rose, religious resentments similarly increased. In the decade of the 1760's fear of Anglican encroachment was at its height, and in the 1770's the dam burst. In New England Jonathan Mayhew, of Boston's West Church (Congregational), led the fight against "all imperious bishops." A powerful polemicist, Mayhew protested the invasion of the Society for the Propagation of the Gospel into New England which was already sufficiently well churched: the Indians needed missionaries, not the Congregationalists! Moreover, any attempt by England to send a bishop to America was an attack upon American liberties, both civil and religious; as such, it must be resisted with all vigor.

In the Middle Colonies, William Livingston continued to be a painful thorn in the Anglicans' side. Dedicated to "opposing oppression and vindicating the liberty of man," Livingston let no spark of suspicion grow cool. Denying that he was against the Church of England as such, he acknowledged his unwavering resistance to "her unreasonable encroachments" and to "all tyrants civil or ecclesiastic." He reported every exercise of Anglican authority in New York, every case of church-state manipulation, and reported it in such a way as to aggravate all dissenters' fears of what the future, under English bishops, might bring.

New York's William Livingston protests the invasion of Anglican missionaries in *A Letter to the . . . Lord Bishop of Landaff* (1768).

If by "the propagation of the gospel in foreign parts" is to be understood the episcopising of dissenters in the American colonies [the Society has] indeed made some attempts toward it. But how the preaching of the gospel by their missionaries in places where it was preached before either the Society or their missionaries had a being can be called "civilizing and converting barbarous infidels," I leave your lordship and the whole world to judge. What barbarians, my lord, have they civilized? What infidels have they converted? The immense sums expended by the Venerable Society are not laid out in missions among the native pagans. . . . They are squandered, ridiculously squandered on missions to places where the gospel was

1. "An Attempt to Land a Bishop" • The fear of episcopacy is clearly seen in this 1769 cartoon and heard in the colonist's cry: "No Lords Spiritual or Temporal in New England!"

preached, and more faithfully preached, before. This, my lord, however people at home may be mendicated and sermonized out of their money, is so notorious here that an attempt to adduce proofs to evince it would be like holding a candle to the sun.

Yale's Ezra Stiles also joined in the battle against episcopacy, recognizing that objections raised even before a bishop arrived were "much founded in the anticipation of futurity." But, he warned, "I have so thoroughly studied the views and ultimate designs of American Episcopalians that I know I am not deceived." Dissenters confidently expected that an episcopate meant at least (1) the loss of their colonial charters, (2) the imposition of taxes for the support of the Anglican Church, clergy, and "bishop's palace," and (3) a restriction of all public offices to members of the Church of England. A convention of delegates assembled at Yale's commencement in 1769, having "reason to dread the establishment of bishops' courts among us," observed: "We have so long tasted the sweets of civil and religious liberty that we cannot be easily prevailed upon to submit to a yoke of bondage, which neither we nor our fathers were able to bear."

Aware of such unrelenting resistance, concerned Anglicans sought to alleviate fears by advocating bishops whose powers were carefully restricted to spiritual matters alone and to Anglicans—or even Anglican clergy—alone. Bishop Joseph Butler, of Durham, England, for example, proposed in 1750 (1) that American bishops have discipline only over ordained clerics of the Church of England; (2) that no interference with local governors or legislatures be permitted; (3) that civil regulations regarding marriages, probation of wills, and the like be unchanged; (4) that the colonies not be charged for maintaining the bishops; and (5) that "no bishops are intended to be settled in places where the government is in the hands of dissenters, as in New England. . . ." But despite so sane a proposal, suspicions would not down. As Jonathan Mayhew pointedly noted, "People are not usually deprived of their liberties all at once, but gradually, by one encroachment after another, as it is found they are disposed to bear them."

The repeal of the Stamp Act prompted Jonathan Mayhew to preach "a thanksgiving discourse" entitled *The Snare Broken,* May 23, 1766.

Having . . . learned from the holy scriptures that wise, brave, and virtuous men were always friends to liberty; that God gave the Israelites a king (or absolute monarch) in his anger, because they had not sense and virtue enough to be like a free commonwealth and to have himself for their king; that the Son of God came down from heaven to make us "free indeed"; and that where the Spirit of the Lord is, there is liberty";—this made me conclude that freedom was a great blessing. Having also, from my childhood up . . . been educated to the love of liberty, though not of licentiousness . . . I would not, I cannot now, though past middle age, relinquish the fair object of my youthful affections: LIBERTY—whose charms, instead of decaying with time in my eyes, have daily captivated me more and more.

While opposition to the coming Anglican bishops was generally political, the desire for bishops in America was generally and sincerely religious. The lack of local episcopal direction made it more difficult to maintain order and discipline within the churches. Further, the logistics of ordination were discouraging. In 1766 an S.P.G. missionary who had encouraged and trained a nephew to take Anglican orders, only to see him shipwrecked and drowned returning to America from his ordination in England, vented his dismay and grief in a poignant letter to the society. It makes no sense, he wrote, "to send three thousand miles across the Atlantic Ocean, at the expense of all we are worth sometimes, and as much more as we have credit for, as well as the risk of our lives, before we can have an ordination." Anglicans needed bishops for their churches, but non-Anglicans feared for their churches and for their civil institutions.

"The Great Fear," as historian Carl Bridenbaugh calls it, bound the colonies together in a mutual anxiety which helped create that unity manifest in 1776. Anglican clergymen, predominantly Tory in the Middle and New England colonies, aggravated those fears as the moment of military clash approached. "The revolution," John Adams wrote, "was in the mind and hearts of the people, and in the union of the colonies." This revolution was accomplished, he observes, before the War for Independence ever began.

Thomas Barton, in a letter to the Society for the Propagation of the Gospel, November 25, 1776, reveals how growing enmity toward England spread also to England's clergy and England's church.

I have been obliged to shut up my churches to avoid the fury of the populace who would not suffer [permit] the liturgy to be used unless the collects and prayers for the King and royal family were omitted, which neither my conscience nor the declaration I made and subscribed to when ordained would allow me to comply with. And although I used every prudent step to give no offence, even to those who usurped authority and rule and exercised the severest tyranny over us, yet my life and property have been threatened upon mere suspicion of being unfriendly to what is called the American cause. Indeed every clergyman of the Church of England who dared to act upon proper principles was marked out for infamy and insult; in consequence of which the missionaries [of the S.P.G.] in particular have suffered greatly. Some of them have been dragged from their horses, assaulted with stones and dirt, ducked in water; obliged to flee for their lives, driven from their habitations and families, laid under arrests and imprisoned!

The second fear, that related to "popery," was no novelty in the Revolutionary period. Waves of anti-Spanish and anti-French feeling swept over the Atlantic seaboard whenever threats or rumors arose suggesting a thrust from Florida, an encirclement from the Ohio or Mississippi Valleys, a sudden descent from Canada. In many of these tense periods colonial America had clung to England for defense. National loyalties and religious fears were then thoroughly fused.

Yet one deed of England's managed—however difficult the task surely was—to fuse anti-Catholic and anti-English sentiments. By the terms of the Peace of Paris in 1763 England fell heir to the vast French territory in Canada, territory that was almost exclusively Catholic. In 1774 Parliament passed the Quebec Act, guaranteeing to Roman Catholics the free exercise of their religion, including the legal collection of tithes in all of Quebec as well as in the American "Old Northwest" (Ohio, Indiana, Illinois, Michigan, and Wisconsin). This "establishment" of Roman Catholic religion, as Alexander Hamilton and others regarded it, touched off a violent reaction among colonial dissenters and Anglicans as well.

All the memories of bloodshed and persecution in sixteenth century Europe were resurrected to do their duty. " . . . The city of Philadelphia may yet experience the carnage of St. Bartholemew's Day," warned the *Pennsylvania Packet*.[1] A South Carolina judge, William Henry Drayton, cautioned that America's whole religious heritage was in danger and might have to be fought for; America must not fall before that "tyranny under which all Europe groaned for many ages." Livingston declared that the British officials had, by this Act, espoused "all the bigotry, all the superstition of the Church of Rome." In Massachusetts, Suffolk County formally resolved in 1774 that the Quebec Act "is dangerous in an extreme degree to the Protestant religion, and to the civil rights of all Americans; and therefore as men and as Protestant Christians, we are indispensably obliged to take all proper measures for our security." One of the "Intolerable Acts" alluded to in the Declaration of Independence, the Quebec Act was officially condemned by the Continental Congress meeting in Philadelphia in the fall of 1774. That this furiously maligned Act could be defended as having preserved religion for the Canadians was too calm a thought for hot tempers in the Anglophobe decade of the 1770's.

---

[1] On August 23, 1572, a council meeting in Paris ordered the slaughter of Huguenots not only in Paris but in the provinces of France as well. Thousands were slain in what came to be called the St. Bartholemew's Day massacre.

On October 21, 1774, the Continental Congress issued a vigorous protest against the Quebec Act.

> . . . We think the Legislature of Great Britain is not authorized by the [English]' Constitution to establish a religion, fraught with sanguinary and impious tenets, or to erect an arbitrary form of government in any quarter of the globe. These rights we, as well as you, deem sacred. And yet sacred as they are, they have with many others been repeatedly and flagrantly violated. . . . Nor can we suppress our astonishment that a British Parliament should ever consent to establish in that country [Canada] a religion that has deluged [England] in blood, and dispersed bigotry, persecution, murder and rebellion through every part of the world. . . .

In Lexington on April 19, 1775, shortly after dawn the shot was fired. Before it was heard round the world, it echoed in the pulpits of New England, the meeting houses of the Middle colonies, the parishes in the South. "The authority of a tyrant is of itself null and void," pronounced Massachusetts' Samuel West in an election sermon in May 1776. And in Virginia the presbytery of Hanover memorialized the Assembly on October 24, 1776, to this effect: we "are governed by the same sentiments which have inspired the United States of America, and are determined that nothing in our power and influence shall be wanting to give success to their common cause." In St. Mary's Catholic Chapel in Philadelphia, Seraphin Bandol commemorated the Fourth of July (1779) by declaring that "the finger of God is still more peculiarly evident in that happy, that glorious revolution, which calls forth this day's festivity." Churchmen of every major persuasion joined in the battle for independence. Catholics, Anglicans, even a regiment from the largely pacifist Quakers, closed ranks with Jewish, Reformed, Lutheran, Baptist, Presbyterian, and Congregational volunteers. With the surrender at Yorktown on October 19, 1781, British fate was sealed and liberty had been won. Would it prevail?

LIBERTY PROCLAIMED

In the Revolutionary period the voices lifted in behalf of liberty were legion. Some were sober, others ecstatic. Some appealed to calm reason, while others aroused the passions. Some dwelt chiefly on liberty in religion, others on liberty in economy and government. But for all—unless lost in the Appalachian wilderness—the last decades of the eighteenth century were times that tried men's souls. Neither summer soldier nor sunshine patriot could meet the test that momentous times imposed.

In the Southern colonies Virginia took and kept the lead in America's march toward liberty. Years before the Revolution, Samuel Davies had made the cause of religious liberty and civil independence one. As the entering wedge into a formidable Anglican establishment this Presbyterian preacher bore heroically the bruises this role brought. He won for dissenters the right to preach in the Old Dominion, ceaselessly pleading the case of those "whose only crime is to follow their conscience and not the direction of their superiors in matters of religion." In 1755, during the French and Indian War, he set a pattern, widely followed twenty years later, when he urged his hearers to "take up arms" in the defense of their homes. This is a Christian duty, he added, and "an honorable part, worthy of a man, a freeman, a Briton, a Christian."

One of Davies's frequent listeners was the youthful Patrick Henry. Like Davies, Henry frequently interceded on behalf of those imprisoned for conscience' sake. Paying fines or defending dissenters in court, he also won for non-Anglican clergymen the right to preach to the Revolutionary troops. And when in St. John's Episcopal Church at Richmond, Virginia, he cried, "Give me liberty or give me death!" the liberty he sought was for both body and soul.

John Leland led Virginia's Baptists in a concerted drive for full liberty, not mere toleration. When the Revolution was over, his vigilance increased as he pushed for complete disestablishment of the Anglican Church. In 1788 Leland headed the group opposing ratification of the Constitution because of its lack of specific guarantees for religious freedom, while James Madison led the faction favoring ratification. The two met for debate, Madison proving so persuasive that he won Leland's support. This fortunate agreement made Virginia's critical support of the Constitution a virtual certainty. In 1791 Leland returned to New England, his original home, there to assist in a longer struggle for disestablishment.

In a letter to George Washington in 1788 Baptist itinerant John Leland spoke for "the General Committee of the Baptists of Virginia."

When the Constitution first made its appearance in Virginia, we as a society feared that the liberty of conscience, dearer to us than property or life, was not sufficiently secured. Perhaps our jealousies were heightened by the usage we received in Virginia, under the regal government, when mobs, fines, bonds, and prisons were our frequent repast. Convinced on the one hand that without an effective national government the States would fall into disunion and all the subsequent evils; and on the other hand fearing that we should be accessory to some religious oppression should any one society in the Union predominate over the rest; yet, amidst all these inquietudes of mind, our consolation arose from the consideration: the plan must be good, for it has the signature of a tried, trusty friend; and if religious liberty is rather insecure in the Constitution, "the administration will certainly prevent all oppression, for a WASHINGTON will preside."

Yet it was an Anglican, not a dissenter, who determined the Constitutional safeguard concerning religion. Charles Pinckney, of South Carolina, proposed that "no religious test shall ever be required as a qualification to any office or public trust under the United States." On August 30, 1787, Pinckney's clause was added to Article VI, along with his proviso that elected officials could be bound to their duties either by "oath or affirmation." This enabled Quakers, whose religious convictions prevented oath-taking, to participate fully in the life of the Federal Government.[2]

Catholic affirmations of liberty came most conspicuously from the Carroll family in Maryland. Charles Carroll, a brilliant lawyer and a signer of the Declaration of Independence, and his distant relative John Carroll, first Catholic bishop in America, both embraced and advanced the cause of liberty. "The definition of freedom," wrote Charles, "is the being governed by laws to which we have given our consent, as the definition of slavery is the very reverse." To his words he brought deeds and—even more important to a penniless people attempting to finance a revolution—his considerable wealth. Praising his "zeal, fortitude, and perseverance" in the "cause of American liberty," John Adams wrote that Charles Carroll "continues to hazard his all, his immense fortune . . . his life." Bishop John Carroll, persuaded that America's newly won revolution was as important to religion as to government, told the pope that in this new nation "free toleration is allowed to Christians of every denomination." He added, "This is a blessing and advantage which it is our duty to preserve and improve."

In Pennsylvania that amiable libertarian Benjamin Franklin likewise lent his impressive weight to the cause. Unmoved by dogma and uninterested in sectarian strife, Franklin favored religion that did not demand political patronage. "When a religion is good," he wrote, "I conceive that it will support itself; and, when it cannot support itself and . . . [is] obliged to call for the help of the civil power, it is a sign, I apprehend, of its being a bad one." While he supported all Pennsylvania's sects—"and we have a great variety"—he joined none. Like many of his prominent contemporaries he believed that reason more than revelation, nature more than the Church, was the proper path to true religion.

In 1774 Franklin, then in England, provided letters of introduction to a twice-married British jack-of-all-trades: Thomas Paine. Letters in hand, Paine sailed for Philadelphia that same year. In two years *Common Sense* appeared (Franklin wrote the introduction) and soon after the famous "Crisis Papers" of the American Revolution. Paine, more radical than Franklin and certainly less prudent, was hostile to much in religion throughout his uneven career. Yet he was not an atheist. Of Quaker origin, Paine like Franklin was a deist, impatient with revelation and intolerant of

---

[2] The contributions of the two greatest Virginians of the Revolutionary period, George Washington and Thomas Jefferson, are considered below, pp. 125 f.

2. *Charles Carroll of Carrollton, Maryland •*
Signer of the Declaration of Independence,
Charles Carroll defended America's liberties
with eloquence.

3. *St. John's Episcopal Church, Rich-*
mond • Here Patrick Henry in
1775 delivered the line known to
every school boy: "Give me liberty
or give me death!"

4. *Archbishop John Carroll of Balti-*
more • America's first Roman
Catholic bishop (and first arch-
bishop as well), John Carroll is
commemorated by the school he
founded: Georgetown University.

religion that played politics or of politics that maneuvered religion. In *Common Sense* he noted: "As to religion, I hold it to be the indispensable duty of government to protect all conscientious professors thereof, and I know no other business which government hath to do therewith."

Obviously the advocacy of liberty by a Franklin or a Paine differed in tone from the advocacy of a Samuel Davies or a John Carroll. To one,

---

Roman Catholicism's first American bishop, John Carroll, wrote in 1791 a "Prayer for the Civil Authorities"; a portion is given here.

We pray Thee, O God of might, wisdom and justice! through whom authority is rightly administered, laws are enacted, and judgment decreed, assist with Thy holy spirit of counsel and fortitude the President of the United States, that his administration may be conducted in righteousness, and be eminently useful to Thy people over whom he presides; by encouraging due respect for virtue and religion; by a faithful execution of the laws of justice and mercy; and by restraining vice and immorality. Let the light of Thy divine wisdom direct the deliberations of Congress, and shine forth in all the proceedings and laws framed for our rule and government, so that they may tend to the preservation of peace, the promotion of national happiness, the increase of industry, sobriety and useful knowledge; and may perpetuate to us the blessing of equal liberty.

---

religion should be free because doctrine mattered so little. To the other, religion should be free because doctrine mattered so much. For the former, dogma was not worth enforcing; for the latter, it was unenforceable. Thus while standing on quite different ground, both the rationalist and the pietist, the churchman and the deist could together affirm the "blessing and advantage of religious liberty."

New England sloughed off its establishment more slowly than others. While Congregationalists inveighed stridently against Anglican encroachments, their voices were muted when discussing Congregational privileges. Dissenters from that establishment (chiefly Baptists, Quakers, and Anglicans) therefore assumed the task of affirming full liberty. A major champion in that undertaking, Isaac Backus, pastor in Middleborough, Massachusetts, was a Congregationalist become Baptist. In 1774 Backus appeared before the Continental Congress in Philadelphia to protest New England's denial of complete freedom of worship. If Boston could throw a rather wild tea party to protest taxation without representation, Baptists and others could justify their moderate protests on precisely the same principle. Dissenters, without representation, were taxed to support an ecclesiastical establishment in which they did not believe and to which they did not belong. Recognizing that the cost of freedom comes high and having seen the nation's dear and bloody price, Backus would not permit the soul's liberty to be compromised or conditioned. We "wrong our consciences in allowing that power to men which . . . belongs only to God."

Liberty proclaimed was not yet liberty secured. To *"secure* the blessings of liberty to ourselves and our posterity" reads the preamble to the Constitution of the United States of America. Sentiments were not enough. Liberty had to become law.

LIBERTY SECURED

The First Continental Congress, gathering in Philadelphia, heard on September 7, 1774, the rector of Christ Church, Jacob Duché, offer prayers and read the Psalm designated in the Book of Common Prayer for that day. Psalm 35 opens: "Plead thou my cause, O Lord, with them that strive with me, and fight thou against them that fight against me." To his wife John Adams wrote, "It seemed as if Heaven had ordained that Psalm to be read on that morning."

This Congress gave its major attention, of course, to forming some kind of alliance or union that could effectively assert and protect the colonists' rights. America's citizens, the First Congress asserted, were "entitled to life, liberty and property; and they had never ceded to any foreign power whatever a right to dispose of either without their consent." An imposing list of grievances was drawn up and the following May designated as the date for the next Congress to convene. On October 6, 1774, the First Continental Congress dissolved.

On May 19, 1775, the Second Continental Congress convened and directed its initial energies to raising an army and organizing a revolution. By August, England, formally proclaiming the colonists to be rebels, proceeded to hire German mercenaries to bolster the British army. In January 1776 Paine's *Common Sense* proclaimed that "the period of debate is closed." And in July, Thomas Jefferson presented to the delegates a document whose second paragraph began: "We hold these truths to be self-evident, that all men are created equal, that they are endowed by their Creator with certain unalienable rights, that among these are life, liberty, and the pursuit of happiness."

The first proclamation of thanksgiving extending to all the colonies was issued on November 1, 1777, by the Second Continental Congress.

> Forasmuch as it is the indispensable duty of all men to adore the superintending Providence of Almighty God; to acknowledge with gratitude their obligation to him for benefits received, and to implore such further blessings as they stand in need of: And it having pleased him in his abundant mercy, not only to continue to us the innumerable bounties of his common providence, but also to smile upon us in the prosecution of a just and

necessary war for the defense and establishment of our unalienable rights and liberties . . .

It is therefore recommended to the legislative or executive powers of these United States to set apart Thursday, the eighteeenth day of December next, for SOLEMN THANKSGIVING and PRAISE.

These carefully weighed words were not lightly received. Nor were the rights of which they spoke cheaply won. On October 19, 1782, when General Lord Cornwallis surrendered to General George Washington, seven years of bitter battle ended—but not before all Europe was involved and all America united. By September 1783 the Peace of Paris was completed and a new nation, stretching from the Atlantic to the Mississippi, from the Great Lakes to Florida, was born.

In 1787 a convention meeting in Philadelphia drafted the Constitution of the United States, then submitted it to the Continental Congress. By the middle of 1788 a sufficient number of states had ratified the vital document. Elections were held early the next year, and George Washington was inaugurated the first president on April 30, 1789.

The Constitution says little about religion, so little in fact that some were reluctant to urge ratification. For most it was enough that religion be free from the state and the state free from religion. Yet some sentiment existed and some hope persisted that religion be favored, possibly even sponsored. Realists could hardly hope that any one church might be formally established, for no one group dominated the thirteen colonies. Furthermore, to grant special favor to one church was to suffer the unrelenting disfavor of every other.

A more plausible scheme, in the minds of a few, was government aid to all religion. Patrick Henry, for example, advocated a general assessment in Virginia for the support of the Christian religion, a proposal that George Washington also, for a time, looked on with favor. Surely contending churches and quarreling sects could agree to this benign plan! No, not at all. Some opposed any alliance between church and state on principle; others opposed it fearing that benefits would be unequal. A large group, outside the ranks of church membership, found Franklin's sentiments congenial: any religion that is good can and should support itself.

Above all, the conviction prevailed that government not be fettered by religion nor religion shackled by government. Article VI of the Constitution looks to the former, the First Amendment to the latter. The provision that "no religious test" be required of any governmental official met with general approval in 1788 (only North Carolina voted against it) and with general assent since. With the exceptions of the presidential elections of 1928 and 1960, little vigorous debate has centered on this portion of Article VI.

The contrary, however, is true of the First Amendment. The stipulation that "Congress shall make no law respecting an establishment of religion, or prohibiting the free exercise thereof" has been a storm center. Theolo-

---

George Washington replied to "the Hebrew Congregation, Newport, Rhode Island," on August 17, 1790.

The Citizens of the United States of America have a right to applaud themselves for having given to mankind examples of an enlarged and liberal policy, a policy worthy of imitation. All possess alike liberty of conscience and immunities of citizenship. It is now no more that toleration is spoken of, as if it was by indulgence of one class of people that another enjoyed the exercise of their inherent natural rights. For happily the government of the United States, which gives to bigotry no sanction, to persecution no assistance, requires only that they who live under its protection should demean themselves as good citizens, in giving it on all occasions their effectual support.

---

gians have wrestled with it, historians have explained it, lawyers have interpreted it—all in such a way as to extract an impressive variety of meanings from those sixteen words. What constitutes an "establishment of religion"? (Tax exemption or military chaplains, for example?) How free can one's free exercise of religion be? (Free to refuse military service or decline health precautions, for example?) What did the founding fathers intend? What do we, their descendants, desire? Such questions only hint at the complexity of the issue in contemporary American society.

But the issue was complex even in the earliest days of the republic. A glance at the first three national administrations reveals that subtleties and contradictions have been with us from the beginning.

After taking the oath of office George Washington, accompanied by the vice-president and the members of Congress, proceeded "to St. Paul's Chapel, to hear divine service, performed by the Chaplain of Congress." These words from the Senate Journal refer to Washington's own church in New York (St. Paul's), a structure within walking distance of Federal Hall. In this service of worship, as in the President's taking his oath on the Bible, no impropriety was perceived or discussed. In October 1789 Washington proclaimed a day of "national thanksgiving" to "that great and glorious Being who is the beneficent Author of all the good that was, that is, or that will be." And in 1795, when threats to the country's peace diminished, he called for days of prayer and thanksgiving.

Without question Washington was kindly disposed toward institutional religion. Baptized and married in the Anglican church in Virginia, he sup-

To all America's Roman Catholics, George Washington offered reassuring words March 12, 1790.

> As mankind becomes more liberal, they will be more apt to allow that all those who conduct themselves as worthy members of the community are equally entitled to the protection of civil government. I hope ever to see America among the foremost nations in examples of justice and liberality. And I presume that your fellow-citizens will not forget the patriotic part which you took in the accomplishment of their Revolution, and the establishment of their government; or the important assistance which they received from a nation in which the Roman Catholic religion is professed.

ported the church of his youth throughout his entire life. After he became President, he continued his attendance at worship when other duties did not interfere. One Sunday when he was in York, Pennsylvania (July 3, 1791), he discovered that there was "no Episcopal minister present in this place." He therefore attended the German Reformed Church, wryly commenting: the services "being in that language not a word of which I understood, I was in no danger of becoming a proselyte to its religion by the eloquence of the preacher."

Even more significant than his Anglican affiliation was his conviction that religion was basic to the origin and to the survival of the United States. In his First Inaugural Address he declared: "No people can be bound to acknowledge and adore the invisible hand which conducts the affairs of men more than the people of the United States. Every step by which they have advanced to the character of an independent nation seems to have been distinguished by some token of providential agency." His Farewell Address even more persuasively extolled religion as the ground from which morality takes its rise, warning that "reason and experience both forbid us to expect that national morality can prevail in exclusion of religious principle."

5. *Christ Church, Alexandria •
Completed shortly before the
American Revolution began,
this church counted George
Washington among its faithful
vestrymen.*

Did Washington, then, favor an alliance of church and state? Not at all. No contemporary could fail to see or to appreciate the first President's unmeasured devotion to religious freedom. "The establishment of civil and religious liberty," he told a New York congregation in 1783, "was the motive which induced me to the field." The same motive that guided him as general directed him as president. Anxious over their liberties, many religious bodies petitioned the president for assurances even as they pledged him their full support. In every case the petitioning group was greatly heartened by a president who would give "to bigotry no sanction, to persecution no assistance."

The second president of the United States, John Adams, was a Congregationalist, moving into that wing of the New England church called Unitarianism. Convinced that reason was the only revelation needed by man, Adams grew impatient over creedal niceties, ecclesiastical decrees, and all

---

John Adams offers to Thomas Jefferson his views on reason and revelation, September 14, 1813.

> The human understanding is a revelation from its Maker which can never be disputed or doubted. There can be no skepticism . . . or incredulity, or infidelity here. No prophecies, no miracles are necessary to prove the celestial communication.
>
> This revelation has made it certain that two and on make three, and that one is not three nor can three be one. We can never be so certain of any prophecy, or of any miracle, or the design of any miracle, as we are from the revelation of nature, i.e., Nature's God, that two and two are equal to four. Miracles or prophecies might frighten us out of our wits; might scare us to death; might induce us to lie, to say that we believe that two and two make five. But we should not believe it. We should know the contrary.

---

the "other trumpery that we find religion encumbered with in these days." Religion is not intended, he wrote, to make us "good riddle solvers or good mystery-mongers, but good men, good magistrates and good subjects, good husbands and good wives, good parents and good children, good masters and good servants." For President Adams the proper companion of religion was not mystery but morality.

While suspicious of denominational dogmatics, Adams was equally suspicious of those devoid of all religion. Religion, he believed, gives strength and purpose to individuals; without it the Adamses "would have been rakes, fops, sots, gamblers." But more significantly religion inspires and directs a nation, a civilization. "Statesmen may plan and speculate for liberty," he wrote to his wife in 1775, "but it is religion and morality alone which can establish the principles upon which freedom can securely stand." Man cannot successfully flaunt God but must intelligently obey Him.

The Bible, "the most republican book in the world," deserves to be read by all. In it can be found "the most perfect philosophy, the most perfect morality, and the most refined policy." But other sacred books ought also to be read, for everyone who can plead in the court of reason and common sense has something to contribute. Of all peoples in the world the Jews, Adams believed, had made the greatest contribution. For they gave "to all mankind the doctrine of a supreme, intelligent . . . almighty Sovereign of the universe, which I believe to be the great essential principle of all morality and consequently of all civilization."

With such views firmly fixed, it is no surprise that Adams gladly enforced the Constitution's guarantees of religious liberty. This he did, adding a hope that "Congress will never meddle with religion further than to say their own prayers, and to fast and give thanks once a year." Then he declared: "Let every colony have its own religion without molestation." And there is the surprise: Adams's sturdy defense of the Congregational establishment in Massachusetts.

The First Amendment prohibited any federal establishment of religion but said nothing about the individual states. This was as it should be, in Adams's opinion. He saw no inconsistency in attacking establishment at the national level while defending it on the state level—at least that sort of "slender" establishment prevailing in Massachusetts. Isaac Backus argued otherwise, protesting the legal obligation "to support a ministry we cannot attend, whilst we demean ourselves as faithful subjects." As the protest grew noisy, Adams calmly observed that one might as well expect a change in the solar system as an alteration in the Congregational establishment. (The race between the two was not very close, for disestablishment came to Massachusetts in 1833.)

Adams's vice-president, leading member of the opposing political party, was Thomas Jefferson. In 1800 Jefferson became president himself, and in his policies yet another attitude toward religion and the state is manifest.

For Jefferson religion in its "pure form" (as taught by Jesus, for example) is good. The difficulty is that simple faith has become barnacled and encrusted with much that is artificial, mystifying, inappropriate, and wholly unnecessary. Partaking of the major motifs of the Age of Enlightenment, Jefferson found the primitive, the original, and the natural to be desirable. On the contrary, the sophisticated, the derivative, and the unnatural—whether in government or in religion—were deplored. "My opinion is," he wrote, "that there would never have been an infidel, if there had never been a priest."

Thomas Jefferson indicates to John Adams his suspicions regarding institutional religion, July 5, 1814.

The Christian priesthood, finding the doctrines of Christ levelled to every understanding, and too plain to need explanation, saw in the mysticism of

Plato materials with which they might build up an artificial system which might, from its indistinctness, admit everlasting controversy, give employment for their order, and introduce it to profit, power and preeminence. The doctrines which flowed from the lips of Jesus himself are within the comprehension of a child; but thousands of volumes have not yet explained the Platonisms engrafted on them; and for this obvious reason that nonsense can never be explained. Their purposes, however, are answered. Plato is canonized; and it is now deemed as impious to question his merits as those of an apostle of Jesus. He is peculiarly appealed to as an advocate of the immortality of the soul; and yet I will venture to say that were there no better arguments than his proof of it, not a man in the world would believe it.

Institutional religion, a secondary growth, therefore bore watching. Thus some of Jefferson's fervency in creating and maintaining religious liberty derives from his uneasy suspicions of what churches and "priestcraft" were up to. That these suspicions did not extend to religion itself is evident not only from his acknowledgement of the Creator in the Declaration of Independence but more patently in his careful attention to the teachings of Jesus. After his retirement from the presidency, he devoted long hours to cutting out verses from the Bible, compiling forty-six pages "of pure and unsophisticated doctrine." These teachings of Jesus, "Jefferson's Bible," he described for John Adams as "the most sublime and benevolent code of morals which has ever been offered to man" (see Fig. 6).

But it is not as a verse cutter that Jefferson made his greatest contribution to the religious history of America. As patron of religious liberty he has no equal among America's presidents. One of the three things he asked to be noted in his epitaph was his authorship of the "statute of Virginia for religious freedom." (The other two were writing the Declaration of Independence and founding the University of Virginia; being president of the United States for eight years he does not bother to mention.)

Twelve years before the adoption of the Federal Constitution, Thomas Jefferson composed this vital "Bill for Establishing Religious Freedom"; it was presented to the Virginia Assembly in 1779.

Well aware that almighty God hath created the mind free; that all attempts to influence it by temporal punishments or burdens, or by civil incapacitations, tend only to beget habits of hypocrisy and meanness, and are a departure from the plan of the Holy Author of our religion, who being Lord both of body and mind, yet chose not to propagate it by coercions on either, as was in his Almighty power to do; that the impious presumption of legislators and rulers, civil as well as ecclesiastical, who being themselves but fallible and uninspired men have assumed dominion over the faith of others, setting up their own opinions and modes of thinking as the only true and infallible, and as such endeavoring to impose

The

Life and Morals

of

Jesus of Nazareth

Extracted textually

from the Gospels

in

Greek, Latin

French & English.

6. *"Jefferson's Bible"* • *After his retirement from the presidency, Jefferson compiled—in four languages—"The Life and Morals of Jesus of Nazareth."*

7. *A Free Nation, 1783*

BRITISH TERRITORY

OREGON COUNTRY

Claimed by Spain and England

Disputed with Great Britain

PACIFIC OCEAN

SPANISH TERRITORY

THE UNITED STATES

ATLANTIC OCEAN

THE UNITED STATES AFTER THE TREATY OF 1783

them on others, hath established and maintained false religions over the greatest part of the world, and through all time . . . and, finally, that truth is great and will prevail if left to herself, that she is the proper and sufficient antagonist to error, and has nothing to fear from the conflict, unless by human interposition disarmed of her natural weapons—free argument and debate—errors ceasing to be dangerous when it is permitted freely to contradict them.

Be it therefore enacted by the General Assembly: That no man shall be compelled to frequent or support any religious worship, place or ministry whatsoever, nor shall be enforced, restrained, molested, or burdened in his body or goods, nor shall otherwise suffer on account of his religious opinions or belief; but that all men shall be free to profess, and by argument to maintain, their opinions in matters of religion, and that the same shall in nowise diminish, enlarge, or affect their civil capacities.

The Virginia act, passed in 1779, marked the beginning of a long career in the service of liberty. When he became president, Jefferson abandoned the precedent set by Washington and Adams of proclaiming days of public prayer, fast, or thanksgiving. "Fasting and prayer," he explained, "are religious exercises" and, as such, belong in the province of religious societies, not of government. And to the Danbury Baptist Association of Connecticut he addressed a letter in 1802 that defined religion as "a matter which lies solely between man and his God." To no other is man accountable for his faith. Government, on the other hand, deals with "actions only, and not opinions." The two realms being therefore inviolate, "I contemplate with solemn reverence that act [the First Amendment] of the whole American people" which built "a wall of separation between Church and State."

Jefferson's role in Virginia no less than his policies as president demonstrate that for him government entwined with religion, in any locale or on any level, was both dangerous and wrong. In this he and John Adams disagreed. They disagreed, strongly and deeply, on a vast number of things, the antagonism between them being for a time bitter and unrestrained. Yet in their later retirement, Adams at Quincy and Jefferson at Monticello, the friendship of these cowarriors in earlier days was renewed. A correspondence—engaging, affectionate, brilliant—sprang up between the two who had helped bring a nation into being and now wondered what would become of it all. Fifty years to the day after signing the Declaration of Independence, both John Adams and Thomas Jefferson died—July 4, 1826. It was then up to others to determine what would become of it all.

12 ❖ Freedom and the Frontier

R ELIGIOUS FREEDOM DID NOT COME at one stroke in 1783, or 1789, or 1791. But, sometimes sputtering and hesitating, oftentimes with enthusiastic dispatch, it eventually came everywhere. Connecticut broke the last formal bonds between church and state in 1818 and Massachusetts did the same in 1833. In Connecticut, Lyman Beecher fought valiantly to prevent the rupture. Nonetheless, it came; and after all was over, Beecher confessed with disarming candor: "For several days I suffered what no tongue can tell *for the best thing that ever happened to the State of Connecticut. It cut the churches loose from dependence on state support. It threw them wholly on their own resources and on God.*" Those resources—theological, psychological, economic—produced religious expressions of undisputed vitality even if somewhat dismaying in variety.

For freedom was, in the new nation, no tired cliché but a prize of war. More than that, it was the excitement of daily decision. A country free from political control! A church free of legal oppression! A society free from titles and hobbling tradition! All this meant little if circumstances constrained men to follow only the familiar paths. But fortunately land was bountiful, natural resources inviting, and strength sufficient. Americans were free to change jobs, free to change climates, free to change creeds. From Jefferson through Jackson, on the frontier and behind it, "freedom's ferment" filled the air.

Religion, as it tried its wings in that exhilarating air, assumed many shapes; among these were utopianism, transcendentalism, methodism, and revivalism. These four modes do not stand in awesome isolation, but rather they blur and overlap. Together they help demonstrate the vigor of religion: religion organized or diffused, orthodox or heterodox, ancient or novel.

UTOPIANISM

In early nineteenth century America two types of utopian visions appear. One saw perfection as the climax of a sure and steady progress. The other saw utopia as the return to a purer, primitive day, now corrupted and almost forgotten. One looked ahead, the other behind; but both looked with assurance to an ideal society on earth. The kingdom of God was within reach, the New Jerusalem was at hand. An age of optimism acknowledged no impossibilities. If men could create a nation of free people where none existed before, why could they not bring heaven to earth?

At no other period in American history were hopes so high nor so well grounded. Problems that seemed insoluble had been solved; barriers that appeared insurmountable had melted away; authoritarian power that was deemed impregnable had been vanquished. Free of European turmoil and entanglement, unfettered by custom, emancipated by law, Americans dreamed dreams and beheld visions. "The time has come," Lyman Beecher declared, "when the experiment is to be made whether the world is to be emancipated and happy, or whether the whole creation shall groan and travail. . . ."

Experiments abounded. Generally utopias were conceived as models both politically and religiously, for the United States was considered exemplary in both. Either by the grace of God or the reason of man, or both, the ideal society was just around the corner. With a little help and a lot of faith, that millenium might be introduced here, now.

An early community of the hopeful, the Shakers, left England for America to prosper for a time in the newly opened country. Under the leadership of "Mother" Ann Lee settlements were made in New England and New York, then (after her death) in Ohio, Indiana, and Kentucky. The harvest of western revivalism in this time awaited those ready to reap it. Shakers, along with innumerable other groups, gained converts from the fervent preaching of Methodists, Baptists, and Presbyterians. Before the middle of the nineteenth century, the Shaker Society reached its peak in growth: a membership of around six thousand.

A simple Shaker dance song, composed in 1849, suggests the lively nature of Shaker rituals.

> Leap and skip ye little band
> Shaker faith will fill the land
> O the comfort life and zeal
> Little Shaker children feel
> Shaking is the work of God
> And it has to spread abroad
> Till the wicked feel and know
> God Almighty reigns below.

As with most utopian efforts property and profit (if any) were held in common. The Shaker community owned all for the good of all. Family life, often the nemesis of this communal leveling, posed no problem for the

Shakers—for there was none. Strict separation between the sexes was observed; there was no marriage, and if a married couple joined the Society, separation was part of the cost of leaving the world behind. New members came, then, only by making converts outside of the community. This burden of proselyting proved too heavy to bear, and the result was a steady decline in Shaker strength after 1860. But their simplicity of life—a simplicity expressed in worship, work, architecture, and design—lingered as a fond memory in more complex times.

Johm Humphrey Noyes, a Dartmouth graduate who planned to enter the ministry, led a faithful flock in 1848 from Putney, Vermont, to Oneida in western New York. Revivalism in New York's "burned-over district" brought added followers to Noyes, who regarded proper social planning as the inevitable consequence of revivalism. Conversion is more than "saving souls"; it enters "into all the affairs of life." And since "religious love is very near neighbor to sexual love," a utopian order, "a divine organization of society," must properly channel both.

In "The Age of Spiritualism" (*The Berean*, 1847) John Humphrey Noyes looks hopefully for vast improvement in the nature of man.

> The whole world seems to be looking for a revolution. Some expect an orthodox millennium; others, a golden age of phrenology; others still, a physiological regeneration of the human race; and not a few are awaiting, in anxious or hopeful suspense, the trump of the Second Advent and the day of judgment. We also are looking for a revolution; and we will endeavor to set forth our idea of the form in which we expect it will appear.
>
> . . . We believe that man can be truly regenerated only by the paramount development of his *spiritual* nature. Accordingly we believe that the great change which is coming will be an outburst of spiritual knowledge and power—a conversion of the world from sensuality, from carnal morality, and from brain-philosophy, to spiritual wisdom and life.

Neither Mormon polygamy nor Shaker celibacy is the divine way, Noyes argued, but rather "complex marriage." Under this arrangement there were no permanent unions, but each woman was treated with the respect due a wife and each man with the loyalty due a husband. Having offspring was a community concern, carefully controlled and regulated by the total group who would rear the community's children. While Noyes bravely endeavored to show the spirituality and rationality of this approach, his fellow citizens showed little sympathy for any tampering with monogamy and traditional family life. Never a large community, Oneida endured only by becoming an economic success in the production of silverware. In 1880, the marriage scheme already abandoned, Oneida Community, Limited, was

1. A Shaker School, Pleasant Hill, Kentucky

2. Shakers at Worship, New Lebanon, New York • *A contemporary observer wrote: "In their marching and dancing they hold their hands before them, and make a motion as of gathering something to themselves: this is called gathering a blessing."*

3. A Shaker Music Hall, Pleasant Hill, Kentucky

formed as a joint-stock company, and another vision of "a system which the whole world would sooner or later adopt" quietly faded away.

By far the most successful of all America's religiously motivated utopias was that founded in 1830 by Joseph Smith, Jr. While the Church of Jesus Christ of Latter-Day Saints, popularly known as Mormonism, originated in the East (Fayette, New York), it left its deepest mark on the West.

From Kirtland Hills, Ohio, where Smith's small community had moved in 1831, Mormons fanned out to colonize the western reaches of Missouri. For eight years loyal members tried to reduce hostile nature and to placate even more hostile neighbors. In 1839 animosities were so great that another move was necessary, this time to Nauvoo, Illinois. Here where the Iowa-Missouri border met the Mississippi River, Joseph Smith proceeded to give solid substance to his vision of a saintly community. The town was carefully laid out, lots were assigned, plans for defense drawn up, and an imposing temple was built.

Like the Oneida community the Mormons held all material goods in common. Property, industry, and finance were vested in the church, which as wise and powerful overseer directed all for the benefit of the total community. Differing from Noyes on the marital question, the Mormons permitted plural marriage. Under certain circumstances approved by the church, the Mormon male might have more than one wife. Though the doctrine did not receive official sanction until 1852, "there is indisputable evidence," (writes official historian B. H. Roberts) "that the revelation making known this marriage law was given to the Prophet as early as 1831." Communal ownership disturbed the non-Mormon neighbors; polygamy, rumored or real, infuriated them. Oneida, by virtue of its small numbers, escaped the grosser forms of persecution. Mormonism, because of its militia, its doctrines, and its size (about 18,000 in 1844), found no such escape.

In June 1844 Joseph Smith, Jr., arrested on a minor charge, was awaiting trial when an angry mob stormed the jail and shot him. His death seemed to spell doom for another utopian dream. But at this critical juncture a sturdy follower, Brigham Young, assumed leadership, preventing further demoralization and necessitating further migration.

For about the only way that Mormons could get along with their fellow Americans, it seemed, was to get as far away from them as possible. In 1847 the long, painful, bleeding exodus began. Somewhere out West, across the wide Missouri, beyond the scorching plains, a Promised Land awaited. From Nauvoo to Omaha, from Omaha to Salt Lake Valley, Young led the weary faithful. To that new Jerusalem settlers flocked from all over America, as well as from England, Scotland, Wales, Germany, and Scandinavia. Before a decade had passed, the desert bloomed and Zion prospered. Against incredible odds and implacable enemies, one utopia survived.

5. *Joseph Smith in Nauvoo, Illinois, 1843*

4. *Winter Quarters, Omaha, Nebraska • This sculpture by Arvard Fairbanks commemorates the Mormon camp near Omaha, 1846–48. The temporary way station became a burial ground for more than six hundred wearied saints.*

6. *Alexander Campbell and his Wife, 1863 • The founder of the Disciples of Christ (and of Bethany College) is seen in an early daguerreotype taken in Bethany, West Virginia.*

7. *Mormons Hauling Wood in Utah, 1870*

Mormon survival and growth rested in part upon careful organization and clear authority. Unlike other experiments on the frontier, Mormonism managed to resist the more disastrous temptations of western individualism and maverick disorder. As Joseph Smith noted in 1843, "There is never but one on earth at a time on whom the power and its keys are conferred." And the Prophet was that one: receiver of revelation, dispenser of divine commands. In the lonesome insecurity of a sprawling continent, such central order and confident assurance had genuine appeal. Authority implies consent; once given, that authority can endow a tender, embryonic community with discipline, determination, and perseverance.

Brigham Young addresses his people in Salt Lake City in 1849 (quoted in Ray B. West, Jr., *Kingdom of the Saints*).

> We have been kicked out of the frying pan into the fire, out of the fire into the middle of the floor, and here we are and here we will stay. God has shown us that this is the spot to locate His people, and here is where they will prosper; He will temper His elements for the good of the saints; He will rebuke the frost and the sterility of the soil, and the land shall become fruitful. Brethren, go to, now, and plant out your fruit seeds.

Some romantics looked ahead to a new age, a "new dawn of human piety." Others, and not all of them romantics, looked longingly to a golden age that had gone but might be revived. The desire to slough off centuries of accumulated rubbish, to return to firmer foundations, reflected a political disdain for monarchies, hereditary titles, landed aristocracies, and the like. In the history of the churches, that disdain was directed toward hierarchies, princely powers, clerical aristocracies, and complex liturgies. Why not a return to primitive Christian society? That is, why not—dismissing all else—return simply to the New Testament?

The movement begun in 1809 by Thomas and Alexander Campbell in Washington County, Pennsylvania, best illustrates this facet of America's religious history. Of Scottish Presbyterian background, the Campbells gathered followers in western Pennsylvania, Ohio, and Virginia who shared their special utopian dream: a church without creed, without label, without loyalty to any but Christ. "To restore the original gospel and order of things" was the motive, and "all that love our Lord Jesus Christ, in sincerity, throughout all the Churches" were to be the means. But this utopian dream, too, in its glimpse of a "holy unity and unanimity in faith and love," fell short of grand realization. Into the fold of the nation's denominations, however, it brought a vigorous new offspring: the Disciples of Christ.

8. *Ralph Waldo Emerson • This statue of New England's most famous transcendentalist is by Daniel Chester French.*

9. *Orestes A. Brownson*

In a basic document called "Declaration and Address," Thomas Campbell in 1809 argues for the restoration of the New Testament church.

> Dearly beloved brethren, why should we deem it a thing incredible that the Church of Christ, in this highly favored country, should resume that original unity, peace, and purity which belong to its constitution and constitute its glory? Or, is there anything that can be justly deemed necessary for this desirable purpose (both to conform to the model and adopt the practice of the primitive Church) expressly exhibited in the New Testament. . . . Were we, then, in our church constitution and managements to exhibit a complete conformity to the apostolic Church, would we not be, in that respect, as perfect as Christ intended we should be? And should not this suffice us?

TRANSCENDENTALISM

Though the frontier seemed to offer more time and space for social experiments than did the settled areas, even the East had its schemes. The New England seedbed, for example, produced many a strange flowering. As Ralph Waldo Emerson wrote in 1840 to Thomas Carlyle: "We are all a little wild here with numberless projects of social reform. Not a reading man but has a draft of a new community in his waist coat pocket." Sharing hopes spawned in an age of romanticism, utopian planners such as Bronson Alcott (father of Louisa May) and George Ripley would dispose of all difficulties, public or private, through a properly conceived social order. Brook Farm, near Boston, was formed, said founder Ripley, "to prepare a society of liberal, intelligent, and cultivated persons, whose relations with each other would permit a more wholesome and simple life than can be led amidst the pressures of our competitive institutions."

Nathaniel Hawthorne in *Blithedale Romance* (1852) alludes to life on Brook Farm.

Often in these years that are darkening around me, I remember our beautiful scheme of a noble and unselfish life, and how fair in that first summer appeared the prospect that it might endure for generations, and be perfected, as the ages rolled by, into the system of a people and a world. Were my former associates now there—were there only three or four of those true-hearted men still laboring in the sun—I sometimes fancy that I should direct my world-weary foot steps thitherward, and entreat them to receive me for old friendship's sake. More and more I feel we struck upon what ought to be a truth. Posterity may dig it up and profit by it.

Also in New England a small but highly creative coterie gave birth to transcendentalism. Part religion, part philosophy, part revolt against doctrine, part adoration of nature, part Puritan and part Oriental, the transcendentalist movement defies simple description. With utopianism it shared the vision of a progressive realization of the beautiful, the good, and the true. With Methodism it rejected a cold critical unfeeling rationalism. And with revivalism it appealed to a free assertiveness, a self-reliance on the part of every true believer. And like all of these, transcendentalism channeled its new understanding into social reform and moral regeneration.

Transcendentalism revolted against Unitarianism, which had itself so recently revolted against the prevailing Congregational orthodoxy. Such persons as Ralph Waldo Emerson, Henry David Thoreau, James Freeman Clark, George Ripley, and Orestes Brownson found little satisfaction or inspiration in Unitarian protests *against*. What positively could be said? What devoutly believed? What cause courageously served? The answers would come not from creeds and constitutions nor from metaphysical speculation but from intuition, from "reason" in the transcendentalist sense of that term. Man was free; but what good is that freedom if he does not respond to all that nature and the universe can teach him? "Let man stand erect, go alone, and possess the universe," said Emerson.

Ralph Waldo Emerson comments on religious ceremonies in "The Lord's Supper" (1832).

> I am not so foolish as to declaim against forms. Forms are as essential as bodies; but to exalt particular forms, to adhere to one form a moment after it is outgrown, is unreasonable, and it is alien to the spirit of Christ. . . . I am not engaged to Christianity by decent forms, or saving ordinances; it is not usage; it is not what I do not understand that binds me to it—let these be the sandy foundations of falsehoods. What I revere and obey in it is its reality, its boundless charity, its deep interior life, the rest it gives to mind, the echo it returns to my thoughts, the perfect accord it makes with my reason . . . Freedom is the essence of this faith. Its institutions then should be as flexible as the wants of men. That form out of which the life and suitableness have departed should be as worthless in its eyes as the dead leaves that are falling around us.

In 1836 Boston's Transcendental Club first gathered in the home of George Ripley. That year alone saw enough conversation started, enough writing published to set the Boston countryside buzzing. By design the Club dipped into every intellectual current. No one could be admitted to the select fellowship if his "presence excluded any one topic." Since a majority of the members were Unitarian clergymen, religion represented a dominant concern. How should the church be reformed? What was the proper view of miracles? Where is the Divine, the Over-Soul, to be found? When is the Kingdom of God to be realized? These and similar queries fired quick minds and facile pens in the movement's brief glory, that "sort of midsummer madness," in Perry Miller's words, "that overtook a few intellectuals in or around Boston about the year 1840."

Ralph Waldo Emerson was the Club's major spokesman. Thirty-three years of age when he met with that first evening symposium in Ripley's home, Emerson had already known disquieting questions and distracting doubts. Four years after his graduation from Harvard in 1825, he assumed ministerial duties in one of Boston's Unitarian churches. But a dislike for public prayers and a discomfort in administering Holy Communion led to his resignation in 1832. While he continued to preach for some years after, he never resumed full pastoral duties.

Like Charles Finney,[1] Emerson was impatient with empty form and dead ritual. Unlike Finney he found the remedy not in a return to Scripture but in a recognition of the divinity within all men. Inspiration was not given to a few men long ago, but is given to all men now. Faith is properly placed not in some external person or platform but in oneself and one's intuitions. There is miracle enough for any man: that "the simplest person who in his

[1] See below, p. 150.

integrity worships God, becomes God; yet for ever and ever the influx of this better and universal self is new and unsearchable."

Emerson's "Address at Harvard Divinity School" (1838) exhibits his confidence in man.

It is the office of a true teacher to show us that God is, not was; that He speaketh, not spake. The true Christianity—a faith like Christ's in the infinitude of man—is lost. None believeth in the soul of man, but only in some man or person old and departed. Ah me! No man goeth alone. All men go in flocks to this saint or that poet, avoiding the God who seeth in secret. They cannot see in secret; they love to be blind in public. They think society wiser than their soul, and know not that one soul, and their soul, is wiser than the whole world.

Another member of this intimate circle, Orestes A. Brownson, made a winding but fascinating pilgrimage through America's religious labyrinth. Reared in Vermont by foster parents, Brownson at the age of nineteen joined a Presbyterian church in northern New York. Contrary to his hopes, the anxieties of soul that drove him into that church neither diminished nor disappeared. Still searching two years later, he tried the Universalists, accepting ordination as a minister in 1826. At first Universalism's affirmation of human nobility together with its denial of eternal damnation contrasted favorably with the rigors of his previous Calvinism. But this, too, soon soured, as all supernaturalism seemed uncertain, or at best irrelevant, to society's painfully prominent injustices. In turning toward socialism and radical reform from 1829 to 1831, Brownson entered the most anti-Christian period of his life.

In his autobiography, *The Convert* (1857), Orestes A. Brownson reveals the depths of his skepticism around 1829.

Failing to find an authority competent to teach me the true sense of a supernatural revelation, I had step by step rejected all such revelation, and brought myself back to simple nature, to the world of the senses, and to this sublunary life. I neither asserted nor denied the existence of God. I neither believed nor disbelieved in a life after death. The position I took was, these are matters of which I know nothing, of which I can know nothing, and therefore are matters of which I will endeavor not to think. Of this world of senses I do and may know something. Here is a work to be done, here is the scene of my labors, and here I will endeavor to love mankind and make them happy.

In 1832 Orestes Brownson became a Unitarian, first accepting the charge of a church in New Hampshire, then two years later, at the suggestion of George Ripley, moving to Massachusetts. None of his passion for social justice lost, Brownson became known for his reforming fervor and humanitarian sympathies. In this role he made his major impact on transcendentalism, seeking to convince as wide an audience as he could reach—by sermon, lecture, article, and conversation—that religion must be the motive force for social advance. The financial panic of 1837 accented his position and increased his audience.

Brownson prefers honest unbelief to dishonest orthodoxy (*The Convert*, 1857).

> I have had my faults, great and grievous faults, as well as others, but I have never had that of disloyalty to principle, or of fearing to own my honest convictions, however unpopular they might be, or however absurd or dangerous the public might regard them. Give me rather the open, honest unbeliever, who pretends to believe nothing more than he really does, than your sleek, canting hypocrite, who rolls up his eyes in holy horror of unbelief, and makes a parade of his orthodoxy, when he believes not a word in the Gospel, and has a heart which is a cage of unclean beasts, out of which more devils need to be cast out than were cast out of the Magdalen. The former may never see God, but the latter deserves the lowest place in hell. There is hope of the conversion of a nation of unbelievers; of the conversion of a nation of hypocrites none.

But Brownson's private pilgrimage was not yet over. Reading even more widely, particularly in European philosophy, the restless wanderer found himself turning back toward supernaturalism, back to what God gives man—grace—and away from the self-reliant divinity within man. "Mere individual reason" is impotent, he wrote, "when it has not, for its guide and support, the reason of God." A long letter written in 1842, later published as "The Mediatorial Life of Jesus," betokened a profound change. In 1844 at Boston, Brownson was baptized and confirmed in the Roman Catholic Church.

In "Catholic Polemics" (1861) Brownson declares that each age must be permitted to defend the faith in its own terms.

> We find no fault with the great men, the great controversialists of other times. They did their work, and they did it well; they vindicated nobly, heroically, and successfully the truth of their age; answered conclusively the objections which they had to answer, and in the form and way most intelligible to those who urged them. It is no reproach to them to say that they have not fully answered objections which were not raised in their time.

What we ask is, that Catholic controversialists be allowed to follow their example, and that we be as free to grapple with the errors and speculations of our age as they were to grapple with the errors and speculations of theirs. They were free to do their work; let us be free to do ours.

While he remained in this church until his death in 1876, Brownson's intellectual and spiritual wanderings were never fully done. His unending concern for the problems of men, the powers of government, the relation between Christianity and civilization brought him into constant conflict with former colleagues and fellow Catholics. The strains to which Catholicism itself was subjected in the stormy papacy of Pius IX (1846–1878) were reflected in Brownson's later life. Moreover, America's religious diversity required adjustments that made the whole era thorny and treacherous. Brownson, his son later wrote, was ever busy defending against Americans his right to be a Catholic, and defending against Catholics his right to be an American.

METHODISM

Methodism is both a denomination and a movement. As a denomination it came to the American religious scene rather late, emerging as an independent entity only after the War of Independence was won. As a movement it came earlier and spread farther.

As a denomination Methodism has a discernible origin and progress. John Wesley broke with the Church of England when clergymen sympathetic to his convictions and sensitive to the colonies' needs were not provided in sufficient number. He therefore personally dispatched laymen and later ordained clergymen to evangelize in America. Under the effective preaching of Francis Asbury, Thomas Coke, William McKendree, Jesse Lee, and others, Methodism was soon winning converts by the thousands. With only a scattered following at the end of the Revolution, the denomination by 1830—only fifty years later—numbered more than a half million. By the middle of the nineteenth century, Methodism was the leading church in a majority of the states.

The denomination's sudden growth is impressive, but even more impressive is the pervasiveness of methodism as a movement. The movement may be characterized by four features: (1) pietism, (2) individualism, (3) reductionism, and (4) perfectionism. As these features dominate much of America's religious history, it is useful to speak of methodism as a movement.[2]

---

[2] When not capitalized, "methodism" refers to the general pietist movement, not to this specific denomination.

Pietism

The wave of pietism that washed over much of western Christendom in the eighteenth century rolled along America's frontiers in the nineteenth century. For pietism the immediate, personal, subjective experiences of religion were central: faith was not an intellectual assent so much as an intimate relationship with the divine. Since religion of the heart outranked religion of the head, no hand-me-down tradition seemed important; no man-made authority in spiritual matters seemed appropriate. Thus man's religious freedom, his freedom of spirit, blended with and augmented his new sense of political freedom. Religious novelty was accepted without shame; religious authority was rejected without fear. For if experience is the bedrock of the religious life, who may tell another what is unreal or untrue?

Individualism

Pietism is thus closely kin to individualism—an individualism that sometimes seemed indifferent to the larger concerns of a people or a nation. Private morality received more attention than public ethics, the redemption of the individual being the prime task of preacher and church. If the heart of man could be subdued, the evils of society would dissolve and sound civic health be restored. In any case, a man's faith is to be left wholly alone—by state and perhaps even by church. Jefferson's dictum that religion lies solely "between man and his God" fell on eager ears in the 1830's, as Jacksonian Democrats viewed impersonal institutions as irrelevant to religion's realm.

Stress on the competence of the individual soon led to scorn for those areas where all men were not competent. Theology was one such area. Dismissed as a professional, artificial activity, theology grew simpler and simpler until it was a question whether any existed at all. Wesley's impatience with the "frothy food" of theological opinion was widely shared, so that what looked like theological harmony on the frontier was often theological vacancy. Doctrine was displaced by congeniality, and social convention more than creedal confession separated "believer" from pagan.

Reductionism

Where every man is his own priest, the laity may rise to the level of the ministry. More often, however, the ministry seeks the theological and moral level of the laity. Along the frontier, therefore, an unlearned, untrained ministry sprang up. Where education was unavailable, it could be readily dismissed. But an untrained, even an illiterate ministry was not necessarily an unworthy or an unfruitful ministry. Consider, for example, Peter Cartwright.

Born in Virginia in 1785, Peter grew up in the wilds of Kentucky, untutored and largely untamed. At the age of sixteen he attended a camp

10. *Brownson Memorial Chapel, Notre Dame University* • *Brownson died in Detroit in 1876, but a decade later was reburied in the crypt-chapel of Sacred Heart Church, Notre Dame University.*

11. *Sacred Heart Church, Notre Dame University*

12. *The Circuit Preacher • The daring and dedication of the Methodist circuit rider became proverbial in the Age of Expansion.*

13. *Baptismal Service, near Morehead, Kentucky • Twentieth century Primitive Baptists carry on in the tradition of their nineteenth century forebears.*

meeting where he joined the ranks of frontier Christians. As a new convert he immediately urged companions and friends to align themselves on his and the church's side. His success was such that the next year, 1802, Methodist authorities granted him a license to "exhort." In 1803 he became an itinerant preacher, traveling into Tennessee, Indiana, and Ohio. Achieving full ministerial status in 1808, he traversed the same circuits until he moved to Illinois in 1824. For almost fifty years he guided religious life in that state.

Peter Cartwright looks back longingly to the "good old days" (preface to his *Autobiography*, 1856).

When I consider the insurmountable disadvantages and difficulties that the early pioneer Methodist preachers labored under in spreading the Gospel in Western wilds in the great valley of the Mississippi, and contrast the disabilities which surround them on every hand with the glorious human advantages that are enjoyed by their present successors, it is confoundingly miraculous to me that our modern preachers cannot preach better, and do more good than they do. Many nights, in early times, the itinerant had to camp out, without fire or food for man or beast. Our pocket Bible, Hymn Book, and Discipline constituted our library. It is true we could not, many of us, conjugate a verb or parse a sentence, and murdered the king's English almost every lick. But there was a Divine unction attended the word preached, and thousands fell under the mighty power of God, and thus the Methodist Episcopal Church was planted firmly in this Western wilderness, and many glorious signs have followed, and will follow, to the end of time.

Cartwright was circuit rider and frontier preacher par excellence. Simple, pious, and unmistakably individualistic, he won an immense popular following. Vigorously opposed to slavery, gambling and drunkenness, he utilized his talents effectively in causes deemed worthy and righteous. His physical might was as proverbial as his forensic power, and one was often the ally of the other. His colorful life was a series of victories: over poverty, over illiteracy, over sin, over Satan. Only one defeat did he know. In 1846 he ran for the United States Congress, but the victory went to his Whig opponent, Abraham Lincoln.

In his autobiography Cartwright noted that he had baptized some twelve thousand persons and had preached over fourteen thousand sermons. Afraid that Methodism would grow soft as America grew sophisticated, Cartwright cautioned against a decline in the camp meeting, where "infidelity quailed before the mighty power of God." The flames of piety must be constantly fanned, the word of God must be regularly and vigorously proclaimed. "I have lived to see this vast Western wilderness rise and improve," he wrote, and all care must be taken that it slip not away from its commitments of faith.

In his *Autobiography* Peter Cartwright offers a lively description of the camp meeting.

> From 1801 for years a blessed revival of religion spread through almost the entire inhabited parts of the West. . . . In this revival originated our camp-meetings, and in both these denominations [Presbyterians and Methodists] they were held every year, and indeed have been ever since, more or less. They would erect their camps with logs or frame them, and cover them with clapboards or shingles. They would also erect a shed, sufficiently large to protect five thousand people from wind and rain . . . here they would collect together from forty to fifty miles around, sometimes further than that. Ten, twenty, and sometimes thirty ministers, of different denominations, would come together and preach night and day, four or five days together; and indeed, I have known these camp-meetings to last three or four weeks, and great good resulted from them. I have seen more than a hundred sinners fall like dead men under one powerful sermon, and I have seen and heard more than five hundred Christians all shouting aloud the high praises of God at once . . . the work went on and spread almost in every direction, gathering additional force, until our country seemed all coming home to God.

Perfectionism

A final feature of the methodist movement, perfectionism, cut a wide swath in nineteenth-century American religion. If utopianism was largely a social ideal, perfectionism was largely a personal one. The Christian justified by the grace of God was not to rest therein; rather he should press on toward sanctification, toward full obedience to the divine command "Be ye therefore perfect, even as your father in heaven is perfect."

This teaching stimulated great moral earnestness and striving in America. Joining a Christian society was the beginning of a redeemed life, not the end. The convert proceeded to reform first himself and then society—to overthrow slavery, to stamp out political corruption, to promote temperance, to eliminate poverty, war, disease and hunger. One minister wrote in 1854: "Nothing short of a general renewal of society ought to satisfy any soldier of Christ." Those pursuing holiness were as leaven in the whole loaf of American culture. By this leavening, might not America itself be made holy?

REVIVALISM

Utopianism and methodism often accompanied the volcanic revivalism that erupted from seaboard to frontier. The nineteenth century saw revivals in

America extended, encouraged, modified, and praised to an extent beyond that ever before witnessed in the history of the western world. Meetings were held in open fields, crude cabins, neoclassical churches, and remodeled theatres. Some revivals were spontaneous outbursts, while others were painstakingly planned and promoted. Some were characterized by emotional excesses (fainting, shouting, jumping), while others were sober and restrained. Some occurred under the leadership of a spectacular itinerant evangelist, while others emerged from a quiet countryside.

Mass evangelism helped the free churches to serve a rootless, sprawling society. Churches severed from all state support competed in the open market, so to speak, for members and money. Parishes were not carefully prescribed; lines of ministerial authority were not laid down. With the country's rapid geographical expansion and growing immigration, new measures of recruitment and propagation were required. Though the methods sometimes seemed boorish and crude, they more often proved to be reforming and effective.

Charles G. Finney ushered in the age of evangelism, employing his "new measures" successfully not only in the boisterous West but also in the sedate East. Born in Connecticut in 1792, Finney taught school in New York and New Jersey before preparing himself for a career in law. Soon after beginning his legal practice, he experienced a dramatic conversion, receiving "a mighty baptism of the Holy Ghost" which changed both his future and America's. Licensed to the Presbyterian ministry in 1824, Charles Finney launched a revivalist career that lasted for fifty years. In the course of that fruitful ministry he was pastor, professor, college president (Oberlin), author, abolitionist, and world traveler.

In 1835, two years after he became professor of theology at newly established Oberlin College, Finney published his *Lectures on Revivals of Religion*. Here, based on his insights and experience, he offered detailed advice for promoting and conducting revivals. Assured that this technique of evangelism was given by God to be used of men, Finney provided this handbook on ways and means. "The connection between the right use of means for a revival and a revival is," he wrote, "as philosophically sure as between the right use of means to raise grain and a crop of wheat." In giving such sure guidance from cause to effect, this powerful preacher of reform and righteousness fired the zeal of the churches' laity and fashioned the pulpit style for many of the clergy.

Charles G. Finney, in *Lectures on Revivals of Religion* (1835), defends revivals as one of God's "new measures."

If we examine the history of the church we shall find that there never has been an extensive reformation, except by new measures. Whenever the churches get settled down into a *form* of doing things, they soon get to rely upon the outward doing of it, and so retain the form of religion while they lose the substance. And then it has always been found impossible to arouse them so as to bring about a reformation of the evils, and produce a revival of religion, by simply pursuing the established form. . . . When [God] has found that a certain mode has lost its influence by having become a form, he brings up some new measure which will BREAK IN upon their lazy habits, and WAKE UP a slumbering church. And great good has resulted.

Perfectionism was preached, individualism was practiced, and once more the redemption of all America was just ahead. Lyman Beecher, at first resisting Finney's revivalist measures, later adopted them with enthusiasm. In New Haven, or Boston, or later in Ohio, Beecher found Finney's evangelism effective. And America was poised on a crested wave of decision, either to be cast up on the shore of salvation or lost in a sea of infidelity. "The religious and political destiny of our nation is to be decided in the West," Beecher wrote, adding this promise and warning: "The capacity of the West for self-destruction, without religious and moral culture, will be as terrific as her capacity for self-preservation, with it, will be glorious."

Hopes for the nation's destiny were often linked with expectations of the Second Coming of Christ. Many viewed the millennium (that thousand-year period of peace and plenty described in the Book of Revelation) as the climax of the American dream. With a little more repentance, a little more reform, with greater piety and morality, the nation might enter that new and glorious, God-ruled age. "If the church will do her duty," Finney declared in 1835, "the millennium may come in this country in three years." And Beecher believed that America was "in the providence of God, destined to lead the way in the moral and political emancipation of the world."

When revivalism and millennialism worked together, the dynamic for social reform was mighty. On the other hand, some viewed the coming of Christ as the prelude to the millennium, something to be expected at any moment, at any place. In this view no steady progress in morals and religion was expected, possibly the opposite. Change would come about not through man's gradual growth but through God's sudden intervention. For these adventists the end of the age was at hand and men could only get ready: "Prepare to meet thy God, O Israel."

In upstate New York, for example, William Miller predicted that Christ's coming would occur sometime between March 21, 1843, and March 21, 1844. Basing this prophecy on the Book of Daniel, Miller's popular lectures attracted those anxious about the approaching end of the world. Shakers, Baptists, Methodists, Congregationalists, the followers of Noyes, and a host of others gave attention to what seemed the most urgent

In a book published in Boston in 1840, William Miller openly predicts the end of the world in three years: *Evidence from Scripture and History of the Second Coming of Christ about the Year 1843.*

If I have erred in my exposition of the prophecies, the time, being so near at hand, will soon expose my folly; but if I have the truth on the subjects treated on these pages, how important the era in which we live! What vast and important changes must soon be realized! and how necessary that every individual be prepared, that that day may not come upon them unawares. . . . After fourteen years' study of the prophecies and other parts of the Bible, I have come to the following conclusions, and do now commit myself into the hands of God as my Judge, in giving publicity to the sentiments herein contained, conscientiously desiring that this little book may be the means to incite others to study the Scriptures, and to see whether these things be so. . . .

of questions: how soon is the world coming to an end? "Signs of the times" were interpreted; biblical materials were read and reread; preparations were made for Christ who "will be revealed in flaming fire, taking vengeance on them that know not God." Obviously such expectations did not lead to long-range programs of social reform. They did, however, electrify the air with excited expectancy. When the prophecies of "flaming fire" failed to come true, visions of inevitable progress became more than ever the mode of the day.

In 1831 one of the most perceptive observers ever to visit America's shores, France's Alexis de Tocqueville, arrived for a ten-month tour, chiefly to investigate the prison system. He investigated far more than that, however, for his keen eye and later his cultivated pen ignored no facet, either of freedom or of frontier. Perhaps it is enough to say that this aristocratic, sophisticated European was not horrified by what he saw. Rather he found both in democracy and in free religion much to commend, much to respect. "I have seen no country," he wrote, where Christianity "presents more distinct, more simple, or more general notions to the mind." Religion "by respecting all democratic tendencies not absolutely contrary to herself" becomes an ally of the "spirit of individual independence" rather than a foe. Not all was wholesome, for in a democracy the

In *Democracy in America* (1835) Alexis de Tocqueville shows how religious conviction strengthens democracy.

It must be acknowledged that equality, which brings great benefits into the world, nevertheless suggests to men (as will be shown hereafter) some very dangerous propensities. It tends to isolate them from each other, to concentrate every man's attention on himself; and it lays open the soul to an inordinate love of material gratification. The greatest advantage of religion is to inspire diametrically contrary principles. There is no religion which does not place the object of man's desires above and beyond the treasures of earth. . . . Religious nations are therefore naturally strong on the very point on which democratic nations are weak; which shows of what importance it is for men to preserve their religion as their condition becomes more equal.

---

clergy "readily adopt the general opinions of their country and their age." But it was a changing country and an unstable age, as Tocqueville also saw. In the molding and fashioning of the future, democracy and religion could work together "toward the unmeasured greatness so indistinctly visible at the end of the long track which humanity has yet to tread."

13 ❖ Manifest Destiny

F ROM THE AGE OF EXPLORATION, through the Age of Colonization, into the Age of Expansion dreams of destiny guided the actions and fired the imaginations of New World pioneers. Like ancient Israelites following the pillar of cloud by day and fire by night, America's explorers, colonists, and citizens were steadied in their journey by the vision ahead. And for them, as for their predecessors approaching Canaan, the hand that led them was the hand of God. Providence knew and Providence directed.

While this assurance undergirded brave men from Columbus on, in the nineteenth century even the timid dared to dream. "The great experiment is now making," Lyman Breecher wrote in 1835; few cared to question or doubt. God had brought His people through famines and plagues, had stayed the hand of proud monarchs, had led His children safely out of the wilderness to the very banks of Jordan. Now, in keeping with His perfect plan, it was time to possess the Promised Land.

What did that land promise? For some the land itself was promise and fulfillment enough. For others the settled, cultivated, possessed land meant a mighty nation, free of tyranny and an agent of liberty to all the world. Still others saw across the Mississippi—America's Jordan—a land to be

---

Samuel Stennett in 1787 wrote these words that for nineteenth-century Americans held a double charm.

> On Jordan's stormy banks I stand
> And cast a wishful eye
> To Canaan's fair and happy land
> Where my possessions lie.
>
> I am bound for the promised land
> I am bound for the promised land
> O who will come and go with me—
> I am bound for the promised land.

---

redeemed, a people to be won. Whether homesteader, nationalist, or missionary, all went out with a sense of destiny. God—or history—was on their side. They knew it and were sustained by it.

ONE LAND, ONE FLAG

This march with time first took the form of major territorial gains. In 1803 by a happy coincidence of good luck and good judgment, a stroke of Thomas Jefferson's pen doubled the territory of the United States. Jefferson's purchase of Louisiana Territory from Napoleon for fifteen million dollars secured navigation and commerce on the Mississippi, preserved the vital port of New Orleans, encouraged exploration of the Far West, and whetted the nation's appetite for a continent stretching from sea to shining sea.

This vast domain, reaching northward into Canada and westward along the river systems of the Mississippi, the Missouri, and the Platte, had for years been contended for by Spain and France. Early in the nineteenth century Napoleon, in need of money for his military exploits, decided to sell more than Jefferson had any plan or dream of buying. The population, largely French, had no fondness for Spanish rule and little more for American. In the chess game of international politics these inhabitants had been the pawns, pushed or traded as the players' interests dictated. The 1803 gambit looked like only another tiresome, temporary shift. But this time Louisiana shifted from Europe's intrigues to America's destiny.

As noted above in Chapter 3, French religion early penetrated the Mississippi Valley, descending from Quebec or moving upstream from New Orleans. Despite the political juggles, the withdrawal of the Jesuits, and the continuing hostility of the Indians, France's hold on the people never faded completely. In New Orleans, for example, the Ursuline convent, reduced in numbers but strong in spirit, hoped to continue its mission under American rule. Appealing to Jefferson for assurance, the sisters welcomed his prompt reply. "The principles of the Constitution and government of the United States," he wrote in 1804, "are a sure guarantee to you" that the convent and its property will be preserved "sacred and inviolate." The French nuns might rest assured that they "will meet with all the protection which my office can give. . . ."

But Louisiana Territory as a whole, largely lawless and unsettled, needed more than a guarantee of the status quo. Louisiana first became a diocese in 1793, when the territory was under Spanish control. Upon his arrival in New Orleans in 1795 the first bishop, Cuban-born Peñalver, found that religion received little reverance or respect. Few took communion, he reported, not even once a year. Attendance at mass was irregular, attention to morality minimal. Fasting "is a thing unknown; and there are other evils which show how little religion exists here among the inhabitants, and which demonstrate that there remains in their bosoms but a slight spark of the faith instilled into them at the baptismal font."

When the territory passed under the American flag eight years later, conditions had hardly improved. To the indifference of the populace and the confusion of politics, French and Spanish clerical strife added its aggravation. By 1805 John Carroll of Baltimore, still the nation's only Catholic bishop, was obliged to add this gigantic expanse to his own sprawling diocese. Searching for an able man to bring order to this difficult diocese,

---

Bishop John Carroll in a letter in 1806 to James Madison, then Secretary of State, tells of problems in Louisiana territory.

I was not so satisfied with the accounts of Louisiana, of the clergymen living there, as would justify a recommendation of any of them for the important trust [office of bishop], which requires not only a virtuous but very prudent conduct, great learning, especially in matters of a religious nature, and sufficient resolution to remove gradually the disorders which have grown up during the relaxed state of civil and ecclesiastical authority. I therefore directed my view to two others, who, though Frenchmen, have been long resident in this country and steady in their attachment to it. But the removal of either of them to Louisiana was rendered impracticable, and circumstances have since occurred which perhaps make it inadviseable, in the opinion of this government, to nominate for the bishop of that country any native of France or Louisiana.

Bishop Carroll at length persuaded William du Bourg to serve as his chief administrator. By this time, 1812, Carroll had convinced Vatican authorities that additional bishops were essential to a rapidly expanding nation. Dioceses were centered in Boston, New York, Philadelphia, and Bardstown (Kentucky), and the able Carroll became America's first archbishop.

Upon Du Bourg's elevation to the episcopate in 1815 he assumed the title of bishop of Louisiana and the Floridas. But since Louisiana was American and Florida Spanish, unified ecclesiastical control was out of the question. In practice the bishop of Havana asserted his rule over Spain's remaining foothold in the eastern part of what is now the United States. How long before that last foothold would slip, Spain could not be sure but the handwriting on the wall offered little comfort. Central and South American colonies were seething with revolt, and Florida had been invaded by Americans repelling Indian forays. Before Florida was lost through force, perhaps it should be sold for profit. In 1819, therefore, at a price of five million dollars the United States acquired the last foreign-owned land east of the Mississippi.

From the Atlantic to the Great Plains one flag waved, one government ruled. Eager settlers began to fill up the void, clear the forest, and cultivate the soil. French and Spanish mixed with German, Irish, and English so that again *e pluribus unum* was a living experience, not a hollow legend. Kentucky and Tennessee, along with Vermont, entered the Union before the eighteenth century closed. Then Ohio (1803) and Louisiana (1812) were followed in quick succession by Indiana (1816), Mississippi (1817), Illinois (1818), Alabama (1819), and the twins of the Great Compromise—Maine (1820) and Missouri (1821). The march was swift, the destiny seemed sure.

In the year that Spain sold Florida to the United States (1819), she also relinquished her claim to the Oregon country held by Great Britain. Five years later Russia likewise yielded her claim, leaving Britain unchallenged in her title to Oregon. Unchallenged, that is, except by that troublesome, upstart nation which in 1812 had again declared war against England. Oregon, i.e., everything north of Spanish California and south of Russian

---

In an 1839 letter to a Massachusetts Congressman, Jason Lee, who later encourged Oregon's first provisional government, prophesies accurately.

> It is believed that if the government of the United States takes such measures in respect to this territory [Oregon] as will secure the rights of the settlers, most of those who are now attached to the mission will remain as permanent settlers in the country after the mission may no longer need their services. Hence it may be safely assumed that ours, in connection with the other settlers already there, is the commencement of a permanent settlement of the country. . . . The country will be settled, and that speedily, from some quarter, and it depends very much upon the speedy action of Congress what that population shall be, and what shall be the fate of the Indian Tribes in that Territory. It may be thought that Oregon is of but little importance; but, rely upon it, there is the germ of a great state.

Alaska, offered attractions to traders, trappers, and explorers even before the War of 1812. The famous Lewis and Clark expedition of 1806, reporting the abundance of fish and game, stimulated extensive commercial activity in a region of growing appeal.

In the 1830's eastern missionaries envisioned a more permanent occupation of Oregon. The evangelists often conceived their mission as a two-fold one: (1) to preach to the native Indians, and (2) to provide a ministry for as well as encouragement to westward-migrating Americans. In 1834 Jason Lee, a Methodist, launched this sort of double-edged mission in Willamette Valley. Two years later Presbyterians Marcus Whitman and Henry Spalding, accompanied by their wives, completed the arduous, dangerous overland journey to Oregon. The two ladies, first white women to cross the Rockies, left careful diaries of their life among the Flathead Indians. If the

In a letter to her mother written a few months before her death (1847) Narcissa Whitman's loneliness and faith are both evident.

> I have been thinking of my beloved parents this evening, of the parting scene and the probability that I shall never see those dear faces again while I live. Sweet as it used to be, when my heart was full to sit down and pour into my mother's bosom all my feelings, both sad and rejoicing, now when far away from the parental roof and thirsting for the same precious privilege, I take my pen and find a sweet relief in giving her my history in the same familiar way. Perhaps no one else feels as I do. It would be indeed a great satisfaction to me to have my mother know how I do from day to day, what my employment and prospects are, but more especially the kind dealings of my heavenly Father towards us continually.

ladies' fears were frequent, they were also justified. For in 1847 the Indians attacked the mission station, killing both of the Whitmans and several others. Ironically mission efforts thus virtually ceased at the very time that Oregon passed into American hands.

Before that diplomatic coup, however, another able missionary penetrated the forbidding country to preach to the capricious Indians. This Belgian Jesuit, Pierre Jean DeSmet, left St. Louis in 1840 for the first of many trips west on behalf of the Flatheads. He became their advocate, not only theologically but financially as well. Seeking adequate support for a permanent mission station beyond the Rocky Mountains, he pleaded the Indian cause at home and abroad.

Pierre Jean DeSmet, S. J., in *Journeys to the Rocky Mountains* (1841) praises the Indians to whom he ministered.

> I was not able to discover among these people [Flatheads] the slightest blameworthy act, unless it was their gambling, in which they often venture everything they possess. These games were unanimously abolished, as soon as I had explained to them that they were contrary to the commandment of God. . . . They are scrupulously honest in their buying and selling; they have never been accused of committing a theft. . . . Slander is unknown even among the women; lying is hateful to them beyond anything else. . . . They are polite, always of a jovial humor, very hospitable, and helpful to one another in their duties. . . . I have often asked myself: "Is it these people whom the civilized nations dare to call by the name of savages?" Wherever I have met Indians in these remote regions [Pierre's Hole, just west of the Teton Mountains], I have found them very teachable in everything adapted to better their condition. The vivacity of their young people is surprising, and the amiability of their characters and their dispositions among themselves are remarkable. People have too long been accustomed

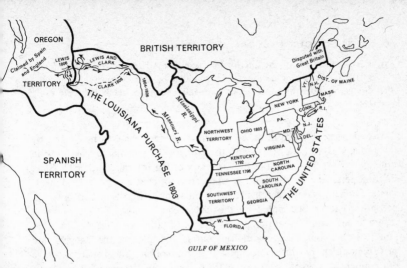

1. Louisiana Purchase, 1803

3. DeSmet with the Indians • On behalf of the United States, Father DeSmet negotiated with Sitting Bull, Chief of the Sioux, as illustrated above.

2. St. Louis Cathedral, New Orleans • The present imposing edifice was built nine years before Louisiana passed into American hands.

4. Pierre Jean DeSmet, S. J.

to judge the savages of the interior by those of the frontier; these last have learned the vices of the whites, who, guided by the insatiable thirst for sordid gain, endeavor to corrupt them and encourage them by their example.

Like Roger Williams in an earlier time, DeSmet came to be trusted by the Indians as an honest man and therefore as an acceptable negotiator in time of war. At the request of the Secretary of the Interior, Father De Smet in 1868 persuaded the Sioux to accept a truce of peace. A delicate, dangerous mission, it was accomplished by a missionary who accepted no compensation except that noted by the peace commissioners. "We are well aware," they wrote, "that our thanks can be of little worth to you, and that you will find your true reward for your labors and for the dangers and privation which you have encountered in the consciousness that you have done much to promote peace on earth and good will to men."

After thirty years of inconclusive negotiation Great Britain and the United States in 1846 signed a treaty that thrust American sovereignty all the way to the Pacific. Oregon Country, extending to 49° north latitude (not to 54° 40′ or fight!), now entered the continental domain. Wagons by the thousands, caravans by the hundreds set out from Independence, Missouri, over an indistinct, treacherous Oregon trail. By 1850 population had boomed to thirteen thousand—about five times what it had been a mere half-dozen years before. Now it was time to build on the foundations carefully laid by Jason Lee.

The remaining territorial steps toward the West were taken at the expense of another new nation, Mexico. In 1821 Mexico wrested its independence from a reluctant Spain. The preceding year the Spanish governor had granted colonization right in Texas to Moses Austin, which rights were actually exercised by Moses' son, Stephen F. Austin. As founder of Texas, Stephen Austin brought land-hungry settlers into this province of Mexico, maintaining peace for years despite the growing population of Americans and the growing suspicions of Mexicans.

Again the tide of destiny moved with colonists hungering for liberty as well as land. In 1835, when Mexico's president swept away the Texans' rights and liberties, the break came. A disastrous defeat at the Alamo (see Fig. 5, Ch. 2) in March 1836 became both rallying point and battle cry. Six weeks later, under Sam Houston, Texas won its independence on the banks of the San Jacinto River. Annexation to the United States was sought but refused, largely because of Congressional reluctance to admit another slave state to the Union. Not until 1845, after nine years as an independent Republic, did Texas win admission.

Some resisted annexation because Mexico was hostile to such a move. By 1845, however, President John Tyler and his successor, James K. Polk, no longer trembled at Mexican hostility; a few even encouraged it. Texas won and Oregon promised, what about Mexico's California? While little was known about the golden West when Polk was elected, mystery only sharpened expansionist desire. California bordered on the Pacific; that, at least, was fairly definite. Therefore, to occupy it would be to thwart or limit empire-building in the Pacific by the European powers. Besides, Mexico's hold was weak, and destiny smiles on the strong.

In 1846 the United States declared war against Mexico. Led by Generals Zachary Taylor and Winfield Scott, American forces received the surrender of Mexico City in September 1847. By terms of the treaty signed early the following year, a desiring, destiny-drawn nation added New Mexico (including Arizona) and upper California to its domain.

But America's military march did not erase Spain's spiritual footprints. Many of those prints were left by an indomitable Franciscan friar, Junípero Serra. Born in Majorca in 1713, Father Serra arrived in California in 1769, and there he remained for most of the final fifteen years of his life. In those years he introduced agriculture, architecture, and Christianity to thousands of western Indians, indelibly marking the Far West with the personality of Spain.

Serra's first and southernmost mission was established in San Diego in 1769. At the northern end of the "chain," San Francisco's Mission Dolores

---

On the expedition from Lower California's Loreto to San Diego (March 28 to July 1, 1769) Father Junípero Serra kept a diary; the final entries appear here.

June 30. We started early, and the first thing was to cross the ravine and climb up the opposite hillside. After a few ups and downs we saw a wondrous sight—a measureless plain stretching out before us which our footsteps had to tread. The hills we left on our right. And over that plain we trudged that day for four hours and a half. But the ravines we had to cross were, and are, quite numerous, without any possibility of avoiding them or flanking them—they are all alike coming straight out of the mountains. And although I continued to pray and resign myself to the will of God, etc., I summoned up all my courage—because you were no sooner out of one ravine than you were into another, and each one was dangerous. At one time I asked the guides: "Is this the last one?" "There are plenty more to come," was their answer. And they were right as events proved. Anyway, like all things in this world, the gullies came to an end. . . .

On July 1, Saturday . . . we started early in the morning on our last day's journey. Already the beginnings of the port we were seeking are partly visible, and already our guides explained to us its entrance and limits . . . we therefore continued on and finally arrived at the said camp, which they were already beginning to call the mission, a little before noon of the above-mentioned day. Thus was our arrival, with all in good health, happy and content, thanks to God, at the famous and wished for Port of San Diego.

---

was built in 1776, a year of some excitement three thousand miles eastward. Between San Diego and San Francisco, Father Serra established seven other missions, the last one (1782) being at San Buenaventura (Ventura). When this sturdy Franciscan died in 1784, he was buried in another of his own missions: Carmel's San Carlos (1771). Successors carried on his work until, in all, twenty-one links formed the great mission chain along California's El Camino Real (see Figs. 5, 6, 7, 8 and 9).

The missions continued for a generation to render good account of themselves, despite troubles within and without. Within the missions the Indians often proved indolent or inconstant. Outside the adobe walls the missionaries found the Spanish civil powers only grudgingly cooperative, sometimes not even that. White colonists at San Jose and Los Angeles seemed more interested in playing cards and guitars than in attending to church, school, or work. And the soldiers by their behavior repeatedly nullified all that the friars proclaimed. While the vast majority of Franciscan fathers persevered at their posts, some sought transfer or relief, some fell ill, and many died.

The cruelest blow yet lay ahead. When Mexico gained its independence in 1821, the tension between civil and spiritual authority intensified rather than declined. New political leaders argued that the missions hindered permanent Mexican colonization, that they held too much land, gained too much wealth, and wielded too much influence. The tone of criticism grew angrier as Mexican opinion against the missions grew stronger. In 1833 Mexico's legislature passed the long-feared act of secularization, confiscating the funds used for the missions, turning the lands and buildings (all but one reserved for a parish church) over to secular uses, and freeing all monks or nuns from their vows. Missionaries were encouraged to leave for Spain, the Mexican government even agreeing to pay the traveling expenses of those "who have not sworn to support the independence."

The full secularization of the missions was barely finished when the war between Mexico and the United States began. How the religious history of California would differ if the American flag had been raised there a dozen years earlier, it is impossible to say. By 1847, when that flag was raised, the backbone of the mission system had been broken, the missionaries had gone home, the Indians had fled. General Kearney could do little but assure all inhabitants that their new sovereign would "respect and protect the religious institutions of California." With the rush for gold in 1849, Spain's old institutions, however protected and respected, could not perform the

---

When the United States took over California, the military governor, S. W. Kearney, assured citizens that religious rights would be guaranteed.

The undersigned is instructed by the President of the United States to respect and protect the religious institutions of California, to take care that the religious rights of its inhabitants are secured in the most ample

5. *Mission San Antonio, 1771 • Founded in the Santa Lucia Mountains south of Carmel, California, the Mission San Antonio de Padua still enjoys a rural setting.*

6. *Mission San Antonio (side view of façade) • Though abandoned for many years, this mission has now been fully restored, most recently in 1949.*

7. *Mission San Luis Rey, 1798 • The eighteenth of the missions in California's chain, San Luis Rey is the largest and one of the most impressive.*

8. *Mission Santa Barbara, 1786 • The present church of this "Queen of the Missions" was begun in 1815 and was completed five years later. In 1950 the façade) was rebuilt, remaining faithful to the original classic design.*

9. *Mission San Miguel, 1797 • The picturesque exterior is more than matched by a richly colored interior provided in 1820 by a Spanish artist working with Indian assistants.*

manner, since the Constitution of the United States allows to every individual the privilege of worshiping his Creator in whatever manner his conscience may dictate. . . . Given at Monterey, Capital of California, this 1st day of March, of the year of our Lord, 1847, and of the Independence of the United States the 71st.

---

heavier tasks now demanded of them. Thus new arrivals turned for religious succor not to Madrid or Mexico City but to Boston, New York, Philadelphia, and Baltimore.

Over the Appalachians, into the valleys, across the plains, and on to the ocean's edge, at every timid step or giant leap, religious leaders summoned all the ingenuity, money, and dedication available. If the dreams for America were to come true, if her great destiny was to be fulfilled, the religious needs of a surging adolescent nation had to be met. But how? Space was immense, time was short, laborers were few. Still, it had to be done.

ONE LORD, ONE FAITH

A heroic saga of America's history, too easily ignored, too frequently overlooked, is the mission to the West. The spiritual needs of both retreating Indian and advancing white tested the mettle of every minister and every church. Where it seemed appropriate, denominations worked together; where it seemed necessary, they worked alone. But all worked, drawn by a mighty challenge that demanded equal might in return.

The term "home missions" encompassed much of the work undertaken. Observers, travelers, returned settlers—all reported to ecclesiastical authorities the opportunities and the needs in the West. As early as 1801 Presbyterians and Congregationalists joined in a Plan of Union so that home mission energies and monies could be pooled. To encourage a continuing cordial relationship between religion and learning, both in the East and in the newly opening West, the American Education Society was created in 1815. The next year, in response to reports that Bibles were scarce in frontier communities, the American Bible Society was formed. In 1822

The scarcity of printed materials hampered all mission effort; John Mason Peck, therefore, asked the Massachusetts Baptist Missionary Society to help (1823).

The experiment I have made has fully answered my most sanguine expectations of the important advantages the cause would derive in Bible societies, and the distribution of mission pamphlets, magazines and tracts. A most important service might be rendered to the cause, if the friends in Boston could supply me with an additional quantity of the back numbers of the magazine, missionary reports, old sermons, tracts, and everything of the like description for gratuitous distribution. These should be packed in a box

10. *Pilgrims of the Plains, 1871*

11. *Across the Continent, 1868*

marked with my name, the freight paid to New Orleans, consigned to some merchant there, and directed to the charge of A. Skinner, St. Louis. I have found the most beneficial effects result from the distribution of a few magazines or tracts after preaching; and as the people in all the settlements seldom hear preaching but once in a month, these silent monitors serve to keep alive impressions and feelings till the return of the preacher.

---

the Society for the Propagation of the Faith was organized in Lyons, France; almost immediately its resources began to stregthen Catholic mission efforts originating in New York, Baltimore, Bardstown, and elsewhere. The American Sunday School Union was formed in 1824, the American Tract Society in 1825, and the American Home Mission Society in 1826. What did all this organization portend?

Among other things it forecast the decline of ecclesiastical disorder and disunity in America. If there was to be a national effort, there had to be national organization. This cooperative trend met some resistance as pockets of vigorous anti-mission sentiment developed. But those who resisted the nation's challenge generally relinquished their importance in the nation's culture. Formation of the broadly based societies, on the other hand, meant that sectarian divisiveness could be transcended for common good. As one theological student observed in 1825, America needed a large mission system "which shall have no sectional interests, no local prejudices, no sectarian views; a system which shall bring the most remote parts of our nation into cordial cooperation, awaken mutual interest in the same grand and harmonious design, produce a new feeling of brotherhood, and thus bind us all together by a new cord of union."

With respectable financial backing, missions to the West brought resident ministers and permanent churches. The touring missionary, the temporary apostle from the East—these were not enough. Sometimes a congregation appealed for a pastor who would be supported jointly by the mission agency and the local church. At other times a society sent out a minister to organize a congregation and build a church, supporting him until the local flock took over. Missionary bishops and supervisory personnel coordinated activities, assisted in emergencies, and observed with wonder a rapidly moving, ever-changing western society. In addition to these cooperative agencies, most denominations by 1850 developed their own boards, bishops, or departments for the evangelization of the West.

Even though conditions were primitive, poverty widespread, and hardship omnipresent, western religion elevated the populace intellectually as well as morally. As in the Age of Colonization, education was considered the handmaiden of religion. The camp meeting, the farmer-preacher, and anti-intellectualism represent, to be sure, one aspect of religion in this age of sudden expansion. But another aspect, not to be glossed over, is religion's pivotal contribution to educational development. Schools in the West were established at every level, with support and personnel usually coming from religious groups.

Missionaries served as school teachers, and public schools often were built under the direction of some clergyman. Parochial schools, especially Lutheran and Catholic, offered elementary education to immigrant groups moving en masse toward the interior. Finally, colleges and seminaries were started by the conviction that in the last analysis the spiritual and intellectual needs of the West could be met only by leadership drawn from and trained in the West.

The *Fourth Report* (1847) of the Society for the Promotion of Collegiate and Theological Education at the West glows with optimism.

> It is therefore an effort of present and most urgent necessity to raise up institutions to do for the mighty West what Yale, and Dartmouth, and Williams, and Amherst have done for New England: to call forth from the bosom of the Western church a learned and pious ministry; to send life, and health, and vigor through the whole system of popular education, and to . . . found society on the lasting basis of religious freedom and evangelical truth. The sun shines not on such another missionary field as the valley of the Mississippi.

Many schools founded in the first half of the nineteenth century failed to survive the financial panics and weakening wars of the century. Nevertheless, to list but a few of the survivors is to be reminded that the mission to the interior brought enlightenment along with evangelism. The western colleges, one reporter observed in 1848, are "known to be places for the diligent inculcation of spiritual Christianity, as well as the truths of science and the grace of literature."

Congregationalists and Presbyterians together founded such colleges as Western Reserve (1826), Knox (1837), Grinnell (1847), Ripon (1851), and the forerunner of the University of California at Berkeley (1855). Methodists were responsible for such pioneer institutions as McKendree (1835), De Pauw (1837), Ohio Wesleyan (1842), Northwestern (1851), and Willamette (1853). Before the Civil War, Baptists had founded, among others, these: Denison (1832), Shurtleff (1835), and Baylor (1845). These four denominations were responsible for about half of all institutions of higher learning begun before 1860. By that year Roman Catholics had started St. Louis University (1832), St. Xavier (1842), Notre Dame (1844), and Santa Clara (1855). Episcopal schools included Kenyon (1826) and the University of the South (1858). With the founding of Wittenberg College in 1845 Lutherans served the needs of German migrants to Ohio. Butler University (1850) became the major western outpost for the Disciples of Christ, while Heidelberg (1851) trained German Reformed youth. Earlham (1850) answered the needs of Indiana Quakers, and in St. Louis the Unitarians encouraged the establishment of Washington University (1853). This abbreviated list, while only hinting at the prodigious activity in education as the West was won, demonstrates an enduring aspect of "home missions." For most of the far-seeing founders of these and other schools, the mission on behalf of Christianity was also a mission on behalf of civilization.

The Sunday School, although an English innovation, flourished in America, where it provided spiritual and intellectual nourishment in communities otherwise deprived. Where ministers were scarce, teachers few, schools scattered, and libraries absent, the school for Sunday scholars—youth and adult—performed a vital function. Requiring no ordained clergy, no sacramental or liturgical authority, Sunday Schools were generally managed by the laity. And as their enrollments grew, the demand for literature also increased.

The Ninth *Annual Report* of the American Sunday-School Union (1833) presented its case for religious education of the young.

> Ought not the influence of the American people, and especially the American church, to be more widely felt by the nations of the earth? A restless spirit of inquiry, a desire for knowledge and liberty, are awakened and are gaining strength in every part of the world. As ancient habits and associations are broken up, new wants and new facilities for supplying them are disclosed. . . .
>
> To meet this new combination of circumstances, the only adequate agency to which we can resort is the Christian education of the world in its childhood—the universal and simultaneous training of the bodies, minds, and hearts of children everywhere to the service of the Lord Jesus Christ, and of course to the most efficient service of mankind, savage and civilized, heathen and Christian. And no agency for this purpose has yet been given to man which may be compared with a good Sunday School.

Denominational publishing houses sought to meet this demand, the Methodists as early as 1789, when their Book Concern was established. The most ambitious literary production, however, came from the American

---

The American Tract Society issued these instructions to its agents in 1851.

> Let the box of books obtained be committed to some one who is willing to take charge of them—furnish the distributors with the requisite quantity for their respective neighborhoods—take an account of volumes delivered to each, and their value—fix the time in which the distribution is to be completed, and see that the amount is returned in volumes or money.

Each distributor having taken in charge a parcel of the volumes as a specimen, let him call upon all families assigned him, explain the nature of the object, and use his influence to induce each family, where practicable, to purchase one of the Libraries, or one or more volumes, not as charity to the Society, but for their own spiritual benefit. Endeavor to do something for the eternal welfare of every individual.

The Sunday School Union in its *Eleventh Annual Report* (1835) promoted religious libraries in the home.

We do know that no books are found in the market at so low a price as those we publish; and we do know that as a whole they form the most complete collection of juvenile religious library books that can be found upon the face of the earth. They are fitted to children and youth of all classes and characters; they have nothing in them offensive to denominational, sectional, or political preferences, or prejudices. They are prepared upon the principle that as a perfect Christian character can be formed in which no denominational trait can be recognized; so a book, exhibiting the simple, saving truths of the gospel, may be made acceptable to any and every Christian mind. Why then should they not be found in the hands of every child that can read them, from border to border, through the whole length and breadth of our land?

Tract Society. Millions of books, tracts, pamphlets, and magazines reached the western frontier through the society's distributors or colporteurs. If Tract Society materials could not be purchased, they were often freely given away. But since everything was sold at cost, prices were amazingly low. Bunyan's *Pilgrim's Progress*, for example, the complete text with eight full-page engravings, sold in 1832 for 37½¢ per copy. A twenty-four volume library sold for $10.00. There was even a "tract of the month," with special dividends for the regular subscriber. Distribution offices and auxiliary societies sprang up all over the country, with circulating libraries also appearing. Special books were printed for children, for non-English-speaking immigrants (French, Spanish, Italian, Dutch, Portugese, Welsh, Danish, Swedish, and German), for the blind, for the Indian in his own dialect, and for the Army and Navy in the Civil War. Together with the denominational houses, the Tract Society brought religious publishing to the peak of its impact on American culture.

Another technique employed before 1850, but used even more extensively after, was church-sponsored colonization. This was especially effective, indeed humane, when the newly arrived were homeless and penniless. Rather than tax further the overcrowded, unsanitary slums of seaboard cities, western colonization helped newcomers to reach free land and fresh air. Arrivals from Germany, for example, were directed by their respective churches to areas where an entire German-speaking community, with a full religious life, could be established. The Mormons went one step further by sending church authorities abroad to organize and persuade prospective immigrants even before they sailed for American shores! While some colonization projects were mismanaged, others brought to troubled travelers a welcome security in the form of familiar liturgy and corporate strength (see also Chapter 15).

In the "era of good feelings," both politically and religiously, this united missionary front shaped the quality no less than the quantity of American religion. The voluntary principle in religion became the unquestioned, and soon the unquestionable, norm. The role of the laity markedly increased,

---

The interdenominational character of the voluntary societies is clearly seen in the *First Annual Report* (1826) of the American Tract Society.

> The bond of their union [the Publishing Committee] is indeed one which the world knows nothing of. Its strength and its endearment have their foundation in the distinguishing characteristics of vital religion. He who doubts the peculiar claims of that religion, and its efficacy on the heart, may believe that in the publication of tracts, different denominations can never cordially harmonize; but he who knows its power, acknowledges its high claims, and has felt its transforming influence will not doubt that, while jarring and dissension reign so predominant among the children of this world, they whose hearts are imbued with the spirit of Jesus, though called by different names, may, when assembled for such an object, find themselves in a hallowed spot, and realize the presence of the Savior himself among them.

---

conspicuously so in the case of women who found that the several societies welcomed their time and talent. In some ecclesiastical circles the growing power of the laymen threatened ministerial prestige and orderly discipline. In others the alliance between clergy and laity worked with smooth efficiency. Indeed, some ministers, who found little opportunity for advancement or recognition in their own denominations, turned eagerly to the more free-wheeling societies where they, too, could make a mark.

Benevolence formed an integral part of American religion in this period, with private philanthropy being conducted on a scale unlike that witnessed anywhere else in the world. Societies were formed, collections were taken, synagogues and churches were pressed to care for the aged, the infirm, the drunkard, the enslaved, the unemployed, the homeless, the lost. The Hebrew Benevolent Society (1822) and the Hebrew Mutual Benefit Society (1826), for example, faced the problem of an increasing immigration of Jews and decreasing funds for helping them. In the years after the Civil War the problems and challenges of philanthropy in every religious group multiplied rapidly.

A New York circular, dated September 3, 1837, encouraged charitable activities among the Jews.

> The undersigned have been appointed an Executive Committee for the purpose of raising funds to aid and assist persons recently arrived from foreign countries, and who may be in a destitute situation.
>
> In addressing you, it is proper to state that a meeting was convened of a number of the House of Israel, at the suggestion of the officers of the several Hebrew Benevolent Societies, to take into consideration the distressed situation of a great number of Israelites, lately arrived in this city [New York] from foreign countries. The funds of the different Societies having been nearly exhausted . . . we trust and pray that this first call ever made in behalf of so great a number of strangers will be answered by the usual liberality of our brethren.
>
> The number already arrived is at least 3 or 400, and the probability that an equal number are now on their way to this country, and mostly bound to the port of New York.

For the sake of a cause larger than any single church, denominational differences were deliberately played down. The American Sunday School Union, as a typical case, stipulated that its Committee of Publication "shall consist of eight members, from at least four different denominations of Christians, and not more than two members from any one denomination." But soon the bark of cooperative charity crashed against two hard rocks: slavery (see Chapter 14) and nativism (see Chapter 15). Not until after World War II did the nation attempt again to climb the heights of religious fellowship.

FROM SHORE TO SHORE—AND MORE

The sentiment for evangelism and expansion carried the cross and the flag farther west even than San Francisco: namely, to Hawaii and Alaska. In the case of Hawaii, the flag followed the cross; in Alaska, the reverse was true.

Through its whaling industry, New England first established American contact with the Hawaiian (or Sandwich) Islands. Thus New England missionaries early resolved to extend the gospel to these distant Pacific isles. In 1819 seven families sailed from Boston on the Yankee clipper *Thaddeus*. After 157 days at sea and an always hazardous turn around Cape Horn, the eager missionaries arrived in Kailua Bay, off the Island of Hawaii. Led by Hiram Bingham of Middlebury College and Asa Thurston of Yale, the young group—most of them newlyweds just out of college —planned the conversion of Polynesian pagans.

Hiram Bingham describes the challenge of Hawaiian missions in *A Residence of Twenty-One Years in the Sandwich Islands* (1847).

The object for which the missionaries felt themselves impelled to visit the Hawaiian race was to honor God, by making known his will, and to benefit those heathen tribes by making them acquainted with the way of life; to turn them from their follies and crimes, idolatries and oppressions, to the service and enjoyment of the living God and adorable Redeemer; to give them the Bible in their own tongue, with ability to read it for themselves; to introduce and extend among them the more useful arts and usages of civilized and Christianized society; and to fill the habitable parts of those important islands with schools and churches, fruitful fields, and pleasant dwellings. To do this, not only were the Spirit and power of the Highest required . . . but . . . the preacher, the translator, the physician, the farmer, the printer, the catechist, the schoolmaster, the Christian wife and mother, the female teacher of heathen wives, mothers, and children were also indispensable.

They could not have arrived at a more opportune time, for the great King Kamehameha I had died just the year before. His death triggered a religious revolution in which ancient gods were toppled and ancient tabus defied. The path thus prepared, the New England way began to transmute the Hawaiian way. Natives learned to sew, sing, read, pray, and keep the Sabbath day holy. And while the work of Christianizing the natives went on, a subtler Americanization of the Islands also took place. Missionaries, pastors, physicians, teachers, traders, travelers—all with tiny threads spun a web pulling Hawaii ever closer to American shores, ever farther from primitive Polynesia.

New England's Congregationalists were joined by other groups from the States, notably the Mormons, who after 1850 grew rapidly. By 1854 the Book of Mormon had been translated into Hawaiian, as had portions of the Bible a generation earlier. In 1850 English was the prevailing language in the Islands, though to preserve a national identity Hawaiian was still taught in the schools. When California and Oregon joined the Union, Hawaii seemed but a simple extension of the westward course of empire. In 1863 Hawaii became "home mission" territory, and the American Board of Commissioners for Foreign Missions withdrew its support. By then American religion and culture were virtually self-sustaining; and annexation, which almost came in 1850, was finally concluded in 1898.

A generation before this annexation the United States made its final great territorial purchase in 1867. For the sum of $7,200,000 Secretary of State William H. Seward bought Alaska from Czar Alexander II, who found Alaska to be troublesome diplomatically and a failure financially.

12. *Kawaiahao Congregational Church, Honolulu* • Built of coral stone in 1841, this early and famous missionary church has sometimes been called the Westminster Abbey of the Hawaiian Islands.

13. *First Chinese Christian Church, Honolulu* • Reflecting the significant immigration from China in the 1850's, this church serves the largest Chinese congregation in Hawaii.

14. *Buddhist Soto Mission, Honolulu* • Along with Protestantism and Roman Catholicism, Japanese Buddhism is a major religious force in the Hawaiian Islands. Here the newest Buddhist shrine is seen.

The United States, recognizing that Britain and Canada had designs of "destiny" too, signed the Treaty of Cession of Russian America. Not a popular purchase, the treaty passed the United States Senate with only a single vote to spare. Serious questions raised then and later about the value of "Seward's icebox" were not fully answered until the days of World War II.

A contemporary account in the Philadelphia *Inquirer* (April 1, 1867) reflects an undecided and uninformed American public (quoted in Virginia H. Reid, *The Purchase of Alaska,* privately printed).

> When the treaty with Russia was read in the Senate in executive session ... it created a general smile, and in some instances ridicule. Had the vote been taken nearly all the Senators would have voted against it as a farce. ... There does not seem to be the slightest prospect that it will be ratified by the Senate. .... Several Senators are today in pursuit of maps and geographies, but at last accounts none of them have been able to locate definitely the limits of Russian America, or to find wherein its value consists, or of a single taxpayer who has ever invested in the territory, or now desires a single dollar to be paid out for any such purpose.

Having made the purchase, the national government proceeded to do virtually nothing about its new empire—not even explore it! The churches first penetrated this vast arctic region, assisting the impoverished, illiterate natives and establishing schools, hospitals, orphanages, and preaching stations. Late in the eighteenth century, while the territory was still Russia's, missionaries (of the Russian Orthodox Church) began work on Kodiak Island, Alaska Peninsula, and elsewhere. The most successful of these men, John Veniaminoff, translated the catechism and portions of the New Testament into the language of the Aleuts, conducted schools for literacy, and became the first Eastern Orthodox bishop in the western hemisphere. Throughout the nineteenth century, even after America's purchase, Russian Orthodoxy remained Alaska's dominant religion.

The major missionary from America's mainland, Sheldon Jackson, had already achieved fame for his work among the Indians and western settlers in the Great Plains. In 1877 he journeyed to Alaska, where he quickly concluded that only wide support, both civil and ecclesiastical, could rescue a destitute populace. Appointed as the United States General Agent of Education, Jackson returned to Alaska in 1885 to fight lawlessness and immorality, witchcraft and slavery, corruption and illiteracy. His introduction of the reindeer from nearby Siberia permanently altered Alaska's economy. Since the white man had so reduced the whale and seal herds as to threaten the Eskimoes with starvation, reindeer became the means of survival. Jackson's experiment was a phenomenal success; if religion had only

15. *Mormon Temple, Laie, Oahu • Beginning its mission in 1850, the Church of Jesus Christ of Latter-day Saints enjoyed great growth in Hawaii. Dedicated in 1919, this was the first Mormon temple built outside the continental United States.*

16. *Russian Orthodox Church in the Aleutian Islands (1938)*

17. *St. Michael's Orthodox Cathedral, Sitka • This famous cathedral, still in use, was started in 1844 and dedicated in 1848—a generation before Alaska's purchase by the United States.*

increased like reindeer, Jackson would be the Paul Bunyan of American missions. Religion, however, grew quite slowly, mainly because (unlike the other areas of the American West) no great migration of permanent settlers advanced toward that northern tundra. The golden West attracted, but the frozen North dismayed.

The perceptive Philip Schaff in 1854 delivered a lecture in Germany that endeavored to interpret the New World to the Old (*America*, 1855).

> For these Americans have not the least desire to rest on the laurels of the past and comfortably enjoy the present; they are full of ambition and national pride, and firmly resolved to soar above the Old World. They are a people of the boldest enterprise and untiring progress—Restlessness and Agitation personified. Even when seated, they push themselves to and fro on their rockingchairs; they live in a state of perpetual excitement in their business, their politics and their religion. . . .
>
> The grandest destiny is evidently reserved for such a people. We can and must, it is true, find fault with many things in them and their institutions—slavery, the lust of conquest, the worship of Mammon, the rage of speculation, political and religious fanaticism and party-spirit, boundless temerity, boasting, quackery, and—to use the American word for it—humbug. . . . But we must not overlook the healthy, vital energies that continually re-act against these diseases: the moral, yea Puritanical earnestness of the American character, its patriotism and love of liberty in connection with deep-rooted reverence for the law of God and authority, its clear, practical understanding, its talent for organization, its inclination for improvement in every sphere, its fresh enthusiasm for great plans and schemes of moral reform, and its willingness to make sacrifices for the promotion of God's kingdom and every good work.

As the nineteenth century opened, the area of the United States was less than one million square miles, the population five million. By the middle of that century the area had expanded to one and one-half million square miles, and the population to more than twenty million. A great nation was in the making; the future looked bright.

In a letter to his brother, 1849, Pierre Jean DeSmet writes proudly of America.

> What nation on earth presents such a spectacle as the United States of America—of a confederated Government, so complicated, over such a vast extent of territory, with so many varied interests, and yet moving so harmoniously? I went within the walls of the Capitol at Washington, and there, under the star-spangled banners that wave amid its domes, I found the representatives of eight Territories and of thirty States or nations—

nations, in many senses, they may be called—that have within them all the germ and sinew to raise a greater people than many of the proud, now tottering, principalities of Europe; all speaking and learning one and the same language, all acting with one heart and all burning with the same enthusiasm—the love and glory of the Great Republic—even while parties do exist and bitter domestic quarrels now and then arise.

Yet, a cloud appeared on the horizon. No bigger than a man's hand in 1800, it was at least that big in 1820. It billowed by 1840, and in 1860 the dark, deadly cloud was ready to burst.

14 ❖ A House of Faith Divided

THE AGE OF EXPANSION was also an Age of Reform. Churches and synagogues cooperatively or separately turned their attention to private vices and social ills. Religiously motivated individuals organized to bring unity and strength into their battle against evil. Horace Mann reformed education; Samuel Gridley Howe transformed treatment of the blind; Timothy Flint wrote against gambling; Lucretia Mott struggled for women's rights; William Ellery Channing called for the abolition of war. Everywhere societies sprang up to serve some humane cause: a New York Association for the Relief of Respectable, Aged, Indigent Females (1814); a Boston Society for the Moral and Religious Instruction of the Poor (1817); a Connecticut Society for the Suppression of Vice and the Promotion of Good Morals (1812); or a Philadelphia Society for Alleviating the Miseries of Public Prisons (1830).

One of the more vigorous reforms concerned intoxicating liquors. The American Temperance Union (1836), along with the Tract Society, the Sunday-School Union, and Catholic temperance societies, joined in a major crusade against alcoholic indulgence. Dr. Benjamin Rush, the only physician to sign the Declaration of Independence, gave his active support to the

---

Benjamin Rush's *Inquiry into the Effects of Ardent Spirits upon the Human Body and Mind* was first published in 1787; by 1850 the American Tract Society had circulated more than 170,000 copies.

Not less destructive are the effects of ardent spirits upon the human mind. They impair the memory, debilitate the understanding, and pervert the moral faculties. . . . But the demoralizing effects of distilled spirits do not stop here. They produce not only falsehood, but fraud, theft, uncleanliness, and murder. Like the demoniac mentioned in the New Testament, their name is "Legion," for they convey into the soul a host of vices and crimes.

1. *Tree of Temperance, 1849
   • This and the following
   figure are characteristic of
   the superabundant tracts
   for the times.*

2. *Tree of Intemperance,
   1855*

crusade by writing and lecturing against the evils of alcohol. Regarding his hope of "checking this evil," Rush declared: "I am disposed to believe that the business must be effected finally by religion alone." Temperance reform, while viewed by some as a misguided attempt to interfere with purely private behavior, was but one more manifestation of American religion's grand design to reform society and elevate humanity.

Bishop Charles P. McIlvaine's twenty-four page pamphlet *Address to the Young Men of the United States on Temperance* was printed by the American Tract Society in 1831 and widely sold at two cents a copy.

> Here, then, are three important points which we may safely assume are unquestionable: that our country is horribly scourged by intemperance; that the time has come when a great effort is demanded for the expulsion of this evil; and that no effort can be effectual without being universal. Hence is deduced, undeniably, the conclusion that it is the duty and the solemn duty of the people in every part of the country to rise up at once, and act vigorously and unitedly in the furtherance of whatever measures are best calculated to promote reformation.

And on most reforms the household of faith was agreed. Liberal Unitarians, evangelical Methodists, southern Anglicans, immigrant Jews, and western Catholics expressed sympathy for and dispensed charity to the aged, the impoverished, the degraded, the imprisoned, the blind, and the insane. When and where they could alleviate the lot of an unfortunate fellow, synagogue and church did so. There was malice toward none, charity for all. Or almost all.

Slavery emerged as the major moral question which soon swept all other crusades aside, breaking the back of the united mission effort, shattering the programs of reform, severing the loyalties to nation, synagogue, church, home. How did this dark disaster come about?

CONSENSUS ON SLAVERY

At the beginning of the nineteenth century it was hard to believe that any such disaster was near. Religious opposition to slavery was general, north and south. Quakers, Presbyterians, Baptists, Methodists, and others publicly denounced slavery, with southern churchmen freely joining in those denunciations. Indeed, before 1830, antislavery societies and antislavery

---

Quaker distress over slavery is revealed in an 1804 petition to Congress submitted by the Philadelphia Yearly Meeting for Sufferings.

> As the representatives of a large body of citizens, we apprehend we have a right by the Constitution to address you in terms of respect, and to claim your attention upon subjects of importance and interesting to the welfare

and happiness of our country. Upon this ground, but more especially from a sense of religious duty and obligation, we again come forward to plead the cause of the African race, who by the opening afresh the traffic in the persons of men and by kidnapping and other disgraceful conduct, are brought under cruel bondage and oppressive slavery. We are not about to condemn all those who hold slaves, believing that there are many well-disposed men who hold those people by inheritance, and may not at present see their way to get rid of them, but it is with regret we observe there are many of another description. We are sensible that Congress are as yet restrained from applying an effectual remedy to this dark and gloomy business. . . . Can it be supposed that the Almighty Creator who made of one blood all nations of the earth beholds with indifference one part of his rational creatures, equally the objects of his love and mercy, held under oppression by another part?

---

propaganda prospered more in the South than in the North. That sudden emancipation would create many problems, all recognized. That gradual emancipation was a necessary aim, all agreed. But around 1830 the testimonies of the faithful began to differ, first with quiet gentleness, soon with rancor and bitterness.

Slavery, once accepted and defended throughout the world, suffered in the generation before Lincoln world-wide abandonment and attack. No European nation allowed it, and all of South America, with the exception of Brazil and Dutch Guiana, had forsaken it. In Haiti a successful Negro rebellion led by Toussaint L'Ouverture freed the slaves at the expense of the French whites. And in the United States the slave trade itself was prohibited in 1808. The tide of events moved swiftly, too swiftly for the easy adjustment of a southern economy dependent on slavery.

Thus placed upon the defensive, the South, joined by some in the North, began to rationalize and support the "dark and gloomy business." At the same time the North, joined by some in the South, began an accelerated campaign against the "peculiar institution." With the abolitionist on one hand and the apologist on the other, earnest souls in the vast middle ground searched for a way out of the dilemma thrust upon them, a dilemma that grew harder each passing year.

With both southern and northern delegates present, the General Assembly of the Presbyterian Church in 1818 unanimously passed this resolution.

We consider the voluntary enslaving of one part of the human race by another as a gross violation of the most precious and sacred rights of human nature; as utterly inconsistent with the law of God, which requires us to love our neighbor as ourselves; and as totally irreconcilable with the spirit and principles of the Gospel of Christ, which enjoin that "all things whatsoever ye would that men should do to you, do ye even so to them."

Every time a new state came into the Union, every time settlers moved out to fresh land, the thorny question of slavery pricked the national conscience more deeply. Should the new territory be slave or free? Was slavery to be extended indefinitely in space and infinitely in time? In the passion to preserve both liberty and union, if one must choose, which came first? These questions acquired additional urgency after Chief Justice Taney's Dred Scott decision in 1857, for his decision seemed to permit slavery to go anywhere and everywhere in the United States. The careful compromises of 1820 and 1850 were now beside the point: how long could a nation endure half slave and half free?

With the founding of William Lloyd Garrison's radically abolitionist *Liberator* in 1831, the voice of antislavery forces grew strong and strident. The New England Anti-Slavery Society came into being that same year, followed two years later by the formation in Philadelphia of the American Anti-Slavery Society. Calling for complete and immediate emancipation, the abolitionists offered no hope for compromise, no hint of moderation. So adamant were the abolitionists against living in a divided house that at times they seemed determined to leave no house standing at all.

In an address to the Massachusetts Anti-Slavery Society in 1853, Wendell Phillips makes the position of the abolitionists crystal clear.

> They print the Bible in every tongue in which man utters his prayers; and get the money to do so by agreeing never to give the book, in the language our mothers taught us, to any negro, free or bond, south of Mason and Dixon's line. The press says, "It is all right"; and the pulpit cries, "Amen." The slave lifts up his imploring eyes, and sees in every face but ours the face of an enemy. Prove to me now that harsh rebuke, indignant denunciation, scathing sarcasm, and pitiless ridicule are wholly and always unjustifiable; else we dare not, in so desperate a case, throw away any weapon which ever broke up the crust of an ignorant prejudice, roused a slumbering conscience, shamed a proud sinner, or changed, in any way, the conduct of a human being. Our aim is to alter public opinion.

The revival preaching of Charles G. Finney won much popular support for antislavery sentiment. At some distance theologically from Boston radicals like Garrison and Wendell Phillips, Finney was at one with them with respect to slavery. Through the broad impact of Finney strong antislavery sentiment built up in the Midwest, especially around abolitionist Oberlin College. Among Finney's followers, Theodore Weld had no equal in vigor

---

Oberlin's antislavery stance is revealed in Charles G. Finney's *Autobiography*.

> This place [Oberlin] became one of the points on "the underground railroad" where escaped slaves on their way to Canada would take refuge, until the way was open to proceed. Several cases occurred [c. 1842] in

which fugitives were pursued by slaveholders; a hue and cry was raised, not only in this neighborhood, but in neighboring towns, by their attempting to carry slaves back into slavery. Slave-catchers found no practical sympathy; and scenes like these aroused public feeling and began to produce a reaction. It set the farmers and people to study more particularly our aims and views; and our school became known and appreciated.

---

and dedication. His powerful writings, *The Bible Against Slavery* (1837) and *Slavery As It Is* (1839), reputedly influenced Harriet Beecher Stowe in her writing of that incomparable catalyst, *Uncle Tom's Cabin* (1852).

James G. Birney, a lawyer, led the abolition movement in Kentucky, while the Quaker sisters Sarah and Angeline Grimké toured New England as agents of the Anti-Slavery Society. Orange Scott, a Methodist pastor, so disturbed the denominational waters that his bishop was visibly relieved when Scott decided to leave his Methodist pulpit for the employ of the Anti-Slavery Society. By arranging lectures at Methodist conferences, however, Scott continued to disturb, drawing large crowds and eventually leading thousands into the abolitionist Wesleyan Methodist Church. "There is a spirit abroad in the land," Albert Barnes of Philadelphia wrote in 1856, and "a voice uttered everywhere against slavery so loud and clear that it will ultimately be regarded."

The radical abolitionists encountered resistance in the North as well as in the South. Weld, repeatedly pursued by mobs, was the target of bricks and eggs when he lectured. The abolitionist paper of James Birney abruptly ceased publication when a Cincinnati mob threw his printing press into the Ohio River. In Alton, Illinois, another printer, the Reverend Elijah P. Lovejoy, resisted a gang protesting his antislavery sentiments. While protecting the press, his third to be destroyed, Lovejoy was killed in November, 1837—America's first martyr to freedom of the press. In May of the

---

Shortly before he was killed on November 7, 1837, Elijah Lovejoy spoke these words.

Why should I flee from Alton? Is this not a free state? . . . Have I not a right to proclaim the protection of its laws? What more can I have in any other place? . . . you may hang me up, as the mob hung up the individuals at Vicksburg! You may burn me at the stake, as they did McIntosh[1] at St. Louis, or you may tar and feather me, or throw me into the Mississippi, as you have threatened to do; but you cannot disgrace me. I, and I alone, can disgrace myself; and the deepest of all disgrace would be at a time like this to deny my Master by forsaking his cause.

---

[1] Francis McIntosh, a free Negro who killed a deputy sheriff in St. Louis, was chained to a tree and burned to death, April 28, 1836.

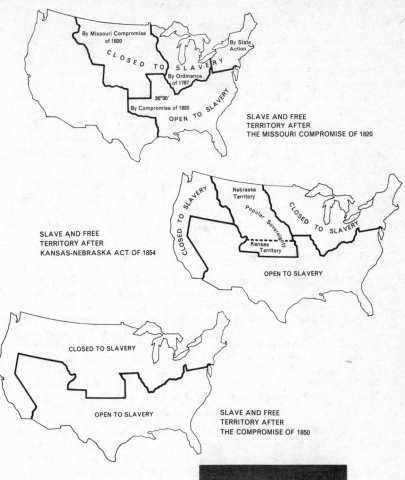

By Missouri Compromise of 1820

By State Action

CLOSED TO SLAVERY

By Ordinance of 1787

36°30'

By Compromise of 1820

OPEN TO SLAVERY

SLAVE AND FREE
TERRITORY AFTER
THE MISSOURI COMPROMISE OF 1820

CLOSED TO SLAVERY

Nebraska Territory

Popular Sovereignty

CLOSED TO SLAVERY

Kansas Territory

OPEN TO SLAVERY

SLAVE AND FREE
TERRITORY AFTER
KANSAS-NEBRASKA ACT OF 1854

CLOSED TO SLAVERY

OPEN TO SLAVERY

SLAVE AND FREE
TERRITORY AFTER
THE COMPROMISE OF 1850

4. *The Reverend Elijah P. Lovejoy,* e d i t o r   a n d *preacher*

following year Garrison was addressing an audience of three thousand in Pennsylvania Hall when a mob tried to break up the meeting. They were unsuccessful, but the next day they burned the Hall to the ground—a hall built for "Free Discussion, Virtue, Liberty and Independence."

Besides the lawless mobs many rational minds in the North counseled greater moderation, slower pace. For abolition seemed to be destroying more than slavery: it was shattering the American dream. "The longer I live," wrote poet James Russell Lowell, "the more I am convinced that the world must be healed by degrees." Brown University's Francis Wayland argued that slavery could be eradicated only by "changing the mind of both master and slave, by teaching the one party the love of justice and the fear of God, and by elevating the other to the proper level of individual responsibility." Obviously such a program took time, but time was fast slipping away.

In the most famous antislavery book of all time, *Uncle Tom's Cabin* (1852), Harriet Beecher Stowe offers a powerful conclusion.

> Christians! every time that you pray that the kingdom of Christ may come, can you forget that prophecy associates, in dread fellowship, the day of vengeance with the year of His redeemed?
>
> A day of grace is yet held out to us. Both North and South have been guilty before God; and the Christian church has a heavy account to answer. Not by combining together, to protect injustice and cruelty, and making a common capital of sin, is this Union to be saved—but by repentance, justice, and mercy; for, not surer is the eternal law by which the millstone sinks in the ocean, than that stronger law, by which injustice and cruelty shall bring on nations the wrath of Almighty God!

Many moderates, north and south, backed the American Colonization Society (organized in 1817), whose purpose was to resettle the freed Negro in Africa—Liberia. But the number colonized was so small and the success so slight that by 1850 this solution was clearly inadequate. Other moderates, faced with costly decisions and difficult judgments, chose the course of silence. Tracts that might alienate North or South on this most sensitive of all points quietly disappeared from publishing lists. And while moderates spoke of the evils within slavery, the institution as such was neither pleaded for nor condemned.

CONFLICT OVER SLAVERY

But moderation did not prevail. As abolitionists and "immediatists" grew more uncompromising, apologists and secessionists grew more extreme. Slavery was first defended as morally neutral: it could be whatever master and bondsman made of it. Since every effort was made to evangelize the slaves, to improve their morals, to teach mercy to the master and obedience to the slave, condemnation of the institution as a whole was inappropriate. Slavery, Bishop John England of Charleston observed in 1840, is not "incompatible with natural law." And when the slave has been justly acquired by the master, then the institution is "lawful not only in the sight of the human tribunal, but also in the eyes of heaven." The Lutheran Synod in South Carolina noted in 1836 "the impropriety and injustice of the interference or intermeddling of any religious or deliberative body with the subject of slavery or slaveholding, emancipation or abolitionism. . . ." Attacking "affected patriots" and "more than rotten-hearted benefactors of this much commiserated race," the synod resolved that it would "not at any time enter into a discussion of slavery."

As apologetics entered a second stage, slavery was defended as soundly biblical. Richard Furman, South Carolina's leading Baptist clergyman, in 1822 pointed out that "the right of holding slaves is clearly established in the Holy Scriptures, both by precept and example." The golden rule, he acknowledged, has been "urged as an unanswerable argument against holding slaves." But that rule is not applied in a vacuum; one must always consider the social context, having "a due regard to justice, propriety and the general good." For example, Furman asks, "A father may very naturally desire that his son be obedient to his orders: is he, therefore, to obey the orders of the son?" Neither the spirit nor the letter of Scripture demands the abolition of slavery.

Southern churchmen found unexpected support from Rabbi Morris J. Raphall of New York. With a knowledge of Hebrew that few dared to question, Raphall early in 1861 confirmed the biblical sanction of slavery. The Ten Commandments themselves ("Thou shalt not covet thy neighbor's . . . male slave or his female slave") support the institution. Since these moral precepts are "acknowledged by Christians as well as Jews" as "the very highest authority," how dare anyone "denounce slaveholding as a sin?" Explaining that he was "no friend to slavery in the abstract, and still less friendly to the practical working of slavery," Rabbi Raphall declared his only function to be that of "a teacher in Israel," giving "the Bible view of slavery."

In a third phase the peculiar institution was defended as a purely economic one, outside the realm of moral and spiritual concerns. Slaves were property; and laws of transfer, use, and disposal of property were matters of civil, not ecclesiastical, jurisdiction. The slave was a thing before he was a person; thus property rights loomed larger than human rights. Slaves were bartered, deeded, auctioned, mortgaged. They were prizes to be given away in contests, stakes to be won or lost in gambling. The market price of slaves, which fluctuated along with that of cotton and tobacco, was discussed in similar terms. While churchmen never wholly accepted this view, the culture they defended did.

More agreeable to religious spokesmen was the final defense of slavery as a positive good. Shifting from the argument based on the slave as property, religious leaders acknowledged the slave as a person. Slavery, they then argued, was a boon to master and bondsman alike. Providence ordained slavery "for the greatest good," argued James Thornwell of Columbia Seminary. "It has been a link in the wondrous chain of Providence. . . . The general operation of the system is kindly and benevolent; it is a real and effective discipline, and without it we are profoundly persuaded that the African race in the midst of us can never be elevated in the scale of being." In New Orleans in 1860 the Reverend B. M. Palmer, standing against the abolitionist spirit which "is undeniably atheistic," declared that the preservation of slavery was a "trust from God."

Peter Cartwright perfectly describes the step-by-step rationalizing defense of slavery (*Autobiography*, 1856).

> Methodism increased and spread; and many Methodist preachers, taken from comparative poverty, not able to own a negro, and who preached loudly against it, improved and became popular among slaveholders; and many of them married into those slaveholding families. . . . Then they began to apologize for the evil; then to justify it, on legal principles; then on Bible principles; till lo and behold! it is not an evil but a good! it is not a curse but a blessing! till really you would think, to hear them, you would go to the devil for not enjoying the labor, toil, and sweat of this degraded race—and all this without rendering them any equivalent whatever!

By 1860 it was obvious to all, as decades earlier it had been obvious to some, that neither side could turn back. Positions were entrenched, passions were inflamed. While every major religious body in America strained with tension in the years 1830–1860, three groups actually split. The Methodists, first to divide, had for years felt the fever of abolition and the fever of secession. In the church as in the nation "reformation or division" became the only alternatives. Bishops exercised every restraint, moderated every resolution, but the spectrum proved too wide. How reconcile "All slaveholding is a sin against God" with "We believe that the Holy Scriptures do unequivocally authorize the relation of master and slave"? It could not be done. Thus in 1844 the Methodist Episcopal Church, South, and its northern counterpart went their separate ways—a separation that lasted until 1939.

The division in Methodism is clearly seen in two statements: (1) the position taken by South Carolina's Methodist Bishop William Capers in 1836; (2) resolutions adopted by the Methodist Anti-slavery Convention meeting in Boston in 1843.

(1) We denounce the principles and opinions of the abolitionists in toto, and do solemly declare our conviction and belief that whether they were originated, as some business men have thought, as a money speculation; or, as some politicians think, for electioneering purposes; or, as we are inclined to believe, in a false philosophy, overreaching and setting aside the Scriptures, through a vain conceit of a higher refinement, they are utterly erroneous and altogether hurtful.

(2) Resolved, that the holding or treating human beings as property, or claiming the right to hold or treat them as property, is a flagrant violation of the law of God: it is sin itself; a sin in the abstract and in the concrete; a sin under all circumstances, and in every person claiming such right, and no apology whatever can be admitted to justify the perpetration.

Resolved, that as the unanimity and harmony of feeling which should ever characterize the people of God cannot exist so long as slavery continues in the Church, we feel it our imperative duty to use all such means as become Christians in seeking its immediate and entire abolition from the Church of which we are members.

The very next year, 1845, the Baptists similarly fell apart. Though the immediate issue was the appointment of a slaveholding missionary, the basic and familiar one was the growing chasm between slavery's friends and slavery's foes. Missionaries and agents who once moved freely through all the states of the Union now found themselves circumscribed, either by preference or by growing hostility. After the 1845 separation, Baptists in the South, like the Methodists, continued special religious and moral instruction among the Negroes, in many instances sharing the same building and the same services.

Contrasting Baptist sentiments are evident in (1) Richard Furman's *Exposition of the Views of the Baptists relative to the Coloured Population* . . . (1823) and (2) John Mason Peck's *Journal* entry for the first day of 1842.

(1) While men remain in the chains of ignorance and error, and under the dominion of tyrant lusts and passions, they cannot be free. And the more freedom of action they have in this state, they are but the more qualified by it to do injury, both to themselves and others. It is, therefore, firmly believed that general emancipation to the Negroes in this country would not, in present circumstances, be for their own happiness as a body, while it would be extremely injurious to the community at large in various ways.

(2) January 1, Nashville. Today I attended for a few moments a sale in the market-place. A negro boy was sold who appeared about twelve years old. He stood by the auctioneer on the market-bench with his hat off, crying and sobbing, his countenance a picture of woe. I know not the circumstances; but it was the first human being I ever saw set up for sale, and it filled me with indescribable emotions. Slavery in Tennessee is cer-

tainly not as oppressive, inhuman and depressing as the state of the poorer classes of society in England, Ireland, and many parts of Continental Europe; yet slavery in its best state is a violation of man's nature and of the Christian law of love.

The last to divide, the Presbyterians, maintained a semblance of North-South unity (in structure but not in sentiment) until 1857. In that year the General Assembly ("New School") expressed its "deep grief" that Southern churchmen tried to defend slavery as "an ordinance of God." This "new doctrine" could not be tolerated, the ruling body announced, because "it is at war with the whole spirit and tenor of the Gospel of love and goodwill, as well as abhorent to the conscience of the Christian world." Under the force of this sharp rebuke twenty-one Southern presbyteries withdrew to form, ultimately, the Presbyterian Church, U. S. Unlike the Methodists, neither the Baptists nor the Presbyterians more than a century later had found their way back together.

In the same newspaper (*New York Evangelist*) on the same day (November 21, 1835) Presbyterians in (1) South Carolina differed sharply with Presbyterians in (2) Michigan.

(1) Resolved, that in the opinion of this presbytery [Charleston Union], the holding of slaves, so far from being a sin in the sight of God, is nowhere condemned in his Holy Word—that it is in accordance with the example, or consistent with the precepts of patriarchs, prophets and apostles; and that it is compatible with the most fraternal regard to the best good of those servants whom God may have committed to our charge, and that, therefore, they who assume the contrary position, and lay it down as a fundamental principle in morals and religion, that all slaveholding is wrong, proceed upon false principles.

(2) Resolved, that this synod [of Michigan] believe the buying, selling and owning of slaves in this country to be A Sin Before God and man: that the system of American slavery is a great moral, political, physical and social evil, and ought to be immediately and universally abandoned—and that it is our duty, by the use of all kind and known means, and especially by cultivating a spirit of sympathy and prayer for the enslaved, and their masters, as well as of general moderation and wisdom in the dissemination of truth and light, to endeavor to hasten the happy day of universal emancipation.

The spectacle of a house of faith divided in a torn and tortured America brought heavy reproach to religion. On the one hand the Bible, or at least the New Testament, extolled liberty for all men; on the other hand the Bible, or at least the Old Testament, justified and endorsed slavery. For one church slavery was a sin, for another a blessing. This minister freed his slaves, while that missionary retained his. Where turn for spiritual inspiration, for moral direction?

Disillusionment penetrated every quarter, but nowhere more deeply than among the Negroes themselves. Religion, Wendell Phillips had observed in 1848, "is the most productive, the most efficient, the deepest idea, and the foundation of American thought and institutions." But for the next fifteen years religion did not seem so to hopeful blacks, slave or free, who suffered one cruel disappointment after another. The best-known of the ex-slave abolitionists, Frederick Douglass, saw little of productivity, efficiency, or depth in America's churches. "Between the Christianity of this land and the Christianity of Christ," he wrote in his autobiography, "I recognize the widest possible difference."

In his autobiography, *Narrative of the Life of . . . An American Slave* (1845), Frederick Douglass recalls his longing for freedom.

I have often, in the deep stillness of a summer's Sabbath, stood all alone upon the lofty banks of that noble bay [Chesapeake], and traced, with saddened heart and tearful eye, the countless number of sails moving off to the mighty ocean. The sight of these always affected me powerfully. My thoughts would compel utterance; and there, with no audience but the Almighty, I would pour out my soul's complaint, in my rude way, with an apostrophe to the moving multitude of ships:

"You are loosed from your moorings, and are free; I am fast in my chains, and am a slave! You move merrily before the gentle gale, and I sadly before the bloody whip! . . . O God, save me! God, deliver me! Let me be free! Is there any God? Why am I a slave? . . . Only think of it; one hundred miles straight north, and I am free! Try it? Yes! God helping me, I will. It cannot be that I shall live and die a slave. I will take to the water. This very bay shall yet bear me into freedom."

While Douglass denounced slaveholding without restraint, he did not go so far as his white friend John Brown, who plotted a violent overthrow of the system. Brown's attack in 1859 on the United States arsenal at Harper's Ferry, "this desperate but sublimely disinterested effort to eman-

5. *Frederick Douglass, ex-slave and abolitionist*

cipate the slaves of Maryland and Virginia" (Douglass), failed in its immediate aim. No emancipation took place, no slave rebellion occurred. But by the time John Brown's body lay a-mouldering in the grave (he was hanged on December 2, 1859), the reverberations of his fanatic action shook North and South, slave and free. Blood was let; a die was cast. The clamor of radical abolition and radical rebellion rose to such a pitch that gentler voices were no longer heard.

Six days before he was hanged in West Virginia, John A. Copeland, one of the Negro participants in John Brown's raid on Harper's Ferry, wrote to his brother (December 10, 1859).

> It was a sense of the wrongs which we have suffered that prompted the noble but unfortunate Captain John Brown and his associates to attempt to give freedom to a small number, at least, of those who are held by cruel and unjust laws, and by no less cruel and unjust men. To this freedom they were entitled by every known principle of justice and humanity, and for the enjoyment of it God created them. And now, dear brother, could I die in a more noble cause? Could I, brother, die in a manner and for a cause which would induce true and honest men more to honor me, and the angels more readily to receive me to their happy home of everlasting joy above? I imagine that I hear you, and all of you, mother, father, sisters and brothers, say: "No, there is not a cause for which we, with less sorrow, could see you die."

LINCOLN AND GOD'S PURPOSES

As impassioned cries became increasingly bitter, the burden of peaceful solution grew heavier. That burden was borne most fully and felt most keenly by Abraham Lincoln. A Kentuckian by birth and by sentiment, Lincoln, later in Illinois and still later in Washington, strained to see both sides of the question. He repeatedly asserted that the North was no more righteous than the South. Each part of the country saw slaveholding from the point of view of its own interest, its own well-being; each resisted threats to its prosperity and security. Thus far the question was moot: a question to be debated on grounds of law, prudence, or custom.

But a larger question loomed: a moral crux, an issue of right and wrong. Here Lincoln's struggle was hardest and his insight keenest. Always recognizing the complexities in limiting or abolishing slavery, Lincoln gradually grew sure of one thing: slavery was wrong. Slavery, he wrote with serene simplicity in 1854, "is founded on the selfishness of man's nature— opposition to it in his love of justice." Defenders of the institution believe that it is good, but if so, then slavery is "strikingly peculiar in this, that it is the only good thing which no man ever seeks the good of for himself."

Debating with Stephen Douglas at Galesburg, Illinois, in 1858, he declared: "I confess myself as belonging to that class in the country who contemplate slavery as a moral, social, and political evil." Lincoln acknowledged a "due regard for its actual existence among us, and the difficulties of getting rid of it in any satisfactory way." Nevertheless, he concluded, I "desire a policy that looks to the prevention of it as a wrong, and looks hopefully to the time when as a wrong it may come to an end."

Pierre Jean DeSmet points to the clear moral issue underlying the Civil War, in a letter to his nephew, April 24, 1863.

The truth is that the present state of the country is due to an angry controversy, long ago begun, on the subject of African slavery. Several compromises between the parties had been entered into, looking to the settlement of the difficulty; but the feeling remained with the one party that *slavery is right,* and with the other that *slavery is wrong.* Those two hostile feelings have culminated in a revolution or rebellion, the most formidable that the world has ever seen. What will be the end of it? No one can say. One thing seems evident, namely, that slavery will be extinguished; for though the General Government does not claim any constitutional power to interfere with the Constitutions in the States, yet, as a war power, as a means of putting down the rebellion, the General Government does claim the power of liberating the slave; and hence the emancipation proclamation of the President more than six months ago.

The "difficulties of getting rid of it" reached monstrous proportions by the time Lincoln assumed the presidency in March 1861. In the preceding decade he had attacked slavery chiefly in the newly settled territories and newly admitted states. Slavery was a snake, he explained, but one attacked a snake on the prairie differently from one found in bed with his children. In the latter instance, "I must be more cautious; I shall in striking the snake also strike the children, or arouse the reptile to bite the children." Slavery already embedded in the South must therefore be approached in one way, but slavery in Kansas or Nebraska in quite another way. Lincoln hoped that slavery, restricted and bottled up, would ultimately wither away. "Let us draw a cordon," he said in 1856, "around the slave states, and the hateful institution, like a reptile poisoning itself, will perish by its own infamy."

On July 10, 1858, Lincoln spoke in Chicago on America's commitment to the principle of equality.

[Stephen Douglas] has said to me that I am a poor hand to quote Scripture. I will try it again, however. It is said in one of the admonitions of the Lord, "As your Father in Heaven is perfect, be ye also perfect." The

Savior, I suppose, did not expect that any human creature could be perfect as the Father in Heaven. . . . He set that up as a standard, and he who did most toward reaching that standard attained the highest degree of moral perfection. So I say in relation to the principle that all men are created equal: let it be as nearly reached as we can.

But the cordon did not hold. The Kansas-Nebraska Act of 1854, the Dred Scott decision of 1857, and the willingness of many to make slavery national and permanent pushed Lincoln toward inescapable conclusions. Slavery must be put on the course to ultimate extinction, else liberty is a lie and freedom a fraud. "A house divided against itself cannot stand," quoted Lincoln in 1858. "I believe this government cannot endure permanently half slave and half free. I do not expect the Union to be dissolved—I do not expect the house to fall—but I do expect it will cease to be divided." But the house, or a part of it, did fall; and the costliest, bloodiest, most soul-searing war of America's history erupted across a morally confused, spiritually perplexed nation.

The Civil War was fought first of all to preserve the Union. Beginning with the firing on Fort Sumter on April 12, 1861, the war was twenty months old before Lincoln on January 1, 1863, signed the Emancipation Proclamation. Then the struggle took on a moral coloration in the eyes of all the world. And for many abolitionists in the North, the War was without essential meaning until the Proclamation for which they had long agitated came forth. Then the War became the only way to enforce a document otherwise devoid of point and power.

By the time of Lincoln's second inauguration in March 1865 the military issue, after horrifying losses on both sides, was gradually becoming clear. For many, however, the moral issue remained cloudy. Nowhere were the ambiguities more eloquently expressed than in Lincoln's own words as he again took the oath of office. "Neither party expected for the war the magnitude, or the duration, which it has already attained. . . . Both [parties] read the same Bible, and pray to the same God; and each invokes His aid against the other. . . . The prayers of both could not be answered; that of neither has been answered fully." Such a confession—that between

---

In New York City, on February 27, 1860, Lincoln lays open the basic quarrel between North and South.

All they [of the South] ask, we [of the North] could readily grant, if we thought slavery was right; all we ask, they could as readily grant, if they thought it wrong. Their thinking it right, and our thinking it wrong, is the precise fact upon which depends the whole controversy. Thinking it right, as they do, they are not to blame for desiring its full recognition, as being right; but thinking it wrong, as we do, can we yield to them? Can we cast our votes with their view, and against our own? . . .

6. Lincoln Writes to the Methodists

Gentlemen.

    In response to your address, allow me to attest the accuracy of its historical statements; indorse the sentiments it expresses; and thank you, in the nation's name for the sure promise it gives.

    Nobly sustained as the government has been by all the churches, I would utter nothing which might, in the least, appear invidious against any. Yet, without this, it may fairly be said that the Methodist Episcopal Church, not less devoted than the best, is, by its greater numbers, the most important of all. It is no fault in others that the Methodist Church sends more soldiers to the field, more nurses to the hospitals, and more prayers to Heaven than any. God bless the Methodist Church— bless all the churches— and blessed be God, Who, in this our great trial, giveth us the churches.

A. Lincoln

May 18. 1864

If our sense of duty forbids this, then let us stand by our duty fearlessly and effectively. . . . Let us have faith that right makes might, and in that faith let us, to the end, dare to do our duty as we understand it.

God's purposes and man's execution of them there is always a difference— would not, as Lincoln recognized, please many men. But to deny that difference, Lincoln wrote to Thurlow Weed a few days later, "is to deny that there is a God governing the world." He added: "It is a truth which I thought needed to be told, and, as whatever humiliation there is in it falls most directly upon myself, I thought others might afford for me to tell it."

7. Civil War Chaplain • The 31st Ohio Volunteers at Camp Dick Robinson, Kentucky, on November 10, 1861, Chaplain L. F. Drake officiating.

8. *"The Emancipator and His Flock"* • *This photograph by J. K. W. Atherton was taken during the 1963 march on Washington (see Chapter 21).*

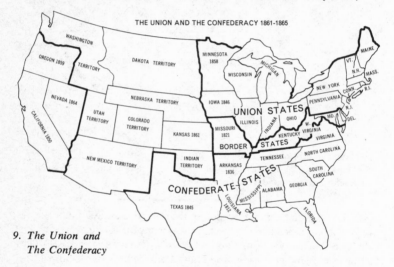

THE UNION AND THE CONFEDERACY 1861-1865

9. *The Union and
The Confederacy*

"TO FINISH THE WORK"

One month after this letter was written, one week after Lee's surrender at Appomattox, Lincoln lay dead. The task of binding up the nation's wounds then fell largely into the hands of strangers to Lincoln's charity and humil-

---

The words of Lincoln's Second Inaugural Address (March 4, 1865) live on.

If we suppose that American slavery is one of those offenses which, in the providence of God, must needs come, but which, having continued through his appointed time, He now wills to remove, and that He gives to both North and South this terrible war, as the woe due to them by whom the offense came, shall we discern therein any departure from those divine attributes which the believers in a Living God always ascribed to Him? Fondly do we hope—fervently do we pray—that this mighty scourge of war may speedily pass away. Yet, if God wills that it continue, until all wealth piled by the bond-man's two hundred and fifty years of unrequited toil shall be sunk, and until every drop of blood drawn with the lash, shall be paid by another drawn by the sword, as was said three thousand years ago, so still it must be said, "The judgments of the Lord are true and righteous altogether."

With malice toward none; with charity for all; with firmness in the right as God gives us to see the right, let us strive on to finish the work we are in. . . .

---

ity. In the decade following Lincoln's death on April 15, 1865, malice more than mercy characterized much of the reconstruction in the South. It was a day of the Northern exploiter—the "carpetbagger"—and of the Southern syncophant—the "scalawag." War's inevitable aftermath of bitterness and desolation was daily aggravated by fraud, plunder, and corruption. In the South the economy was in collapse, leadership in prison or exile, and education in chaos. While Northern manufacturing, banking, and mining progressed, poverty still hung as a pall over all the Confederacy.

In the work of reconstruction religion had much to do but limited resources for doing it. Church funds, like college funds, had been dissipated by the military effort and the political collapse. Denominational schools closed their doors, publishing houses fought to survive, and church bodies struggled with alien or shattered organization. Northern churchmen

---

Bishops of the Methodist Episcopal Church, South, sent this pastoral letter in 1865 to the clergy of their respective dioceses.

. . . We must express with regret our apprehension that a large portion, if not a majority, of Northern Methodists have become incurably radical. They teach for doctrine the commandments of men. They preach another gospel. They have incorporated social dogmas and political tests into their church creeds. They have gone on to impose conditions upon discipleship that Christ did not impose. Their pulpits are perverted to agitations and questions not healthful to personal piety, but promotive of political and ecclesiastical discord. . . .

The conduct of certain Northern Methodist bishops and preachers in taking advantage of the confusion incident to a state of war to intrude themselves into several of our houses of worship, and in continuing to hold these places against the wishes and protests of the congregations and rightful owners, causes us sorrow and pain. . . . They are not only using, to our deprivation and exclusion, churches and parsonages which we have built, but have proceeded to set up claim to them as their property; by what shadow of right, legal or moral, we are at a loss to conceive.

---

brought personnel and funds, but sometimes both seemed an arm of political "reconquest." A spirit of righteous vengeance so marred some Northern efforts that bitterness sank deeper into the Southern soul. When "treason" had been properly repented of, Southern sin would be generously forgiven. Many overlooked that difference between God's purposes and one's own.

While the conquered South received several types of missions, Northern efforts in Negro education were the most enduring. Before cannons had cooled, the American Missionary Association, backed principally by Congregationalists, started important industrial and agricultural schools in the South. By 1870 some twenty schools, including major institutions like Fisk (Tennessee) and Hampton (Virginia), were founded by this one group alone. The Freedmen's Aid Society (Methodist) and the American Baptist Home Mission Board likewise invested heavily in increased educational opportunities for the Negro. Fifteen years after Appomattox, Negro freedmen beheld an array of institutions and colleges which a generation earlier would have been unthinkable.

On the elementary level, where needs were greatest, large-scale efforts were also made. Both governmental agencies and private philanthropy built and staffed schools, recruited and trained Negro leadership. A wealthy financier, George Peabody, set up the Peabody Education Fund, which for generations quietly elevated Southern education in general and Negro education in particular. The Negro's eagerness for education was phenomenal. "It was a whole race trying to go to school," Booker T. Washington commented. "Few were too young, and none too old, to make the attempt to learn." "The great ambition of the older people," he added, "was to try to read the Bible before they died."

Hampton Institute, founded in 1868, led in the promotion of Negro education; the words here are of its first president, Samuel C. Armstrong.

"It is for us to finish the work which they so nobly began," said Lincoln at Gettysburg. The duty of the hour is construction, to build up. With all credit to the pluck and heroic self-help of the Southern people and to Northern enterprise for railroad, mineral and other commercial development, the great constructive force in the South and everywhere is the Christian Teacher. *"In hoc signo vinces"* is as true now as in the days of Constantine. Let us make teachers, and we will make the people.

The Hampton Institute should be pushed steadily, not to larger but to better, more thorough effort, and placed on a solid foundation. It is big enough, but its work is only begun. Its work, with that of other like schools, is on the line of Providential purpose in ending the great struggle as it did—the redemption of both races from the evils of slavery, which, while to the Negro educative up to a certain point, was a curse to the country. God said, "Let my people go," and it had to be done.

10. *African Methodist Episcopal Zion Church, New York City, 1867*

11. *Bethune-C o o k m a n College, Daytona Beach, Florida, 1943*

12. *Freedmen School, Vicksburg, Mississippi, 1866*

The Negro also acclaimed his ecclesiastical independence. In the church he found the equality and dignity denied by the state. Where only God was master, color caused no fear and service brought no servility. The freedman, therefore, gradually abandoned the white-dominated churches, forming his own congregation and often his own ecclesiastical superstructure as well. Organization, especially among the numerous Negro Baptists, remained quite loose for decades. Negro Methodists generally joined either the African Methodist Episcopal Church (organized in the North in 1816) or the African Methodist Episcopal Zion (formed in 1821). Throughout the nineteenth century Negro church life found expression chiefly under Baptist and Methodist labels, though some found spiritual homes among Presbyterians, Episcopalians, and Roman Catholics.

Despite the degradation of slavery, the toll of war (some 186,000 colored troops served in the Union army), and the tortuous course of Reconstruction, religion steadily prospered within the Negro community. Throughout the nineteenth century the church affiliation of Negroes multiplied six times (from about 5 per cent to about 30 per cent of the population). The church served as social and educational center no less than as house of worship. And the ministry offered the Negro virtually his only professional opportunity. To the thousands in the pew, the churches granted security, status, and spiritual food. The God of Abraham, Isaac,

---

Before Emancipation, Richard Allen (1760–1831), founder of the African Methodist Episcopal Church, in an undated sermon encouraged "the People of Color" to look beyond present miseries to future glories.

> I mention experience to you that your hearts may not sink at the discouraging prospects you may have, and that you may put your trust in God, who sees your condition, and as a merciful father pitieth his children, so doth God pity them that love Him. . . . As life is short and uncertain, and the chief end of our being in this world is to be prepared for a better, I wish you to think of this more than anything else; then you will have a view of that freedom which the sons of God enjoy; and if the troubles of your condition end with your lives, you will be admitted to the freedom which God hath prepared for those of all colors that love him. Here the power of the most cruel master ends, and all sorrow and tears are wiped away.

---

and Jacob had delivered them from Egypt's bondage; yet their full inheritance in the Promised Land was far, far away. A century after Appomattox the mournful magnificence of the Negro spiritual was still relevant.

This spiritual was written by an anonymous Negro slave in Guilford County, North Carolina, around 1825.

> Deep river, my home is over Jordan,
> Deep river, Lord, I want to cross over into camp-ground
> O don't you want to go to that gospel feast,
> To that promised land, where all is peace.
> Lord, I want to cross over into camp-ground.
> Lord, I want to cross over into camp-ground.
> Lord, I want to cross over into camp-ground.

For while some assured the freedman of all his American rights, others compromised and whittled away those liberties until the Negro, though no longer a slave, was clearly not yet free. By a series of Southern "black codes" and a sequence of adverse judicial decisions, the Negro was gradually abandoned to a limbo of semicitizenship. Churches, north and south, seemed less sure than Lincoln of the moral issue involved. The announcement made to the world on July 4, 1776, that "all men are created equal" is, said Lincoln, "the father of all moral principle." All who come to America—of whatever race, lineage, or nation—"have a right to claim it as if they were blood of the blood, flesh of the flesh, of the men who wrote that Declaration, and so they are." In that great Declaration, he concluded, we find an electric cord "that links the hearts of patriotic and liberty-loving men together, that will link those patriotic hearts as long as the love of freedom exists in the minds of men throughout the world."

15 ❖ The Making of America: Immigration and Assimilation

"THE HOMELESS, TEMPEST-TOST"

THE HISTORY OF THE UNITED STATES is a history of immigration. Colonial immigrants set the pattern followed and intensified during the nineteenth and early twentieth centuries. From 1815 to the first World War, a century later, approximately thirty million persons sailed for American shores. Affecting the nation's history and culture in every respect, the immigrant transformed that culture even as he was transformed by it.

Of Jewish heritage, Emma Lazarus in 1883 wrote a sonnet entitled "The New Colossus" which was inscribed on the Statue of Liberty. The poem concludes:

> Give me your tired, your poor,
> Your huddled masses yearning to breathe free,
> The wretched refuse of your teeming shore,
> Send these, the homeless, tempest-tost to me,
> I lift my lamp beside the golden door.

From 1815 to 1860 five million immigrants settled in America, the largest bloc coming from Ireland (2 million), the next largest from Germany (1.5 million). England, Wales, and Scotland also dispatched sizeable numbers in the pre-Civil War period, with smaller groups coming from Switzerland, Norway, Sweden, and the Netherlands. Between 1860 and 1890 the number of new arrivals rose to ten million, and in the brief period from 1890 to World War I the figure zoomed to fifteen million. In this third period the majority emigrated from southern or eastern Europe—Italy, Austria-Hungary, Rumania, Greece, Turkey, and Russia (see Fig. 2 and 6).

In the tumult of transplanting, religion often provided personal security and ethnic cohesion. In a new land and among strange people, removed from ancestral home and family ties, the uprooted immigrant turned to the synagogue and church for the comfort of the familiar, for the assurance of continuity in a life severely disjoined. When so much was different, when

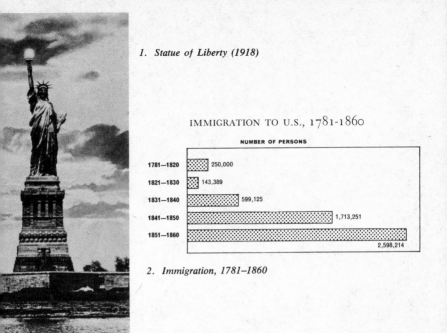

1. Statue of Liberty (1918)

IMMIGRATION TO U.S., 1781-1860

NUMBER OF PERSONS

1781—1820	250,000
1821—1830	143,389
1831—1840	599,125
1841—1850	1,713,251
1851—1860	2,598,214

2. Immigration, 1781–1860

3. Immigrant Leave-Taking, Cahirciveen, Ireland, 1866

4. An Italian Family Comes to America

5. *Immigrants on Ellis Island Await Entry, October 30, 1912*

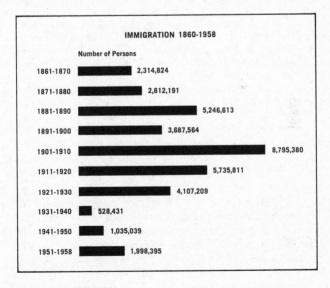

IMMIGRATION 1860-1958

Number of Persons

Years	Number of Persons
1861-1870	2,314,824
1871-1880	2,812,191
1881-1890	5,246,613
1891-1900	3,687,564
1901-1910	8,795,380
1911-1920	5,735,811
1921-1930	4,107,209
1931-1940	528,431
1941-1950	1,035,039
1951-1958	1,998,395

6. *Immigration, 1860–1958*

so many adjustments were demanded, when one's whole world had been turned inside out, calm confidence was found—if at all—in an enduring faith.

Strangely, however, those elements that granted security to the first-generation immigrant often took it away from the second generation. Those born in America found security more by identifying with their new nation than by retreating to liturgy or life distinctly "old world." Second-generation immigrants therefore faced a hard choice: abandon a foreign worship for an "American faith," or accommodate that exotic religion to its new environment. Both courses were taken. While some sons and daughters turned away from old-country ways to prove that they too "belonged" in America, others modernized or Americanized their synagogues and churches. Both groups found themselves opposed not only by the older generation but even more vigorously by newly arriving immigrants who instinctively, hungrily reached for the familiar, the tried, the trusted.

Marcus Lee Hansen wrote movingly of *The Immigrant in American History* (republished, 1964).

> The odyssey of the immigrant began when he first dreamed of that far-off land. Week after week that dream became more real, speculation crystallized into action and, finally, the day of departure arrived. There was a "last" time for everything—a last Sunday in the church with the village pastor extending a special blessing; a last visit to the tavern where the whole company solemnly drank to the success of the undertaking; a last stroll through the winding lanes or along the river's bank; a last night beneath the paternal roof. To hide neighborhood doubts once the decision was made, tradition decreed that festivity should reign. In Germany, orchestras and bands of singers serenaded until the doors were opened and all thronged in for a shake of the hand and a final word of encouragement. In Ireland, where friends felt they were being deprived of what every respectable citizen owed his community—a wake—they proceeded to turn the leave taking into a night of jollification unrestrained by the presence of a corpse. Shortly after sunrise, to the pealing of the village bells, the procession started, accompanied for a mile or two along the highway by the now weeping relatives and strangers.

The great wave of Irish that arrived before the Civil War posed special problems for Roman Catholicism. The very magnitude of the influx taxed resources to and beyond their limits. The urgency of spiritual needs, moreover, could not be divorced from physical needs obvious in every seaboard city, in every malignant slum. To alleviate the serious social ills Archbishop John Ireland of St. Paul promoted Irish colonization in the uncrowded interior of America. Though some feared that scattered immigrants might be lost to the Church, Ireland successfully planted several colonies in southern Minnesota in the 1870's and 1880's. The Irish Catholic Colonization Society, which he helped found, arranged for cheap railroad transportation from the seaboard as well as for easy payment on land settled and farmed. Archbishop Ireland provided a priest in each colony to aid and advise the settlers in every aspect of their new life (see Fig. 3).

Despite the energy and devotion poured into this venture, most of the Irish, recalling the dreary, impoverished farm life behind, remained in the cities. There the major crises of immigration and assimilation were squarely met, as church and parochial school took up their ponderous tasks. The Church's ministry to the Irish, while demanding enough, soon expanded to include Germans, French (especially from Canada), Italians, Poles, Austrians, Hungarians, and many others. With greater membership came graver problems.

Samuel Gompers, who helped organize the American Federation of Labor in 1886, tells how America, through song, attracted laborer and industrialist alike (*Seventy Years of Life and Labor*, 1925).

> It was typical of the feeling among English wage earners of my boyhood days that the two most popular songs were "The Slave Ship" and "To the West." I learned both and sang them with a fervor in which all my feeling quivered and throbbed. I could throw back my head and sing:
>> To the west, to the west, to the land of the free,
>> Where mighty Missouri rolls down to the sea,
>> Where a man is a man, if he's willing to toil,
>> And the humblest may gather the fruits of the soil.
>> Where children are blessings, and he who has most
>> Has aid for his fortune and riches to boast.
>> Where the young may exult and the aged may rest,
>> Away, far away, to the land of the west.
> The song expressed my feeling of America, and my desire to go there rose with the ringing chorus:
>> Away! far away, let us hope for the best
>> And build up a home in the land of the west.
> Years afterward Andrew Carnegie told me this song had inspired his father with a desire to come to America. . . .
> In the years that followed there grew in me a feeling of pride and ownership in the Red, White, and Blue, until the time came when I looked up at it under foreign skies, from the ramparts of a great world war, and felt it in my heart to say: "America is more than a name. America is an ideal. America is the apotheosis of all that is right."

Judaism in America, augmented before the Civil War by an influx of German-speaking Jews, received after that war even greater numbers from eastern Europe. Again the challenges to the religious leadership were momentous, but no central organization directed the immigration, colonization, or preservation of the Jewish people. Instead a myriad of organizations, some religious and some secular, sprang up. Wherever a *minyan* (ritual group of ten men) was found, at least a synagogue could be organized and Judaic worship begun. Apart from the cities, however, Jews frequently lacked even that much spiritual direction. Though some wished to lose themselves in American culture, many were anxious to save themselves and their ancient faith from that absorbing culture.

While nineteenth-century immigration brought dramatic increases to both Catholicism and Judaism, Protestant ranks were also swelled by Lutherans from Germany and Scandinavia, Reformed from Holland and Switzerland, Episcopalians from England, and a variety of sectarians from most of Europe. Protestants carried on vigorous missionary and benevolent activity among co-religionists and non-Protestants alike, dispensing charity, increasing literacy, and seeking converts fervently. For all American religion, immigration constituted a momentous challenge. To some, however, it loomed as a horrendous threat.

"AMERICA FOR AMERICANS"

When a normal fear of the strange and foreign becomes an abnormal hatred of the strange and foreign, then American democracy receives its severest test. The nineteenth century saw two such severe testing times, one shortly before the Civil War and the other near the end of the century. In both periods nativism fed on fears, biases, and aspirations that marched under the banner of religion. And in both periods the American dream almost turned to nightmare.

The American hierarchy in a pastoral letter (1833) to all Catholics in the United States noted growing Protestant hostility.

We notice, with regret, a spirit exhibited by some of the conductors of the press, engaged in the interests of those brethren separated from our communion, which has, within a few years become more unkind and unjust in our regard. Not only do they assail us and our institutions in a style of vituperation and offense, misrepresent our tenets, vilify our practices, repeat the hundred times refuted calumnies of days of angry and bitter contention in other lands, but they have even denounced you and us as enemies to the liberties of the republic, and have openly proclaimed the fancied necessity of not only obstructing our progress, but of using their best efforts to extirpate our religion. . . . We are too well known to our fellow-citizens to render it now necessary that we should exhibit the utter want of any ground upon which such charges could rest. We, therefore, advise you to heed them not: but to continue, while you serve your God with fidelity, to discharge honestly, faithfully, and with affectionate attachment, your duties to the government under which you live, so that we may, in common with our fellow-citizens, sustain that edifice of rational liberty in which we find such excellent protection.

As long as Roman Catholics were few in number, they aroused little direct animosity and harassment. The Catholicism of Spain, the prelates of France, the pronouncements of the pope—these could be and were roundly denounced. But the Catholics living in America? Well, there weren't many, and the good patriot John Carroll seemed to have everything under control. From the 1830's on, however, Catholic membership rose rapidly, making the Roman church by 1850 the largest religious group in the United States. The creation of new parishes, the promotion of schools and seminaries, the publication of newspapers and journals proved that Catholicism in America was on the move. Where would the expansion end? Were men's liberties in danger? Was America's destiny secure?

In a sermon preached in Rome in 1887 James Cardinal Gibbons defended America's freedom in religion.

> For myself, as a citizen of the United States, without closing my eyes to our defects as a nation, I proclaim, with a deep sense of pride and gratitude, and in this great capitol of Christendom, that I belong to a country where the civil government holds over us the aegis of its protection without interfering in the legitimate exercise of our sublime mission as ministers of the Gospel of Jesus Christ.
>
> Our country has liberty without license, authority without despotism. Hers is no spirit of exclusiveness. She has no frowning fortifications to repel the invader, for we are at peace with all the world. In the consciousness of her strength and of her good will to all nations she rests secure. Her harbors are open in the Atlantic and Pacific to welcome the honest immigrant who comes to advance his temporal interest and to find a peaceful home.

Anti-Catholicism moved from intemperate propaganda to violent attack. An Ursuline convent in Massachusetts was burned in 1834. A decade later riots broke out in Philadelphia, resulting in the total destruction of St. Michael's and St. Augustine's Churches. While mob action was everywhere deplored, oratory and press kept passions high and rumors rampant.

Of all the printed testimonies to this hysteria, the most scurrilous (and now thoroughly discredited) was a small book entitled *Awful Disclosures of the Hotel Dieu Nunnery of Montreal,* first published in 1836. Purporting to be by an ex-nun, Maria Monk, the book seemed to confirm every suspicion ever harbored by non-Catholics. That three hundred thousand copies

8. *The Promised Land, 1870 •
Thomas Nast's cartoon suggests that with Garibaldi's capture of Italy the pope will
take over the United States
which has been "promised" to
him.*

7. *"The Aim of Pope Pius IX" •* This
1855 cartoon advertises a new book,
Danger in the Dark, *which in wild
tones warns against "Anti-Republic
Romanism."*

10. *Attack on the Public Schools, 1870 •
Thomas Nast represents Catholicism as
preparing for a full attack on the
American public school.*

9. *Night Rider of the
Ku Klux Klan*

of this lurid volume were sold prior to the Civil War testifies both to its influence and to the broad base of anti-Catholic, nativist sentiment.

Though reactions to the influx of Catholic immigrants took many forms, three areas of searing friction appeared. The first was economic. Cheap Irish labor threatened to undercut native American labor. When the local brickmakers of Charlestown, Massachusetts, felt trapped by the competition of Irish labor, they responded by burning the convent. The financial panic of 1837 resulted in a shortage of jobs which in turn produced greater resentment against increased competition in the labor market. As complaints and bitterness grew, "native American" associations multiplied and resistance became resolute.

Second, Catholicism appeared peculiarly vulnerable in the political area, both for its tight hierarchical organization and for its alliance with anti-democratic governments abroad. The opinion prevailed, occasionally buttressed by a Church pronouncement, that the American pattern of religious liberty was theoretically and ultimately unacceptable to Roman Catholicism. Moreover, the "trusteeism" controversy (concerning the right of Catholic laity to control parish finances and to select their own ministers) persuaded many non-Catholics that the Church was fundamentally undemocratic and *ipso facto* un-American. This prolonged dispute, extending throughout the first half of the nineteenth century, created temporary schisms within Catholic parishes themselves (e.g., in New Orleans, Charleston, Norfolk, Buffalo) even as it fed the flames of nativism.

Education constituted a third area of tension. Both Germans (Lutheran as well as Catholic) and Irish found the American public school either (1) inadequate in its religious instruction or (2) biased in that instruction. Controversy waxed hottest in New York and Philadelphia as ecclesiastical

---

In their 1866 Pastoral Letter, the Catholic hierarchy in America recognized the need for a separate system of education.

> We recur to the subject of the education of youth . . . for the purpose of reiterating the admonition . . . in regard to the establishment and support of Parochial Schools; and of renewing the expression of our conviction that

11. James Cardinal Gibbons, Archbishop of Baltimore

12. *Polish Catholics in Buffalo • The priest blesses the food on the Saturday before Easter (1943).*

religious teaching and religious training should form part of every system of school education. Every day's experience renders it evident that to develop the intellect and store it with knowledge, while the heart and its affections are left without the control of religious principle, sustained by religious practices, is to mistake the nature and object of education; as well as to prepare for parent and child the most bitter disappointment in the future, and for society the most disastrous results.

---

authorities sought to obtain public funds for the Catholic schools. Failing in this, Church leaders sought permission for Catholic children in public

---

Judge Alphonso Taft (father of President William Howard Taft) in 1870 issued a strong dissent in the Cincinnati Superior Court; his dissent was later upheld by the Ohio Supreme Court.

It is said that the Catholic clergy demand their share of the [public school] fund, to be used in carrying on schools under their control. That cannot be done under the Constitution. But this affords no reason why the Board of Education shall not grant to the Catholic people what the Bill of Rights guarantees to every sect, that their rights of conscience shall not be violated, and that they shall not be compelled to attend any form of worship, or to maintain it against their consent, or be compelled to submit to religious preferences shown by the government to other religious societies. . . .

Another numerous class of heavy tax-payers, the Jews, object to the old rule [permitting daily reading from the King James version of the Bible]. . . . Like the majority of us, the Jews have received their faith from their ancestors, and according to that historic faith, the assertion in the New Testament that Jesus of Nazareth is God is blasphemy against the God of Israel. If a Protestant Christian would object to have the common schools daily opened with the forms of worship peculiar to the Catholic Church which worships the same Triune God with him, how much more serious must be the objection of the Jew to be compelled to attend, or support, the worship of a being as God, whose divinity and supernatural history he denies? . . .

No sect can, because it includes a majority of a community or a majority of the citizens of the state, claim any preference whatsoever. It cannot claim that its mode of worship or its religion shall prevail in the common schools.

---

schools at least to hear scripture from a Catholic Bible. John Hughes, bishop (later archbishop) of New York, led a vigorous fight for a share of public school monies, contending that the city's Public School Society was really Protestant and that public school texts were openly anti-Catholic. Failing to win major concessions, the Church began to build its own ambitious and expensive separate school system. Far from quieting all criticism, however, the establishment of the parochial schools appeared to cast reproach upon the public schools themselves. The nation's main agency of assimilation and Americanization was being bypassed. Was it being undermined? Was unity still possible? Was America still one? (See Fig. 10).

The Order of the Star-Spangled Banner (1849), nucleus of the Know-Nothing party, expressed these sentiments in its constitution.

The object of this organization shall be to protect every American citizen in the legal and proper exercise of all his civil and religious rights and privileges; to resist the insidious policy of the Church of Rome, and all other foreign influence against our republican institutions in all lawful ways; to place in all offices of honor, trust, or profit, in the gift of the people, or by appointment, none but native-born Protestant citizens, and to protect, preserve, and uphold the Union of these states and the Constitution of the same.

These deeply disturbing questions, widely discussed in pulpit, press, and political assembly, led to the major political expression of American nativism: the Know-Nothing or American party, created in 1854. Exercising real power only briefly, the party won quick successes at the polls. But on the critical issues of slavery and secession, Know-Nothingism lost so much relevance and appeal that by 1860 it was politically dead. Moreover, its denial of the democratic faith moved men to seek saner solutions for problems that proved as persistent as they were complex.

Lincoln's views on the Know-Nothings are found in his letter to Joshua Speed, August 24, 1855.

> I am not a Know-nothing. That is certain. How could I be? How can any one who abhors the oppression of Negroes be in favor of degrading classes of white people? Our progress in degeneracy appears to me to be pretty rapid. As a nation, we began by declaring that "all men are created equal." We now practically read it "all men are created equal, except Negroes." When the Know-Nothings get control, it will read "all men are created equal except Negroes, and foreigners and Catholics." When it comes to this I should prefer emigrating to some country where they make no pretense of loving liberty—to Russia, for instance, where despotism can be taken pure, and without the base alloy of hypocrisy.

Following four bitter years of war, the nation busied itself for a time binding its own bleeding wounds. But in the 1880's resistance to immigration mounted again. In California, for example, the influx of Chinese provoked resentments that ultimately cut off further immigration from China. The Irish Catholic immigrant opposed cheap Chinese labor in much the same way he had been opposed in the East a generation earlier. To be anti-Chinese was to be pro-Irish, pro-Catholic, pro-organized labor. To be pro-Chinese was to be aligned with Protestantism and the business community against Irish Catholicism and the Workingmen's Party (led by Dennis Kearney). Gradually, however, when the need for cheap labor declined and the Protestant vision of ten thousand Chinese converts dimmed, defense of continued immigration all but disappeared. As mob violence grew and anti-Oriental feeling soared, the federal government in May 1882 passed the first of a series of Exclusion Acts, halting all further immigration from China.

Meanwhile, Easterners again resisted the growing "foreignness" of urban population. Political fears of the radicalism, socialism, and anarchism found or suspected among new arrivals aggravated the religious fears. Riots, strikes, and intemperate words convinced many Americans that revolution was being smuggled into their very midst. Anti-Catholicism erupted once more, with parochial schools and organized labor again becoming battle stations. The appointment in 1893 of Cardinal Satolli as the first Apostolic Delegate to the United States spurred rumors of papal designs on American liberties.

Anti-Semitism likewise increased in proportion to the growing Jewish

13. *Greek Orthodox C h u r c h in Amoskaag, New Hampshire*

14. *Rabbi Isaac M. Wise*

15. *Russian Orthodox Church in Pittsburgh, Pennsylvania (1938)*

population. Jews, resented as either too expert at capitalism or too crafty in socialism, incurred greater resentment when they joined Catholics in protesting Bible reading in the public schools. International intrigue, notably in the world of finance, was laid at the door of the Jewish banker, merchant, or even pawnbroker. The evils of the big city—and there were many—were too readily attributed to the Jewishness of the city. Finally, racist theories used against the Negro and the Oriental now proved useful against the Jew, as prejudices mounted and stereotypes hardened.

Isaac M. Wise, the first rabbi to visit the White House, tells of this experience in his *Reminiscences,* first published serially 1874–1875.

> [1850] A fire was burning in the grate opposite the door, chairs stood on both sides, and a man sat in front of the fire, with his back to the door. Without turning around to see who it might be, he called out: "Step up closer, gentlemen; it is cold today."
>
> We took our positions on either side of the grate, and I knew not that I was standing before the President [Zachary Taylor]. "Mr. President, I have the honor of introducing to you my friend from Albany," said [Senator William H.] Seward. The President extended his hand, and asked us to be seated. After catechising me in true American fashion, he said: "I suppose you have never seen a President of the United States, and for that reason you have paid me a visit." "I beg pardon, Your Excellency," said I, "I had the honor of speaking with your predecessor, James K. Polk. My object in coming has been to see the hero of Buena Vista." Hereupon the old war horse arose and bowed graciously. "Mr. Seward," said he, "your friend seems to be very polite."
>
> The old man became so talkative that I ventured to say: "Your Excellency, it has afforded me the keenest pleasure to form the acquaintance of the hero-President—a unique and magnificent personality. Permit me, however, to say that I believe you have never seen a person of my kind." He looked at me dumbfounded. "I have seen people of all sorts and conditions," said he, "and would like to know what you mean." "Certainly," said I, "I am a rabbi." "You are right; I have never seen a rabbi." He now extended his hand a second time, and began the conversation anew.

As eastern European immigration swelled, doctrines of Nordic supremacy and Anglo-Saxon superiority drew attentive audiences. Blond, blue-eyed Protestants would save America; dark, sloe-eyed Slavs would ruin it. Slavic strikers were shot in Pennsylvania, Italians were lynched in New Orleans, and anti-Jewish riots broke out in the South. In 1894 the Immigration Destruction League, formed in New England, urged that only the better "stocks" be henceforth admitted to America. Early in the twentieth century some social scientists supported restrictionist demands, and shortly after World War I a revived Ku Klux Klan intimidated the "foreigner" in general—the Negro, the Catholic, and the Jew in particular (see Fig. 9).

Some nativist drives were unmistakably religious in origin and motive. The American Protective Association, founded in Clinton, Iowa, in 1887, directed its propaganda specifically against the "Catholic menace." Unlike the Know-Nothings, the A.P.A. solicited and obtained foreign memberships, most of its support coming from immigrants of German, Scandinavian, Canadian, and British background. A.P.A. members swore to resist the growth of Catholicism, pledging that they would not employ Roman Catholics, nor help build their churches, nor vote for any Roman Catholic, nor "countenance the nomination, in any caucus or convention, of a Roman Catholic for any office in the gift of the American people." Within a decade the A.P.A., having reached the peak of its power, rapidly declined; yet the mood it represented endured for decades—indeed, for generations.

World War I widened social fissures that could in calmer days be ignored. Ties with the old country were still strong, and new loyalties were compromised by old memories. Theodore Roosevelt spoke impatiently of "hyphenated Americans," and in 1916 Woodrow Wilson wrote intemperately to a pro-German Irish agitator: "I should feel deeply mortified to have you or anybody like you vote for me. Since you have access to many disloyal Americans and I have not, I will ask you to convey this message to them."

A nation at war now saw ethnic diversity as a threat to its security. Furthermore, social reformers and city planners argued that the spiraling problems of poverty, sanitation, education, slums, disease, immorality, and crime could not be solved as long as thousands of immigrants annually poured off the ships into the overburdened cities. In 1921, therefore, Congress passed the first of a series of acts restricting immigration both in number and in kind. With the adoption of the National Origins Act of 1924 a quota system favorable to northern and western European countries was the official federal policy until 1965. The mighty river of immigration that for three hundred years had cascaded into the United States now became a tiny trickle. Freedom's lamp still burned brightly on Liberty Island, but on nearby Ellis Island, where so many immigrants had been received, the gates closed at last in 1954. As they swung shut, a magnificent chapter of American history, even of world history, came to an end.

"AND CROWN THY GOOD"

For the long-established citizen the assimilation of newcomers proceeded slowly. Differences of dress, speech, custom and diet constantly called attention to the strangers sojourning "with thee in your land." But for the immigrant, Americanization and assimilation seemed much too fast—not nearly slow enough! Dutchman, Pole, or Russian hastened from the boat to the nearest church or synagogue only to discover an unfamiliar institution. The Lutheran sat down to a service conducted in English—a language he hardly knew. The Polish Catholic found himself surrounded by sculptured saints he never heard of, preached to by Irish clerics he could not understand. Jews from Russia were first perplexed, then angered by the novelties confronting them in the Ashkenazim (German) congregation. For all these America was too quickly embraced, ancestral way too lightly forsaken.

New times demand new thoughts, Isaac Wise argued in *The Israelite* I (1855).

> Poor philosophers, who maintain that our ideas and conceptions should be the same as those of our forefathers. We fly to distant territories on the wings of fire and water, we speak into distant lands by the terrible force of lightning, we enlist the sun in our service to paint our pictures, we propel cities across the ocean in as short time as our fathers went from Dan to Jerusalem. The tremendous thunderbolt is feared no longer; man has wrested it from the powerful hands of Jupiter. Still we are required to think and feel as our good forefathers did. What nonsense!
>
> Distant nations have come into close contact, exchanged ideas, revolutionized each other's thoughts, feelings, and conceptions; superstitions between nations are *railroaded* and *steamboated* away, the partition wall between man and man totters and falls.

Among the Reformed Protestants from Holland, for example, those arriving in mid-nineteenth century felt little kinship with their coreligionists long in America. The latter sang hymns (not psalms), permitted choirs, ignored revered creeds and doctrines, abandoned the Dutch language, and even tolerated membership in Masonic lodges. The church they found in America was not the church they left behind in Holland. Yet both were Dutch Reformed Churches. What to do except start a True Dutch Reformed Church (1864) which would be what every pious Dutch immigrant expected his Church to be?

Coming from so many contrasting cultures, Catholics sometimes found the ethnic pull stronger than the ecclesiastical one. German Catholics wanted German priests and bishops as well as the use of their own language wherever the vernacular was permitted. To a lesser degree the Portuguese, the French, and the Italians voiced similar sentiments. Wisely resisting that normal desire, the Roman Catholic Church promoted the Americanization and assimilation of the whole. Polish Catholics, chafing under this policy, in 1907 established their own organization: the Polish National Catholic Church (see Fig. 12).

The problems facing the eastern European Jews were severest of all. The older Jewish immigrants, predominantly German, had begun a major reform in Judaism's doctrine and practice when the flood of newer immigrants arrived. These Jews found little community among their German coreligionists. Services in English were held on Sunday, not on the Sabbath;

children attended Sunday Schools, not Talmud Torah Schools. Dietary and other regulations of the Torah (Law) were modified, ignored, or interpreted symbolically. Instrumental music was introduced, and seating by families rather than by sexes practiced. The eastern European Jew happening into a reform German synagogue might fear that by mistake he had stumbled upon a Protestant church.

Solomon Schechter in his Inaugural Address at Jewish Theological Seminary in New York, 1902, describes the course he will pursue as president.

> But first let me say a few words about the general religious tendency this Seminary [Jewish Theological] will follow. I am not unaware that this is a very delicate point, and prudence would dictate silence or evasion. But life would hardly be worth living without occasional blundering, "the only relief from dull correctness." Besides, if there be in American history one fact more clearly proved than any other it is that "Know-nothingism" was an absolute and miserable failure. I must not fall into the same error. And thus, sincerely asking forgiveness of all my dearest friends and dearest enemies with whom it may be my misfortune to differ, I declare, in all humility, but most emphatically, that I do know something. And this is that the religion in which the Jewish ministry should be trained must be specifically and purely Jewish, without any alloy or adulteration. Judaism must stand or fall by that which distinguishes it from other religions as well as by that which it has in common with them. Judaism is *not* a religion which does not oppose itself to anything in particular. Judaism is opposed to any number of things, and says distinctly "thou shalt not." It permeates the whole of your life. It demands control over all your actions, and interferes even with your menu. It sanctifies the seasons, and regulates your history, both in the past and in the future. . . . In a word, Judaism is absolutely incompatible with the abandonment of the Torah.

While part of the Germanic reform was conscious Americanization, the movement was broader than that. Ghettoized Judaism had, of necessity, held itself rigid and unchanging for centuries. In the liberalism of nineteenth-century western Europe, however, Jews breathing a freer, cleaner air began to take their legitimate place in the modern world. Modernizing Judaism—making it relevant to an urban, industrial, secularized world—had already begun in Germany before the major migrations to America. Rabbis coming from this atmosphere simply carried on the program in America, adjusting it to the challenges and freedoms offered in a ghettoless land. By 1873 a Union of American Hebrew Congregations was formed with Hebrew Union College of Cincinnati founded two years later. Under the direction of a native rabbinate the twin task of reformation and Americanization could be carried forward.

For Jews as for so many others America was a great new laboratory for social and spiritual experiment. There one might, with God's help, perfect a product so awe-inspiring, so unmistakably superior that all the nation, indeed all the world, would be enthralled. America was still a place where old men could dream and young men behold visions. Isaac M. Wise, who went to Cincinnati as rabbi in 1854, was wholly American in his high hopes, his heady optimism. Judaism, reformed of its archaic limitations, ennobled in its ethical ideals, cultured in its every fibre, could elevate all America. Such a religion could become, Wise believed, the religion of all mankind.

In *Reminiscences* Rabbi Wise pleaded for Americanization.

> The Jew must be Americanized, I said to myself, for every German book, every German word reminds him of the old disgrace. If he continues under German influences, as they are now in this country, he must become either a bigot or an atheist, a satellite or tyrant. He will never be aroused to self-consciousness or to independent thought. The Jew must become an American, in order to gain the proud self-consciousness of the free-born man.
>
> From that hour I began to Americanize with all my might and was as enthusiastic for this as I was for Reform.

But then came the flood of immigrants not tuned to western Europe's reform, not partners in Wise's dream. Fleeing the ghettoes or the brutal pogroms, these Jews asked only to pursue peacefully their ancient faith in all its purity and strength-giving familiarity. Each ethnic group, if not each ship's company, preferred its own synagogue, its own cantor, and, when available, its own rabbi. As a measure of the growing diversity, New York City had only fourteen synagogues in the 1850's, but by the end of that century some three hundred separate congregations were scattered about the city.

In an address delivered in Indianapolis (1904), Solomon Schechter spoke on Americanization.

> There is nothing in American citizenship which is incompatible with our observing the dietary laws, our sanctifying the Sabbath, our fixing a Mezuzah on our doorposts, our refraining from unleavened bread on Passover, or our perpetuating any other law essential to the preservation of Judaism. On the other hand, it is now generally recognized by the leading thinkers that the institutions and observances of religion are part of its nature, a fact that the moribund rationalism of a half century ago failed to realize. In certain parts of Europe every step in our civil and social emancipation demanded from us a corresponding sacrifice of a portion of the glorious heritage bequeathed to us by our fathers. Jews in America, thank

God, are no longer haunted by such fears. We live in a commonwealth in which by the blessing of God and the wisdom of the Fathers of the Constitution, each man abiding by its laws, has the inalienable right of living in accordance with the dictates of his own conscience. In this great, glorious and free country we Jews need not sacrifice a single iota of our Torah; and, in the enjoyment of absolute equality with our fellow citizens, we can live to carry out those ideals for which our ancestors so often had to die.

Religious life demanded more than the synagogue. Funeral associations, benevolent societies, and, above all, schools were required to maintain the traditional life. Schools presented the hardest problem, as resources both in leadership and money were meager. A school providing only Hebrew language and literature was not enough, since it failed to meet the standards set by state law. A school competing with public education was, on the other hand, too much, since it exceeded the resources of immigrant Jewry. Varied experiments at every level resulted in Jewish religious education being largely a part-time, after-public-school activity. Only a minority, however, met even this minimum in the education of their children.

Mary Antin, who arrived from Russia in 1894 as a young girl, tells what free education meant (*The Promised Land,* 1911).

> As we moved along in a little procession, I was delighted with the illumination of the streets. So many lamps, and they burned until morning, my father said, and so people did not need to carry lanterns. In America, then, everything was free, as we had heard in Russia. Light was free; the streets were as bright as a synagogue on a holy day. Music was free; we had been serenaded, to our gaping delight, by a brass band of many pieces, soon after our installation on Union Place [Boston].
>
> Education was free. That subject my father had written about repeatedly, as comprising his chief hope for us children, the essence of American opportunity, the treasure that no thief could touch, not even misfortune or poverty. It was the one thing he was able to promise us when he sent for us; surer, safer than bread or shelter.

Synagogue life itself took one of three paths. Orthodox Judaism maintained the ritual laws of behavior (*kashruth*) in a tightly knit communal society, where food was properly prepared, the Hebrew language carefully preserved, and the Law strictly interpreted. Reform, as noted above, moved rapidly toward a reinterpretation of Jewish doctrine and a modification of Jewish practice. Between these two, Conservative Judaism arose. Conservatism, which was less rigid than Orthodoxy and more traditional than Reform, served as a bridge between newer and older immigrants and maintained the Jew's religious life across much of suburban America.

16. *Jewish Market, New York City's East Side, 1900*

17. *Synagogue Weekday Service, Colchester, Connecticut, 1940*

18. *Rabbi Solomon Schechter*

19. *Rabbi Inspects Kosher Wine Shop, New York City, 1942*

Under the early leadership of Rabbi Sabato Morais and the later leadership of such men as Solomon Schechter and Cyrus Adler, the Conservative movement gained great influence. New York's Jewish Theological Seminary, over which Schechter presided from 1902 to 1915, trained an English-speaking rabbinate that saved many eastern European immigrants from a radical abandonment of their faith. Conservative Judaism also saved many second- and third-generation suburbanites from a too easy exchange of religious peculiarity for cultural conformity. In the campaign to keep Americanization from becoming absorption Solomon Schechter emerged with the clearest, most commanding voice. "We must leave off talking about Occidentalizing our religion," he wrote, remembering that the "Torah gave spiritual accommodation for thousands of years to all sorts and conditions of men . . . and it should also prove broad enough to harbor the different minds of the present century." A sermon in English is fine; renunciation of history is folly.

As Americanization proceeded, Judaism adapted to its new culture and assisted that culture toward richer expression. Though much about American civilization was novel and strange, at its very center stood something marvelously familiar and old: the God of Abraham, Isaac, and Jacob.

What, after all, did Americanization mean? Must one surrender his beard, his beads, his shawl, his crucifix to become an American? Must he forget the Irish songs he knew, the Hungarian music he loved, the Mosaic laws he honored, the Norwegian bread he brought, the Italian holidays he celebrated, or any of a dozen more festivities, fashions, or mores? How much must the melting pot melt?

In his introduction to the *Life of Father Hecker* (1891) Bishop John Ireland suggests what Americanization might mean for Roman Catholics.

The American people hold these [natural and social virtues] in highest esteem. They are the virtues that are most apparent, and are seemingly the most needed for the building up and the preservation of an earthly commonwealth. Truthfulness, honesty in business dealings, loyalty to law and social order, temperance, respect for the rights of others, and the like virtues are prescribed by reason before the voice of revelation is heard . . . It will be a difficult task to persuade the American that a church which will not enforce those primary virtues can enforce others which she herself declares to be higher and more arduous; and as he has implicit confidence in the destiny of his country to produce a high order of social existence, his first test of a religion will be its power in this direction.

The immigrants' answers to these questions were not uniform—not for Protestants, Catholics, or Jews. And answers imposed from without tended to be unhelpful and unavailing. Gradually, the immigrants, by actions more than words, revealed what they thought it meant to be an American. In the most general terms it meant a share in the national dream, as inheritors of the American past and as stockholders in the American future. In economic terms this suggested the right to property, employment, and investment enjoyed by other citizens. In political terms it meant the privileges of suffrage and the protection of constitutional liberties.

In religious terms it involved at least three things. First, it meant something about freedom in religion, a freedom that in law and in fact exceeded what most nineteenth-century arrivals had ever experienced. Americanization meant accepting, enjoying, and ultimately defending this freedom. It could be accepted initially as a simple acknowledgment that in the United States no official religion had the protection and support of the state. The Swedish Lutheran, the Italian Catholic, the Greek Orthodox could preceive the difference immediately. And strange and radical though it was, they accepted it. (To enjoy it took a little more time, as it had for Lyman Beecher.) The recruitment of members, the gathering of support, the competition against heresy, heterodoxy, and indifference—these might not look like rare joys. But after a time few were willing to trade this purifying effort for the corrupting patronage of government, the malignant hatreds bred by persecution, or the adulterating confusion of political with spiritual. Ultimately what may have been accepted as an onerous necessity came to be defended as the dearest liberty.

Second, Americanization had some relevance to language. English enjoyed no special sanctity, just currency. To participate fully in America one must learn English. This simple fact was readily perceived and readily acknowledged—except in religion. Though the battle for the ancestral tongue might be fought in the market place, assembly, or school, the issue was religion: its preservation and its perpetuation. Yet on these very grounds—religion's survival and growth—the argument for English was won. For only the first-generation immigrant found strength and appeal in maintenance of the older tongue. Some churches and synagogues went through the motions for another generation or more, aided by the church schools; gradually, however, the language wall began to crumble. Prayers were translated, hymns received English words, and in at least one service the sermon would be in English.

Language was widely considered the key to ethnic unity and cultural cohesion. But other old-world ties persisted: holidays, parades, dances, special rites, fraternal or military orders, even social and personal habits. In this last category of public and private morality Americanization made its third demand on the nineteenth-century immigrant. A kind of frontier, frugal, aggressive "Methodist Puritanism" permeated much of American life. Lutherans accustomed to friendly picnics on Sunday afternoons, with beer and wine for all, found their midwestern neighbors shocked and scandalized. Temperance and strict sabbath observance, the norm in many regions, became the law in some. "Blue laws," elaborately detailed, demanded a moral conformity often in the narrowest terms.

A concert pianist from Paris, on tour in the United States in 1846, lit a cigar on the streets of Boston. He describes his experience:

> I had not proceeded ten feet when a constable stopped me, shocked.
> "Sir, smoking is forbidden."
> "You are joking, constable."
> "Not at all. Smoking in the streets is forbidden. If you cannot contain yourself, go home to smoke. . . . Your infraction is all the more shocking and blameworthy on Sunday, the day consecrated to the glory of God."
> I could not help but consider this taboo, in the land of all the liberties, tyrannical. But I had to obey.

While one need not surrender cigar-smoking to be Americanized, immigrant institutions generally sought the favor and good will of the older population. In this way a pervading Anglo-American morality infiltrated the moral and religious codes of many old-world settlers. As Archbishop Ireland noted in 1891, "An honest ballot and social decorum among Catholics will do more for God's glory and the salvation of souls than midnight flagellations or Compostellan pilgrimages."

If church and synagogue membership were voluntary, then it ought to be meaningful: discipline was demanded, moral achievement was expected. The immigrant's religion, it was assumed, would be a power for reform and reconstruction in America—otherwise it was not religion. All liberty's children were invited to shape their nation's destiny.

At the laying of the cornerstone for the Catholic University of America in 1888 John Lancaster Spalding spoke of the relationship between Christianity and democracy.

> The special significance of our American Catholic history is not found in the phases of our life which attract attention, and are a common theme for declamation; but it lies in the fact that our example proves that the Church can thrive where it is neither protected nor persecuted, but is simply left to itself to manage its own affairs and to do its work. Such an experiment had never been made when we became an independent people, and its success is of world-wide import, because this is the modern tendency and the position toward the Church which all nations will sooner or later assume; just as they all will be finally forced to accept popular rule. The great underlying principle of democracy—that men are brothers and have equal rights, and that God clothes the soul with freedom—is a truth taught by Christ, is a truth proclaimed by the Church; and the faith of all Christians in this principle, in spite of hesitations and misgivings, of oppositions and obstacles and inconceivable difficulties, has finally given to it its modern vigor and beneficent power.

---

16 ✤ A Changing Order: Factory and Town

DIAGNOSIS IS THE PROPER PRELUDE to cure. But when symptoms are numerous and complex, then diagnosis is difficult and consensus is elusive. So it proved in American society in the late nineteenth century. Newspaper headlines, pulpit alarms, and civic resolutions bewailed the ill-health to which a dizzying succession of symptoms witnessed: strikes, riots, panics, sweat shops, slums, illiteracy, immorality, poverty, bribery, and graft. What was the cause, and where was the cure?

From 1860 to 1900 the nation's urban population more than doubled, creating "big city" problems inland as well as in the coastal centers. Immigration itself was part of a European move from farm to city—an Irish or Polish farm to an American city. But native Americans also left the rural areas, especially in the Middle West, to augment the city's fast growing population. By the end of the century Chicago was the nation's second largest city, with rapid growth notable in Detroit, Milwaukee, Minneapolis, St. Paul, Indianapolis, Cleveland, Columbus, Toledo, Kansas City, and Omaha.

In the same forty-year span the industrial revolution likewise radically altered American life. "Revolution" was not too strong a word for the changes in transportation (steam engine, combustion engine, electric engine), communication (telegraph, telephone, transatlantic cable, wireless, typewriter, linotype presses), agriculture (binders, improved harvesters, threshers, cutters), and domestic life (electric light, sewing machine, phonograph). The greatest revolution, however, was in the labor market itself, where thousands of propertyless men traded only their skills and their sweat.

All three—immigration, urbanization, industrialization—heightened the ills and multiplied the symptoms. For the sores of the city the immigrant was often held responsible; for the fevers of the factory the city itself received blame. So complex were the ultimate causes that enemies of the city or the factory or the immigrant seized their chance to single out a scapegoat for all social disorder.

To these ills, whatever their cause, religion could not long remain indifferent. Some callousness and some complacency, particularly just after the Civil War, did characterize the churches' attitude. As the social distresses persisted, however, leaders probed for solution or cure. Convictions about the perfectability of men and the benevolence of God reinforced America's persisting optimism that free men could create the finest society. If one still believed in a utopia, he now also believed in America. He did not, therefore, flee to the mountains or empty plains to fashion his ideal society. Rather he stayed with thronging humanity, there to work and pray for a better order.

Was religion relevant to the economic, the social, the political crises? Could physicians cure sickness of class, race, and slum? Was there any balm in Gilead? A healing ministry offered to American society two contrasting (but not contradictory) remedies: one for the individual; a second for the social structures themselves.

REDEMPTION OF PERSONS

From the first signs of social corruption in colonial New England through the fluctuating fortunes of revolution, expansion, civil strife, immigration, and industrialization, one cure was repeatedly urged: change the hearts of men. Then and only then do you change the health of society. As one cannot make a silk purse from a sow's ear, it was argued, so one cannot elevate or redeem a society whose members wallow in stubborn sin. This curative procedure bore the respectability of age, the glory of repeated triumph. With little disposition to abandon it after the Civil War, religious leaders nevertheless recognized the necessity for new means and new measures to reach the individual. Along with the old techniques, therefore, came experimental approaches to problems posed by factory and town.

Mass Evangelism

Whitefield, Dwight, Finney, and others in an earlier time unified society, resisted infidelity, and extended Christianity. After the Civil War was the revival obsolete? Dwight L. Moody provided the most resounding negative to that question.

A Boston shoe clerk, Moody, impressed by the earnestness of his Sunday School teacher, joined the Congregational Church when he was eighteen years of age. Later that same year, 1856, he left for Chicago to make his own way in the world of business, but money-making soon took second place to religious teaching. Moody spent his after-business hours organiz-

---

The gospel of personal redemption is proudly proclaimed by Dwight L. Moody (*Moody's Great Sermons,* 1899).

Now, let me say, my friends, if you want that love of God in your hearts, all you have to do is to open the door and let it shine in. It will

1. Dwight L. Moody's Sunday School Class, Chicago, 1876 • In this lithograph, entitled "Will It Pay?", Moody stands in the center rear.

2. Moody's strong ally, Ira D. Sankey

3. Moody preaches at the Hippodrome, New York City, 1875–76

4. Twentieth Century Revivalism (Washington, D. C., 1939)

shine in as the sun shines in a dark room. Let him have full possession of your hearts. Some people have an idea they had something to do to bring about reconciliation. God is already reconciled. There is not anything for you to do but believe that God is reconciled.

---

ing Sunday Schools, distributing tracts, raising money for church buildings, and ministering in a dozen ways to Chicago's disheartened and dispossessed. By 1860 he emerged from "the hardest struggle I ever had in my life" with the decision to give himself fully to the cause of religion (see Fig. 3).

During the Civil War he worked in the army camps, offering aid to the wounded and guidance to the confused. After that conflict, he returned to the slums of Chicago to direct relief, establish missions, and acquire a reputation for efficient advancement of the Christian cause. Moody won his great fame as a revivalist, however, far from Chicago. In 1875, after conducting amazingly successful evangelistic meetings in Great Britain, he returned to America to become a hero at home no less than abroad.

Ira D. Sankey, the song leader whom Moody took along to England, shared in this shower of fame. Sankey's hymns (those he sang and those he wrote) introduced an impressive novelty into American revivalism. Henceforth, no revivalist dared enter the arena of mass evangelism unless armed with a musical ally (see Fig. 2).

Unordained and uneducated (he never finished the seventh grade), Moody nonetheless made impressive contributions both to religion and to education. In religion he renewed and sharpened the demands of a gospel of charity and brotherhood. To a society threatened by bitter division, he offered the unifying theme of a God who loved all the world. The theme seemed more plausible, the message more winsome when presented in the quiet, restrained, homey manner that Moody regularly employed. No hysterics were countenanced, no excesses of emotion encouraged. A simple gospel, simply presented was for many enough.

In education Moody likewise left a permanent mark. Aware that his hearers no longer shared a common religious heritage or common intellectual assumptions, Moody pleaded "for teachers who shall teach and show what the gospel is." In 1879 he founded a school for girls near his old home at Northfield, Massachusetts; the Mount Hermon School for boys opened two years later. In 1889 he transformed Chicago's Evangelization Society into a coeducational religious school, later know as the Moody Bible Institute. From these centers, as from the impact of his revivals and the influence of his prominent supporters (Cyrus McCormick, John Wanamaker, Anson G. Phelps, T. DeWitt Talmadge, Phillips Brooks, James McCosh, and Henry Ward Beecher, among others), Moody's name spread around the world.

Moody saw reform as possible only when "the Reformer gets into [men's] hearts." This was the business of religion: to change men, not to upset political, social, and economic apple carts. Popular pulpit orators generally followed the same path. The persuasive Phillips Brooks, rector of Boston's Trinity Church, maintained that the churches' vital business was to redeem the hearts of men. Patience, prayer, Bible reading and church-going constituted the route to a better world. And Henry Ward Beecher, of Brooklyn's Plymouth Church, found a man's poverty to be the result of his sin, his prosperity the mark of his virtue. ". . . Where you find the most religion there you will find the most worldly prosperity—in communities, I mean, not in single persons." "Until the heart is made right," said Moody, "all else will be wrong."

Reforms

Even those concerned primarily with private morality and personal sin agreed that group action against sin was occasionally desirable. Two areas, Sunday observance and temperance, occupied many who fretted over America's changing mores. Sunday proved troublesome simply because its observance differed so widely. The "continental Sunday" featured sports, games, parties and recreation, while the "puritan Sunday" turned from all unnecessary labor and frivolous activity. As these two traditions in Christendom collided, each fought for its own method of keeping "the sabbath day holy."

Preserving Sunday as a day of religion and rest turned into a major crusade. Violations of the expected decorum intensified attacks on the city, the factory, and the immigrant as destroying "the very foundations of public morality and private virtue." Resisting every breach in the wall, pietist churches reluctantly retreated before Sunday newspapers, Sunday sports, Sunday business. Conservative churches even supported labor's struggle for a six-day week, hoping that religion could then find a place along with rest and relaxation. For some a man's Americanism was measured by his Sunday habits. And for the Reverend Josiah Strong "there is, perhaps, no better index of general morality than Sabbath observance."

Attracting more attention, winning more votes, exuding more zeal, the temperance crusade achieved nationwide prominence in the years before and immediately after World War I. Sentiment for temperance was old, but the vigor and extent of organized sentiment was new. The National Temperance Society and Publishing House was founded in 1865, the Prohibition Party in 1869, the Catholic Total Abstinence Union of America in 1872, the Women's Christian Temperance Union (WCTU) in 1874, and the Anti-Saloon League of America in 1895. Some worked for moderation, others for abstinence; some attacked the saloon, others aided the victim; some thought political action desirable, others placed emphasis on "moral suasion."

Francis E. Willard organized a following to promote the prohibition cause (*Do Everything: A Handbook for the World's White Ribboners,* 1895).

> Whenever in any country the Government allies itself with the effort to secure Prohibition we cooperate with "the powers that be" to the utmost of our own power. We cannot consent, as an organization, to stand in relations of equal friendliness towards one party that ignores, another that opposes, and a third that espouses the cause of Prohibition. We have, therefore, in some countries favored the formation of a new party . . . made up of a body of voters who are committed to protect the home and to outlaw the dram shop. This party always places equal suffrage for man and woman as a plank in its platform, and is strongly sympathetic with the cause of labor and purity. Indeed, it may be said to be the political exponent of the modern spirit. Whether it comes to power or not, such a party, in the widest sense, is an educator of public opinion. . . .

Despite differing views temperance crusaders reached into every parish, town square, and polling place. Francis E. Willard, president of the WCTU, James Roosevelt Bayley, Catholic bishop of Newark, and Wayne B. Wheeler, of the Anti-Saloon League, argued for control or abolition of the liquor traffic. States, counties, and friends separated into the "wets" and "drys" as the crusade became more blatantly political, less obviously moral. In 1919 the evangelical churches (chiefly Baptist and Methodist) supporting the Anti-Saloon League won their victory as the Eighteenth Amendment became law (see Figs. 5 and 7).

The sweets of a victory that lasted only until 1933 soured even before that fourteen-year period ended. As gangsterism, bribery, and willful violation of the law characterized much of prohibition's "era of excess," the disenchanted turned away from what Richard Hofstadter called "the final assertion of the rural Protestant mind against the urban and polyglot culture that had emerged." Though the experiment "noble in motive" failed, the problem of alcoholism remained. Repeal was a victory for the cities, but this victory, like that of 1919, mixed sweet with sour.

Philanthropy

Charity, like prohibition, developed large-scale organization in this period. The magnitude of philanthropy reflected the magnitude of personal fortunes accumulated in the late nineteenth century. While religious scruples may have been dim as money was accumulated, they sparkled as money was dispensed. Denominational schools, churches, hospitals, and orphanages benefited handsomely from the gifts of Rockefeller, McCormick, Wanamaker, Cooke, Drew, Crozer, Stanford, Schiff, Rosenwald, and a great many others.

5. Frances W. Willard, Statuary Hall, United States Capitol

6. Woman's Holy War (Currier & Ives, 1874)

7. Local Option Election, Chillicote, Missouri, 1908

8. "Now Will You Be Good?" New York Herald, March 15, 1908

For Andrew Carnegie, an impoverished Scottish immigrant, the hand of Providence upheld his own enormous fortune. Writing on the "gospel of wealth," Carnegie argued that those who prosper through industry and virtue must be stewards of all they possess. A free individual in a freely competitive society is yet bound by love to contribute to the general welfare. More than 350 million dollars flowed from Carnegie into colleges, libraries, scientific research and the Endowment for International Peace. His conviction that wealth came as a providential reward and that virtue always prospers was readily popularized. Russell H. Conwell's famous lecture, "Acres of Diamonds," echoing many of Carnegie's views, earned enough to launch Temple University.

Russell H. Conwell's "Acres of Diamonds" lecture was first delivered in 1868.

> Money is power, and you ought to be reasonably ambitious to have it. You ought because you can do more good with it than you could without it. Money printed your Bible, money builds your churches, money sends your missionaries, and money pays your preachers. . . .
>
> I say, then, you ought to have money. If you can honestly attain unto riches in Philadelphia, it is your Christian and godly duty to do so. It is an awful mistake of these pious people to think you must be awfully poor in order to be pious.

New Organizations

Neither revivals nor reforms faced the problems of city and industry as squarely as new agencies and institutions created for this purpose. While both the Young Men's and Young Women's Christian Associations were founded before the Civil War, their influence and work in America became significant only after that war. Similarly, the Young Men's and Young Women's Hebrew Associations acquired real stature in the postwar period. The YMHA and the YWHA first assisted the assimilation of immigrants; afterward they developed the Jewish Center, where a community's entire social, cultural, and religious life was nourished.

The YMCA and YWCA, working first among the poor, ministered to a variety of needs. The homeless were housed, the jobless employed, the unskilled trained, the lonely and bored entertained. Evangelism, "our one and only object," carried workers to jails, hospitals, poorhouses, rescue missions, even to sailors on the docks (see Fig. 9). Tracts by the tons found their way to boarding houses, railway stations, Sunday Schools, gynmasiums, and lecture halls. But "Y" evangelism was broadly and humanely conceived. To meet the need for an indoor winter substitute for football, an enterprising YMCA secretary, James Naismith, invented

9. *"The Floating Church of Our Saviour for Seamen,"
New York "Y" Association*

10. *YMCA in World War I • A recreation hall at Camp MacArthur, Waco,
Texas, 1917.*

basketball in 1891. On campuses and battlefields no less than in suburbs and slums, Hebrew and Christian Associations overrode barriers of race and even of creed, contributing effectively to responsible democracy (see Fig. 10).

Catholic monastic orders served the dispossessed and wayward, but lay organizations such as the Society of St. Vincent de Paul and the Knights of Columbus also assumed a vital role. The Society, French in origin, began its work in the United States in 1845. Within twenty years some seventy-five chapters or conferences around the country rescued the fallen or, preferably, prevented their fall. Industrial schools and boarding homes gave youth the security, the training, the hope to lead lives of usefulness and reputation.

Catholic social action received recognition in the 1866 pastoral letter of the American hierarchy.

> We have noticed, with the most sincere satisfaction and gratitude to God, the great increase among us of Societies and Associations, especially of those composed of young and middle-aged men, conducted in strict accordance with the principles of Catholic religion, and with an immediate view to their own sanctification. We cannot but anticipate the most beneficial results to the cause of morality and religion from the conduct and example of those who thus combine together to encourage one another in the frequentation of the sacraments, and in the works of Christian charity. We urge their extension, and especially of the Society of St. Vincent of Paul and of Young Men's Catholic Associations, in all the dioceses and parishes of the country, not only as useful auxiliaries to the Parochial clergy, in the care of the poor, and of destitute and vagrant children, but also as one of the most important means of diminishing the vices and scandals of which we have spoken.

A distinctly American enterprise, the Knights of Columbus, beginning in 1882 as a kind of group insurance venture, soon included education, charity, and social service among its concerns. Under the leadership of Patrick H. Callahan, the Knights during World War I operated over three hundred recreational centers for servicemen in the States and a like number abroad.

The Catholic Young Men's National Union, formed in 1875, offered wholesome recreation, night school education, and vocational training, affirming again that prevention was preferable to cure. The Sisters of Charity, the Sisters of Mercy, the Sisters of St. Joseph, among countless others, ministered to young women, providing superior care and correction. Finally, a National Conference of Catholic Charities, organized in 1910, guided the treatment of those hastening ills found "where wealth accumulates and men decay."

New York's Chautauqua summer assembly, begun in 1874, instructed adults in their spiritual heritage. "The most American thing in America" (said Theodore Roosevelt), Chautauqua brought inspiration and appreciation of the Christian faith to masses of citizens. To serve a similar function among the disparate groups of Judaism the Jewish Chautauqua Society was launched in 1893. "Our leadership is vain without the following of an intelligent laity," declared the Society's founder, Rabbi Henry Berkowitz. Moving beyond the bounds of its own laity, Jewish Chautauqua also bridged the chasm of ignorance between Gentile and Jew.

Rabbi Henry Berkowitz promoted the Jewish Chautauqua Society (*The Beloved Rabbi,* 1923).

The Torch is a symbol of our [Jewish Chautauqua] society. Let its light shine afar, radiating throughout the land and unto all the inhabitants thereof the sublime truths of Israel's prophets and sages. They first discerned the great purpose and goal of human endeavor to be the attainment of universal freedom through social justice as the end of war and the basis of enduring peace.

In steadfast loyalty to that sublime purpose Israel has endured through the changes of time and all the trials of martyrdom. And now, under the providence of God, in this day, we in America shall not fail to be dedicated, with all the accumulated experience and deepened consecration of the generations, to renewed service in the cause of mankind.

In addition to these auxiliary organizations two new entities, each with its own cult and ministry, arose in this period. The Salvation Army, organized in England by William and Catherine Booth in 1865, came to America shortly thereafter. Suffering at first from internal disorganization and external suspicions, the Army soon won wide respect. Under the leadership of the Booth family, the American branch overcame the abuse, the ridicule, and the hostility that first greeted it. Ministering to "the lowest fallen, the most depraved, and the most neglected," the Salvation Army rescued a level of society that others were unable or unwilling to reach. Saloons and street corners became preaching stations, with women—the "hallelujah lasses"—doing most of the speaking. The bass drum and the cymbal drew some, but clear and simple charity drew even more. The sick were visited, the hungry fed, the naked clothed. Slum brigades fought filth and disease, while Rescue Homes for prostitutes sprang up across the nation. Services then provided by no other agency—legal advice, first aid, life insurance, even a missing persons department—were extended to the submerged tenth of the city's population. "The lowest fallen" had found a fold (see Figs. 12 and 13).

11. *Evangeline Booth, about 1914*

12. *Salvation Army Center, San Francisco, 1939*

13. *Salvation Army Street Service, San Francisco, 1939*

In *The Salvation Army in the United States* (1899) Booth Tucker tells something of the Army's appeal.

> "We could manage pretty well without food," said a converted hobo to me one day. "We became accustomed to the gnawings of hunger. But it was the awful longing for *sleep* that we could not endure. At first they would allow us to spend the night in the empty wagons and freight cars. That was bad enough. . . . But after a time the police received orders to prevent us from using carts or even the doorsteps. All night we would be compelled to keep moving. The longing for sleep at such times would be terrible. . . ."
>
> Our [Salvation Army] Shelters for the homeless poor have been greatly appreciated. Here, for ten cents a night, or for its equivalent in work, we have been able nightly to harbor thousands of destitute persons as well as to provide a clean and comfortable resting place for the multitudes of working men whose employment is irregular and whose wages are low.

A second new organization appealed to a different stratum of urban society. Christian Science, begun by Mary Baker Eddy in 1866, rescued city dwellers not from vice and vermin so much as from anxiety and tension. No place for quiet repose, the city-imposed pressures that drove some to drink, others to despair. Congregationalism's Josiah Strong, much concerned about the effect of city life on the nation, wrote: ". . . It is evident that the intensity of modern life has already worked, and continues to work, important changes in men's nervous organization. The American people are rapidly becoming the most nervous, the most highly organized, in the world, if, indeed, they are not already such." If anxiety could be dispelled, if pain could be forgotten, if evil could be conquered, if death was but an illusion, the city-sufferer was ready to listen. Through her writings, most notably *Science and Health, with Key to the Scriptures,* Mrs. Eddy won a following in Lynn, Massachusetts, then Boston, Chicago, and from city to city across the country. "Life, Truth and Love," she wrote, can when properly understood conquer and destroy "sin, sickness and death." Those suffering pain too keen to ignore and poverty too debasing to shrug off felt little attraction toward Christian Science. But others, in the enlarging middle class, saw hope in a religion that offered health, comfort, and peace (see Fig. 16).

Mary Baker Eddy describes her own experience in *Science and Health, with Key to the Scriptures* (1875).

> I subscribed to an Orthodox creed in early youth, and strictly adhered to it through many years; but when all earthly means had failed to restore my health, I caught the first gleam of what interprets God as higher than man-

made creeds. This vision took me away from human beliefs, and gave the spiritual import of all things from the Divine Mind expressed through Science. This gave me a new sense of Life, of God, and healed me.

Ever since then my highest creed has been Divine Science, which, reduced to human apprehensions, I have named Christian Science. This Sacred Science teaches man that God is his only Life, and that this Life is Truth and Love; that God is to be understood and demonstrated, instead of believed and feared; that divine understanding casts out human error and heals the sick.

REDEMPTION OF SOCIETY

As America's social disorders mounted, many became convinced that the basic illness was public, not private. Salvation of souls was commendable, but salvation of the system was imperative. Let us suppose, in Moody's terms, that the heart of a man be changed. Then let us suppose he is returned to the twelve-hour day, seven-day week at the steel mill; his wife and even his small children, taken from school, are employed elsewhere to help sustain the family; all return to a squalid, sunless, depressing tenement to make their devotions before falling wearily onto a blanket spread on a cold floor. The man's heart has been changed, but for how long and to what end? Has all duty been done, all redeeming effort been exhausted?

Sociology, both as a word and as a field of study, developed in the nineteenth century, drawing attention to the effects of environment on the moral, intellectual, and spiritual life of man. Convinced that man motivated by religion could alter his environment, Jewish and Christian reformers also acknowledged that environment could alter, deform, or degrade a man—even a religious man. The application of newly discovered sociological and economic principles to America's crises came to be known, in Protestant circles, as the "social gospel." But under whatever banner, leaders from every religious tradition explored ways to sanctify the social order (see Fig. 14).

Industrial problems

Industry's development led to an accumulation of vast wealth on the one hand and an aggregation of a vast laboring force on the other. In the small-farm, independent-artisan days of the early republic, society escaped a massive struggle between labor and capital. But between the Civil War and World War I the specter of class war loomed. Unionization, wage scales, working hours, working conditions, monopoly, private property, single tax, tariff, free competition, free silver—these issues set debtor against creditor, labor against capital, citizen against citizen.

The rights and responsibilities of labor involved synagogue and church most deeply and raised the moral issues most inescapably. In the 1880's

14. Sweatshops of New York City, 1888

16. Mary Baker Eddy Enters her Carriage, 1910

15. Washington Gladden in His Study, Columbus, Ohio

17. "The Boss": Corruption in The City • Cartoon by Walter Appleton Clark in Collier's Weekly, November 10, 1906.

strikes, lockouts, boycotts, and riots plunged America into industrial war. Since the employer was generally a native, the employee generally an immigrant, "the ominous separation of the American people into two nations" rested on ethnic and religious differences as well as on economics. With labor accused of pushing toward socialism, with business charged with retreating toward feudalism, democracy itself was endangered.

Much of Protestantism, especially that of a far earlier immigration, defended the position of the business community. Here its major membership and support lay, and here divine favor seemed to rest on thrift, industry, and faithful church attendance. The laboring man, charged with spending more time in saloons and union associations than in churches, could hardly hope to prosper. "Change your hearts." But labor's heart was hardening against what looked like at best the indifference of religion, at worst its collusion with a systematic exploitation.

A few prophets stood against the current, their very isolation increasing their eminence. Washington Gladden, Congregationalist pastor in Columbus, Ohio, called for a religion of relevance, a Christianity applied to the no-longer-to-be-ignored ugly sores of modern life. "The one thing needful," he announced, "is the application to all human relations of the Christian law of brotherhood" (see Fig. 15).

When an 1884 coal strike involved members of his own congregation, Gladden struggled to bring some good will and brotherhood. "The doctrine which bases all the relations of employer and employed upon self-interest is," he wrote, "a doctrine of the pit; it has been bringing hell to earth in large instalments for a good many years." Defending labor's right to organize and showing that increased production brought no increase in wages, Gladden recommended a profit-sharing system and a reduction in working hours without a reduction in pay. Both labor and capital must be checked by the commonweal, looking toward that day when honorable cooperation replaces fierce competition.

Washington Gladden defends the labor union in *Social Facts and Forces* (1897).

> So long as the present organization of industry continues, the right of working men to combine must be frankly and fully conceded. In view of the stupendous combinations of capital, the refusal to permit the combination of laborers is a gross injustice. . . . A large number of the most bitter and destructive conflicts between labor and capital have been fought on this issue. In every such conflict my sympathies are wholly with the working men. The attempt to deprive them of the right to stand together for their own defense is one that they ought to resist by all lawful means, and they ought to know that all men who hate oppression are on their side.

Walter Rauschenbusch, Baptist pastor and later seminary professor, spoke powerfully for the application of Christian principles to social and economic life. If religion has power, then it must use that power for a worthy social order. For "the religious spirit always intensifies thought, enlarges hope, unfetters daring, evokes the willingness to sacrifice, and gives coherence in the fight. Under the warm breath of religious faith, all social institutions become plastic."

Admitting that labor unions seek the welfare of their own groups, Rauschenbusch pointed out that few loyalties have been world-wide. "Christian love itself checks its pace when it crosses the threshold of its own particular Church," he confessed. "Why should we demand of one of the lowest classes, fighting on the borderland of poverty, an unselfish devotion to all society which the upper classes have never shown?" The unions, he argued, stand "for human life against profits." Capitalism "makes the margin of life narrow in order to make the margin of profit wide."

In his *Prayers of the Social Awakening* (1909) Walter Rauschenbusch offered a petition on behalf of "children who work."

For Children Who Work

O Thou great Father of the weak, lay thy hand tenderly on all the little children on earth and bless them. Bless our own children, who are life of our life, and who have become the heart of our heart. Bless every little child-friend that has leaned against our knee and refreshed our soul by its smiling trustfulness. Be good to all children who long in vain for human love, or for flowers and water, and the sweet breast of Nature. But bless with a sevenfold blessing the young lives whose slender shoulders are already bowed beneath the yoke of toil, and whose glad growth is being stunted forever. Suffer not their little bodies to be utterly sapped, and their minds to be given over to stupidity and the vices of an empty soul. We have all jointly deserved the millstone of thy wrath for making these little ones to stumble and fall. Grant all employers of labor stout hearts to resist enrichment at such a price. Grant to all citizens and officers of state which now permit this wrong the grace of holy anger. Help us to realize that every child of our nation is in very truth our child, a member of our great family. By the Holy Child that nestled in Mary's bosom; by the memories of our own childhood joys and sorrows; by the sacred possibilities that slumber in every child, we beseech thee to save us from killing the sweetness of young life by the greed of gain.

Radically critical of the greed he saw in the economic realm, Rauschenbusch was equally critical of the complacency he found in the religious realm. Modern-day revivalists, he scornfully observed, produce only "skin-deep changes. Things have simmered down to signing a card, shaking hands, or being introduced to the evangelist." A torn and bleeding society, rent by industrial war, needed more than that. So did religion. "If we seek to keep Christian doctrine unchanged, we shall ensure its abandonment."

Catholicism, drawing more support in America from the working classes, generally defended labor's position. Papal pronouncements, notably the encyclical of Pope Leo XIII issued in 1891, strengthened Catholics in America. *Rerum novarum* elevated the whole dispute to the higher ground of social justice. The pope even justified state intervention into industry's affairs that evils might be remedied, dangers decreased. This important step helped remove the terrifying tag of "socialism" from any suggestion that public authority should mediate, inspect, supervise, or legislate in industrial concerns.

A few years before Leo's encyclical the American hierarchy prevented an open condemnation of the Knights of Labor, then the major association of workingmen in the United States. When Archbishop James Gibbons went to Rome in 1887 to receive his cardinal's hat, his timely defense of the Knights averted a double loss: to the laborer, his union; to the Church, the workers' sympathies and affection. Other members of the hierarchy, notably John Ireland, John J. Keane, and John L. Spalding, also recognized the legitimacy of associations that granted dignity and security to labor.

In 1887 James Cardinal Gibbons memorialized the Holy See, defending the Knights of Labor.

A third danger [in condemning the Knights of Labor]—and the one which most keenly touches our hearts—is the risk of losing the love of the children of the Church, and of pushing them into an attitude of resistance against their Mother. The world presents no more beautiful spectacle than that of their filial devotion and obedience; but it is well to recognize that, in our age and country, obedience cannot be blind. We would greatly deceive ourselves if we expected it. Our Catholic working men sincerely believe that they are only seeking justice, and seeking it by legitimate means. A condemnation would be considered both false and unjust, and, therefore, not binding. We might preach to them submission and confidence in the Church's judgment, but these good dispositions could hardly go so far. They love the Church, and they wish to save their souls, but they must also earn their living, and labor is now so organized that without belonging to the organization it is almost impossible to earn one's living.

Espousing the Judeo-Christian view of man, Archbishop Ireland deplored the tendency to view labor as a mere commodity to be bargained and bartered for as cheaply as possible. "I hate that view of labor," he wrote, "which makes it a mechanical force, like the rotation of a railroad engine or a turbine, purchaseable at mere market value. I must see at all times the living generator of labor—the man, my own brother and the child of the Supreme God—and in availing myself of human labor I must keep well in mind the dignity and rights of man."

Urban problems

In health, housing, morals, education, and a host of other areas the metropolis confronted church and synagogue with tasks of staggering proportion. These tasks became either opportunities or burdens: opportunities when religion met the challenge, burdens of guilt and shame when problems outran solutions. The immigrant journalist Jacob Riis pictured tenement life in New York in *How the Other Half Lives*; no rosy tones brightened his palette.

In *How the Other Half Lives* (1890) Jacob Riis described the churches' losing battle in the slums.

> Where God builds a church the devil builds next door a saloon, is an old saying that has lost its point in New York. Either the devil was on the ground first, or he has been doing a good deal more in the way of building. I tried once to find out how the account stood, and counted to 111 Protestant churches, chapels and places of worship of every kind below Fourteenth Street, 4,065 saloons. The worst half of the tenement population lives down there, and it has to this day the worst half of the saloons. Uptown the account stands a little better, but there are easily ten saloons to every church today. I am afraid, too, that the congregations are larger by a good deal; certainly the attendance is steadier and the contributions more liberal the week round, Sunday included.

To correct industrial abuses the reformers frequently looked to the national government for help. But in urban crime and sin the city governments were often part of the corruption. Political machines, fraudulent voting, and demagoguery scarcely encouraged moral crusades at the local level. The city corporations can use their power, Washington Gladden sadly observed, "to undermine morality, to debauch the consciences of citizens, to lower the standards of business integrity and to pervert the judgment of the youth. . . . I can think of few influences that would more effectively uplift and confirm social morality than that of a good city government" (see Fig. 17).

Washington Gladden analyzed the effect of the city on human lives in *Social Facts and Forces* (1897).

> So it is that this great political organism [the city], to which enormous power is and must be entrusted, becomes in so many cases an engine of

extortion and oppression. The public health is sacrificed through defective drainage, and uncleansed streets and impure water; the slums that breed physical and moral pestilence are left untouched; all the manifold beneficent provision that the city might make for the welfare of its citizens is neglected; for even supposing that these people could conceive of such beneficence, who would entrust them with the means of realizing it? Evidently, so long as the kind of men are in control of our city governments whom we are now wont to see in power, the fewer the functions we commit to them the better. So long as the civic corporation consists of people who buy school sites for more than the owners ask for them and sell the most precious franchises for a song, it is idle to think of realizing for ourselves, through the medium of the city, those beautiful gains of civilization of which we have been thinking.

The most conspicuous inhumanity of the city was the atrocious housing. Cheerless slums bred disease, encouraged vice, and destroyed human aspiration. Mortality figures, when compared block by block, demonstrated the lethal character of the tenements, where one of every five babies died in infancy. Drunkenness, prostitution, and capital crime tripled as one crossed the discernible line between respectable housing and slum. As for the aspirations of the human race in such an environment, Bishop Spalding eloquently described their pathetic withering away. The tenements, said Jacob Riis, are "dark and deadly dens" where the home loses its sanctity, character is smothered, and children are "damned rather than born" into the world.

John Lancaster Spalding shows the slums shriveling the human spirit in *The Religious Mission* (1880).

There the home is not owned; it cannot be transmitted; it has no mystery; it has no charm. It is a rented room in some promiscuous tenement; it is a shanty in some filthy street or alley. The good and the bad are huddled together; and the poisoned air does no sooner take the bloom from the cheek of childhood than the presence of sin and misery withers the freshness of the heart. The children rush from the narrow quarters and stifling air into the street, and the gutters are their playgrounds. The sounds that greet their ears are the yells of the hawkers of wares and the blasphemous and obscene oaths of the rabble. Through all the changing year they see only the dirty street and the dingy houses. Spring and summer, and autumn and winter, enacting, as they pass over the great world's stage, the divine drama of God to soften and purify the human heart, come and go, and come again, but for these poor waifs no flowers bloom, no birds sing, no brook murmurs. . . .

18. **Home Mission Chapel Car** • *Before the days of airplanes and superhighways, missions often reached Western towns and cities by rail. The car shown above was not "retired" until 1946.*

19. **Urban Worship in Chicago, 1942** • *Sunday services at St. Elizabeth's Roman Catholic Church, South Side.*

IT MUST BE DONE

20. **The Reverend C. H. Parkhurst Cleans Up New York City** • *Thomas Nast shows Presbyterian Parkhurst dropping Tammany Hall's D[e-Lancey] Nicoll in the slot, 1892.*

Settlement houses relieved—as best they could—the terrors, the temptations, the degradation of slum living. Before this institution was born, a missionary visiting the city slum returned each night to his own safer, cleaner part of town. "Suppose," asked one reformer, "that the Lord, when he came on the earth, had come a day at a time and brought his lunch with him, and then gone home to heaven nights?" The point was clear: compassionate neighbor-love comes only from a neighbor. The settlement house moving into the slum became a school, a church, a library, a bath house, a theatre, an art gallery, a bank, a hospital, a refuge, a hope. Whatever it needed to be, it was.

Jane Addams founded the most famous of all, Hull House, on South Halsted Street in Chicago. Begun in 1889, Hull House attracted statewide, then nationwide, and finally worldwide attention as it suffered with its neighbors. While no specific religious instruction was offered, Jane Addams saw Christianity as "a simple and natural expression in the social organism itself." In harmony with the Quaker principles of her father, Miss Addams determined to recognize "the good in every man, even the meanest." Spiritual force, she wrote, is necessary for the success of any settlement; in Hull House "there must be the overmastering belief that all that is noblest in life is common to men as men." Her energies as wide as her sympathies, she threw herself into the battle for social justice, women's rights, civil liberties, child welfare, and international peace—all with unstinted dedication.

Jane Addams described the Settlement House in *Philanthropy and Social Progress* (1893).

> The Settlement, then, is an experimental effort to aid in the solution of the social and industrial problems which are engendered by the modern conditions of life in a great city. It insists that these problems are not confined to any one portion of a city. It is an attempt to relieve, at the same time, the over-accumulation at one end of society and the destitution at the other; but it assumes that this over-accumulation and destitution is most sorely felt in the things that pertain to social and educational advantage. . . . It must be grounded in a philosophy whose foundation is on the solidarity of the human race, a philosophy which will not waver when that race happens to be represented by a drunken woman or an idiot boy. Its residents must be emptied of all conceit of opinion and all self-assertion, and ready to arouse and interpret the public opinion of their neighborhood. They must be content to live quietly side by side with their neighbors until they grow into a sense of relationship and mutual interests. . . . The highest moralists have taught that without the advance and improvement of the whole no man can hope for any lasting improvement in his own moral or material individual condition. The subjective necessity for Social Settlements is identical with that necessity which urges us on toward social and individual salvation.

Gradually the voices of lonely prophets and the examples of heroic saints made their mark. Progressivism in American politics took cues from religious reformers. Seminaries sensitized the social consciences of the next generation's ministry. Denominations directed their corporate attention to the human condition. And at the turn of the century millions read Charles M. Sheldon's fantastically popular best seller *In His Steps*. In this novel the Congregational pastor from Topeka, Kansas, persuaded ordinary men and women in ordinary congregations to apply their religion with extraordinary verve.

Charles M. Sheldon's *In His Steps* was first published serially in 1896; by 1960 over twenty million copies had been sold. Here the fictional Reverend Henry Maxwell speaks.

"What I am going to propose now is something which ought not to appear unusual or at all impossible of execution. Yet I am aware that it will be so regarded by a large number, perhaps, of the members of this church. But in order that we may have a thorough understanding of what we are considering, I will put my proposition very plainly, perhaps bluntly. I want volunteers from the First Church who will pledge themselves, earnestly and honestly for an entire year, not to do anything without first asking the question, 'What would Jesus do?' And after asking that question, each one will follow Jesus as exactly as he knows how, no matter what the result may be."

By 1920 Protestants, Jews, and Catholics had all officially endorsed momentous programs of social reform. In 1908 over twelve million Protestants created a Federal Council of Churches, one of its major purposes being to relate religion powerfully to society's problems. Adopting a "social creed of the churches," the new group pointed to "the mighty task of putting conscience and justice and love into a 'Christian' civilization." Four years later, in 1912, the Council urged social justice in all areas of life. "The final message" breathing through every issue, motivating every concern, was still redemption: "the redemption of the individual in the world, and through him of the world itself, and there is no redemption of either without the redemption of the other."

In 1918 the Central Conference of American Rabbis likewise confronted that "mighty task" of implementing conscience, justice, and love. Declaring that "the dignity of the individual soul before God cannot be lost sight of before men," the Conference argued for a "fundamental reconstruction of our economic organization." In the early 1930's other Jews joined in urging reforms in wages, working conditions, unions, child labor, housing, and civil liberties—resting their case, too, on each human being's "inherent infinite moral worth."

21. *First Jewish Community Center, New York City • Covenant Hall on Orchard Street, founded in 1852, included the Maimonides Free Library, shown here.*

22. *Catholic Social Action Leader: John A. Ryan*

23. *Protestant Social Action Leader: G. Bromley Oxnam*

Under the progressive leadership of Monsignor John A. Ryan, American Catholicism in 1919 made its most significant statement regarding "social reconstruction." To administer many humanitarian efforts required by World War I, America's Roman Catholics had already formed the National Catholic War Council. When the war ended, Ryan, professor at Catholic University of America, presented to the council a program for peace. Recognizing that the "only safeguard of peace is social justice and a contented people," the council's controlling bishops approved Ryan's plan of reform. Catholic social action, temporarily channeled through the War Council, in the 1920's received a permanent institutional base: the National Catholic Welfare Conference.

Literature, lobbies, schools, and annual institutes educated a vast public —Catholic and non-Catholic—in the "principles of charity and justice that have always been held and taught by the Catholic Church." Until his death in 1945 John A. Ryan, "Right Reverend New Dealer," played a major part in this broad, patient process of education. From *A Living Wage* (1906) to his autobiography, *Social Doctrine in Action* (1949), the blunt, bold, restless monsignor rarely permitted the conscience of his Church or his nation to rest. For Ryan the state represented more an instrument for the common good than an agent for individual suppression. And the Church stood as an engine for justice, not as a refuge of reaction. Ryan's voice and pen, Franklin Roosevelt noted in 1939, created for men "an opportunity to share in the things that enrich and ennoble human life."

Before the roaring twenties had spent their fury, both city and factory responded to the persuasive voice of organized religion. Civic reform, as in The Reverend Charles Parkhurst's campaign to clean up New York, came often at the instigation of synagogues and churches. Mayor Tom L. Johnson of Cleveland and Mayor Samuel L. Jones of Toledo freely acknowledged the religious source of their humanitarian and moral reforms. Industrial improvements proceeded from the Unions for Practical Progress, the Social Action Commissions, the Departments of Social Justice, and other centers where religious leadership was determinative. Pulpit pronouncements reached beyond cushioned pew to unsanitary slum, unsafe factory or mine. And from the inspiration of quiet worship, the faithful moved out to a needy world.

Meeting a multitude of needs and fending off a barrage of criticism, advocates of social redemption had little time to develop a full theology. Moreover, the growing prestige of science, the application of Darwin's theses to politics, economics, and religion, and the increasing use of literary and historical criteria in biblical study created theological problems not to be solved in a single decade or a single generation. The search for a new theology was made nonetheless, and by none more earnestly than Rauschenbusch in his *Theology for the Social Gospel* (1917). Interpreting the Kingdom of God as "humanity organized according to the will of

God," Rauschenbusch saw the kingdom as the elevation of human personality, an escape from bigotry, oppression, obligarchy, and monopoly toward a "reign of love [that] tends toward the progressive unity of mankind." The Kingdom of God, he concluded, "embraces the whole of human life," for it is nothing less than the "transfiguration of the social order."

In the first quarter of the twentieth century Protestants, Jews, and Catholics all demonstrated their keen social concern: (1) A Social Creed of the Churches, adopted by the (Protestant) Federal Council of Churches in 1908; (2) A Statement adopted by the Central Conference of American Rabbis in 1918; and (3) The Bishop's Program of Social Reconstruction, adopted by the Administrative Committee of the National Catholic War Council in 1919.

---

(1) We deem it the duty of all Christian people to concern themselves directly with certain practical industrial problems. To us it seems that the churches must stand:

For equal rights and complete justice for all men in all stations of life.

For the rights of all men to the opportunity for self-maintenance, a right ever to be wisely and strongly safeguarded against encroachments of every kind. For the right of workers to some protection against the hardships often resulting from the swift crises of industrial change.

For the principle of conciliation and arbitration in industrial dissensions.

For the protection of the worker from dangerous machinery, occupational disease, injuries and mortality.

For the abolition of child labor.

For such regulation of the conditions of toil for women as shall safeguard the physical and moral health of the community.

For the suppression of the "sweating system" [working under the most adverse conditions, e.g., factories in tenement homes].

For the gradual and reasonable reduction of the hours of labor to the lowest practicable point, and for that degree of leisure for all which is a condition of the highest human life.

For a release from employment one day in seven.

For a living wage as a minimum in every industry, and for the highest wage that each industry can afford.

For the most equitable division of the products of industry that can ultimately be devised.

For suitable provision for the old age of the workers and for those incapacitated by injury.

For the abatement of poverty.

---

(2) The ideal of social justice has always been an integral part of Judaism. It is in accordance with tradition, therefore, that the Central Conference of

American Rabbis submits the following declaration of principles as a program for the attainment of which the followers of our faith should strive:

1. A more equitable distribution of the profits of industry.
2. A minimum wage which will insure for all workers a fair standard of living.
3. The legal enactment of an eight hour day as a maximum for all industrial workers.
4. A compulsory one-day-of-rest-in-seven for all workers.
5. Regulation of industrial conditions to give all workers a safe and sanitary working environment, with particular reference to the special needs of women.
6. Abolition of child labor and raising the standard of age wherever the legal age limit is lower than is consistent with moral and physical health.
7. Adequate workmen's compensation for industrial accidents and occupational diseases.
8. Legislative provision for universal workmen's health insurance and careful study of social insurance methods for meeting the contingencies of unemployment and old age.
9. An adequate, permanent national system of public employment bureaus to make possible the proper distribution of the labor forces of Amercia.
10. Recognition of the right of labor to organize and to bargain collectively.
11. The application of the principles of mediation, conciliation and arbitration to industrial disputes.
12. Proper housing for working-people, secured through government regulation when necessary.
13. The preservation and integrity of the home by a system of mother's pensions.
14. Constructive care of dependents, defectives and criminals, with the aim of restoring them to normal life wherever possible.

---

(3) "Society," said Pope Leo XIII, "can be healed in no other way than by a return to Christian life and Christian institutions." The truth of these words is more widely perceived today than when they were written, more than twenty-seven years ago. Changes in our economic and political systems will have only partial and feeble efficiency if they be not reinforced by the Christian view of work and wealth. Neither the moderate reforms advocated in this paper nor any other program of betterment or reconstruction will prove reasonably effective without a reform in the spirit of both labor and capital. The laborer must come to realize that he owes his employer and society an honest day's work in return for a fair wage, and that conditions cannot be substantially improved until he roots out the desire to get a maximum of return for a minimum of service. The capitalist must likewise get a new viewpoint. He needs to learn the long-forgotten truth that wealth is stewardship, that profit-making is not the basic justifica-

tion of business enterprise, and that there are such things as fair profits, fair interest, and fair prices. Above and before all, he must cultivate and strengthen within his mind the truth which many of his class have begun to grasp for the first time during the present war; namely, that the laborer is a human being, not merely an instrument of production; and that the laborer's right to a decent livelihood is the first moral charge upon industry. . . . This is the human and Christian, in contrast to the purely commercial and pagan, ethics of industry.

PART IV

This Nation Under God:
At Worship

17 ❖ The Word

WHEN THE PRESIDENT OF THE UNITED STATES raises his right hand to take the most solemn oath of office, he places his left hand on the most sacred book for Americans: the Bible. This public act symbolizes a people's private rootage in the Hebrew-Christian scriptures. But were that ceremony abandoned, the very mountains, rivers, and towns would echo the biblical heritage. Place names—nine "Canaans," eleven "Beulahs," twenty-one "Sharons"—repeat from coast to coast a scriptural refrain. Rehoboth may be found in Massachusetts and Maryland; Ebenezer in Mississippi, New York, and South Carolina; Palestine in Arkansas, Illinois, Ohio, and Texas. There is a Jordan Dam in Alabama, a Jordan River in Utah, a Jordan Valley in Oregon, not to mention towns of Jordan in Minnesota, Montana, and New York. St. Paul brightens Minnesota, the Sangre de Cristo (Blood of Christ) Mountains rise in Colorado, Our Lady of Mercy (Merced) River flows in California, and in Utah one may even visit a national park named Zion.

The superficialities of topography, however, only hint at the Bible's full impact on the nation. The book flavored the common man's speech, inspired the artist's brush, determined the poet's imagery, bestowed purpose upon a people. It is *the* book. And the American people, more than they know, are a people of that book.

THE BIBLE IN AMERICAN LIFE

Unspoken assumptions more than dogmatic assertions reveal the theological foundations of a people. In the wellsprings of the American's behavior and belief, the Bible's muted voice is heard.

History

The American conviction of movement, progress, and destiny represents a particular view of history. History has direction, events have meaning, the past fashions the present, and today shapes tomorrow. All this, obvious and familiar, breathes the biblical heritage. "In the beginning, God . . ." Out of chaos, order. Out of the slavery, Canaan. Out of the folly of idolatry and sin, the emancipation of the chosen. Out of the oppression of powerful enemies, deliverance and redemption, vindication and blessedness. God was in the fiery furnace, said the author of Daniel; therefore senseless suffering made sense. God was in Christ, said the author of Corinthians; thereby death lost its sting. God was in the world, said the authors of Jewish and Christian scripture; therefore aimless whirl became purpose and plan.

Not a circle but a line, history had a beginning and an end, an alpha and an omega. All history had meaning, but not all meaning was found in history. For God was beyond history as well as in it. But one read history as he read nature, as he read scripture, as he read himself—through a veil. Knowing that he now saw through a glass darkly, one pursued his course, steadied by the assurance that "in the fullness of time" all truth would be known, and all history's puzzling pieces would fit.

From Jamestown to Plymouth, from Boston to Newcastle, from St. Mary's City to Providence, the biblical view of history prevailed. Because it prevailed, a scattered people found strength to form a more perfect union. If calamity struck, it was God's call to profounder repentance, purer zeal. If good fortune came, it was God's bounty poured out upon an obedient people. Found faithful over a few things, the servant nation was challenged to be faithful over much. And in the nineteenth-century expansion across the continent and over the seas, divine largess was evident to all.

In the twentieth century, confidence in the biblical view of history faltered. President Wilson's idealism brought sarcasm and cynical rebuke. Crumbling traditions of morality and changing attitudes toward authority turned the 1920's into an irrational binge of sensuality. The havoc of the Great Crash, followed by the horror of the Second World War left a nation reeling off center, uncertain of its purpose and unsure of its judgment. As national goals were re-examined, many turned again to a biblical sense of destiny, a biblical base for patient humility.

Morality

The monotheism of the Judeo-Christian heritage is ethical in origin and ethical in effect. Ancient Israel's great prophets saw the oneness of God as the necessary consequence of universal moral demands. From all men—Ethiopians, Medes, Jews—justice and righteousness demanded the same. To all men, even Nineveh's unrepentant crowd, the promises of a God who made Pleiades and Orion offered the same. And if the God of Abraham, Isaac, and Jacob could not be bought off, hoodwinked, or traded in for a more indulgent deity, then morality must be taken seriously.

This intimate bond between religion and morality gave essential cohesion to America's democratic society. Each citizen bore responsibility, moral no less than political. Of course, Americans, like all other fallible souls, concentrated more readily on the fluff and foam of ethical demands, often forgetting the "weightier matters of the law." Such moral evasion, however, found little scriptural sanction. In the eighth century B.C. Micah summarized the moral law in words carved all over America: "It has been told thee, O man, what is good, and what the Lord doth require of thee: Only to do justly, and to love mercy, and to walk humbly with thy God."

In America, therefore, religions so diverse, so fractious, so splintered made common moral demands. Puritanism no less than perfectionism, deism no less that pietism, Catholicism no less than Judaism accepted the great moral commands and honored the great moral teachers. For all its variety religion in America searched for its own confirmation in its ability to change man's lives. Neither mysticism nor passive resignation, neither sacramentalism nor tradition, but voluntary, active, responsible behavior marked the concern of the nation's faithful. Morality became the measure of all things.

Culture

In the century following the Civil War a whole new way of life evolved. Revolutions in industry, in agriculture, in science, in international affairs made the child of the twentieth century a stranger to his forebears. Life did not greatly differ from Cato's farm to Lincoln's, but a mere century after Lincoln all was new. Transportation and communication made only snail-paced advances from Cicero's Senate to Henry Clay's, but the drastic changes in the succeeding hundred years provoked wonder, rapture, or fright.

Inevitable questions arose: can an ancient volume, written in a far-removed pastoral age, speak to a spiraling, rocketing, technological age? Can atomic physics and biblical ethics both be true? Who is to say how the earth was made: geology or Genesis? Which tells more of the nature of man: Darwin's barnacles or Tennessee's Bibles? Who best judges the whereabouts of God: the soaring cosmonaut or the plodding cleric? Which will save civilization: science or religion?

Throughout the century after Charles Darwin's *Origin of Species* burst upon an unsuspecting world in 1859 these questions challenged the minds and burned the hearts of men. While the whole theological fortress was under attack, the crucial rampart for many was the Bible. If this bastion fell, all else collapsed. But even before the battle could begin, dissension arose within the gates. Some suggested that the Bible may not be without error, that it may not be authoritative, that it may not be the sole repository of truth.

Especially for Protestantism the question of an infallible book loomed large. Torn by contrary views and aroused by intemperate controversy, "fundamentalists" at one extreme drew up against "modernists" at the other, each term, of course, being hurled by the opposing force at the "enemy within." Between the extremes many mediated wherever possible, looking for ways to embrace both the Bible and the modern world without alienating the affections of either.

Unfriendly observers might characterize fundamentalism as a rigid, uncritical, naïve worship of "an inerrant book"; modernism as a weak, uncritical, naïve worship of "an omniscient science." The friendly critic, on the other hand, might describe fundamentalism as an honorable defense of Christian revelation, the supernatural realm, and the faith "once delivered unto the saints"; modernism as an honorable offense, relating Christianity to the newest discoveries of science and the newest needs of society. To choose one's weapons and labels was the first step in a bruising theological brawl.

Harry Emerson Fosdick comments in *The Modern Use of the Bible* (1925) on new ways of understanding biblical writing.

> The old Book has moved into a new world. There are sharp contrasts between some ways of thinking in the Bible and our own. There is no use obscuring the fact. We would better set it out in the clear light and deal with it. For if we who are the disciples of the Lord do not do it in the interests of his people and his cause, it will be ruinously done for us by those who are his enemies. . . .
>
> If there are new ways of approaching men's minds, new methods of argument and apologetic, let us have them and not fight like fools with bows and arrows at Verdun, when the One we are fighting for is so worthy of the best that we can do. If there are new powers disclosed by science, let us have them and put them at the disposal of the Lord of life to make our service more efficient! All that we know at the service of the Highest we know—that is the ideal!

The most famous clash, though not the most significant in American religion, occurred in Dayton, Tennessee, in the hot summer of 1925. John Scopes, a young high school teacher of biology, was tried for violating the state law that prohibited the teaching of evolution. Because of the star performers at the trial, the "Scopes Trial" drew nationwide attention. William Jennings Bryan, three-time candidate for president of the United States and national spokesman for fundamentalism, served as prosecuting attorney, while the defense of Scopes fell to Chicago's brilliant, well-known lawyer Clarence Darrow. To heighten the drama even further, Henry L. Mencken, the nation's most erudite, volatile, and uninhibited reporter, covered the trial for the *Baltimore Sun*.

The immediate issue before the court was, of course, whether John Scopes had violated Tennessee law. But the issue before the country was far larger than that—as Darrow and Bryan both readily recognized. For Bryan the whole trial was trumped up so as to destroy the Bible and ridicule religion. "My only purpose in coming to Dayton," Bryan declared with a glance at Darrow, was "to protect the word of God against the greatest atheist or agnostic in the United States!" The courtroom burst with applause (see Fig. 1).

For Darrow nothing less than intellectual freedom was on trial. The Bible was not being destroyed, Darrow argued, but learning and common sense were. He concluded one of his passionate declamations for the defense in these words: "After awhile, your Honor, it is the setting of man against man and creed against creed until with flying banners and beating drums we are marching backward to the glorious ages of the Sixteenth Century when bigots lighted fagots to burn the men who dared to bring any intelligence and enlightenment and culture to the human mind." The courtroom did not burst with applause, but most of the country did.

When all was over, Scopes was found guilty and a token fine was imposed. But the nation as a whole assessed guilt and innocence differently. Outside of Dayton fundamentalism lost its case. After the 1920's fundamentalism no longer seriously contended for the mind of America, though the dying body flailed out here and there to wreck a career or divide a denomination or denounce an enemy.

Which is not to say that the victory went to modernism, for it did not. The closing decade of the nineteenth century saw several trials not as spectacular as Dayton's but ultimately more costly to the nation's religious life. As suspect pastors and professors were evicted from positions of responsibility, denominations busied themselves with morbid introspection and bled themselves of creative individuals. Presbyterians, Baptists,

1. William Jennings Bryan, 1919 • Bryan here receives a silver loving cup from the National Dry Federation (of which he was then president) for his gallantry in the cause of prohibition.

Methodists, Episcopalians, and Disciples of Christ, in some degree, all suffered dissension and recrimination.

Gradually the extremes withered away as fundamentalists began to adopt critical methods in biblical study, as modernists began to acknowledge that salvation by science was a ridiculous expectation. Harry Emerson Fosdick, a storm center himself, in the 1930's said of his own liberal wing: "We have at times gotten so low down that we talked as though the highest compliment that could be paid Almighty God was that a few scientists believed in Him." And John G. Machen of Princeton Theological Seminary, at the head of the fundamentalist charge, by that time also dropped the virulent hostility characteristic of the controversy a decade earlier. If positions remained the same, assurances that all who differed were traitors began to waver or fade.

John Gresham Machen comments in *The Christian Faith in the Modern World* (1936) on the inspiration of the biblical writing.

> What, then, shall we think about the Bible? I will tell you very plainly what I think we ought to think. I will tell you very plainly what I think about it. I hold that the Biblical writers, after having been prepared for their task by the providential ordering of their lives, received, in addition to all that, a blessed and wonderful and supernatural guidance and impulsion by the Spirit of God, so that they were preserved from the errors that appear in other books and thus the resulting book, the Bible, is in all its parts the very Word of God, completely true in what it says regarding matters of fact and completely authoritative in its commands.
>
> That is the doctrine of full or "plenary" inspiration of Holy Scripture.

Catholicism revealed similar tensions. In 1893 Pope Leo XIII issued an encyclical, *Providentissimus Deus*, which encouraged a search for a purer biblical text but discouraged investigation behind the manuscripts to lost "originals." Private study, moreover, must always be under the guidance of "our Holy Mother the Church, whose place it is to judge of the true sense and interpretation of the Scriptures." Leo further averred that it is "absolutely wrong" to declare "that the sacred writer has erred." The Holy Spirit employed fallible men, it is true, but by supernatural power "He so moved and impelled them to write—He so assisted them when writing," that the results were "apt words" and "infallible truth."

Pope Leo XIII in *Providentissimus Deus* (1893) writes on biblical inspiration and authority.

> For all the books which the Church receives as sacred and canonical are written wholly and entirely, with all their parts, at the dictation of the Holy Spirit; and so far is it from being possible that any error can exist with inspiration, that inspiration not only is essentially incompatible with

error, but excludes and rejects it as absolutely and necessarily as it is impossible that God Himself, the supreme Truth, can utter that which is not true. This is the ancient and unchanging faith of the Church, solemnly defined in the Councils of Florence and Trent, and finally confirmed and more expressly formulated by the Council of the Vatican [1870]. . . . It follows that those who maintain that an error is possible in any genuine passage of the sacred writings either pervert the Catholic notion of inspiration or make God the author of such error.

On the fiftieth anniversary of Leo's encyclical, Pope Pius XII issued *Divino afflante spiritu* ("Inspired by the Divine Spirit"), which gave great impetus to Catholic biblical scholarship. Acknowledging that many problems of translation and of interpretation remained unsolved, Pius urged Catholic scholars on to the waiting tasks. At the same time he warned the overly cautious to abandon their automatic suspicion of anything new. All human knowledge, the pontiff observed, "even the non-sacred, has indeed its own proper dignity and excellence, being a finite participation in the infinite knowledge of God."

Pope Pius XII in *Divino afflante spiritu* (1943) declares the necessity of biblical study and contemporary investigation.

What is the literal sense of a passage is not always as obvious in the speeches and writings of the ancient authors of the East, as it is in the works of our own time. For what they wished to express is not to be determined by the rules of grammar and philology alone, nor solely by the context; the interpreter must, as it were, go back wholly in spirit to those remote centuries of the East and with the aid of history, archaeology, ethnology, and other sciences, accurately determine what modes of writing, so to speak, the authors of that ancient period would be likely to use, and in fact did use. . . . Nevertheless, no one, who has a correct idea of biblical inspiration, will be surprised to find, even in the Sacred Writers, as in other ancient authors, certain fixed ways of expounding and narrating, certain definite idioms, especially of a kind peculiar to the Semitic tongues, so-called approximations, and certain hyperbolical modes of expression, nay, at times, even paradoxical, which even help to impress the ideas more deeply on the mind.

Spurred by such encouragement, the Church's contribution to biblical study escaped "the mentality of the beleaguered fortress." New societies, new seminary offerings, new archaeological investigations, new translations testified to a new spirit after World War I. "No one who accepts the Bible as the word of God can feel comfortable when this book is praised by every one and read and understood by almost no one." These words, while written by a Catholic, just as readily reflect the contemporary opinion of Protestant or Jew.

Jewish biblical studies also showed the same stresses of Christianity. Orthodox Judaism, maintaining centuries-old traditions, accepted the Bible as the revealed will of God. It was to be read and studied only in Hebrew; it was to be obeyed in every particular. Reform Judaism as early as 1885

Herman Wouk in *This Is My God* (1959) comments on the nature and content of the Torah from the viewpoint of Orthodox Judaism.

> [Moses'] law comprises five books of the Bible, the first five: Genesis, Exodus, Leviticus, Numbers, and Deuteronomy. For the Jewish people these five are one book, the Torah, the heart of Scripture; given to Israel at Sinai, and binding to this hour on the descendants of those who were there.
>
> If one asks who legislated this law, the answer is Moses. If one asks what his authority was, the answer is that we believe he was inspired by Providence and we know he was elected by Israel to write founding statutes that have virtually spanned recorded time. We call art inspired when passing years cannot dim it. It is no proof of Moses' inspiration that his law still lives—nothing can prove that if his words do not—but the rock-like strength of his law at least makes it one of the marvels of history.

---

declared that the Bible reflects "the primitive ideas of its own age" and at times uses "miraculous narratives" to convey its conceptions of divine providence and justice. With respect to the laws of Moses (the Torah), "We accept as binding only its moral laws and maintain only such ceremonials as elevate and sanctify our lives." Occupying a middle position, Conservative Judasim followed more closely the ceremonial as well as the ethical demands of the Torah. Recognizing the evolving nature of religion, however, Conservative Jews proved ready to adapt to changing needs.

The Central Conference of American Rabbis (Reform Judaism) in 1937 offered this comment on the origin and authority of the Torah.

> God reveals Himself not only in the majesty, beauty and orderliness of nature, but also in the vision and moral striving of the human spirit. Revelation is a continuous process, confined to no one group and to no one age. Yet the people of Israel, through its prophets and sages, achieved unique insight in the realm of religious truth. The Torah, both written and oral [tradition], enshrines Israel's ever-growing consciousness of God and of moral law. It preserves the historical precedents, sanctions the norms of Jewish life, and seeks to mold it in the patterns of goodness and holiness. Being products of historical processes, certain of its laws have lost their binding force with the passing of the conditions that brought them forth.

But as a depository of permanent spiritual ideals, the Torah remains the dynamic source of the life of Israel. Each age has the obligation to adapt the teachings of the Torah to its basic needs in consonance with the genius of Judaism.

Jewish biblical studies also include the oral traditions based on written law. The voluminous Talmud contains the opinions, maxims, rules, and reminiscences of about a thousand rabbis over a period of almost as many years. This "Oral Torah" or "Traditional Lore," like the "Written Torah," commands allegiance varying in degree and kind. Yet its very purpose, to keep Judaism flexible and relevant to successive ages, was at the heart of the twentieth-century controversy about a sacred book: how was it to be studied? in what language was it to be read? what authority and significance did it have? With these questions in their hearts Christians and Jews first sought agreement among themselves in order to face bravely the absurdities that a modern world presented.

Rabbi Hillel summarizes the meaning of the Torah or Law of Moses (taken from the Talmud).

A heathen came to Hillel and asked to be converted to Judaism, provided he be taught all the tenets and principles of Judaism while standing on one foot. Hillel agreed, and said to him: "Do not unto others what thou wouldst not have others do unto you. This is the whole Torah, the rest is merely a commentary on it."

THE BIBLE IN AMERICAN LITERATURE

Marking the beginning of American publishing, the *Bay Psalm Book*, published in 1640, also initiated the enduring alliance between biblical influences and American literature. Novelist, dramatist, versifier, and poet reflect biblical style, image, rhetoric, and idea. A nation without a history, by claiming Jehovah's eternal promise, swiftly acquired a hoary past: you shall be my people, and I will be your God. A people without other unifying heritage or common tradition responded to the symbols, the ceremonies, the personalities, and the events of Palestine's ancient lore.

From Anne Bradstreet and Edward Taylor through Herman Melville and Nathaniel Hawthorne to William Faulkner and Robert Penn Warren, biblical imagery and even biblical theology steadily flow, depositing scriptural silt in unlikely places. When John Steinbeck writes *The Pearl*, he assumes a general awareness of the "pearl of great price" and of the eagerness with which it was sought. When Faulkner entitles a novel *Absalom! Absalom!*, readers readily supply the necessary context of powerful father and rebellious son, of evil Amnon and abused Tamar. When

In William Faulkner's *The Bear* one of the characters speaks of "some things He said in the Book."

> "And I know what you will say now: That if truth is one thing to me and another thing to you, how will we choose which is truth? You dont need to choose. The heart already knows. He didn't have His Book written to be read by what must elect and choose, but by the heart, not by the wise of the earth because maybe they dont need it or maybe the wise no longer have any heart, but by the doomed and lowly of the earth who have nothing else to read with but the heart. Because the men who wrote His Book for Him were writing about truth and there is only one truth and it covers all things that touch the heart."

Ernest Hemingway portrays the indomitable Santiago, carrying his boat's heavy mast like a cross up steep Golgotha, the parallels and allusions need no prompter. When Saul Bellow refers to Daniel and Nebuchadnezzar in *Henderson the Rain King*, he provides no glossary, for none is needed. And when Archibald MacLeish presents *J.B.* on Broadway, he can be assured that the original biblical drama will, for good or ill, affect his play's impact and reception.

In James Baldwin's *Go Tell It On the Mountain* (1953) the boy preacher expounds on Isaiah 6:5.

> "For God had a plan. He would not suffer the soul of man to die, but had prepared a plan for his salvation. In the beginning, way back there at the laying of the foundations of the world, God had a plan, *amen!* to bring all flesh to a knowledge of the truth. In the beginning was the Word and the Word was with God and the Word was God—yes, and in Him was life, *hallelujah!* and this life was the light of men. Dearly beloved, when God saw how men's hearts waxed evil, how they turned aside, each to his own way, how they married and gave in marriage, how they feasted on ungodly meat and drink, and lusted, and blasphemed, and lifted up their hearts in sinful pride against the Lord—oh, then, the Son of God, the blessed lamb that taketh away the sins of the world, this Son of God who was the Word made flesh, the fulfillment of promise—oh, then, He turned to His Father, crying: 'Father, prepare me a body and I'll go down and redeem sinful man.' "

The preceding paragraph is not a parade of orthodoxies. Biblical symbol may protest a prevailing orthodoxy, may ridicule a patent superficiality, may probe behind or beyond the trite convention. But the point remains: American literature employs biblical thought because there reside those mysteries and marvels confronting all men in life and in death. With the crises of the soul every serious artist is concerned. And as he attempts to communicate, he discovers that patriarchs, prophets, and apostles are still heroic messengers of faith, that Eden's bowers still bloom, that the City of David still beckons, the star over Bethlehem still shines.

More than mere literary allusion is involved. In contemporary America one's views of man, nature, and God may reflect or recoil from biblical views, but they cannot ignore the Jewish and Christian heritage. Is man the glory or the folly of the universe? Is he perfect or perfectible, sinful but redeemable, amoral and contemptible? To what does man owe his ultimate loyalty? What is the source of his values, the sanction for his conduct? What, if anything, does he mean by "God"? To this last question the poet Edwin Arlington Robinson offered an answer in *King Jasper*:

> I don't say what God is, but it's a name
> That somehow answers us when we are driven
> To feel and think how little we have to do
> With what we are.

Reaching for expression of ultimates, the artist in America adopts the only metaphysics meaningful to him and his public: biblical thought.

Arthur Miller's play *After the Fall*, opened in the new Repertory Theater of New York City's Lincoln Center early in 1964. In a special foreword to the play Miller wrote:

> The first real "story" in the Bible is the murder of Abel. Before this drama there is only a featureless Paradise. But in that Eden there was peace because man had no consciousness of himself nor any knowledge of sex or his separateness from plants or other animals. Presumably we are being told that the human being becomes "himself" in the act of becoming aware of his sinfulness. He "is" what he is ashamed of.
>
> After all, the infraction of Eve is that she opened up the knowledge of good and evil. She presented Adam with a choice. So that where choice begins, Paradise ends, Innocence ends, for what is Paradise but the absence of any need to choose this action? And two alternatives open out to Eden. One is Cain's alternative . . . to express without limit one's unbridled inner compulsion, in this case to murder, and to plead unawareness as a virtue and a defense. The other course is what roars through the rest of the Bible and all history—the struggle of the human race through the millenia to pacify the destructive impulses of man, to express his wishes for greatness, for wealth, for accomplishment, for love, but without turning law and peace into chaos.

The decade of the 1920's, when the "modern temper" rejected traditional morality and T. S. Eliot wrote *The Waste Land*, reflected little biblical light. A flirtation with Marxism in the 1930's occupied some but not all of the literary establishment. But as war clouds gathered and debas-

2. *"Moses," Lee Lawrie*

3. *"Ezekiel," Lee Lawrie*

4. *"Hagar and Ishmael," Benjamin West*

5. *"Jonah," Albert Pinkham Ryder*

6. "Holy Family," John Trumbull

8. "Visit of Nicodemus to Christ," John LaFarge

7. "The Prodigal Son," Heinz Warneke

9. *"The Crucifixion,"* Rico Lebrun

10. *"Our Saviour with Little Children,"* John Trumbull

ing ideologies prospered, biblical views of man and of history won new respect and voice. Phyllis McGinley's "Carol with Variations" saw little harmony between the modern temper and an ancient one. And Ludwig Lewisohn wrote in *The Last Days of Shylock* of that "intelligible and eternal world of values" which must "stream into the world of the senses and touch it and heal it and mayhap save it. . . ."

In the depth of World War II, if not before, the force behind Aldous Huxley's quiet understatement struck home: "The abolition of God left a perceptible void." Postwar literature and art, saturated with despair and nauseated by dread, thrashed about for an exit. Suspicious of any message-bearing novel, play, or poem, many artists declared the only message to be that there was no message. But others returned to "the pit from which we were digged"—the biblical heritage.

Henry Roth's only novel *Call it Sleep*, first published in 1934, enjoyed a remarkable revival a generation later. In 1965 he commented on the writing of that book.

> I finished it when I was 27, and for the 3½ years up till then I was in a sort of general mystical state. I had a sense about the unifying force of some power I neither knew nor had to bother to know. It was part of having been an Orthodox Jew. I wasn't formally religious any more, but still the Hebrew uprightness of that orthodoxy was diffused in me. I could see a gleam wherever I looked. Most writers have to rely on their environments to feed them. I didn't then. Something inside fed me.

The American-born Anglican T. S. Eliot, weary of the inanities and sterility of religionless culture, explored with new hope and searching sensitivity the richness of Christian litany and life. Robert Frost in *A Masque of Reason* probed Job-like the perennial mysteries of the universe. In *Sunday Morning* Wallace Stevens despaired of that frivolous modernity that drowns out "the holy hush of ancient sacrifice." Thomas Merton, Catholic contemplative, called for poets for whom "the whole world and all the incidents of life tend to be sacraments—signs of God, signs of His love working in the world."

In the American novel, too, the time of defensive reaction against religion's heritage had passed. The Bible obstructing knowledge, religion perverting justice, clergymen reveling in ignorance, avarice, and sloth—this was truth, to be sure, but it was never the whole truth. Edwin O'Connor's *Edge of Sadness* (1961), Conrad Richter's *A Simple Honorable Man* (1962), and Noah Gordon's *The Rabbi* (1965) all found faith more than buffoonery and fraud. Contemporary literature seemed less willing, in Walter Lippmann's words, to trade "a majestic faith for a trivial illusion."

18 ❖ The Belief

IN ONE RESPECT Americans seem a peculiarly nondogmatic people, wary of theological system, averse to metaphysical speculation. But in another respect they appear ever eager to state their convictions and declare their beliefs, responding with hurt or surprise if everyone does not fully agree with them. Americans do not want to be found guilty either of believing too much or of believing too little.

Suspicions against systematic theology did not prevail until the nineteenth century. Then a combination of rationalistic deism and romantic pietism made "metaphysical" a dishonorable word and theory an unprofitable servant. Religion was simply morality or simply feeling or simply habit; in any case, it was simple. And all attempts to explain, to expound, to analyze, or to theorize were—almost by definition—obstructive and vain.

Earlier generations in America exhibited no such hostility to speculation. The English Puritans, the Scottish realists, the German confessionalists "justified the ways of God to man" with acumen, earnestness, and verve. To be sure, much early American theology was imported, as was inevitable in a civilization hardly begun. Yet British and Continental thought emerged from the crucible of American experience always in altered form. If it is too much to claim an American theology, it is only enough to recognize that theology was shaped by America even as it helped to transform that wilderness.

Benjamin Franklin wrote to Yale's President Ezra Stiles, March 9, 1790.

> You desire to know something of my religion. It is the first time I have been questioned upon it. But I cannot take your curiosity amiss, and shall endeavor in a few words to gratify it. Here is my creed. I believe in one God, Creator of the Universe. That he governs it by his Providence. That he ought to be worshipped. That the most acceptable service we render to him is doing good to his other children. That the soul of man is immortal, and will be treated in justice in another life respecting its conduct in this. These I take to be the fundamental principles of all sound religion, and I regard them as you do in whatever sect I meet with them.

After a constitution had been written and a new nation born, theology confronted a proliferating religious diversity amply nourished by a continuing religious freedom. In such a context theology was free: free to stagnate, hibernate, or explore. It did all three.

Stagnation came about in two ways. First, the gradual, steady surrender of intellectual standards for the clergy undercut religious leadership in national life. Second, theology was often reduced to a soft sentimentality, to a good neighbor policy, or to an endorsement of material success. Obedience to Ecclesiastes' command came all too easily: "Drink thy wine with a merry heart, for God has already approved what you do."

Isolation from the social and intellectual currents of America produced a kind of hibernated theology. Immigrants fearful of a new society or natives resentful of a changing one often withdrew into their own institutional or ethnic shell. After a generation or two, few lines of communication were still open between creed and culture. Like a cyst an insulated, hardened theology continued to exist, but the nation's lifeblood drew from it neither health nor strength. Within the closed circle the creed was comfortingly familiar; outside, it was painfully irrelevant.

William O. Douglas, Associate Justice of the U. S. Supreme Court, speaks of the "faith of our fathers" and of his own as well.

. . . One day in a moment of great crisis I came to understand the words of my father: "If I die it will be glory, if I live it will be grace." That was his evening star. The faith in a power greater than man. That was the faith of our fathers. A belief in a God who controlled man in the universe, that manifested itself in different ways to different people. It was written by scholars and learned men in dozens of different creeds. But riding high above all secular controversies was a faith in One who was the Creator, the Giver of Life, the Omnipotent.

A great many others, however, found America's freedom to be—above all else—a challenge to discover and explore. For these theology was more a probe than a pattern; it invited intellectual daring rather than supine surrender. If liberty meant only lethargy, then freedom's bell was not worth ringing. And theology lost its majesty if it traded the law of inertia for the logos of God.[1]

Edith Hamilton, classicist and writer, suggests that creeds must be incentives to action more than refuges of reason.

The truths of the spirit are proved not by reasoning about them, but only by acting upon them. Their life is dependent upon what we do about them.

---

[1] Theology consists of two Greek words: *theos* (God) and *logos* (reason). One word therefore combines the infinite mystery of the universe with the finite exploration of that universe.

Mercy, gentleness, forgiveness, patience—if we do not show them they will cease to be. Upon us depends the reality of God here on the earth today. "If we love one another God dwelleth in us." Lives are the proof of the reality of God. . . .

God leaves us free. We are free to choose Him or reject Him. No tremendous miracle will come down from heaven to compel us to accept as a fact a Being powerful enough to work it. What would that kind of belief do toward making love or compassion a reality? God puts the truth of Himself into our hands. We must carry the burden of the proof, for His Truth can be proved in no other way. "Glorious is the venture," Socrates said.

Most twentieth-century theology in America has been of this experimental and exploratory type. With a desire not so much to rewrite the ancient creeds as to infuse them with new understanding, theology in the United States bound itself to no narrowly prescribed course.

Americans, when asked what they believe, rarely answer in traditional creedal forms. Something more is expected than a mere recitation of the Apostles' Creed, or Maimonides' Principles, or the Augsburg Confession. And that something is the anticipation that deepest convictions arise from and reflect personal experiences and private hopes. The result is still theology. Indeed, it is usually still Judeo-Christian theology, but the American experience and the American dream are unmistakably stamped upon it. In the informal but clearly personal creeds of Benjamin Franklin, William O. Douglas, Edith Hamilton, and Clarence Randall the private wrestle with theology is readily apparent.

Industrialist and lawyer Clarence Randall argues for the compatibility of freedom and faith.

That the world has meaning seems much more reasonable to me than the hideous concept that everything which surrounds me came about by cosmic accident. This thought again takes me to God, to the conviction that outside of myself there is a source of strength infinitely greater than any within me. I want my life to be in parallel with that eternal power for good.

Not for a moment, however, do I doubt that I am free to accept or reject God, or to make individual choices as to what is good and bad in life. In fact, it is only because I know that I am free to accept God voluntarily that I believe in Him. Unless I am free, I am nothing.

Nor is a more professional theological tussle immune to such personal daring. Resisting the stagnation of archaic thought, the hibernation of irrelevant creed, earnest theologians push ahead the frontiers of religious understanding. In contemporary America Abraham Heschel, Reinhold Niebuhr, and Gustave Weigel (among others) make possible this growing edge in religious thought.

ABRAHAM HESCHEL

Born in Warsaw in 1907, Abraham Heschel, after earning his doctorate at Berlin University, assisted Germany's Jews to revive their cultural and religious life. In 1938, however, Heschel along with all other Polish Jews was expelled from Germany. After a brief period in Poland he came to the United States in 1940, teaching first in Cincinnati's Hebrew Union College, then in 1945 in New York's Jewish Theological Seminary as professor of Jewish ethics and mysticism.

Heschel is not interested in offering answers to questions that nobody asks. Much contemporary religious activity, he recognizes, consists in just this: giving responses that were pertinent a century ago but not now. Thus the sorry state of modern man and his faith. Religion has declined in the present day, Heschel notes, "not because it was refuted, but because it became irrelevant, dull, oppressive, insipid." If answers are to speak to man, they must arise from the most urgent, awesome, terrifying experiences that modern man passes through. Religion is not an avenue of escape from the world but an awareness of and response to reality beyond ourselves.

But does man need such awareness? Does he need to respond to something outside himself? What does he need? Or is religion something more than the satisfaction of a need? Perhaps, Heschel suggests, man must recognize in his own nature not his needs but his anxiety to be needed. "Happiness, in fact, may be defined as the certainty of being needed." Here is a need unlike all others, "striving to give rather than to obtain satisfaction." Religion is so constituted as to meet man's natural anxiety. "Religion begins with the certainty that something is asked of us. . . ." God is in search of man, Heschel declares, and man is a need of God.

Abraham Heschel writes in *Man is Not Alone* (1951) of "the sense for the sacred."

> The course in which human life moves is, like the orbit of heavenly bodies, an ellipse, not a circle. We are attached to two centers: to the focus of our self and to the focus of God. . . .
>
> Horrified by the discovery of man's power to bring about the annihilation of organic life on this planet, we are today beginning to comprehend that the sense for the sacred is as vital to us as the light of the sun; that the enjoyment of beauty, possessions and safety in civilized society depends upon man's sense for the sacredness of life, upon reverence for this spark of light in the darkness of selfishness; that once we permit this spark to be quenched, the darkness falls upon us like thunder.

. . . The true foundation upon which our cities stand is a handful of spiritual ideas. All our life hangs by a thread—the faithfulness of man to the concern of God.

It is no artificial exercise to offer answers regarding evil. For questions about evil surely arise "in a civilization where factories were established in order to exterminate millions of men, women, and children; where soap was made of human flesh." If modern man has become hardened to horror, at least he can be horrified at the loss of his sense of horror. And if intelligence can be used to distinguish white from black, beauty from ugliness, pleasure from pain, that same intelligence must discern right from wrong. "The fate of mankind depends upon the realization that the distinction between good and evil, right and wrong, is superior to all other distinctions." The choice involved is none other than the choice between life and death.

Abraham Heschel states in *God In Search of Man* (1955) his theory of religion.

> Most theories of religion start out with defining the religious situation as man's search for God and maintain the axiom that God is silent, hidden and unconcerned with man's search for Him. Now, in adopting that axiom, the answer is given before the question is asked. To Biblical thinking, the definition is incomplete and the axiom false. The Bible speaks not only of man's search for God but also of *God's search for man*. "Thou dost hunt me like a lion," exclaimed Job (10:16).
>
> . . . This is the mysterious paradox of Biblical faith: *God is pursuing man*. It is as if God were unwilling to be alone, and He had chosen man to serve Him. Our seeking him is not only man's but also His concern, and must not be considered an exclusively human affair. His will is involved in our yearnings. All of human history as described in the Bible may be summarized in one phrase: *God is in search of man*.

So grave is the choice, so terrifying the evil, that except for the clear commands of God, man's steps would falter, his spirit fail. But if God demands obedience, then somehow it must be possible for man to give it. Besides, it is not a great abstraction called Evil which man resists and overcomes, but the tangible, day-by-day evils that come his way. These he can meet in partnership with God; these he can overcome. Obedience brings on further obedience, but "the reward of a transgression is a transgression."

In *God in Search of Man* Abraham Heschel warns the theologian, among others, against the subtle snare of self-deception.

> Intellectual honesty is one of the supreme goals of philosophy of religion, just as self-deception is the chief source of corruption in religious thinking, more deadly than error. Hypocrisy rather than heresy is the cause of spiritual decay. "Thou desirest truth in the inwardness" of man (Psalm 51:8).
>
> Rabbi Bunam of Przyscha used to give the following definition of a hasid [pious man]. According to medieval sources, a hasid is he who does more than the law requires. Now, this is the law: Thou shalt not deceive thy fellow-man (Leviticus 25:17). A hasid goes beyond the law; he will not even deceive his own self.

What of freedom: is this not a real question, an ultimate concern? Who is free—the man who follows the laws of nature, the man who obeys his own will, the man who acts without cause or motive? Here Heschel distinguishes between a process and an event. The former term describes that which is regular, typical, uniform, ordinary, in accordance with a fixed law or pattern. Event, on the other hand, refers to the irregular, unique, sudden, inexplicable, and extraordinary. Science, interested in what can be uniformly predicted or repeated, confines its attention to process, ignoring and sometimes denying the event. But art and religion concern themselves with the indefinable and unpredictable event—that rare occurrence which gives meaning and focus to the whole dull, repetitive process.

Now freedom is an event. Rather than exist, it *happens*. It happens in those creative moments when man rises above himself, above his self-willing, above all that binds him to routine, mechanical, predictable process. Freedom is, in short, "a spiritual event." In Greek thought the world or the cosmos evolve by process, but in Hebrew thought the creation of the world was an event. An act of freedom, God's freedom, happened, and a world with room for freedom began to be. Man is free to choose, above all else to respond to God, for only then does he become responsible. His highest freedom comes in the same way that religion itself arises: in man's awareness that he is an object of God's concern.

This, Heschel argues, is the great message of the ancient prophets and of the entire biblical record: God cares. And it is a message that modern man would still hear. God is not Aristotle's indifferent, abstract Unmoved Mover; He is the concerned, immediate "Most Moved Mover." There is no concept of a chosen God, only of a chosen people. God seeks, God chooses, God cares. He makes a covenant with man in time, but a covenant that binds for eternity. And a major measure of the Bible's enduring worth is that it records the wonder of God speaking to man and of man in a matchless moment of freedom responding to God. "The Bible is a seed; God is the sun, but we are the soil. Every generation is expected to bring forth new understanding and new realization."

In different words, theology must explore.

REINHOLD NIEBUHR

A native of Missouri, Reinhold Niebuhr grew up in the atmosphere of small-town evangelical piety. An undistinguished student in college and seminary, Niebuhr moved on to the Divinity School of Yale University, where he took a Master of Arts degree in 1915. Here "the whole world of philosophical and theological learning" was opened to him; nevertheless, Niebuhr, partly by preference and partly by necessity, turned from an academic career to a pastorate in Detroit, Michigan. Thirteen years there in the heart of the pressing problems of industry and city opened up another whole world: that of the social, economic, and political forces which modern man wields or beneath which he falls. In 1928 the pastor became a professor (of Christian ethics) in New York's Union Theological Seminary; Niebuhr maintained this institutional connection for the remainder of his professional life.

One of Niebuhr's appeals is that his own spiritual pilgrimage was so tortuous, yet so candidly confessed. Every change of mind or heart or tactic stands fully documented, openly acknowledged. The simple sentimentalist, the hearty optimist, the glum obscurantist can, should they choose, follow this pilgrim's progress, with carefully marked short cuts pointed out here and there.

Niebuhr's major shift was from a soft, naïve idealism to a stern, complex realism. One can maintain that "every day in every way we are getting better and better" only by ignoring most of what goes on in the world and in the human heart. Facing facts means facing man's perversity and society's folly. And while such facts may not remove all optimism, they incline one to be more hopeful about the promises of God than the attainments of man. Niebuhr described himself as a long-term optimist (God's time), a short-range pessimist (man's time).

Reinhold Niebuhr in *Leaves from the Notebook of a Tamed Cynic* (1929) also cautions against costly deceptions.

One of the most fruitful sources of self-deception in the ministry is the proclamation of great ideals and principles without any clue to their relation to the controversial issues of the day. The minister feels very heroic in uttering the ideals because he knows that some rather dangerous immediate consequences are involved in their application. But he doesn't make the application clear, and those who hear his words are either unable to see the immediate issue involved, or they are unconsciously grateful to the preacher for not belaboring a contemporaneous issue which they know to be involved but would rather not face.

To the ancient query whether man is the glory or folly of the universe, Niebuhr answers that he is both. Man is a child of nature, but he is also "a spirit who stands outside of nature, life, himself, his reason and the world." It is dangerous distortion to view man as wholly beast or wholly angel. His uniqueness, his hope, his misery all stem from his citizenship in two worlds, his bondage both to God and mammon. "Man is mortal. That is his fate. Man pretends not to be mortal. That is his sin."

If we would know more about man, we should know more about history. For it is in the dramatic dialogues and dialectic of history, the absurdities and incredibilities of history, that man is best revealed. "Man is primarily a historical creature." But what pattern or meaning does man find in history? Only that which by faith he brings to the whirling jumble of events. For Niebuhr "the life, death, and resurrection of Christ represent an event in history, in and through which a disclosure of the whole meaning of history occurs." This disclosure, however, is apprehended only through faith, only by an affirmation of the whole man, and not by an analytical, objective exercise of reason alone.

When it comes to understanding America's history and man's present posture in that tradition, Niebuhr offers exciting insights. Responding to Henry Ford's harsh industrialism, Protestantism's unrealistic liberalism, and Wall Street's unrestrained capitalism, Niebuhr in the early 1930's called for honest appraisal of history's real forces, of man's true tendencies. Enough of self-delusion and sentimental fluff. Science, sanitation, and education will not, cannot make a perfect world. Neither pietism nor pacifism squarely meet the unavoidable facts of war, greed, exploitation, prejudice, poverty, cruelty, injustice, and lust. We tell men to love, to imitate Christ, and all will be well. But Christ loved, and all was not well: he ended nailed to a cross. In the social order, therefore, the most one can hope for is the attainment and preservation of justice. Rarely is the choice before us a clear one between good and evil, but rather it is an ambiguous one between lesser evils, between degrees of violence to an ethic of love.

Reinhold Niebuhr in *The Children of Light and the Children of Darkness* (1944) comments on the contribution of profound religion to genuine democracy.

Democracy therefore requires something more than a religious devotion to moral ideals. It requires religious humility. Every absolute devotion to relative political ends (and all political ends are relative) is a threat to communal peace. But religious humility is no simple moral or political achievement. It springs only from the depth of a religion which confronts the individual with a more ultimate majesty and purity than all human majesties and values, and persuades him to confess: "Why callest thou me good? there is none good but one, that is, God."

The real point of contact between democracy and profound religion is in the spirit of humility which democracy requires and which must be one of the fruits of religion. Democratic life requires a spirit of tolerant cooperation between individuals and groups which can be achieved by neither moral cynics, who know no law beyond their own interest, nor by moral idealists, who acknowledge such a law but are unconscious of the corruption which insinuates itself into the statement of it by even the most disinterested idealists.

The problem, then, is one of power: how to balance competing forces, how to protect contending factions. And the best hope for meeting that problem is democracy. "Man's capacity for justice makes democracy possible; but man's inclination to injustice makes democracy necessary." When men have uncontrolled or unlimited power, as in totalitarian society, the inclinations to injustice expand and ripen, yielding their rotten fruit. When society takes too hopeful a view of man's love of justice, then chaos and confusion await, as democracy degenerates into anarchy. The Christian view of man is therefore acutely relevant: both angel and beast. Because he is a child of nature, man tempers his optimism; because he is a child of God, he escapes from cynicism.

Reinhold Niebuhr in *Christianity and Crisis* (January 24, 1955) distinguishes between genuine religion and the noise made in its name.

A visitor to our shores would probably come to the same conclusion at which St. Paul arrived in regard to the Athenians, namely, that we are "very religious." But the judgment might not imply a compliment any more than Paul wanted to so imply when he called attention to the worship of many gods in Athens, including the "unknown god." Our religiosity seems to have as little to do with the Christian faith as the religiosity of the Athenians.

. . . For whether it is in ourselves, or in mankind, or in civilization, or in America, that we are asked to have faith, the admonition always points to an object of faith that is less than God. . . . The question is whether a generation which has lost its faith in all the gods of the nineteenth century, that is, in "history," or "progress," or "enlightenment," or the "perfectibility of man," is not expressing its desire to believe in something, to be committed somehow, even though it is not willing to be committed to a God who can be known only through repentance, and whose majesty judges all human pretensions. It is precisely faith in this God which is avoided in all this religiosity.

Like Abraham Heschel, Niebuhr is anxious not to deceive himself. Man's power to judge himself is cloyed by his capacity to deceive himself. So also the institutions of religion and the "children of light" as a group: self-deception comes too easily. Even America as a nation falls into this ready trap, a trap made deeper by the very grandeur of our hopes. We were, writes Niebuhr, "a messianic nation from our birth . . . born to exemplify the virtues of democracy and to extend the frontiers of the principles of self-government throughout the world." New England's Puritanism together with the Enlightenment's Jeffersonianism convinced the nation that its light was not to be hid under a bushel; America was, in John Winthrop's words, "a city set upon a hill."

While a sense of mission can inspire, it can also delude. A nation may conceal its lust for power under a thin veil of moral idealism, of spiritual mission. A nation may also interpret its mission in rigid terms no longer relevant to the "unpredictable contingencies of history." Part of the task of a creative, probing theology is to help the American people, "living on the edge of the abyss of nuclear catastrophe," to face disquieting complexity with courage. The age of innocence is past; the time for self-righteousness has never come, nor will it do so. The religious heritage of America does not make the nation infallible; it ought to make the nation humble. Pride, the original and persisting sin of mankind, is most corrupting when it disguises itself as religion. Man is not God, but he needs God. Niebuhr, said Abraham Heschel, "speaks of the eternal in a world of spiritual absenteeism."

GUSTAVE WEIGEL

From his native state of New York (Buffalo, 1906) Gustave Weigel migrated to Maryland to prepare himself for admission to the Society of Jesus. At the age of twenty-two he graduated from Woodstock College with a Bachelor of Arts degree. Advanced studies were pursued abroad, chiefly at Gregorian University in Rome. From 1937 to 1948 the Jesuit scholar taught dogmatic theology at the Universidad Católica de Chile, from which in 1956 he received an honorary degree. In 1948 Weigel assumed the post of professor of ecclesiology at Woodstock College, remaining in this position until his death early in 1964.

Weigel shared with Niebuhr and Heschel an eagerness to communicate. He, as a Catholic, wished to communicate with the Protestant and the Jew. He, as an American, wished to communicate with his fellow citizens, particularly with those hostile toward or indifferent to all religious orientation. Communication is a necessary aspect of proselytizing, to be sure, but communication can also aim at understanding and acceptance. Because even with our different world views we must yet live together, "we are all anxious to live in such a way that there will be peace and harmonious

1. *Gustave Weigel, S. J.*
   1906-1964

2. *Abraham Heschel*
   1907-1973

3. *Reinhold Niebuhr*
   1892-1971

collaboration in our coexistence." To that end we must talk with each other. If we cannot convert, at least we can converse.

The modern world is one of competing faiths: religious faiths and secular faiths, false faiths and saving faiths. What are the features of a faith sure enough to save? For one thing, such a faith will make life worth living, offering goals that are worthy and channeling human drives toward the constructive and general good. This does not mean that utopia arrives; earth "is not heaven, but there is no reason why it should be hell." A saving faith, moreover, manifests "an openness to all things good." If a faith is to be creative and alive, it must "be open to embrace every form of human good." Weigel is willing even to adopt Nietzsche's "wild saying" that "faith must be a yes-response to life and all that is in it." No stagnation of theology here, no retreat from fresh complexities to older, idealized simplicities. Finally, the faith which modern man needs and will respond to is one that "preserves the beneficial insights of a former time and pushes them into a yet fuller insight for the present." The theology that fails to probe has begun to die; with it dies the culture which it has spawned and nurtured.

Gustave Weigel in *The Modern God: Faith in a Secular Culture* (1963) discusses the changing role of Christianity in western culture.

> The collapse of Christian belief as the pattern for Western society was rooted in Christendom's refusal to accept the discoveries of the renaissance of the fifteenth, sixteenth and seventeenth centuries. In those days the esthetic and philosophical achievements of the non-Christian Greeks were seen again and they were alluring to the European. The Christendom of that time was slow in giving these wonderful things a home in its own house. Although it finally did accept them, there was a long period of suspicion and hostility.
>
> . . . It is true that within the last fifty years the churches have embraced science nor do they any longer heap insult and abuse on it. They even flatter it. But it is too late. Science gave a new faith to the West, and although . . . this faith did not succeed in destroying the old faith, it certainly robbed it of its controlling power.

If theology has health-giving words for America's culture, it should offer them quickly. For Weigel saw signs of a decaying moral framework, a shrinking moral consensus. Religion's voice is hesitant and divided, so that "there is no effective general guidance for our young people and for our morally obtuse citizens." We can, as a nation, still agree on some things: e.g., murder is not approved. But can we still agree on "honesty, sobriety, industriousness, self-reliance and regard for the neighbor's personal dignity [that] certainly were elements in the American consensus of the past"?

We are, by common acknowledgment, a pluralistic society. The signs of a diversified pluralism abound, but what are the signs of cohesive society? Enlightened and emancipated as they were, the founding fathers were able to say, "We hold these truths." What truths do we, their children, hold in common?

This admittedly is more a political than a theological problem, a task for state more than for church. Yet is a creative theology irrelevant to the challenge or inimical to the task? Weigel sees religion as offering aid in two complementary ways. One, a purely intellectual activity, is a probe for that objective moral truth arising from the very nature of man. We teach the biological, psychological and sociological truths about man; can we not as interdependent citizens teach the ethical truths? If there is no moral minimum, no ethical polar star, then at what point does pluralism become nihilism?

Religion can also aid, more concretely, more forthrightly, by seeking consensus within its own ranks. A worthy beginning is made when bitterness, hostility, and ignorance give way to charity, friendship, and understanding. Gustave Weigel did more than urge such a step: he took it. Writing an "ecumenical primer for Catholics," he brought his own communion to an awareness of what promises and pitfalls the twentieth century held for moral or spiritual consensus. Those outside his own Church he paid the compliment of seeking to know by acquaintance, not being content with hackneyed descriptions and half-truth stereotypes. "That non-Catholics do not know more of the Catholic idiom is regrettable," he wrote, "but that the Catholics do not know the language of their non-Catholic milieu is tragic."

Gustave Weigel in *Catholic Theology in Dialogue* (1961) comments on the importance of and technique for dialogue.

If I plan a love feast to entertain my Jewish friend, my friendship is short-sighted if all the dishes on the table are such that the Jew cannot partake of them by reason of his own religious commitments. My love feast will be a harrowing occasion for him and rouse in him the suspicion that his very Jewishness is consciously or unconsciously under attack. This is no way to make friends and influence people.

. . . The one thing we must all remember is that the purpose of the Ecumenical Movement is conversation. . . . We must with patience and forbearance overcome the difficulties which stand in the way of meeting. If my friend is embarrassed when in my house, I shall hold converse with him elsewhere. The conversation is important, not the place where it is to be held.

Is it, then, the business of religious faith to save America? No, Weigel responds without hesitation. The role of the churches has always been, is now, "to be the locus where man meets God and dedicates himself to do His purposes." One must be careful to distinguish his religious from his patriotic loyalties. While on occasion the two may run a parallel course, the separation must be kept safe and sure. "Religion is good just because it is religion. It is not good because it is good for my country. It would be good even if my country drew from it no benefit whatever." To be sure, the New Testament promises that if we seek first the Kingdom of God, all other things will be added unto us. "But what we seek must be the Kingdom of God and not the other things."

Gustave Weigel in *Faith and Understanding in America* (1959) points to religion's inviolate freedom and indestructible force.

The State can try to persuade but it is not equipped to achieve persuasion without fail. Schools and social media of suggestion can be monopolized by governments, but they cannot control the spirit of man without his consent. The police can throw our bodies into jails; they can torture us into specious submission—but they cannot hold on to the soul which flows through the torturers' grasping fist. It is the indestructible free spirit of man which ultimately unseats the tyrant, for the tyrant cannot crush it because he cannot touch it. . . . The strength of religion is not derived from any police power. All religions have this in common that they move the inward will through the excitation of an inward vision. The sharper the vision, the more dynamic is the influence of the religion on the will and behavior of the believer. . . . The secular affairs of men will not move fruitfully unless the secular order leans on the spiritual.

---

19 ❖ The Liturgy

L ITURGY, LITERALLY THE "work of the people," constitutes the outward and public expression of religion's principal rhythms.[1] And
while some religious groups are considered "nonliturgical" (meaning that
their service is informal and without prescribed order), all churches and
synagogues manifest some rhythm in their services of worship. The flux
may only be from one revival to the next, from one moment of dedication
to the next, from one quiet and honest meditation to the next, but in each
case rhythm is there. In this sense all American religion is liturgical: people
are at work together praising God, "practicing the presence of God." Recalling a common heritage, anticipating a common destiny, the community
of faith expresses its noblest ideals in liturgical acts and deeds.

Historic religions such as Judaism and Christianity draw rhythms from a
corporate tradition remembered and revered. The Jews honor the exodus
from Egypt, the law given at Sinai, the tabernacle and Aaron's high priesthood, the temples before and after the exile into Babylonia, Esther's protection of her people, Judas Maccabeus' deliverance of Israel, and other
critical events in their history. In Christianity's storehouse of historical
treasure liturgy centers on the birth, ministry, death, and resurrection of
Christ, though the lives of apostles and later saints also receive liturgical
attention. The "mystic chords of memory" bind a people religiously no less
than politically.

The rhythms of America's religious life may be viewed under four aspects: of the day, the week, the year, and the span of life itself.

DAILY DEVOTION

For centuries the devout Jew has punctuated the day with three periods of
religious devotion. In the morning, at noon, and at night prayers of intercession and praise are offered, accompanied morning and evening by the

---

[1] Of course all life is enriched by rhythm: of wakefulness and sleep, of work
and play, winter and summer, sorrow and joy, youth and old age. A dazing and
stupefying monotony is thereby exchanged for the mystery and magic of change.
Religion's rhythms may be those of life, of calendar, or history.

Shema: "Hear, O Israel, the Lord is our God, the Lord is One." Prayers, known as the Eighteen, exalt the God of Abraham, Isaac, and Jacob, "great, mighty, revered God, supreme over all." Other daily devotion among Jews, as among Christians, is drawn from the Book of Psalms, a repository of great antiquity and inexhaustible vitality.

From the eighteenth century to the twentieth the Constitution of the Presbyterian Church, U. S. A., gave these instructions regarding private devotions.

1. Besides the public worship in congregations, it is the indispensable duty of each person, alone, in secret, and of every family, by itself, in private, to pray to and worship God.

2. Secret worship is most plainly enjoined by our Lord. In this duty every one, apart by himself, is to spend some time in prayer, reading the Scriptures, holy meditation and serious self-examination. The many advantages arising from a conscientious discharge of these duties are best known to those who are found in the faithful discharge of them.

3. Family worship, which ought to be performed by every family, ordinarily morning and evening, consists in prayer, reading the Scriptures, and singing praises.

Jewish worship, the major external influence on early Christian worship, shaped the rhythm of the Christian's day even as it obviously determined the weekly rhythm. The three periods of prayer became six, then eight in the Western church, with the first daily office beginning after midnight (nocturns, or matins) and the last one coming at bedtime (compline). The faithful in the Middle Ages could also pray privately (though "with the church"), for which purpose richly illustrated Books of Hours came into use. Frequent daily services in Latin failed to attract a large lay attendance, increasing sentiment for fewer services and for those services to be conducted in the language of the people.

The Protestant Episcopal Church, for whom English was already the liturgical language, reduced the eight daily offices to two: Morning and Evening Prayer. Others select a single office (e.g., vespers) for a time of corporate devotion. Still others, by printed schedule or public announcement, encourage a regular reading of Scripture, along with daily meditation and prayer "with the church." Throughout much of Judaism and Christianity family devotions, bedtime prayers, mealtime blessings, personal or public meditations bring to the secular routine a spiritual dimension that redeems the day.

1. *Grace Before Meal (Carroll County, Georgia)*

2. *Jewish Chaplain reading the Holy Scriptures (Fort Benjamin Harrison, Indiana)*

3. *Private Prayer (First Wesleyan Methodist Church, Washington, D. C.)*

4. *Weekly Worship (Moravian Sunday School, Lititz, Pennsylvania)*

The general confession prescribed for both Morning and Evening Prayer, Book of Common Prayer, Protestant Episcopal Church, U. S. A.

Almighty and most merciful Father: We have erred and strayed from thy ways like lost sheep. We have followed too much the devices and desires of our own hearts. We have offended against thy holy laws. We have left undone those things which we ought to have done; And we have done those things which we ought not to have done; And there is no health in us. But thou, O Lord, have mercy upon us, miserable offenders. Spare thou those, O God, who confess their faults. Restore thou those who are penitent; According to thy promises declared unto mankind in Christ Jesus our Lord. And grant, O most merciful Father, for his sake; That we may hereafter live a godly, righteous, and sober life, To the glory of thy holy Name. Amen.

WEEKLY WORSHIP

". . . And on the seventh day He rested." The one-day-in-seven set aside for rest, relaxation, and worship is built into American life. No federal law demands it, no constitutional clause insures it, but the rhythm is there. On a Sabbath evening or a Sunday morning some sixty million Americans gather to render their service of worship. Some sit in the midst of monumental art, hearing musical masterpieces masterfully performed. Plain walls and bare floors encompass others who find comfort and strength in the words they hear, the hymns they sing, the hope they share. In some services of worship the mood is emotionally extravagant and ecstatic; the mood in others is rationally severe and analytic. For some worshipers the heart of the service is what is said; for others what is done matters most. A service may instruct or inspire, comfort or disturb, exalt the divine or elevate the human.

Protestant and Jewish worship centers on instruction through the Word. In the synagogue the Torah holds the most honored place, receives the most reverent devotion. In much (but not all) of Protestantism the open Bible or centered pulpit holds a similar rank. A liturgical renewal sweeping through American religious life distinguishes between instruction (man-directed) and adoration (God-directed). A large element of Jewish and Protestant worship includes prayer, praise, thanksgiving, and dedication that are directed primarily toward the divine. In some services instruction and adoration hold equal rank; in others the balance is uneven.

Traditionally, and for the most part contemporaneously, the sermon occupies the major position in the weekly worship of Protestants and Jews. The sermon is an exercise in theology. That is, it is an effort to make meaningful and relevant the biblical revelation, to present the Word, the logos, that challenges and transforms. While the sermon may be, and often is, a bit of everything (language analysis, historical research, literary judgment, anecdote, humor, harangue, review of the week, hints for the future, sociological, political, and psychological commentary), it is at best a proclamation of God's good tidings to all men.

The sermon, its import and nature, is defined in the 1956 Constitution of the Presbyterian Church, U. S. A.

1. The preaching of the Word being an institution of God for the salvation of men, great attention should be paid to the manner of performing it. Every minister ought to give diligent application to it; and endeavor to prove himself a workman that needeth not to be ashamed, rightly dividing the word of truth.

2. The subject of a sermon should be some verse or verses of Scripture; and its object, to explain, defend, and apply some part of the system of divine truth; or, to point out the nature, and state the bounds and obligation of some duty. A text should not be merely a motto, but should fairly contain the doctrine proposed to be handled. It is proper also that large portions of Scripture be sometimes expounded, and particularly improved [used to good purpose], for the instruction of the people in the meaning and use of the sacred oracles.

In Catholicism—both Western (Roman) and Eastern (Greek)—the mass constitutes the central focus of worship. Though other elements are present, including a sermon at "high mass," the climax is the sacrificial offering of Christ's body and blood, really present in the transformed wine and wafer. Not the pulpit but the altar is the architectural, theological and liturgical center.

The Mass can be many things, but above all else it is "a true and living sacrifice" offered to God for the benefit of the living and the dead. The atoning death of Christ on the cross, His sacrifice, is re-presented on the altar. Calvary is seen again, not as a mere recollection of history, but as an ever present, recurring redemption. So central a place does the mass occupy in Eastern Christendom that it is simply "the Divine Liturgy." But in all Catholicism, East or West, this signal service includes all the major elements of worship: prayer, praise, instruction, offering, healing, communion, and blessing.

Twenty centuries of liturgical development in Christianity have introduced great complexity and variety in the ritual of the mass. Yet, the essential ingredients are unvarying. Also, missals and other aids in worship guide the congregation, notably in those special prayers (collects) and readings (lections) which vary according to the day. In the present century, reformers of the liturgy seek ways to increase congregational partici-

6. Sunday Mass (Chicago, Illinois)

5. Crowded House of Worship (New York Avenue Presbyterian Church, Washington, D. C.)

7. Sabbath Service (University of Massachusetts)

8. *Easter in Washington, D. C.*
(The Reverend Peter Mar-
shall)

9. *Passover in Korea*

10. *Mid-week Prayer Meeting (Heard County, Georgia)*

pation in and understanding of the mass. Vatican Council II greatly assisted this effort when it authorized the use of the vernacular in large portions of the service. In 1964, America's Roman Catholics for the first time joined in the celebration of mass in English.

The mass of the Roman rite consists of three basic actions: (a) preparation, (b) consecration, and (c) communion. The Ante-mass, which leads into the actual canon of the mass, may include a solemn procession of entry (Introit), a humble beseeching of mercy (Kyrie eleison), an exulting song of praise (Gloria in excelsis Deo), a didactic reading of Scripture, other hymns and prayers concluding with a corporate affirmation of faith: I believe (Credo). The instructional portion of the Ante-mass may also include a sermon which would then follow readings from the Epistle (Old Testament or writings of the Apostles) and the Gospel (Matthew, Mark, Luke, John).

In the mass (Roman) the Gloria, though omitted on certain occasions, normally follows the Introit and the Kyrie eleison ("Lord, have mercy").

> Glory be to God on high, and on earth peace to men who are God's friends. We praise thee, we adore thee, we glorify thee, we give thanks for thy great glory: Lord God, heavenly King, God the almighty Father. Lord Jesus Christ, only-begotten Son; Lord God, Lamb of God, Son of the Father, who takest away the sins of the world, have mercy upon us; thou who takest away the sins of the world, receive our prayer; thou who sittest at the right hand of the Father, have mercy upon us. For thou alone art the Holy One, thou alone art Lord, thou alone art the Most High: Jesus Christ, with the Holy Spirit: in the glory of God the Father. Amen.

The mass proper begins with the preparation. While an offertory anthem is heard, a collection representing the dedication and participation of the faithful is gathered. At the altar the priest also makes his offering, not of material possessions but of the bread and the chalice. The people are prepared in heart and in mind; the elements to be consecrated are prepared on the altar; the blessing of God is sought upon "this unblemished sacrificial offering."

A prayer of preparation for the mass (Roman rite).

> Take away from us our iniquities, we implore Thee, Lord, that with pure minds we may worthily enter into the holy of holies. Through Christ our Lord. Amen.
>
> We implore Thee, Lord, by the merits of Thy saints, whose relics are here, and of all the saints, that Thou would deign to forgive me all my sins. Amen.

11. *Jewish New Year Services (Camp Gordon Johnston, Florida)*

12. *Easter in Italy (U. S. Fifth Army)*

In consecration, the great Eucharistic prayer is offered and the dramatic climax of the mass is reached. Though this portion of the mass is in form a series of several prayers, there is essentially only a single intercession, a central transaction. On behalf of the people ("thy whole household"), the priest makes an offering to God "which we entreat Thee to accept." It is accepted, making of that which is offered "a thing consecrated and approved . . . the body and blood of Thy dearly beloved Son." The bread, now the host, is elevated above the altar for all to see. So also the chalice. Then host and chalice are raised together (the "little elevation") in invitation to the faithful to share in the spiritual food.

Communion constitutes the final portion of the mass. The bread is broken over the chalice ("fracture of the host") and, as a portion is dropped within, the priest prays: "May this sacramental mingling of the Body and Blood of our Lord Jesus Christ be for us who receive it a source of eternal life." After the litany "O Lamb of God" (Agnus Dei), prayers to Christ are offered. The celebrant then receives the host and drinks the contents of the chalice. As the faithful come forward to kneel at the altar rail, each receives a portion of the consecrated host. After all have communed, the sacred vessels are returned to the altar: the mass is done. The congregation being dismissed (Ite, Missa est) voice their thanks to God (Deo gratias) and receive a final blessing: "May almighty God bless you: the Father, the Son [sign of the cross made here], and the Holy Spirit." And all the people say, "Amen."

In the Mass according to the Greek liturgy, the priest offers this prayer as he distributes the host (which has been dipped into the chalice):

> I believe, O Lord, and I confess, that Thou art indeed the Christ, the Son of the Living God, who didst come into the world to save sinners, of whom I am the chief. Likewise do I believe that this is truly Thy Most Pure Body and that this is verily Thy precious Blood.
>
> Make me this day, O Son of God, a sharer in Thy Mystic Supper, for I will not reveal the mystery to Thine enemies, nor will I give Thee a kiss, like unto Judas, but like unto the Good Thief, I will confess Thee: Remember me, O Lord, in Thy kingdom. Grant, O Lord, that the participation in Thy Holy Mysteries may not be for me a cause of judgment and condemnation, but for the healing of my soul and body.

THE LITURGICAL YEAR

"In the seventh month, on the first day of the month, you shall have a rest-day, a day of remembrance, horn-blowing, and holy assembly." Thus does the Book of Leviticus prescribe the ritual observance of the Jewish New Year. With the blowing of the ram's horn (shofar) in the fall of the year, a ten-day period ("the High Holy Days") of discipline, contrition, and confession begins. The most solemn Day of Atonement (Yom Kippur) marks the end of Judaism's major annual event.

Rosh Hashana, or the New Year, corresponds roughly to the harvest and in-gathering, recalling the days when Jews were primarily an agricultural people. It is not, however, a time of revelry and abandon but of sober preparation for the ten "Days of Awe." The blowing of the shophar, noted one of Judaism's great philosophers, is "analogous to the trumpet blasts which announce the coronation of a king. On Rosh Hashana we remember that God created the world and assumed the role of its Sovereign, and in the sounding of the *shofar* we acknowledge Him as our King." The horn-blowing also serves as a reminder of that day of final judgment when God weighs the deeds of men and of nations.

Judaism's longest and most solemn liturgy is voiced on Yom Kippur. Eating, drinking, and all sensual pleasure are forsaken as penitents all day long repair to the synagogue's somber prayers and soulful music. The impurity and impotence of man confront the majesty and power of God.

> Yet even now, saith the Lord,
> Turn ye unto Me with all your heart,
> And with fasting, and with weeping, and with lamentation;
> And rend your heart, and not your garments,
> And turn unto the Lord your God. [Joel 2:12–13]

Yom Kippur creates solemnity but drives away despair. As sure as God is powerful, so also is He merciful. For a people in covenant with such a God there is, under any circumstance, reason for hope. And at the waning of the day, when the Book of Jonah is read, the faithful remember that even the wicked of Nineveh repented and found forgiveness.

The feast of Passover, coming in the spring, marks the other crest in the rhythm of the Jewish religious year. Celebrating the deliverance of the Jews from Egyptian bondage, the passover meal is essentially a liturgy of the home rather than of the synagogue. In orthodox Judaism the preparations may serve as a ritualized spring house cleaning, for all the house must be carefully cleansed of any leaven (yeast) or leavened food. Regular dinnerware used throughout the year is put away, as china and crockery reserved

---

When at the beginning of the passover feast (seder) the unleavened bread (matzo) is uncovered, these words are recited by the head of the family:

This is the bread of affliction that our fathers ate in the land of Egypt. All who are hungered—let them come and eat: all who are needy—let them come and celebrate the Passover. Now we are here, but next year may we be in the land of Israel! Now we are slaves, but next year may we be free men!

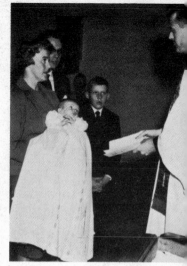

14. Baptism in Greenland (Thule Air Force Base)

13. Confirmation among Oregon Indians (St. Andrew's Mission Church)

15. Baptism on the High Seas (U. S. S. Columbus)

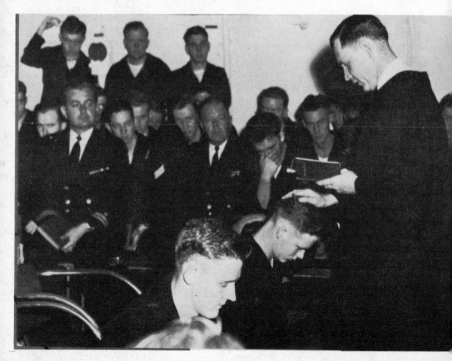

16. *Confirmation in North Carolina (Seymour Johnson Air Force Base)*

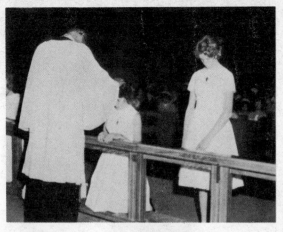

17. *First Communion (Turner Air Force Base, Georgia)*

18. *Jewish Chaplain reads Memorial Service for fallen Soldier (Pusan, Korea)*

19. Protestant Funeral (Lincoln Air Force Base, Nebraska)

21. Communion below the Seas
(U.S.S. Orion, Submarine
Squadron Six)

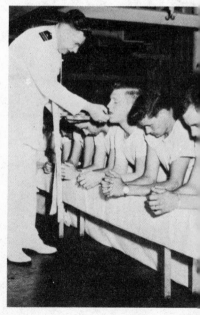

20. Catholic Chaplain administers
Extreme Unction (Luxembourg)

only for the Passover is taken from its storage. Unleavened bread (matzo) is prepared, candles are lighted, and children coached to ask the four ritual questions during the feast (seder).

"Wherein is this night different from all other nights?" the youngest child (six years old, at least) respectfully inquires. Why the unleavened bread? the bitter herbs? the dipping of the herbs? the reclining posture? Patiently, as for the first time, the father tells the story of the exodus out of Egypt and away from the oppression, the death angel taking the first-born son of Egyptian households but "passing over" the Jewish homes marked with the blood of a sacrificial lamb. All this, with other rich detail and meaningful symbol, is set down in the *Haggada Shel Pesah,* "probably the best-loved single piece of Hebrew liturgy." Before many seders have passed, the Jewish boy or girl has blended the ancient past into the rhythm of the pulsating present.

Following the Passover meal this song is sung:

Who knows One? One I know!
One is our God in Heaven and on Earth.

Who knows Two? Two I know!
Two are the Tables of Covenant:
One is our God in Heaven and on Earth.

Who knows Three? Three I know!
Three are the Fathers:
Two the Tables of Covenant:
One is our God in Heaven and on Earth.

Who knows Four? Four I know!
Four are the Mothers:
Three are the Fathers:
Two the Tables of Covenant:
One is our God in Heaven and on Earth.

Who knows Five? Five I know!
Five are the Books of the Law:
Four are the Mothers:
Three are the Fathers:
Two the Tables of Covenant:
One is our God in Heaven and on Earth.

[13 verses in all]

The twin peaks of the Christian year, Christmas and Easter, mark the liturgical celebration of the Incarnation and the Atonement. Christmas is introduced by a preparatory period of Advent (twenty-eight days), and Lent (forty days) prepares the way for Easter. The dates chosen to commemorate the birth of Christ (December 25 in the West, January 6 in the East) do not pretend to correspond to the actual date of birth, for this is not known. Rather the chosen dates denoted a rejection of sun worship and its festivals of the winter solstice; Christianity, displacing pagan rites, continued its conquest of the Gentile world.

From about the eighth century on, the Advent season in the West marked the beginning of the Christian year. Preparation for Christmas is generally joyful, extolling the redemption brought by Bethlehem's babe. Christ's coming also calls to mind a Second Coming, a judgment, which tempers joy with awe and repentance. Christmas, i.e., "Christ's mass," is celebrated in story, song, sermon, prayer and pageant. While most of the popular piety centers on the shepherds watching their flocks, angels an-

---

A Christmas song written by Martin Luther in 1534 for his own children; J. S. Bach composed several settings for the hymn.

> From heaven above to earth I come
> To bear good news to every home;
> Glad tidings of great joy I bring,
> Whereof I now will say and sing:
>
> To you this night is born a child
> Of Mary, chosen virgin mild;
> This little child, of lowly birth,
> Shall be the joy of all the earth.
>
> This is the Christ, our God and Lord,
> Who in all need shall aid afford;
> He will himself your Savior be
> From all your sins to set you free.
>
> He will on you the gifts bestow
> Prepared by God for all below,
> That in His kingdom, bright and fair,
> You may with us His glory share.

[15 verses in all]

---

nouncing glad tidings, and kings presenting their gifts, the churches' liturgy returns to the theological import of the event. The Christian year begins, as indeed the Christian religion begins, with the Incarnation: "In the beginning was the Word, and the Word was with God, and the Word was God. . . . And the Word was made flesh, and dwelt among us (and we beheld his glory, the glory as of the only begotten of the Father), full of grace and truth" (John 1 : 1,14). God came into the world in order to reconcile the word unto himself. Christmas, if not for the churches the "season to be jolly," is for them the season of joy. For it announces the good news, the glad tidings, the gospel: that the Word became flesh and dwelt among us.

Easter takes its name from an Anglo-Saxon festival of spring, once more blending the rhythms of nature with the events of history. But unlike Christmas which became a festival in the fourth century, Easter was celebrated from the start of Christian history. Every Sunday, indeed, commemorated the resurrection that occurred "on the first day of the week." So crucial is this celebration to the Christian life that Eastern Orthodoxy counts it as the proper beginning of the church year. In any case, Christmas is incomplete without Easter, the Incarnation unfinished without Atonement.

An Easter hymn written by St. Ambrose, fourth-century bishop of Milan; translated by Francis X. Weiser.

> O mystery great and glorious,
> That mortal flesh should conquer death
> And all our human pains and wounds
> The Lord should heal by bearing them.
>
> Behold how man, though crushed by death,
> Now doth arise and live with Christ,
> While death, repelled and robbed of might,
> Dies from its own malignant sting.

Associated with the Jewish Passover, the Easter festival marked a deliverance not from Egyptian slavery but from sin and death. It signified a new covenant, a new testament with God made possible by the vicarious sacrifice of the "lamb without blemish," "wounded for our transgressions and bruised for our iniquities." The seventh day of the week, the Sabbath, commemorated God's creation of the world; the first day of the week, Sunday, commemorated God's re-creation and redemption of that world. Behold, said St. Paul, "old things are passed away; all things are become new."

If Christmas marks the doctrinal beginning of Christianity, Easter marks the actual entrance into its corporate life. For from earliest days Easter was the special time to instruct, baptize, confirm, and receive new members of the flock. One ritually participated in the death and resurrection of Christ, as he was buried with Him in baptism, then raised with Him to walk in newness of life. "Good Friday" is good because, for all its dark tragedy, God on that day pointed out the path to redemption. "And I, if I be lifted up from the earth, will draw all men unto me." As Passover was for the Jew a time for remembering, so Easter was for the Christian. "Christ our Passover is sacrificed for us: therefore let us keep the feast, not with old leaven, neither with the leaven of malice and wickedness, but with the unleavened bread of sincerity and truth" (I Cor. 5 : 7).

For both Christian and Jew many other fasts, feasts, and festivals illumine life's "long days' journey into night." But the stars of brightest magnitude, Passover and Yom Kippur, Easter and Christmas, steady, sustain, and direct the pilgrim through each passing year.

LITURGY AND LIFE

Life processes also have their rhythms, from the short pace of heartbeat and respiration to the longer span of growth and decay. If ever a man is religious, he is so during natural crises of life. If ever a religion serves basic needs, it is in time of dangerous passage: from the womb to the world, from childhood to adulthood, and from the world to the grave. While there are other "rites of passage" (to use the anthropologist's term), these three sufficiently demonstrate the ministry of faith to the mystery of life.

The birth of a child is a trauma for all concerned: society, parent, and infant. No religion can ignore an event of such social and personal significance, certainly not Judaism and Christianity for whom personality itself is sacred. The child born within the pale of these historic faiths is received

---

"Prayer for the New Born Daughter," to be offered at the public naming of a child in Judaism (Conservative).

> May He who blessed our fathers Abraham, Isaac, and Jacob, bless——, his wife——, and their new born daughter. Her name shall be——. May the parents be privileged to rear their daughter to womanhood imbued with the love of Torah and the performance of good deeds. Let us say: Amen.

---

into or cared for by the whole believing community. The giving of a name is a public act, a perpetual reminder of the context into which one was born. This "Christian" name (in America even Jews are sometimes asked, "What is your Christian name?") grants identity and relationship in a world that tries to destroy both.

For much of Christendom the baptism of the child is his admission into the Church, his assurance of eternal salvation. For others this baptism is the first step in a process not complete until the gift of grace is later confirmed and acknowledged by further action of the church. And for still others baptism is inappropriate for the infant, since he can neither receive instruction nor make his own profession of faith.

These words are addressed to the infant's sponsors at the time of his baptism; from *The Occasional Services and Additional Orders* (Lutheran), 1962.

Since in Christian love you present this child for Holy Baptism, I charge you that you diligently and faithfully teach him the Ten Commandments, the Creed, and the Lord's Prayer; and, that, as he grows in years, you place in his hands the Holy Scriptures, bring him to the services of God's house, and provide for his instruction in the Christian Faith; that, abiding in the covenant of his Baptism and in communion with the Church, he may be brought up to lead a godly life until the day of Jesus Christ.

When one comes to the "years of discretion," leaving childhood fancies behind, religion once more responds to life's biological rhythms. In Judaism's *bar mizva* ("son of command"), the boy becomes a man as he assumes a responsible role in the life of the synagogue. Since he may now publicly read from the Torah, he is obliged to be loyal to that Law. Taking on some of the aspects of a "family Fourth of July," *bar mizva* includes joyful feasting in the company of relatives and friends. But when the celebration is over, the duty remains: "Therefore, keep those words of Mine in your heart and in your soul. You shall bind them as a sign upon your hand; they shall be as frontlets between your eyes."

Like *bar mizva,* Christian confirmation usually occurs in the early teens. Also like *bar mizva,* it normally follows a period of more of less intensive instruction and study. The assumption of adult responsibilities and religious duties is signaled by partaking of the bread and wine that symbolize or constitute the body and blood of Christ. "First Communion," too, can be a joyous, festive occasion, a time for food and gifts, for the best wishes of family and friends. Still, the liturgy would insure that it be something more.

The Ritual of the Methodist Church (1939) provides for the reception of new members.

Beloved in the Lord, you are come hither seeking union with the Church of God. We rejoice that you are minded to undertake the privileges and the duties of membership in the Church. Before you are fully admitted thereto, you should here publicly renew your vows, confess your faith, and declare your purpose, by answering the following questions:

Do you here in the presence of God and this Congregation renew the solemn promise and vow that was made at your Baptism?

Response: I do.

Do you confess Jesus Christ as your Savior and Lord and pledge your allegiance to His kingdom?

R.: I do.

Do you receive and profess the Christian faith as contained in the New Testament of our Lord Jesus Christ?

R.: I do.

Will you be loyal to The Methodist Church, and uphold it by your prayers, your presence, your gifts, and your service?

R.: I will.

In the Book of Common Prayer (Episcopal) the candidate for confirmation must, among other things, assume as his own the three promises made for him at baptism. "First, that I should renounce the devil and all his works, the pomps and vanity of this wicked world, and all the sinful lusts of the flesh; Secondly, that I should believe all the Articles of the Christian Faith; And, Thirdly, that I should keep God's holy will and commandments, and walk in the same all the days of my life." The minister then asks, "Do you not think you are bound so to do?" And the candidate replies, "Yes, verily; and by God's help so I will. . . ."

The final ministrations of religion come at the time of death. "Last rites" are administered to the deceased, and restorative words are spoken to the living. But while religion in the Western world offers strength and hope, it does not deny or sentimentalize the fact of death. Orthodox Judaism calmly sets down the method of burial, the manner and duration of mourning. Grief is expressed not through an elaborate, expensive funeral; indeed, austerity is prescribed—a shroud and plain wooden coffin, quickly buried. To voice his sincerest sorrow, the observant Jew privately mourns at home for seven days, receiving the condolences of friends. For thirty more days entertainment is shunned while prayers in the synagogue, especially the Kaddish, are publicly offered. If one has lost a mother or a father, the mourning period continues for a year.

While practices among Christians show wide variety, the prevailing mood is that long ago voiced: "O death, where is thy sting? O grave, where is thy victory? . . . Thanks be to God who gives us the victory through our Lord Jesus Christ" (I Cor. 15 : 55, 57). This confidence expresses itself in the recitation of scripture and the singing of hymns, the comforting words of exhortation, the calm words of prayer. Because of differing views regarding the nature of the hereafter, Protestantism omits prayers for the dead which Catholicism includes.

The requiem mass[2] offers the most elaborate liturgical structure. The ordinary of the mass is followed with some omissions (e.g., the Gloria) and some additions (readings and collects chosen for their appropriateness to the occasion). The Roman missal also provides for a mass to be said on the third, seventh, and thirtieth day after burial, as well as on

---

[2] Requiem mass is so called from the first words of the Introit and the concluding prayer of absolution: *Requiem aeternam dona eis* (Eternal rest grant to them).

anniversaries thereafter, "birthdays in eternity." The promise of Christ, "I will not leave you comfortless," is never more urgently claimed than at those severe separations of parent from child, husband from wife, friend from friend. Once more, the rhythms of life are sustained by the dynamics of faith.

When liturgy and ceremony become the objects of conscious attention, it is often a spirit of iconoclasm[3] that is responsible. In twentieth-century America, however, revived attention has been given to liturgy with the aim of building up instead of tearing down. The liturgical "renewal" or "renaissance" of recent years is less an escape into empty form than it is a search for unifying symbol. Liturgy attempts to reach the whole man (his reason, his senses, his emotions) in order to turn him toward a "wholly other" God. By means of liturgy, "the work of the people," servants are found for the work of God.

[3] Image-breaking, literally; thus, opposing accepted patterns and modes of behavior or thought.

20 ❖ The House

I F LITURGY is figuratively "the work of the people," architecture is literally so. The most social of all the arts, architecture is today as it was in former times a community enterprise. And because it requires a corporate effort along with a combination of talent, the resulting creation boldly proclaims the community's commitment. The synagogue and church themselves call to wonder and worship.

Not that religion is confined to terrestrial quarters, to appointed hours, or to stated forms. Both Judaism and Christianity pay homage to a God limitless and unconfined. Every day is holy and the whole world a temple. Nevertheless religious life requires a focus, a center, a source from which it may radiate to all the rest of life. America's churches and synagogues (for the construction of which about one billion dollars are annually expended) continue to be the most obvious as well as the most logical loci for religion.

However important to the national economy, church architecture has far greater significance for faith itself. Winston Churchill once remarked that first we shape our dwellings, then our dwellings proceed to shape us. If this be true of political structures (of which he was speaking), it is even more applicable to ecclesiastical structures. The intimacy, for example, between liturgy and architecture is so close that chaos results when the two have not walked hand in hand. And if liturgy has neglected to shape its own house, then the building soon shapes the liturgy.

Reinhold Niebuhr decries church architecture in America in *Essays in Applied Christianity* (1959).

In a sense the formless exuberance of American church architecture in 'most of the churches built between 1870 and 1930 is a perfect expression of the formlessness inside the church. . . . A vital Christianity will express itself in new architectural forms or in novel adaptations of old forms to the 'new' realities of a technical society. But American church architecture in the period mentioned revealed no discipline of any kind. It was merely the expression of free imagination and the fruit of some architect's conviction that a church should not look like a grain elevator. Therefore it was distinguished from the latter by as many turrets, arches, and other curious gingerbread as the architect could dream up.

The synagogue of Judaism bears little resemblance to the temple of Solomon or Herod. Nor can it, for the worship within is so different. The temple of antiquity, always part market place and part slaughter house, centered upon rituals of animal sacrifice and priestly intercession. The open-air brazen altar would be singularly superfluous in the modern American synagogue. Similarly, if there is no high priest to intercede annually in the innermost Holy of Holies, then it is pointless to build such a secluded sanctuary.[1]

If the Eucharist is the highest peak in Christian worship, architecture must reflect that fact; else it will blur or erase it. If the sermon is the climactic ritual, then structure and design must proceed accordingly. If liturgy is performed for the people, one building plan is appropriate; if performed by the people, then quite another is called for. In some religious bodies (e.g., Christian Science and Quaker) no official clergy presides. An architecture which ignores this can hardly succeed. Other groups emphasizing lecture and discussion scarcely benefit from divided chancel and distant altar. In church architecture, if nowhere else, "form follows function."

Otto Spaeth, founder of the Liturgical Arts Society, urges a contemporary religious architecture (in J. K. Shear, *Religious Buildings for Today*).

It seems to me that the first requirement of a church or temple today is that it be of today, contemporary, a structure embracing the total life of the parishioner. That parishioner drives a streamlined car to work in an office or factory where everything has been designed for maximum efficiency and comfort. He travels in streamlined trains and jet-propelled planes. Yet every Sunday he is asked to hurl himself back centuries to say his prayers in the pious gloom of a Gothic or Romanesque past. The clear implication is that God does not exist today: He is made out to be a senile old gentleman dwelling among the antiques of his residence, one whom we visit each week out of sentiment and then forget since he obviously has no relation to the normal part of our lives.

The church's structure not only sustains and reinforces the liturgy, it also stimulates and shapes the theology. This it may do in such obvious ways as providing built-in symbolism (see Figs. 16, 21), but also in the somewhat subtler way of the House itself becoming a symbol. Thus the building opening itself to nature and the world suggests one kind of theology, while

---

[1] In America today the term "temple" is used by Reformed Jews for their houses of worship, the term "synagogue" by Orthodox Jews.

the heavy, barricaded fortress implies another. One church reaches for heaven, a second clasps the earth. One synagogue embraces the intellectual, artistic, and social life along with the spiritual, while another structure more narrowly defines its function. The very pillars and walls declare their theology.

What do America's religious buildings say? Is there an American architectural style for the House of God? In general, no. The diversity of faiths, together with the diversity of races and origins, virtually preclude a unified architectural expression. Sharp jabs, sometimes good-humored and sometimes not, at "American grotesque," "post-office baroque," and "frontier gothic" take aim at the mixture and dilution of historic styles. On the other hand, the United States offers excellent artistic imitations of the styles of other lands and other ages: the Spanish mission, the French Gothic, the Greek Temple. America in the twentieth century even imitates America of the nineteenth and eighteenth centuries.

Yet also in the twentieth century new creativity appears. While the concern that the ecclesiastical structure "look like a church" may be legitimate, the determination that it function like a church is now deemed more urgent. Liturgist and theologian work with artist and architect to produce a House appropriate to the time, place, use, and creed. The result of this willingness to experiment is at least an honest reflection of the talents and convictions of those responsible for it. Generally it is more: a living symbol calling to faith in terms that twentieth-century man heeds. He sees his world, not some other, embodied in the glass, the steel, the concrete, the wood. And he sees faith vital enough to create anew, to fashion a fresh world, to bestow a present beauty upon a distracted people. Rather than a museum, the house of God becomes a message.

Creativity, of course, does not mean uniformity; no new "creative style" emerges. Yesterday's diversity will be no less under the inspiration of today's creative urge: it will probably be more. Yet a purposiveness in design and an honesty in structure grant meaning to the variety. Since it is impossible to think creatively about religious architecture without also thinking creatively about theology and worship, a renaissance in construction may likewise be a renaissance in consecration.

Max Abramovitz, leading architect and sometime professor of fine arts, calls for creative synagogue architecture (in T. F. Hamlin, *Form and Function in Twentieth Century Architecture*).

Today, consistent with a world-wide interest in honest architectural expression, free of false stylistic trends, the problem of the architectural solution of the synagogue or temple should resolve into one of good design; it is concerned primarily with the requirements of space, utility and character. There is a growing trend away from the styles of yesterday. Along with

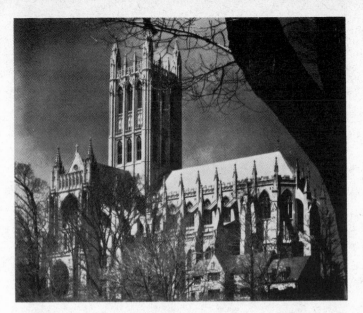

1. *Washington Cathedral • Officially designated the Cathedral Church of St. Peter and St. Paul, the Washington Cathedral has been under construction since 1907. An Episcopal church, it seeks to be a "House of Prayer for all People."*

3. *National Shrine of the Immaculate Conception, side view*

2. *National Shrine of the Immaculate Conception • The largest Catholic Church in the United States, the National Shrine is dedicated to the Blessed Virgin Mary as Patroness of the country. Completed in 1959, the church is Byzantine in design.*

4. *Hillcrest Jewish Center, Jamaica, New York • Designed by Sam J. Glaberson and built in 1950, this Jewish Centers carries its symbolism not only externally (see at left) but in the very design of the sanctuary itself (see following figure).*

5. *Hillcrest Jewish Center (interior)*

6. *The Wayfarers' Chapel (façade)*

7. *The Wayfarer's Chapel, Portuguese Bend, California • Designed by Lloyd Wright (son of Frank Lloyd Wright) in 1951, this Swedenborgian house of worship minimizes the distinction between man and nature. As is seen particularly in the preceding figure, the church is open to all the world.*

8. *Trinity Lutheran Church, Walnut Creek, California • The firm of Skidmore, Owings & Merrill working closely with the congregation produced a church of notable simplicity and appeal. Members of the church carved the three rough-hewn crosses themselves.*

9. *Trinity Lutheran Church (chancel)*

10. *Calvary Baptist Church, San Bernardino, California • Taking advantage of the surrounding natural beauty, this church, dedicated in 1965, provides both intimacy and openness in its sanctuary.*

11. *Calvary Baptist Church (interior)*

the knowledge of science and technology, there has come to the people of today a new confidence in their own strength and power. Today we can create an architecture to fit our age and need not ape the past.

Architecture determines the location of more than walls and beams. Tables, pulpits, altars, and other furnishings play their role not by accident but by design. In Judaism, Catholicism, and Protestantism conformity in internal architecture generally exceeds that found in the external structure. Yet even within the houses of worship significant deviations of design appear in contemporary America.

In the synagogue the two necessary and therefore ever-present appointments for worship are the Ark of the Covenant (where the Torah is kept) and the almemar, or reading desk (where the Torah is read). Traditionally the ark and the desk have been far enough apart to permit ceremonial processions from one to the other, with major attention given to the transporting of the Torah. In Reform temples, however, the ark and the desk (which can serve also as a pulpit) may both be at the front of an auditorium-like building. Here ceremony and procession yield in prominence to reading and instruction. Orthodox practice, moreover, calls for separate seating of the sexes, while in Reform design mixed seating prevails. Like a church, a synagogue too has trouble always "looking like a synagogue," as accompanying illustrations suggest. (Compare Figs. 4, 12, and 15.)

While little representational art decorates either synagogue or temple, the furnishings themselves are rich with symbolic meaning and evocative power. The seven-branched candlestick (menorah), symbol of the spiritual light God sheds on and through Israel, usually flanks the Ark of the Covenant. In front of the ark itself the eternal light hangs, reminding the worshiper that the Torah is a source of unceasing illumination and inspiration. And above the ark representations of the two tables of law given on Mount Sinai reaffirm the divine origin of Judaism's message. The most familiar symbol of all, the six-pointed star or shield of David, representing all Israel, may be found in many places inside and outside the synagogue—even in the design of the building itself (see Figs. 4 and 5).

The center of Catholic worship is the altar. But the position of the altar may vary according to the structure of the building or the desires of the worshipers. In the most familiar plan the altar stands on a platform at one end of a rectangle. The congregation sits facing the altar. The pulpit is off to one side, raised or suspended over the heads of the worshipers, perhaps almost halfway up the length of the rectangle. The most interesting contemporary variant of this design makes the altar the architectural as well as the liturgical center. The congregation sits on several sides of the altar, thus participating more fully in the rites celebrated there. Among the effects of this plan is to restrict the size of congregation to the few hundred (instead of the few thousand) who can actually join with the priest in the Eucharis-

12. *B'nai Israel, Milburn, New Jersey • Architecture reinforces theology as the Ark's thrust from the center of the building is seen. The sculpture thereon symbolizes the burning bush. (Percival Goodman, architect, 1951.)*

13. *Priory Church of St. Mary and St. Louis, Creve Coeur, Missouri • Completed in 1962, this dramatic structure of concrete and glass opens like a flower in the midst of the Benedictine monastic enclosure. Designed by Hellmuth, Obata & Kassabaum of St. Louis, the priory church has a central altar totally surrounded by the congregation.*

14. *Priory Church of St. Mary and St. Louis (interior)*

tic liturgy. The mass again becomes a meal, the parish membership a worshiping community. Churches of traditional plan may also encourage this intimacy through the modesty and simplicity of design (see Fig. 13 and 14).

Edward J. Sutfin and Maurice Lavanoux, prominent Roman Catholic authorities, show why church architecture cannot imitate (in Albert Christ-Janer, *et al., Modern Church Architecture*).

> But even if we could duplicate a medieval cathedral exactly, stone by stone, we would still be unable to relive the spirit of its age. Our copy would be no more than a curiosity, a museum piece rather than living architecture. It must be kept in mind that the Church ever brings forth new and old treasures. The sacramental and liturgical life are old, but vital and dynamic. The presentation of this heritage, however, is dated by the "new" and the "now" of the contemporary stage of development of the city of God. Thus the "new" treasures of Romanesque, Gothic, Renaissance, and Baroque could be expressed by the architectural styles of each of these succeeding periods; whereas these same styles are now "old" and "traditional." The main thing to be understood is that new architectural treasure must be authentic and genuine. If it is so, living people will embrace it as their own.

Symbolism within the churches of Catholicism is inexhaustibly rich: murals, frescoes, stained windows, mosaic floors, statuary, and pictures. In America the abundant use of large paintings is especially characteristic of Eastern Orthodoxy, the separation of nave from sanctuary being made by a curtain or partition (iconostasis) normally filled with paintings. Statues of the four evangelists, the apostles, the saints, the martyrs adorn side chapels, external friezes, the main sanctuary, and nave. Often the representational art contains symbols that aid in identification of the person or event portrayed even as they carry their own meaning. In other places, notably on the vestments and altar cloths, symbols stand alone.

The central symbol in Catholicism is the crucifix. Artists have for centuries sought to capture the serenity or agony, the humanity or divinity of Christ upon the cross. The crucifix generally hangs over the altar, portraying Golgotha's historic sacrifice as the mass repeats the daily sacrifice. Second in prominence only to the crucified Christ, the Madonna and Child or the Blessed Virgin alone dominate much of Catholicism's religious art. Symbolizing the merciful, the protective, the compassionate, Mary is daily implored to "pray for us sinners now and in the hour our death." The dove, representing the Holy Spirit, also receives prominent artistic expression, usually in conjunction with specific events such as the baptism of Jesus and the miraculous preaching at Pentecost.

15. Beth El, Flint, Michigan • In this contemporary synagogue, "strength and beauty" are also found in the restrained symbolism of the façade.

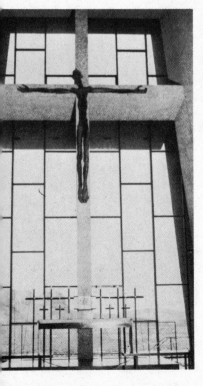

17. Chapel of the Holy Cross, Sedona, Arizona • Completed in 1956, this striking chapel was designed to be a shrine "where God can be worshipped as a contemporary." Sculptor Keith Monroe designed the attenuated and painfully strained figure of Christ (see above).

16. Chapel of the Holy Cross (altar)

Maurice Lavanoux pleads for honesty and creativity in Catholic architecture (in T. F. Hamlin, *Form and Function in Twentieth Century Arhitecture*).

It was of course possible to reproduce faithfully all the elements which made the Gothic period great—but only when funds were plentiful and craftsmen available. The real danger was apparent when the hopes and desires of both client and architect went far beyond the means available to carry then out. This difficulty bred a spirit of compromise which tended to justify make-shifts; in consequence the land was dotted with pseudo-this and pseudo-that churches which, by their very nature and construction, belied all the principles which had actuated and guided the builders of old. A further danger arose from the fact that this stage-scenery architecture brought into play efforts to camouflage the weaknesses of the construction in order to make the building look like the real thing. In addition to the structural lie thus perpetrated, this adherence to the past for sentimental reasons cost all concerned a great deal of wasted money; for that reason the work of creative artists could not find a place in such a scheme.

For Protestantism the proclamation of the word is the traditional center in architecture and worship. Preaching becomes the principal sacrament, the major means for the dispensation of divine grace. The pulpit therefore stands as silent symbol even as it serves as active agent of the Word expounded, "improved," and applied. Reflecting this prominence given to preaching, much Protestant architecture resembled that of lecture or concert hall where hearing was the prime consideration. Indeed, so suitable were such halls for Protestant services that in the nineteenth and twentieth centuries they were often taken over by large urban congregations. Groups constructing their own church buildings might follow the "Akron plan," calling for pews radiating around the pulpit platform with the floor inclined that all might see and hear. This plan also provided for Sunday School rooms immediately adjacent to the "auditorium," with movable partitions permitting an enlargement of seating space when necessary.

Leading Protestant theologian Paul Tillich discusses the possibility of a "Protestant architectural language" (in Albert Christ-Janer, *et al., Modern Church Architecture*).

Today, genuine Protestant church architecture is possible, perhaps for the first time in our history. For the early experiments were too swiftly engulfed by eclecticism to act as evolutionary factors in developing a recognizable Protestant architectural language.

Even today, however, many congregations and ministers still assume that the choice between modern and imitative-traditional architecture is merely

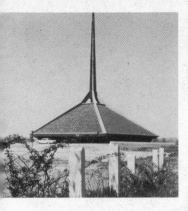

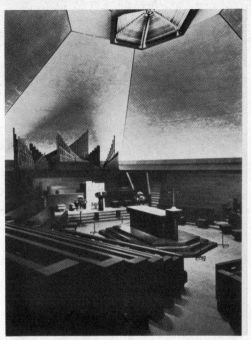

18. North Christian Church, Columbus, Indiana • In 1964, one of the nation's leading architectural firms, Eero Saarinen & Associates, designed both exterior and interior.

19. North Christian Church (interior)

20. First Baptist Church, Bloomington, Indiana • In its stark simplicity this sanctuary, dedicated in 1956, suggests something of the clear and austere demands of discipleship. The Lord's Supper is celebrated around what is clearly a table rather than an altar.

21. First Baptist Church (chancel)

22. *Unity Temple, Oak Park, Illinois • Near the beginning of the twentieth century, Frank Lloyd Wright designed this church which is notable, among other things, for its deliberate rejection of symbolism and historical tradition.*

23. *Unity Temple (interior)*

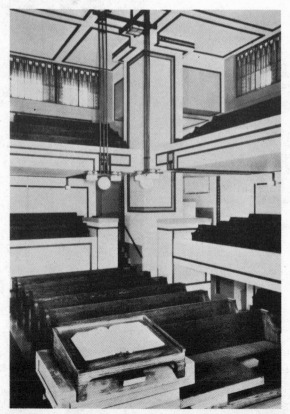

24. *Concordia Senior College Chapel, Fort Wayne, Indiana* • *Unlike most
college campuses in America, Concordia was built (in 1957) with unity and
harmony of design. The chapel, whose altar is illumined by natural light,
stands between the library and dining hall of the campus.*

25. *Concordia Senior College Chapel*
    (nave)

26. *Concordia Senior College Chapel*
    (chancel)

a matter of taste and preference. They fail to see that only by the creation of new forms can Protestant churches achieve an honest expression of their faith.

This expression should be made real, even if many experiments are necessary and some end in failure. An element of risk is unavoidable in the building of sacred places, just as a risk must be taken in every act of faith.

For some the service of preaching seemed to minimize the service of worship. Little if any symbolism, little if any liturgy inspired the person in the pew to an adoration and glorification of God. Could the listener become a worshiper? To solve this problem the architect, the liturgist, and the theologian once more worked together. One popular solution called for a visual center of worship besides the preacher in his striped (or checkered, or subdued, or gowned) single-breasted suit. The auditorium became a sanctuary with symbols of the Christian faith in full evidence. The pulpit was moved to one side, with a lectern on the other side, and the cross, or the open word, or a stained window, or a panorama of nature held the worshiper's attention (see Figs. 18 and 19).

Protestant ventures in the use of symbols have widely varied, some conscientiously resisting them as distracting and dangerous. Idolatry arises when one confuses the physical symbol with that incorporeal reality which it represents. To avoid symbols is to spurn this danger. But there are dangers in thoroughgoing iconoclasm, too, for through the senses as well as through the intellect God speaks to man. Most Protestants find meaning in baptism and communion; some extend the use of symbols beyond these to sculpture, painting, mosaic, bas-relief, and the like.

While Judaism, Catholicism, and Protestantism each has its architectural problems to solve, America's pluralistic society presents even more problems. What if one wishes to represent successfully all three religious traditions? Can the Ark, the altar, and the pulpit all be central? Does the cross of Christ blend with the shield of David? The pulpit platform with the iconostasis? Nowhere but in America would an architect be expected to find his way through this puzzle, for nowhere else has the plurality of faith been so openly acknowledged, so fervently preserved.

Two clear alternatives present themselves in the effort to represent the historic faiths of all America. One adopted at Brandeis University, for example, consists in portraying the three traditions side by side in an architectural style that is consistent but which permits the liturgical emphases of each tradition to express themselves (see Fig. 29). The other, employed regularly by the military services, requires a building which permits maximum flexibility in the interior arrangements and foci of worship (see Fig. 28). Neither plan attempts to blend or blur the liturgical heritage.

A third alternative, less clear in direction, seeks a synthesis in its archi-

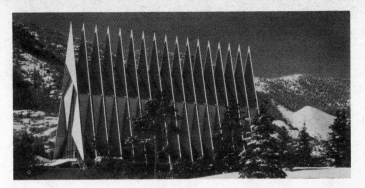

27. *Chapel, U. S. Air Force Academy, Colorado • Using the most modern of materials, the firm of Skidmore, Owings and Merrill built the Air Force Chapel in a manner reminiscient of a most venerable style: the Gothic. Its silhouetted peaks and its structural bays help the worshipper contrast his finitude with an infinity beyond.*

28. *Inter-Faith Chapel, U. S. Merchant Marine Academy, Kings Point, Long Island, New York • The rotating chancel area solves the problem of multiple liturgical demand made upon the military chapel.*

29. *The Three Chapels, Brandeis University, Waltham, Massachusetts • Religious diversity on the college campus finds its most ambitious architectural solution on the Brandeis grounds where Protestant, Jewish and Catholic chapels were erected, 1954-56.*

tectural expression. Is it possible to erect a structure that is religious without its being of a specific religion? Is there a Judeo-Christian House of God? While attempts to answer these questions with bricks and mortar have been made, the necessity of divorcing liturgy from history is probably too heavy a burden for religious architecture to bear. Having a religion without having any religion in particular is, said George Santayana, like trying to speak a language without speaking any language in particular. And a house of God that does not assist in the specific worship of that God loses much of its reason for being.

The dean of Harvard Divinity School, Samuel H. Miller, writes of the need for a powerful symbol in modern life in *The Dilemma of Modern Belief* (1963).

What we are seeking is fundamentally *a reconciling image,* although the descriptive adjective is far from strong enough to describe the dynamic energy inherent in true symbols. Usually we consider a symbol or an image as a static object, a picture of a particular sort. Actually, however, even advertising in its crassest efforts deliberately counts on the dynamic intensity of certain images. Few of them have reconciling power. What we need is an image of such interest and depth that it can redeem life from superficiality and relate us again to the depths of our origin and the ground of our existence.

. . . In the West, since the fall of Greece and Rome, the reconciling image has been the passion of Jesus Christ, symbolized by the crucifix and elaborated in the manifold events of his life, death, and resurrection. The long and extremely significant development of that image, its seemingly inexhaustible supply of new perspectives and fresh stimulation in the opening up of man's consciousness and the world derived from it, is the story of our Western history.

PART V

This Nation Under God:
At Work

21 ❖ The Mission at Home

A NATION'S WORSHIP is best revealed in a nation's work; or, in the words of an early Christian apostle, faith without works is dead. Religion that ministers beyond institutional boundaries, faith that transcends parochial walls, finds ears eager to hear and hearts ready to be healed. Modern man swiftly shuns the insular religious community busy contemplating and flattering itself, but he responds to faith lost in service to a great cause. When the church and synagogue thrust themselves into the center of life rather than retreat to a cozy corner of life, they still transform. Then religion, ceasing to be a mere relic of the past, becomes powerful reality in the present.

PEACE AND WAR

The twentieth century opened on a confident note: a new millennium seemed ready to dawn. The age of the giants had come to America. Industry grew rich, labor grew strong, cities grew big, and the nation's government tried to keep up with its enlarging, noisy brood. The simple success of the "splendid little war" in 1898 increased the brood and here and there troubled a conscience.

The nineteenth-century peace movements, having lost much momentum in the Civil War era, regained strength as the century ended. The Universal Peace Congress held in Chicago in 1893 stimulated popular interest, as did the Lake Mohonk Arbitration Conferences begun by Albert K. Smiley in 1895. When a Hague Conference of twenty-six nations in 1899 formulated plans for universal peace, hopes soared that heaven drew near. Peace, seen more as a personal than a political question, seemed within easy grasp. Philanthropy, notably that of Andrew Carnegie, aided the churches in their corporate quest for international understanding, as Christian and Jew proclaimed the glad tidings of peace on earth.

Re-elected in 1916 because "he kept us out of war," Woodrow Wilson, Presbyterian educator-become-President, found himself nonetheless surrounded by war. If the nation could not preserve peace without a war, perhaps it could through war win an enduring peace. The idealism infusing

World War I was not Wilson's alone: it was a people's—a people still riding the future's wave, still basking under Divine benevolence. A war to end all wars: that was worth fighting. A world made safe for democracy: that was worth fashioning.

But for most, World War I seriously, even tragically, interrupted the mission of America—the mission to its own people and to the world. And when that war ended, Wilson resumed the work in the name of a nation of law and a God of love. Hailed on all sides as a peacemaker par excellence, President Woodrow Wilson personified the aspirations of a confident people. If America's competing colonies, divergent minorities, and clashing creeds could live in peace, then why not a world likewise ordered and blessed?

Whatever the shortcomings of the Treaty of Versailles, the churches clung hopefully to the promise offered in the last of Wilson's Fourteen Points: the League of Nations. The Federal Council of Churches, for example, exclaimed in a cable to President Wilson, then in Paris, that the League constituted the "political expression of the Kingdom of God on earth." Representing Catholicism, Judaism, and Protestantism, the influential Church Peace Union pressed vigorously for American support of and entry into the League. By a proportion of more than twenty to one, America's clergymen of all faiths endorsed the League.

President Woodrow Wilson spoke before the Senate on July 10, 1919, endeavoring to enlist its support for the League of Nations. His high view of America's destiny in the international scene was widely shared by his fellow citizens.

> Our participation in the war established our position among the nations and nothing but our own mistaken action can alter it. . . . We answered the call of duty in a way so spirited, so utterly without thought of what we spent of blood or treasure, so effective, so worthy of the admiration of true men everywhere, so wrought out of the stuff of all that was heroic, that the whole world saw at last, in the flesh, in noble action, a great ideal asserted and vindicated, by a Nation they had deemed material and now found to be compact of the spiritual forces that must free men of every nation from every unworthy bondage. It is thus that a new role and a new responsibility have come to this great Nation that we honor and which we would all wish to lift to yet higher levels of service and achievement.
>
> The stage is set, the destiny disclosed. It has come about by no plan of our conceiving, but by the hand of God who led us into this way. We cannot turn back. We can only go forward, with lifted eyes and freshened spirit, to follow the vision. It was of this that we dreamed at our birth. America shall in truth show the way. The light streams upon the path ahead, and nowhere else.

1. *Woodrow Wilson's Tomb, Washington Cathedral*

When the United States Senate blocked this avenue toward international understanding, churches and synagogues continued to press for alternatives to repeated war. Disarmament seemed a hopeful path. If armies and navies were reduced, also stores of ammunition and fire power diminished, would not peace be brought nearer thereby? If one cannot beat all swords into ploughshares (armored tanks and battleships present a problem), then perhaps he can at least dispose of the swords. The Washington Disarma-

---

One of America's great Quaker philosophers, Rufus Jones (1863–1948), explains his understanding of the pacifist way of life in *The New Quest* (1928).

> Pacifism means *peace-making*. The pacifist is literally a peace-maker. He is not a passive or negative person who proposes to lie back and do nothing in the face of injustice, unrighteousness and rampant evil. He stands for "the fiery positive." Pacifism is not a theory; it is a way of life. It is something you *are and do*. . . .
>
> St. Paul knew enough about the forces of evil to know that they could be conquered only by greater *forces*, and so he set forth his famous method—

"overcome evil with good." There is no other way to overcome it. Something else, something better, must be put in its place. . . .

We shall not get very far with phrases like "passive resistance" or "non-resistance," or "the use of force is immoral." One can neither train a life nor build a world on those or any other slogans. . . . There would be little use having our Government and all the other governments of the world adopt abstract resolutions to the effect that military force shall be outlawed and shall never be resorted to again, if at the same time all the selfish and unjust methods of life and business and social relations were left to work just as they are now working. War is a fruit which grows and ripens like other fruit. No magic phrase, no written scrap of paper, will stop the ripening of it if the tree which bears it is planted and watered and kept in the sunshine and warm air. The axe must first be laid to the root of the tree.

---

ment Conference, gathering nine nations to the American capital late in 1921, resulted largely from pressures exerted by organized religion. As early as June 5, 1921, a "Reduction of Armament Sunday" called thousands of priests, rabbis, and ministers to a cause they considered altogether righteous and critically relevant. More than twenty thousand clergymen petitioned President Harding to call a conference on international disarmament. Yielding to these and other pressures, Harding called the Conference for November 12, 1921. The churches promptly named November 6 as a day of prayer for all delegates attending.

Most disarmament conferences only talk about disarmament vaguely. But Secretary of State Charles Evans Hughes electrified his audience by suggesting that disarmament actually begin according to a definite, detailed plan. For this conference called by American officials and sustained by American convictions the churches prayed, preached, and lobbied, maintaining public interest until Senate ratification was secure.

Hopes rose even higher in 1928 when the Briand-Kellogg peace treaty (Pact of Paris) outlawed war as an instrument of national policy. The promise of this agreement, asserted the General Conference of Southern Methodism, is illumined by "the light that shone in Bethlehem." Church delegations by the dozens called on America's Secretary of State Frank Kellogg, assuring him of their enthusiastic support for this "great step forward in human history." Fifteen nations of the world had agreed to renounce war! "The rosy dawn of a new peace consciousness is at hand," the moderator of northern Presbyterians exulted.

Pacifist sentiment spread rapidly in the 1930's. Not only the historic "peace churches" such as the Quakers or Mennonites but also most others encouraged or advocated pacifism. Numbers of ministers declared themselves unable ever again to sanction or support war. Nearly all organizations pressing for peace drew their strength from the ranks of religion.

In one of the two most significant encyclicals of his brief pontificate (1958–1963) Pope John XXIII addressed himself to the urgent questions of peace and war. *Pacem in Terris* (*Peace on Earth*) includes the following comment on disarmament (1963).

> All must realize that there is no hope of putting an end to the building up of armaments, nor of reducing the present stocks, nor, still less—and this is the main point—of abolishing them altogether, unless the process is complete and thorough and unless it proceeds from inner conviction: unless, that is, everyone sincerely cooperates to banish the fear and anxious expectation of war with which men are oppressed. If this is to come about, the fundamental principle on which our present peace depends must be replaced by another, which declares that the true and solid peace of nations consists not in equality of arms but in mutual trust alone. We believe that this can be brought to pass, and we consider that, since it concerns a matter not only demanded by right reason but also eminently desirable in itself, it will prove to be the source of many benefits.

How naïve or uncritical was this religious commitment to peace? War was evil, but was it the greatest evil? Peace was good, but was it the ultimate good? Sharp debates pricked the consciences and punctured the composures of editors, theologians, pastors, and parishioners. Often the condemnation of any and all war showed little awareness of or concern for the larger world. Thus religious pacifism sometimes allied itself with political isolationism. But as brutal injustices and insatiable ambitions grew more obvious, absolute pacifism grew harder to defend. How should Ethiopia endure Mussolini's aggression, China withstand Japan's invasion, Poland meet Hitler's blitzkrieg? With resignation and love, or with resistance and sword? Micah's ancient command to love mercy also included an injunction to "do justly." What did justice demand?

The wide divergence of religious opinion narrowed following England and France's 1939 declaration of war against the Axis powers. But the relative merits of neutrality, nonbelligerency, and open combat continued to be debated in America until December 7, 1941. Then Pearl Harbor's dark disaster mobilized public opinion in a day. The question was no longer that of peace or war, but a more treacherously difficult one: can mankind, by war, ever bring about a world of peace?

In World War II organized religion followed two broad approaches. In one, churches and synagogues directly bolstered the war effort, hoping to bring hostilities to a quick and successful end. Ministries of faith offered consolation, guidance, inspiration, and a community of moral strength. Bandages wrapped, supplies sent, entertainment provided, Bibles dispatched, prayers offered, plaques hung, services held—these and countless other activities characterized religion's mission in wartime.

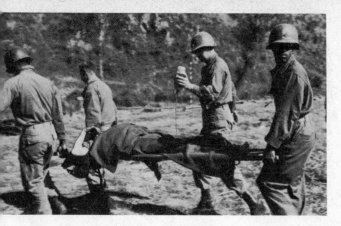

2. *Chaplain Carries Plasma in Korea (1951)*

3. *Confession on the Battlefield, Korea (1951)*

4. *Chaplain Aids the Wounded in France (1944)*

5. *Sunday Services at Augusta Bay, Sicily (U. S. S. Columbus)*

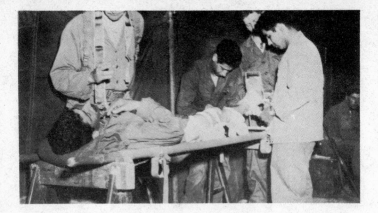

6. *Wounded Soldier Receives Blessing, Korea (1951)*

7. *Easter Sunday, O'Reilly General Hospital, Springfield, Missouri*

8. *Aboard the U. S. S. Tanner, 1961*

9. *Services for the 102nd Infantry Division, war-torn church in Ubach, Germany*

New York City Synagogue, 1944

11. *D-Day service, June 6, 1944*

More than eight thousand ministers, rabbis, and priests served as chaplains in World War II. Confession was heard on battlefields, hymns were sung on armored decks, sermons were preached in arctic snows, communion was offered in front-line hospitals, and scripture was read at many an unmarked, but not unhallowed, grave. Chaplains lived in tents, trailers, ships, planes, foxholes, and open fields; they also died there, none more bravely than the four who stood arm in arm on the deck of the *Dorchester* as she slowly sank into the Atlantic.

The other approach of American religion was to seek, almost as soon as war began, the path to a just and durable peace. Some years before he became Secretary of State (1952–1959), John Foster Dulles, vigorous Presbyterian layman, directed a commission of churchmen in considering the grounds of a proper peace. Participation in the war gave the United States, Reinhold Niebuhr argued, a better chance to secure the peace. ". . . We belong in the same world, are part of the same family, still have faith in God and the dignity of man, and must share with them [nations at war] the problems and tasks of the world." Aloof and indifferent to the bleeding wounds of a warring world, America could not have served, for it could not have felt. Through the tragedy of participation, out of the sacrifice of commitment, comprehension and then compassion could come. We were indeed "part of the same family."

If participation brought identity, it failed to bring either the power or wisdom to effect enduring peace. And if the idealism of Wilson's Fourteen Points seemed too hopefully naïve, the cynicism of "unconditional surrender" seemed too hopelessly barren. Deeply rooted hopes for "just and durable peace" began to flower only after the germination of the United Nations in San Francisco in 1945.

Meanwhile, a war won, the task of mending men and nations began. Veterans, sometimes more shattered in spirit than in body, returned to ways of life rudely interrupted, to ways of devotion sometimes abandoned. Religion, seeking to prove that right makes might in a world where the opposite was ever more plausible, proclaimed anew the power of faith to heal, even to transform. Yet, sobered by two costly wars and an economic depression, America's religious leaders no longer took refuge in a simple ethic of "Be good, and you'll be happy." Moral choices were too complex, the path to righteousness too obscure to suppose that the "old-time religion" possessed ready-made solutions to war-made problems.

And if personal problems were intricate, how much more were international conflicts a maze of dark mystery. Was it possible to forgive nations as well as men, to mend broken economies no less than broken bones, to restore morale along with morals? Was it possible to speak to a waiting world the ancient words:

Comfort ye, comfort ye my people,
says your God.

Speak tenderly to Jerusalem,
and cry to her
that her warfare is ended,
that her iniquity is pardoned. . . .

The moral vision of these words found expression in the Marshall Plan, the Relief and Rehabilitation Agency (UNRRA), the Children's Emergency Fund (UNICEF), the World Health Organization, and an intensified missionary effort of the churches.

The development of nuclear power, threatening the annihilation of civilizations if not civilization itself, made conscientious re-examinations of war and peace even more agonizing. Serene peace or total war now became a question of uneasy peace and limited war. And none pretended that the question was merely academic. On August 6, 1945, a single bomb killed 78,150 persons, injuring 37,425 others. A Judeo-Christian heritage that commanded men to love mercy and hate evil now called men to find some way out of unmeasured savagery. Over all the rebuilding of a postwar world, a mushroom cloud cast its sinister shadow.

Like a great many other religious leaders in the United States, the rabbis of the Central Conference addressed themselves to the intensified threats posed by nuclear war. A portion of their 1959 message follows.

As rabbis representing the oldest continuing moral and ethical tradition in human thought, we appeal at this critical juncture in the world's affairs to the reason and conscience of men everywhere—and especially to the leaders of the nations. The Biblical forevision of universal doom has become all too realistic a possibility in our time. We must come to our senses without delay if we are to achieve some measure of safety from destruction for mankind and a modicum of sanity in the relations between nations. There is no longer any substance in the formulas of national prestige, interest and security when placed above the survival and welfare of all humanity. . . .

What is requisite is that mood of humility which is willing to recognize that all men and nations are fallible. God was not always on the side of Israel, nor has He been or ever will be on the side of any nation. He judges all men and nations, and weighs their actions on the scales of justice. There are wrongs being committed by all nations, which sooner or later will have to be corrected if tensions are to be lessened and peace becomes less precarious.

A 1957 message of the National Council of Churches, while recognizing the military and scientific importance of nuclear power, declared the world's fundamental crisis to be "moral and spiritual." In such a crisis religion, the Council noted, must remind all that "God wills for man to live in love and reconciliation." Judaism's Martin Buber argued that the time had come to turn from war games, from this nuclear "gambling, the stake of which is the life of the human race, and in which both partners must lose." And in 1959 John Cogley, former editor of *Commonweal,* maintained that total disarmament, "man's ancient dream," is the only possible course for rational, moral men.

Yet only in the 1960s and 70s did national sentiment against war become a demonstrative public passion. Indochina and Vietnam, for all their tragic failure as foreign policy, may have succeeded in one thing: namely, giving war a bad name. America's "brightest and best" as well as her dedicated and devout found themselves mired in a war they could not end, found themselves inflicting wounds they could not heal. In a growing revulsion prompted chiefly by the young, an embittered America slowly turned more and more toward peace marches and peace symbols or, at least, away from war chants and body counts. Was there at last a chance for abstract pacifist principle to become concrete political fact?

"WITH LIBERTY AND JUSTICE FOR ALL"

Two world wars in two generations left little easy optimism. What hopes war clouds did not dampen, a bleak and gloomy Great Depression did. As optimism faded, confidence in religion's power to transform likewise lessened. So keen was the suffering in the 1930's, so oppressive the poverty that many despaired of traditional techniques of amelioration. Some, despairing of even the nation's basic structure, urged revolution rather than reform.

On the whole, Americans found it easier to tame hostile frontiers than to solve economic crises. This was also true of the churches. Ministers and missionaries, voluntary societies and denominational boards knew how to direct expansion, cut forests, and ford streams. But how does one shore up a faltering industry, stimulate a lagging economy, bring about a return to prosperity? More immediately, how does one gain a living wage, feed a starving child, shelter a dispossessed family? If religion had any good news, eager ears strained to hear it.

In 1931 the National Catholic Welfare Conference, the Federal Council of Churches, and the Central Conference of American Rabbis held a Conference on the Permanent Preventives of Unemployment. The 1931 encyclical *Quadragesimo Anno*[1] of Pope Pius XI was applied wherever relevant to America's economic woes. And three years later a Committee of Religion and Welfare Activity began to alleviate suffering and promote the common good. But an uneasiness pervaded: how competent was the spiritual order to repair or replace the malfunctioning temporal order?

---

[1] So-called because it was issued on the fortieth anniversary of the significant encyclical of Leo XIII, *Rerum novarum*, which dealt with social and economic problems.

The encyclical of Pope Pius XI *Quadragesimo Anno* (1931), or *On Reconstructing the Social Order,* testified to Catholicism's continuing concern for the economic status of man.

> Since the present system of economy is founded chiefly upon ownership and labor, the principles of right reason, that is, of Christian social philosophy, must be kept in mind regarding ownership and labor and their association together, and must be put into actual practice. First, so as to avoid the reefs of individualism and collectivism, the two-fold character, that is individual and social, both of capital or ownership and of work or labor, must be given due and rightful weight. Relations of one to the other must be made to conform to the laws of strictest justice—commutative justice, as it is called—with the support, however, of Christian charity. Free competition, kept with definite and due limits, and still more economic dictatorship, must be effectively brought under public authority in these matters which pertain to the latter's function. The public institutions themselves, of peoples, moreover, ought to make all human society conform to the needs of the common good; that is, to the norm of social justice. If this is done, that most important division of social life, namely, economic activity, cannot fail likewise to return to right and sound order.

During the depression churches and synagogues dispensed their dwindling resources effectively and humanely. Without fanfare or fuss charity found its way from altar to hearth, from the community at worship to the family at home. The Mormons most conspicuously made each ecclesiastical division an agent of economic aid. Food was canned, stored, distributed, and consumed in a manner as thrifty as it was orderly. Judaism, hardly recovered from helping the indigent immigrant, fought for the survival of the unemployed. The Roman Catholic Church steadily urged that "social justice" be more than mere sloganeering and resolution-passing. The formation of the Association of Catholic Trade Unionists in 1937 provided one avenue for this church's concrete and constructive direction.

Yet economic dislocation remained staggeringly severe, the obstacles confronting voluntary charity were overwhelmingly great. The perennial temptation reappeared: since we cannot do everything, why do anything? Some churches contented themselves by suggesting simple solutions to complex problems, by offering archaic nostrums for modern ills. Even in the depths of the depression, prohibition for many Protestants remained the most urgent social issue. A southern churchman, asked to explain the causes of America's economic disaster, replied not too helpfully, "Sin." A kind of retreat of religion—churches withdrawing from effective involvement in the nation's social order—often took place.

New sects or cults protesting against society, against the prevailing order, against traditional forms obviously represent such a retreat. Some saw the approaching end of the world as sufficient argument against undertaking social reforms. Others, finding the secular·world evil and unrepentant, sought only to escape its pollution and save themselves. A few, as in the nineteenth century, deemed it best to build a new social order in minature off somewhere in deserts or in hills; there the forces of production, distribution, and consumption could be closely watched and carefully controlled. Finally, several new movements urged only adjustment within, a fresh mental power won, a comforting vision secured, a quieting peace restored. For all these the nation's social and economic order was at best irrelevant to religion; at worst, insidious.

Most of the older religious fellowships, on the other hand, while admitting the larger relevance, often confessed impotence or puzzlement regarding society's problems. And so another type of retreat resulted: a surrender to the overarching state of the basic responsibility for welfare, relief, and reform. Even churches traditionally conservative and individualistic increasingly sought government aid and intervention in the years of depression. The *Alabama Baptist* declared in 1933:"The old capitalistic system failed; the whole banking system failed; the government itself fairly tottered, and there is no where else to go except with the President. . . ." Some of the principles of the New Deal are "very similar" to some of the principles of the Old Book, declared Southern Presbyterian Walter L. Lingle. And in 1937 five hundred young Methodists, meeting in Lynchburg, Vir-

13. *Holiness Mission in Farm Area, New York-Pennsylvania border*

12. *Evicted Sharecropper Reads his Bible, Butler County, Missouri (1939)*

15. Japanese-Americans forcefully Evacuated from Los Angeles, 1942

14. Interracial Camp, Tusten, New York (1943)

16. Navaho Indians at Protestant Service, Phoenix, Arizona (1964)

17. Papago Indians learn under Catholic Direction

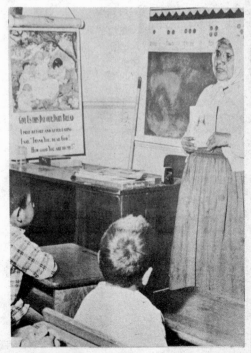

18. *Indian Children at Santa Cruz, Arizona*

19. *Jesuit Missionary aids Tony Good Buffalo, St. Francis Mission, South Dakota (1955)*

20. *Franciscan Sisters at the South Dakota Mission (1955)*

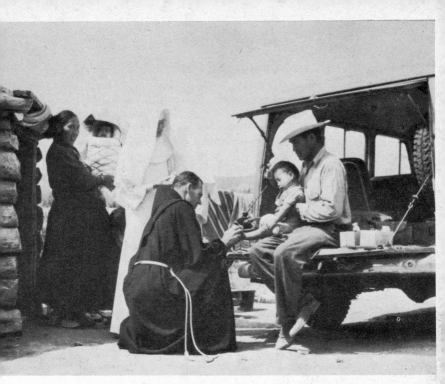

21. *Medical Care given on Navaho Reservation, St. Isabel's Mission (1956)*

22. *Flood Relief for Missouri River Victims (1952)*

ginia, looked beyond even the national government to "a world economic and social order in which service shall be the motive, cooperation the means, and universal equality and plenty the end of all production."

The task of reform was larger than the local church, larger than an association or assembly of churches, larger even than organized religion itself. Yet the ideals that directed national reform and determined national goals continued to arise as they had in the past: out of insights, commitments, and purposes basically spiritual.

These insights, commitments, and purposes were sorely tried in the major social crisis following World War II: the crisis of race. Jefferson's pivotal phrase "all men are created equal" proved easier to ridicule than to realize. For nearly two centuries Americans struggled with its meaning, pursued or fled its implications. Negro, Mexican, and Oriental servicemen returning from battle fought for equal terms, since those who fell in battle had given in equal measure. Together the living and the dead hastened an understanding of "liberty and justice for all." For justice, if not wholly blind, was surely color-blind.

At the very beginning of World War II the nation, in panic and distrust, relocated thousands of Japanese living on the West Coast. Fearful of sabotage or insurrection following the attack of December 7, 1941, authorities arranged for Japanese-Americans to be confined in camps far from the Pacific coast. Not only the Japanese alien but in some cases also the citizen of Japanese ancestry endured abuse. German-Americans, of course, had not been held responsible for Hitler's madness, nor Italian-Americans for Mussolini's aggression. But Japanese-Americans were concentrated geographically and, even more convenient, were identifiable physically. While some leaders protested this unjust deportation, the pressures and passions of a wartime emergency carried churches and general public along in an unthinking rush. In the detention camps a ministry of religion did what it could to bind these bloodless wounds of war, long in healing (see Fig. 15).

So swift and so new was this crisis of the Japanese that many in America remained virtually ignorant of it. The same was true, to a degree, of other regional frictions: Mexican-Americans in the southwest, Italian-Americans in the northeast, Indian-Americans (the most abused of all) in scattered, neglected reservations across the land. In the 1950's and 1960's, however, none could remain unaware of America's greatest race crisis since Emancipation. With the 1954 decision of the United States Supreme Court setting aside the "separate but equal" doctrine in public education, a racial revolution began. And the passage of an encompassing Civil Rights Act ten years later extended the revolution into housing, employment, voting, and public accommodations. In the churches, the streets, the courts, and the jails Negroes (and others) sang the hymn of revolution: "We Shall Overcome."

Conferences and crusades, marches and mass meetings, protests and prayers formed a holy alliance against continued legal discrimination and compulsory segregation. "The first step," said America's Roman Catholic bishops in 1963, "is to treat all men and women as persons." But it was a big step, for some a frightening step, requiring both the political authority of the state and the spiritual authority of the church. "Without recognition of individual dignity and compassion for suffering," the bishops added, "small wonder that social justice becomes merely a political matter and we remain as a nation morally tortured by racial injustice. . . ."

Ministers and rabbis, Negro and white, testified in city councils, church services, jail cells. Churches, both white and Negro, served as stations for protest, as servants to understanding. Seminary students stood together— Protestant, Catholic, Jew—in all-night vigils at the nation's capital, identifying themselves with the cause of justice for all. And the religious press added its powerful voice, calling the conscience of a people to "Equality Now!" Biblical faith affirmed it, America's democratic faith demanded it, all citizens deserved it: equality now.

The Jewish B'nai B'rith ("Sons of the Covenant") typified the many organizations seeking to dissolve those irrational barriers erected between man and man. Organized in the nineteenth century, B'nai B'rith together with its twentieth-century offspring, the Anti-Defamation League, directed much of its energy against symptoms of anti-Semitism. But its purposes were regularly broader than that. Utilizing the most advanced techniques of mass communication, B'nai B'rith with artistry, imagination, skill, and steady purpose promoted the kinship of mankind. "Who is my neighbor?" one ancient Jew asked another. Modern Jews of B'nai B'rith suggested an answer.

A Negro Baptist, Martin Luther King, represented within Christendom the most dramatic leadership of the racial revolution. Southern born and bred (Atlanta, Georgia, 1929), King received his ministerial education at Morehouse College in Georgia and Crozer Theological Seminary in Pennsylvania. After advanced graduate work at Boston University, King went to Montgomery, Alabama, in 1954 as pastor of the Dexter Avenue Baptist Church. He soon found himself, almost by accident, in the eye of a gathering storm. On December 1, 1955, a Negro citizen of Montgomery boarded a city bus and sat down in the first available seat. This simple action lacks the startling drama associated with revolution; yet because Mrs. Rosa Parks refused to yield her seat to a white male who boarded later, a way of life was threatened and a social structure challenged. Under the leadership of Martin Luther King this personal, spontaneous protest became a city-wide, deliberate bus boycott that lasted 381 days. Gradually, King wrote, the Negro community "came to see that it was ultimately more honorable to walk the streets in dignity than to ride the buses in humiliation."

23. Bus Boycott, Montgomery, Alabama (1956)

24. Bombed Birmingham Baptist Church (1963)

25. Fire Hoses in Birmingham, Alabama (1963)

26. *Martin Luther King addresses marchers in Washington, D. C. (1963)*

27. *Ministers pray on steps of Supreme Court, 1964, marking tenth Anniversary of School Desegregation Decision*

Martin Luther King spoke in 1960 of his "pilgrimage to nonviolence."

> . . . The nonviolent approach does not immediately change the heart of the oppressor. It first does something to the hearts and souls of those committed to it. It gives them new self-respect; it calls up resources of strength and courage that they did not know they had. Finally, it reaches the opponent and so stirs his conscience that reconciliation becomes a reality.

And as Governor William Bradford long ago had written, "Out of small beginnings. . . ." The bus boycott demonstrated the effectiveness of organized protest, the hopefulness of nonviolence, the sustaining power of faith. With "no plan except prayer [and] no policy except love," as Saunders Redding later wrote, King went from church to church and from village to metropolis, transforming "an irate, sullen people into a glorious righteous multitude." After Montgomery, then Albany. Then Meridian, Jackson, Atlanta, St. Augustine, Harlem, and a climactic march on Washington in August 1963. Ridiculed, bombed, cursed, knifed, and jailed, King somehow kept his poise and held to his purpose. Then, three days before Palm Sunday 1968, in Memphis, Tennessee, King fell before an assassin's rifle shot. This cruel calamity renewed men's skepticism about that day when "love and brotherhood will shine over our great nation."

In his book *Why We Can't Wait* (1964) Martin Luther King speaks on behalf of twenty million American Negroes.

> The Negro is saying that the time has come for our nation to take that firm stride into freedom—not simply toward freedom—which will pay a long-overdue debt to its citizens of color. . . . The Negro knows he is right. He has not organized for conquest or to gain spoils or to enslave those who have injured him. His goal is not to capture that which belongs to someone else. He merely wants and will have what is honorably his. When these long withheld rights and privileges are looked upon as prizes he seeks from impertinent greed, only one answer can come from the depths of a Negro's being . . . : "If this be treason, make the most of it."

When the U.S. Senate passed the Civil Rights bill in July 1964, the effective lobbying of religious bodies was openly acknowledged: the pressure of B'nai B'rith, the National Catholic Welfare Conference, the National Council of Churches, and of yet other groups had been felt. In 1969, a churchman, Father Theodore M. Hesburgh of Notre Dame University, even became chairman of the federal Civil Rights Commission: he also became by far its most courageous spokesman. And in a time when consciences were newly sensitized to ethnic neglect, other minorities—conspicuously that "second largest minority," Mexican-Americans—began to call for and, to a degree, to receive their rightful inheritance. Among Chicanos as among Blacks, religion was being invited to make its voice heard far beyond the sanctuary: in the streets, in the markets, in the school, and even in the fields.

In the 1970s the Roman Catholic labor leader Cesar Chavez attracted national attention in his battle for the farm workers—chiefly Mexican-Americans—of the Southwest. In Coachella, California, he and his union received the annual Reinhold Niebuhr award, July 13, 1973.

Reinhold Niebuhr Award of 1973 to
CESAR CHAVEZ AND THE MEMBERS OF THE NATIONAL FARM WORKERS' UNION brave fighters for social justice and representative of all those who, within our American society, have suffered great wrongs; spokesmen for the oppressed, they have wielded power non-violently and responsibly, reminding us by word and deed that economic injustice bears down with particular force on racial minorities; leaders of a struggle to redress one of America's momentous social problems, they have moved with that combination of social passion and effective realism which was characteristic of Reinhold Niebuhr's many battles.

On the limits of liberty and justice, honorable men, committed men deeply disagree. For the extension of liberty may somehow diminish justice, or an even distribution of justice may limit liberty. Neither is ever perfectly achieved; nevertheless the American credo calls for loyalty to both as long-range ideals and as short-range practical programs. In loyalty to America's creed as well as to their own, synagogues and churches could not escape the demands of liberty under justice for all.

Freedom of religion in America includes, of course, the right of religion to be inane, impotent, and toothless: to be, in short, what Marx called the opiate of the people. That freedom, however, can also be used to proclaim repentance, reform, and, if need be, even revolution. The struggle for "liberty and justice for all" is never wholly won, but only when that struggle ceases is the battle wholly lost.

In July 1964 President Lyndon B. Johnson signed the Civil Rights Bill. On the evening of the signing he took time to address the nation, concluding with these observations.

My fellow citizens, we have come now to a time of testing. We must not fail.

Let us close the springs of racial poison. Let us pray for wise and understanding hearts. Let us lay aside irrelevant differences and make our nation whole.

28. *Dr. Billy Graham in Balboa Stadium, San Diego, California (1964)*

Let us hasten that day when our unmeasured strength and our unbounded spirit will be free to do the great works ordained to this nation by the just and wise God who is the Father of us all.

PROSPERITY AND CONFORMITY

In executing its mission at home American religion grew in size, wealth, and popularity. If elsewhere optimism sometimes failed and confidence faltered, the church statistician had no reason for postwar gloom as he tallied membership lists, added up weekly donations, and counted full pews. Each growing suburb boasted of its new schools, efficient fire stations, and convenient churches. Atheism was "out"; religion was "in."

Mass revivalism once more gained favor, notably under the persuasive preaching of Billy Graham. Born in North Carolina in 1918, Graham grew up in a Presbyterian stronghold but later became a Baptist. Like all successful revivalists, however, Graham wore denominational labels lightly: "I much prefer being called a 'Christian.'" Personable in the pulpit and skillful in organization, the tall, broad-shouldered, wavy-haired Graham launched city-wide crusades on an amazing scale. In 1949 an eight-week Los Angeles revival resulted in three thousand persons making or renewing religious commitments. After Los Angeles came Boston, where in 1950 success abounded. Then Portland, Oregon, and a decision to undertake a regular radio program, The Hour of Decision. In quick succession, Graham and his team—for now there was an organization—filled the halls, churches, tabernacles, or stadiums of Minneapolis, Atlanta, Fort Worth, Shreveport, Memphis, Seattle, Houston, Pittsburgh, Dallas, and Detroit. And when the New York World's Fair opened in 1964, Billy Graham's personal pavilion beckoned the anxious and concerned.

While Graham's popularity was seldom questioned, most everything else about him was. Did statistics of "conversion" indicate changed values, conviction, and behavior? Did the inspiration of the revival endure after tent and team left town? Was there an alliance between conservative theology and conservative political or economic philosophy? How helpful was Graham's message for the problems of the city, the crises of race, the threats of war? While many vigorously debated these questions, others did not bother to raise them at all. For these persons the method and mood of mass revivalism belonged to a faded and better forgotten past. To them it seemed that the music was still Sankey's, the theology still Moody's.

In other social circles men and women looked to religion not as a way of changing the world but as offering a shelter and refuge from that ever more complex and confusing world. Joshua Liebman for Judaism (*Peace of Mind*), Norman Vincent Peale for Protestantism (*Power of Positive Thinking*), and Fulton J. Sheen for Roman Catholicism (*Peace of Soul*) represented, in varying degrees, that aspect of religion concerned more with the "haven of rest" than with "the armor of God." Bewildered by industrial might and urban maze, intimidated by political power and nuclear threat, millions sought sanity and calm in the ancient promise "Thou dost keep him in perfect peace, whose mind is stayed on Thee."

Norman Vincent Peale's *Power of Positive Thinking* (1952), breaking record after record in nonfiction sales, encouraged other entries in the field of self-help through an amalgam of popular psychology and popular piety. The opening paragraph of Peale's best seller reads:

> Believe in yourself! Have faith in your abilities! Without a humble but reasonable confidence in your own powers you cannot be successful or happy. But with sound self-confidence you can succeed. A sense of inferiority and inadequacy interferes with the attainment of your hopes, but self-confidence leads to self-realization and successful achievement. Because of the importance of this mental attitude, this book will help you believe in yourself and release your inner powers.

As the percentage of Americans affiliated with organized religion grew (over 60 per cent in the 1960's), the general respectability of church membership correspondingly increased. Churches and synagogues basking in the sunshine of "success" felt occasional uneasiness about their exalted status. Arthur Cohen asked: "How much wealth, comfort, and security can any religion take without becoming supremely cheap and smug?" In times of prosperity more than in adversity institutional religion had to guard against being dulled or absorbed by the surrounding culture. Yet this smug comfort gave way in the late 60s and 70s—gave way with precipitate and alarming swiftness—to anxieties, self-doubts, and harsh criticisms of institutional religion in America. Both church membership and church attendance leveled off or even began a gradual decline. More disturbing, however, was the growing conclusion that religion all across the nation was "losing its influence." Most Americans, the Gallup polls revealed, saw the churches as outmoded and irrelevant, increasingly impotent in comparison with the towering power structures of modern life. Many of the churches, for their part, saw a populace increasingly sensual or cynical, prone to translate the "abundant life" into terms of status, stocks, and material possessions. Whatever the merits of the case, the local church watched uneasily as its congregation grew smaller, as its coffers grew lighter, and as its voice grew weaker. Young men turned away from seminaries and from ministerial careers; men already in the ministry—and Roman Catholic priests were particularly visible in this regard—turned to other vocations, or to none. Americans seemed to have moved rapidly into a post-Protestant and then post-Christian and finally thoroughly secular era. What roots remained to nourish, what fixed stars served to guide? In the wake of Watergate, a moral miasma seeped over a land that had forgotten, in Lincoln's words, "whence it had come and whither it was tending."

Following the nationally televised funeral service for Dwight D. Eisenhower, James Reston made the following comments in *The New York Times* (April 2, 1969):

The trend toward a secular society in America is clear, but when television demonstrates on a great occasion that it has the capacity to bring the whole nation into a common experience—almost to make us all part of a single congregation—then we find that at least the remnants of a common faith still exist.

The choir at the National Cathedral in Washington sang the old hymn. The opening line is: "Faith of our Fathers, living still," and despite all the modern denials of the point, it is probably still true. The first line of the chorus, however, is different: "Faith of our Fathers, Holy Faith, we will be true to thee till death"—and that is clearly not true for most Americans.

Nevertheless, for believers and unbelievers alike, some facts are plain. The political life and spirit of this country were based on religious convictions. America's view of the individual was grounded on the principle, clearly expressed by the Founding Fathers, that man was a symbol of his Creator, and therefore possessed certain inalienable rights which no temporal authority had the right to violate.

That this conviction helped shape our laws and sustained American men and women in their struggle to discipline themselves and conquer a continent even the most atheistic historian would defend. And this raises a question which cannot be avoided: If religion was so important in the building of the Republic, how could it be irrelevant to the maintenance of the Republic?

---

22 ❖ The Mission Abroad

E<small>VEN BEFORE THE CONQUEST</small> of its own continent was complete, this nation dispatched monies, missionaries, and matériel around the world. In addition to Hawaii and Alaska, considered above in chapter 13, nations in all "four corners" received American personnel and supplies: medical, educational, cultural, and theological. Long before the Marshall Plan, scores of mission plans rendered assistance abroad. And before political programs of technical assistance existed, ecclesiastical programs of spiritual assistance reached fields and farms throughout the world. Japan, China, Burma, and India, the Philippines and Southeast Asia, Turkey, Palestine, and Africa, Central and South America—these and other territories received hospital and school, chapel and convent, vision and love.

In the nineteenth century the Protestant mission abroad was largely an Anglo-American effort. In the twentieth century the humanitarian and mission efforts of Judaism and Catholicism were financed chiefly by America's citizens. To what end and with what result?

WORLD EVANGELISM

However much the missionary acts as teacher, doctor, or technical assistant, he remains primarily a missionary, an evangelist. The vision which takes him to interior Brazil, northern Rhodesia, or primitive Borneo is a vision he wants to share. Yet no effective missionary separates precept from practice. A gospel of love, everyone ultimately grants, must be presented in love. It must be presented, that is, with a readiness to extend whatever love demands: from a pump that brings unpolluted water into a village to a plan that can drive infanticide out of a culture.

In the 1930's Protestant missions suffered from the prevalent pessimism of the time. A Laymen's Inquiry investigated the effectiveness of the foreign mission effort as the economic reversal of the decade reduced missionary expenditures. World War II, moreover, seriously impaired or altogether curtailed several ambitious programs. Nevertheless in the postwar world mission programs were rapidly rebuilt. By 1960 the United States was providing at least one half of all Protestant personnel (more than twenty thousand) engaged in mission work anywhere in the world. In financial support the American effort was even more impressive: more than 80 per cent (about 150 million dollars) of the support for all Protestant missions came from the United States.

The titanic task of ministering to immigrant multitudes left America's Roman Catholics with little resources for overseas evangelism. But gradually between the World Wars and more swiftly after World War II America's Catholic missions grew. By 1960 almost seven thousand Roman Catholic missionaries (mostly members of monastic orders) departed from America for stations throughout the world. While this contribution in personnel amounts to only about one ninth of the total Catholic effort, the financial contribution approximates one half of Catholicism's total mission work. The Catholic Foreign Missionary Society of America (the "Maryknoll Fathers"), founded in 1911, contributed most conspicuously to the missionary force. Beginning in 1920 the Foreign Mission Sisters of St. Dominic, with headquarters also at Maryknoll, New York, joined in the world-wide enterprise.

One expression of mission zeal, the Student Volunteer Movement (1886), won wide acclaim for the calibre of personnel that it recruited through the colleges and universities. An American innovation, it was flattered by imitation in the British Isles, Holland, Germany, Norway, Sweden, Denmark, Finland, Switzerland, and South Africa. Under the dynamic, tireless leadership of John R. Mott the SVM, dedicated to the "evangelization of the world in this generation," developed Missionary Departments in both the YMCA and the YWCA. Encouraging extensive missionary study by young people all over North America, the movement even before World War I sent more than five thousand volunteers into foreign missions. After that war the numbers increased and the tactics altered, but the purpose remained steady. America needs thousands of missionary ambassadors, John Mott declared in 1932, men and women who are ambassadors "in the finest and richest content of the term." These people interpret the best side of the nation that sent them "and, likewise, the best side of the one which has received them." By mediation, by example, by instruction, and by their actual presence Catholic and Protestant missionaries proclaimed a "fellowship or brotherhood which transcends all national and racial boundaries."

In the first half of the twentieth century no American had greater influence on the course and intensity of world evangelism than John R. Mott. In *The Present World Situation* (1914) he wrote:

> What then will afford a helpful environment and ensure right feeling and relationships between nations and races? The only program which can meet all the alarming facts of the situation is the world-wide spread of Christi-

1. *Methodist baptism in Liberia (1962)*

2. *Methodist choir in Liberia (1962)*

anity in its purest form. In other words, this is not a matter of external arrangements. The disposition of men must be changed. Their motive life must be influenced. The springs of conduct must be touched. A new spirit must be imparted. All this is only tantamount to saying that the influence of the life and spirit as well as the principles of Jesus Christ, the source of superhuman life and energy, must be brought to bear on all men individually and upon all their relationships.

The present world situation is unprecedented not only in opportunity and in danger, but also in urgency. From the point of view of the Christian Church the present moment is incomparably the most critical and urgent it has ever known. This is true because so many nations just now in a plastic condition are soon to become set unchangeably. Shall Christian or unchristian influences determine their character and destiny? The answer to this question cannot be deferred.

One of Protestanism's most ambitious mission commitments was to China. Teachers, doctors, ministers, and rural workers poured into that vast reach of four million square miles. Reports of one-half million converts and over five thousand churches by 1923 offered some measure of the impact. In the single year 1922 more than $740,000 in voluntary offerings flowed from the United States into the Chinese mission. In operation at that time were 219 kindergartens, more than 7,000 elementary schools,

3. *John Scott Everton, U. S. Ambassador to Burma, speaks at church convention in Burma (1962)*

4. *Baptists baptize in Tukuyu, Tanganyika (1962)*

333 high schools, and 42 teacher training schools. In little more than a century American Protestantism established 24 colleges and 125 seminaries or Bible training schools in China alone. Eleven medical schools and about 400 physicians joined in a ministry to the whole man. Also, by 1923 the American Bible Society had sent nearly twenty thousand Bibles to China, along with some two million copies of portions of the Bible. Finally, the first quarter of the present century saw 44 orphanages established, 17 leper colonies, and 12 institutions for the deaf and the blind.

But by the end of that decade the peak of the mission effort in China had been reached. Civil disorder, antiforeign and anti-Christian outbreaks, the experiments with communism, the impending Japanese invasion—all blunted an enduring effectiveness. Criticism also was heard: against superficial evangelization, of excessive financial demands made on converts, and of the tendency of Chinese Christians to become less Chinese in outlook and interest.

Whatever improvements might have been made, the chance to make them was brutally cut off: first in 1937 by the invading armies of Japan, then again in 1949 by the Communist revolution of Mao Tse-tung. With the People's Republic firmly in power, virtually every Christian missionary had been forced out of China by 1951. Soon all mission welfare and educational activities were taken over by the government, leaving only the Bible schools and publishing houses to the churches' control.

In the aftermath of the Chinese mission's collapse, earnest churchmen asked, "What went wrong?" Some untoward events were beyond forseeing or controlling, but others were not. Missionaries benefited from Western-imposed treaties that, being unfair to China, created deep, lasting resentment against "imperialism" and "its religion." Moreover, native leadership was not trained early enough or in large enough number to insure a church capable of "self-support, self-government, and self-propagation." Weakness from within coupled with steady hostility from without resulted in a serious decline in church membership, church activities, and theological training. Nonetheless, though choked, stifled, and shouted down, a small voice still speaks in China, reaffirming the missionary's finer message of a fellowship or brotherhood transcending nation and race.

In *Re-Thinking Missions: A Laymen's Inquiry After One Hundred Years* (1932) the fundamental question "Should missions continue?" was asked and answered.

As to the first and most searching question put to us, whether these missions should in our judgment any longer go on, we may say that this question has been with us, honestly and objectively entertained, throughout our inquiry. As the inquiry closes, we may confess that this formidable question has not proved to be highly significant. It is somewhat like asking

5. *Maryknoll missionary with the Quechus Indians in the Andes Mountains*

7. *Native Clergy trained in Maryknoll School, Molina, Chile*

6. *Roman Catholics revive faith in Guatemala*

8. Baptists conduct class in El Salvador

whether good-will should continue or cease to express itself. Like other works, organized by men's hands, missions might conceivably ossify in unadaptable forms and deserve to perish. But at the center of the religious mission, though it takes the special form of promoting one's own type of thought and practice, there is an always valid impulse of love to men: one offers one's own faith simply because that is the best one has to offer. It is always reasonable to ask whether this good-will might take quite different shape: but to ask whether it should cease to operate would seem to suppose that the very substance of friendship among men and races might somehow be mistaken.

America's Roman Catholics evangelized with special force in Latin America. After World War II the Church in the United States committed virtually one third of its total foreign mission force to the Americas to the south. Nominally Roman Catholic since Spain's conquest in the sixteenth century, Latin America lacked both a strong Catholic witness and a secure ecclesiastical tradition. Anticlericalism, erupting time and again, provoked political crises even as it precluded a stable, fruitful relationship between clergy and laity. The condition of the native Indians, moreover—their vast number, their geographical isolation, their educational level, their social status—made conversion in depth difficult. American missionaries, therefore, even in the 1960's still looked upon Latin America as a prime challenge for evangelism.

South and Central America, as well as the West Indies, received Catholic missionaries from the United States: over two thousand in the 1960's. Over five hundred worked in Puerto Rico alone, about three hundred in Brazil. Franciscans, Redemptorists, and especially Maryknoll Fathers led in this evangelical effort. In 1960 the National Catholic Welfare Confer-

---

The first formal movement for foreign missions by American Catholics resulted in 1911 in the formation of the Catholic Foreign Mission Society of America at Maryknoll, New York. Cardinal Gibbons, whose words are quoted below, helped bring the organization into being.

> The priests of the United States number more than 17,000, but I am informed that there are hardly sixteen on the foreign missions. . . . we must confess that as a Catholic body we have only begun, while our Protestant fellow-countrymen have passed the century mark in foreign mission work and are represented today in the heathen world by some thousands of missioners, who are backed by yearly contributions running up into the millions.
>
> A seminary, such as that contemplated, if established with the goodwill of the entire American Hierarchy, can hardly fail to draw, emphatically, the attention of American Catholics.
>
> "It is time," to use the words of the Apostolic Delegate, "that the American Church should begin to move in this direction."

---

ence, recognizing the scope and significance of this Western Hemisphere venture, organized a Latin American Bureau with Father John J. Considine, himself a Maryknoll priest, as its first head.

The gigantic needs in Latin America demanded gigantic response. In 1946 Considine called for forty thousand new priests or missionaries to meet the chronic clerical shortage. Despite the four centuries of settlement to the south, the percentage of natives receiving ordination remained pitifully small. In Brazil, for example, where 36 per cent of the population is Negro or mulatto, only 2 per cent of the priests come from these groups. The preponderance of priests continued, therefore, to be either "imports" from the north or of European descent. As in China, so in Latin America: the permanent strength of the church depended upon a trained, literate, moral, native clergy. And where China displayed a general fear of the foreign, Latin America's suspicion of the foreigner was especially acute wherever that northern colossus, the United States, was directly involved.

Other missionaries labored in Latin America: notably, Pentecostals and similar fundamentalist sects. Moving on a wave of popular preaching in street, slum, farm, and factory, the *Evangelicos* reached all classes, all races. And where private wrong was a key to so much public woe— alcoholism in Chile, for instance—the sects were strikingly effective. One

9. Lutherans distribute food in Hong Kong

10. In Hong Kong, clothing dispensed by Lutheran World Federation

11. Seventh-day Adventists provide medical care in Korea

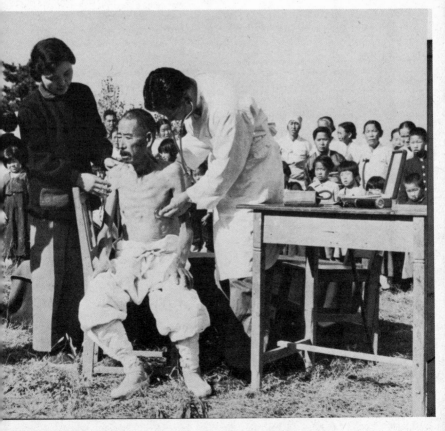

12. In 1940, this Seventh-day Adventist Hospital opened in Bangkok, Thailand

13. Christian canteen in Haiti

14. Adventists give medical attention to isolated tribes of Amazon River

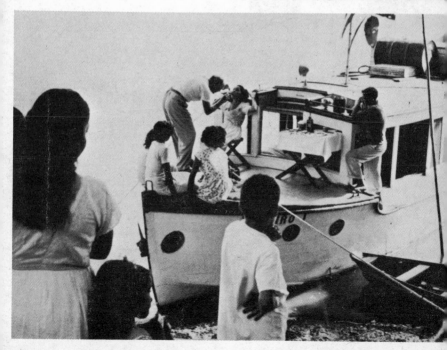

15. *Leper Colony in northern Rhodesia, served by Adventists*

16. *Baptist Nurse operates Baby Clinic in Vanga, Congo*

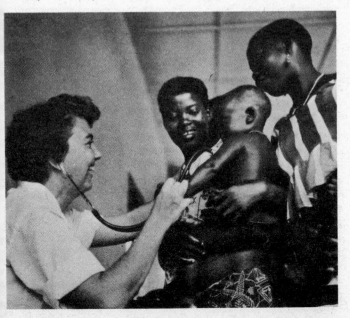

Jesuit missionary noted in 1963: "The Evangelical movement . . . is a powerful spiritual force moved forward by a popular enthusiasm. . . . [It] is a phenomenon worthy of admiration." America's missionaries, confronted by a continent where religion, in the words of Lord Bryce, "seems to be regarded merely as a harmless Old World affair which belongs to the past order of things," turned with renewed vigor to their monumental task. Freeing itself of entangling political alliances, Christianity in South America stood upon the threshold of a new age.

RESCUE AND RELIEF

Abroad, America's religious forces often assumed responsibilities not borne at home. The larger tasks sometimes resulted from emergencies of plague or persecution, of social chaos or starvation. When one maintained a separate colony or community, cut off from any major cultural or political stream, wider responsibilities were inevitable. Often religion abroad did alone what at home government, school, hospital, community chest, and church jointly undertook. Proceeding from a wellspring of good will, missions rarely limited the dispensation of that good will to things solely spiritual. "The welfare of the individual's soul," commented the Laymen's Inquiry of 1932, "cannot be secured in complete independence of the welfare of his body, his mind, his general social context."

World mission, therefore, usually included world rehabilitation. At the same time, many engaged in social reconstruction did not regard their labors as "missions" in the traditional sense of seeking conversions. In the days after World War II national and international agencies, often cooperating with synagogues and churches, directed much of the world's recovery from war and preparations for peace. Red Cross, CARE, Church World Service, Catholic Relief Services, Lutheran World Relief, Meals for Millions, and special agencies of the United Nations gave more than two billion dollars worth of aid from 1954 to 1964. Thus the mission of American religion was allied with a broad, even "secular" benevolence toward humanity. In the words of Vice-President Hubert Humphrey, "The cause is mankind."

And in that cause the services rendered, the money spent, the lives given under the inspiration of religion are beyond calculation. A cup of cold milk found its way into the parched hands of a pregnant Arab woman. A shot of penicillin wrought its healing miracle in the blood stream of a North African boy. In India a simple demonstration in the proper use of fertilizer increased the village food supply by 300 per cent. In the central Congo a world of words and infinite wonder opened up to a group of girls taught to read. And in communities across America a refugee family was clothed and sheltered, a job was provided, a new life begun. It was an old but never dull story: the blind see, the lame walk, the deaf hear, the naked are clothed, the poor are lifted up.

17. *Smallpox Inoculation in Liberia*

18. *In Miami, Florida, Cuban Refugees are served by Church World Service (1961)*

19. *Catholic Relief Services reach Far East*

20. Surplus Food "Donated By the American People to the People of Ghana"

21. Food Sacks become quilts in Korea

22. Methodist Appeal for Congo and Rhodesia, 1961

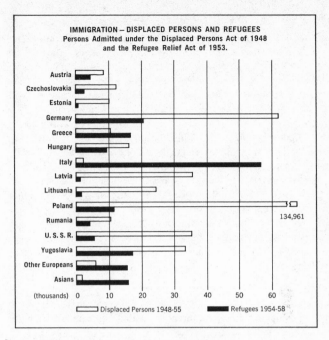

IMMIGRATION — DISPLACED PERSONS AND REFUGEES
Persons Admitted under the Displaced Persons Act of 1948
and the Refugee Relief Act of 1953.

Austria
Czechoslovakia
Estonia
Germany
Greece
Hungary
Italy
Latvia
Lithuania
Poland   134,961
Rumania
U. S. S. R.
Yugoslavia
Other Europeans
Asians

(thousands) 0   10   20   30   40   50   60

☐ Displaced Persons 1948-55   ■ Refugees 1954-58

23. *Displaced Persons and Refugees to America*

24. *Former Flight Surgeon becomes Missionary Doctor in Tanganyika*

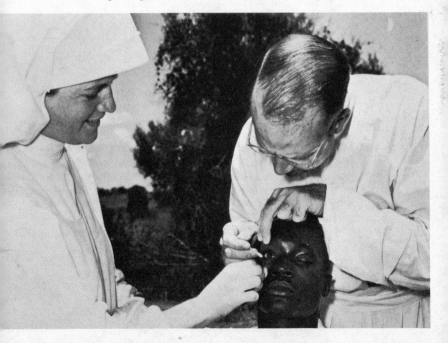

Two of America's smaller religious groups established particularly enviable records in rescue and relief. The Friends, or "Quakers," through the American Friends Service Committee, rendered service so conspicuous that in 1947 their committee received the Nobel Peace Prize. Though AFSC maintained no institutions of its own, it administered benevolence with integrity and bestowed upon the degraded a measure of human dignity. The other group, Seventh-day Adventists, supported hospitals, orphanages, schools, food factories, and publishing houses around the world; many larger denominations strained to match their bold dedication. And while the Adventists, like the Quakers, condemned war, they, also like the Quakers, plunged bravely into the slimy wake left by brutality and hate.

In the Nazi devastation of Europe's Jews man's inhumanity to man reached its most sickening dimension. After World War II, when the monstrous nature of Hitler's horror became fully and generally known, forces and funds were gathered to save those who somehow survived. Nowhere was action more prodigious or philanthropy more generous than among American Jewry.

The American Jewish Committee, organized in 1906, declared in 1954 its continuing opposition to immigration policies that discriminated on the basis of race, creed, and national origin.

> We re-affirm our objection to the McCarran-Walter Act of 1952 on the grounds that it is a law of exclusion rather than of immigration; that it is based on un-American racial premises; that it establishes unnecessarily harsh rules for deportation without adequate procedural safeguards; and that, contrary to American principles, it creates invidious distinctions between native-born and naturalized citizens.
>
> We urge the Congress to adopt an enlightened and liberal immigration and nationality policy in order to bring this vital aspect of American life into consonance with traditional American ideals and principles, and thus advance our relations with the other nations of the free world.

Judaism's dedication to charity is of long standing. "If there be among you a needy man, one of thy brethren, within any of thy gates, in thy land which the Lord thy God giveth thee, thou shalt not harden thy heart, nor shut thy hand from thy needy brother; but thou shalt surely open thy hand unto him . . ." (Deuteronomy 15:7f.). *Zedakah,* or righteousness, is understood more as action than attitude: one's relationship to God is measured by his responsibility toward man.

In the 1930's when Hitler's growing power took an increasingly anti-Semitic turn, America's Jews warned of dark disaster ahead. If Hitler could not be stopped, then a way to rescue threatened minorities had to be found. In the United States communities of concern moved to resettle Europe's

25. *"Meals for Millions" Serve Congolese Children, 1960*

26. *Methodist at work in Milk Feeding Station, Seoul, Korea*

refugees in Palestine, America, or elsewhere. Between 1936 and 1943 some 150,000 Jewish refugees entered the United States, assisted by private, voluntary contributions from citizens of the United States. The American Jewish Conference, coordinating the resources of several constituent organizations, directed much of this rescue work. At the same time it sought a more permanent solution when peace should eventually come. At

---

Rabbi Stephen Wise proclaimed the cause of humanitarianism and justice from the pulpit of New York City's Free Synagogue and in the public press. Valiantly, but largely in vain, he warned of Hitler's mounting horrors. These words were spoken in 1942, seven years before Wise's death.

> We would not be worthy of our Jewish fellowship if we did not lift up our voices in solemn lamentation and mournful protest over the oceanic wrongs done to our brother-Jews wherever Nazis live and rule. We would not be equal to our American citizenship if we did not tonight with one voice ask our great-hearted, liberty-loving fellow Americans to join with us in solemn condemnation of the infamy of the Axis in dooming unarmed and defenseless men, women and children by the hundred thousands to suffering, torture and death. . . .
>
> . . . We are asking our Government and the United Nations [the Allies] to serve notice upon the Nazi despots that the horror of Nazi mistreatment of civilians should cease, whether of Jews, Protestants or Catholics, whether Poles, Czechs or Greeks, and that as our President [Franklin Roosevelt] has put it, "The American people will hold the perpetrators to strict accountability in a day of reckoning which will surely come."

---

the creation of the United Nations Organization in 1945 the Conference fought to protect Jewish rights in Europe as well as in the Commonwealth in Palestine.

The establishment of the state of Israel in 1948 enlarged American Jewry's opportunity for social service and philanthropy. In that year alone the United Jewish Appeal raised approximately $148,000,000—an amazing sum from only five million people. Food, clothing, and medical supplies, housing, rescue ships, and transportation, resettlement and relief—these suggest the breadth of responsibilities discharged with signal honor. Israel, the chief but not sole beneficiary of these world-wide efforts, grew in population from little more than one-half million in 1948 to one and one-half million in 1953 and two and one-half million a decade later.

The Christian rescue of the Jew was faltering, especially in the 1930's when small steps might have accomplished great good. Scattered voices in America, calling for international sanction, pronounced the strongest of moral judgments. But isolationist sentiment, coupled with indifference or unbelief, prevented definitive, determinative action by America's churches.

27. B'nai B'rith Food Ship to an
    Independent Israel, 1948

28. Clothing Collected for earth-
    quake-damaged Chile, 1960

29. Jews in U. S. A. seek relief for
    Jews in U. S. S. R., April,
    1964 • left to right: Rabbi
    Uri Miller, President of the
    Synagogue Council of Amer-
    ica; Abraham Ribicoff, Sena-
    tor from Connecticut; L. A.
    K a t z , President of B'nai
    B'rith; Arthur Goldberg, Am-
    bassador to The United Na-
    tions.

30. Freedom of Religion restored
    to Austria • American sol-
    diers make a Jewish service
    once again possible in Hitler-
    dominated Europe: Salzburg,
    Austria, September 8, 1945.

New York's Rabbi Stephen Wise wrote in 1949 of his "deep disappointment over the failure of American Christendom to bestir itself . . . in the hour of our greatest need." In 1938 Unitarian John Haynes Holmes had concluded that the only thing to be done about Germany's Jews was to "get them out." "They must be rescued, as the residents of a burning house, trapped by devouring flames, are rescued by firemen." But the vast majority did not get out. And by the time the gas ovens finally cooled, six million Jews had perished. Buchenwald, Dachau, and Belsen became mocking monuments to the perversity of man.

UNITY AND UNDERSTANDING

Religion in America strives for unity and understanding throughout the world. It is not enough to bind up wounds if those wounds can in the first place be prevented. It is not enough to rescue men from the furies of hate if hate itself can be dissolved. Within the Judeo-Christian tradition men seek those moral maxims and foundational wisdom that build bridges of sympathy and understanding over chasms of cruelty and despair.

Broader than peace and war or rescue and relief, the basic issue is found in the familiar question "And who is my neighbor?" An ancient Talmudic parable tells of a traveler approaching an oasis in the desert. From a distance he saw a wild animal moving among the palm trees; drawing nearer, he saw that it was not an animal but a man. Drawing nearer still, he saw that the man was his brother.

Historically, religion has been a bar to brotherhood as often as a boon. Holy wars, fervent crusades, and heresy hunts stain the tapestry of world civilization. In America the book of martyrs is fortunately short. But as previously noted, the story of white against black, Protestant against Catholic, Christian against Jew makes a book far too long. In the twentieth century, however, greater charity at home raised hopes for greater unity abroad.

In 1945 San Francisco saw a new organization dedicated to world understanding come into being: the United Nations. To "save succeeding generations from the scourge of war" and to "reaffirm faith in fundamental human rights" were among the chartered aims of the UN. In 1948 the General Assembly adopted a Universal Declaration of Human Rights, affirming that a "recognition of the inherent dignity and of the equal and inalienable rights of all members of the human family is the foundation of freedom, justice, and peace in the world." Special agencies of that world organization such as the World Health Organization, the Children's Emergency Fund, and UNESCO (United Nations Educational, Scientific and Cultural Organization) sought to grant that "inherent dignity" and to preserve those "inalienable rights." To this cause America's churches and synagogues gave steady support, recognizing that these humane instruments extended helpful hands to the "needy brother."

In Amsterdam the first Assembly of the World Council of Churches met in 1948 to seek a unity in all Christendom. "There are times," the Assembly noted, "when the bitter conflicts which divide men are more nearly transcended and more quickly healed within the Christian community than outside it." Acknowledging, however, that the churches have been guilty "both of indifference and of failure," the delegates confessed that loyalty to "our own economic or national or racial interests" has often superseded a loyalty to God. Division, bickering, and sectarian jealousies, furthermore, prevent the voice of faith from being heard above the clamor of cruel hate. "But there is a word of God for our world. It is that the world is in the hands of the living God, whose will for it is wholly good. . . ."

The World Council of Churches, in its First Assembly meeting at Amsterdam in 1948, recognized its responsibility for promoting world understanding.

> The establishment of the World Council of Churches can be made of great moment for the life of the nations. It is a living expression of this [supranational] fellowship, transcending race and nation, class and culture, knit together in faith, service and understanding. Its aim will be to hasten international reconciliation through its own members and through the co-operation of all Christian churches and of all men of goodwill. It will strive to see international differences in the light of God's design, remembering that normally there are Christians on both sides of every frontier. It should not weary in the effort to state the Christian understanding of the will of God and to promote its application to national and international policy.

In 1962 Roman Catholics met for their first ecumenical council in the twentieth century (and only their third in more than four hundred years). Vatican II, while deeply concerned with internal renewal and reform, turned its face squarely toward the world "outside the walls." Under the gentle but persistent prodding of Pope John XXIII over two thousand bishops of all races, regions, and cultures confronted the challenge of mission in its broadest sense to the world in its farthest reach. Relations of Catholic to non-Catholic, of Christian to Jew, and of member to stranger received

Pope Paul VI opened the Second Session of Vatican II on September 29, 1963, with an address, from which the following is selected.

> Let the world know this: The Church looks at the world with profound understanding, with sincere admiration and with the sincere intention not of conquering it, but of serving it; not of despising it, but of appreciating it; not of condemning it, but of strengthening and saving it.
>
> From the window of the council, opened wide on the world, the Church looks towards some categories of persons with particular solicitude: It looks towards the poor, the needy, the afflicted, the hungry, the suffering and sorrowing. Humanity belongs to the Church, by the right which the Gospel gives her. She likes to repeat to all who make up the human race: "Come unto me, all. . . ."

repeated attention. An American *peritus* (expert) at Vatican II, John Courtney Murray, wrote: "The question today is, whether the Church should extend her pastoral solicitude beyond her own boundaries and assume an active patronage of the freedom of the human person, who was created by God as his image, who was redeemed by the blood of Christ, who stands today under a massive threat to everything that human dignity and personal freedom mean." That indeed was the question of the 1960's, the answer determining in great measure the contribution of American religion to universal unity and understanding.

So far as the American scene was concerned, any offer of spiritual succor to a suffering world was severely compromised by this nation's protracted military involvement in Southeast Asia. So much disunity and misunderstanding seemed tied to American planes, American arms, American might. The roles of healer and teacher, of food supplier and peace keeper, were denied, at least for a time, to a world as much in need as ever for that which could bind up rather than tear down. The image that was so tarnished abroad seemed as badly blemished at home. To speak of national purpose or mission abroad was to invite ridicule or despair. Government was an object of suspicion, all authority an invitation to rebellion, and an older generation—which seemed responsible for so many mistakes—the subject of derision. The nation, no less than the world around it, was wounded. Perhaps neither foreign nor domestic policies could remain oblivious to the moral and spiritual dimensions—and consequences. Perhaps priorities were badly misaligned and perspectives falsely perceived.

In his book, *The Crippled Giant* (1972), Senator J. William Fulbright speaks of the material and spiritual drain resulting from "the neglected American agenda."

> Someday the war in Vietnam will be over and, like a dreamer awakening from a nightmare, Americans will be able to look around and see that the sun still rises and sets, that life has gone on in their country and the world, leaving a profusion

of tasks and opportunities on the neglected American agenda. Some of the problems we will face then, such as the population explosion and the world's food supply, may seem almost hopeless, but at least we will be free to act upon them and, human ingenuity being what it is, perhaps it will prove possible to do things that now seem beyond us. One wonders what the world would be like if, say, half of the human inventiveness that goes for weapons and war—to say nothing of the resources—were being applied to human needs and satisfactions. . . .

Defining our priorities is more a matter of moral accounting than of cost accounting. The latter may help us determine what we are able to pay for, but it cannot help us to decide what we want and what we need and what we are willing to pay for. It cannot help the five-sixths of us who are affluent to decide whether we are willing to pay for programs which will create opportunity for the one-sixth who are poor; that is a matter of moral accounting. It cannot help us to decide whether winning a military victory over a poor and backward Asian nation is more important to us than rebuilding our cities and purifying our poisoned air and lakes and rivers; that too is a matter of moral accounting.

On a global scale, what were the churches' responsibilities and what were the possibilities? Evangelism, as has been noted, continued into the twentieth century to be a major response of American religion. For many, however, the spread of a gospel carried the additional obligation of the application of that message to particular international aches. In South Africa, for example, where an especially regressive policy of racial segregation (apartheid) prevailed, did the churches have a precisely defined commitment? Some churches condemning official government policy on the one hand discovered, to their embarrassment, that on the other hand their investment portfolios gave implicit support to the regime in the Republic of South Africa. Other churches argued that the disorder in our own racial house gave America's religious spokesman no firm platform for public pronouncements. Still others, as Alan Paton was to write of some South African churches, did not "want these matters discussed at all, reckoning that such discussion is an obstacle to reconciliation, as though we could perhaps be reconciled if we lowered our sights, and concentrated on those things we could all agree about, such as cruelty to children, care for the aged, concern for the poor, and rape and murder." In such fashion, the churches' contribution to world understanding was often muted or mutually nullifying—whether it be in Bangladesh, the Middle East, Latin America, or remote corners of the planet. In the 1970s the lowering of Washington's barriers to Moscow and Peking raised the hope of new possibilities for rational dialogue among nations and possibly even a measure of moral progress among men.

In *Christianity and Crisis* (1969), Alan Paton, well-known for his novels as well as his firm opposition to apartheid, wrote of the churches' struggle over governmental race policy. The suffering witness of some South African Christians spurred many American churches and even the World Council of Churches itself into conscientious response. Paton writes:

In many countries the discussion of love and justice in the light of the gospel is perennial, and by no means always productive. But in South Africa we add to it the electric ingredient of race, and the whole debate sparks, crackles and explodes. . . .

For us to rediscover the gospel could be a shattering experience. It could either shatter us or shatter the nice safe world. And as for us, what would we do? Whatever we did, it would lie between two extremes. The one extreme is to forswear the world. The other is to practice upon ourselves the supreme self-deception, namely that the gospel is really the nice safe world after all. . . .

We believe in large measure what we want to believe, but at the same time we want our beliefs to be true and good. Therefore we devote endless time, even our whole lives, to the proof that our actions are the consequences of our highest beliefs. The virtue of humility, the practice of self-criticism, fall into desuetude; complacency and self-satisfaction are rife; and against the critics of our society, our anger is intense. . . .

Are we so bad then? We are not innately worse than anyone else. Many of us are made worse because of two environmental factors, our fear for our own survival and our fear of offending the Government. But there is a stirring among us, a recognition that life is not really worth living, unless we retain that sense of our value and significance which the gospel gives to us, a recognition—and painful it can be—that Christianity had a cross in it and can never become a kind of bonhomie, a recognition that life is something more than survival, and lastly, a dawning realization of the possible truth of that strange saying, that perfect love casts out fear.

Because of the cost in human suffering and because of the cost to America's self-esteem, the nation's involvement in Southeast Asia continued to be the paramount world concern. This foreign affair above all other "affairs" became a watershed in the public's understanding of both the perils and the limits of military power. But that affair also became a watershed in the public assessment of national morality. The idealism of a Woodrow Wilson seemed far removed from the banal sloganeering and corrosive rhetoric of later governmental spokesmen. The integrity of a John Adams seemed out of place in an era of practiced deception, international prevarication, and wholesale espionage at home and abroad. Most of all, the moral and spiritual sensitivity of an Abraham Lincoln did not easily comport with a prideful self-righteousness and a vengeful unleashing of insensate power. In 1967 three religious voices (Protestant, Jewish and Roman Catholic) declared that the nation's military "presence" in Southeast Asia presented the religiously committed citizen with a "crisis of conscience." America's potential for war is admittedly great, noted Rabbi Abraham Heschel, but her "peace potential is even greater."

If the churches and synagogues across the United States could somehow assist in replacing a war-torn world with a warless one, then the entire "mission abroad" would ever after be bathed in a strange and wonderful light.

In the book alluded to above, *Vietnam: Crisis of Conscience* (1967), Robert McAfee Brown, Abraham Joshua Heschel, and Michael Novak sought to arouse the religious community to a politically effective, spiritually based opposition to the Vietnam War. Robert Brown here summarizes the "ongoing responsibility" of institutional religion in America.

We have an obligation, Christians and Jews alike, to get on record and insist that our fellow citizens do likewise. Silence and inaction are no longer merely irresponsible. They are immoral. . . .

We of the churches and synagogues, who should for years have been sensitizing the conscience of the nation, bear a particularly heavy burden of guilt for what has happened so far, and therefore bear a particularly heavy burden of responsibility for righting that wrong, and initiating a new direction.

The word that is spoken to us, and must be spoken to our nation through us, is an old word. It is a biblical word, one that dominates both the Jewish and the Christian Scriptures. It is the word "Repent!" Before we dismiss it as old-fashioned, we should be reminded of what it means. It means "Turn about, begin again, make a fresh start." That is what we are called upon to do. It is not easy for the individual, it is harder for the church or synagogue, it is hardest of all for the nation. But there is no hope, literally no hope, save on the other side of that.

23 ❖ Education

IN THE FIRST 250 years of this country's history, religion and education were intimate and interdependent. On every level, from primary school to college, the church's hand was felt, its voice was heard. Religion dictated the choice of books, the course of study, the ends in view. Normally clergymen served as administrators or teachers; often they were also the fund-raisers and custodians. In prenational days religion was indeed the major prop of colonial education. But even in the early decades of the nation's independence a pervasive "nonsectarian," Protestant-oriented, religious aura surrounded virtually all instruction, public or private.

In 1959 Nathan M. Pusey, president of Harvard University, offered these observations to the graduating class.

> The standards of the scholar, the mature scholar who at his best has also become a mature person, continue to impress us—his patience, honesty, industry, his sense of "standard," his sympathy, his humility, his vision of something better beyond the tawdry and the broken.
>
> And somewhere here too it seems to me inevitable one must, as he grows, come upon an even more important matter—the serious confrontation of the question of God. Like moral character, this subject is much less frequent and much less easy in our conversations than it appears to have been to those who were here before us a hundred, two hundred, or three hundred years ago. Perhaps college age is not now the best time for it. But it would seem to me that the finest fruit of serious learning should be the ability to speak the word God without reserve or embarrassment, certainly without adolescent resentment; rather with some sense of communion, with reverence and with joy.

After the Civil War, however, a quiet revolution began. The gradual secularization of education, first in the cities, then in the hamlets, spread across the land. The forces responsible for this basic change included (1) the growing prestige of a naturalized science and a scientized philosophy,

374

(2) the increasing pluralism or religious diversity of American society that weakened or challenged the older Protestant orientation, and (3) added anxiety about the "wall of separation" between church and state. These forces moving in unconscious concert caused institutional religion to lose its leadership in American education. Clergymen steadily disappeared from governing boards of colleges and universities, as well as from superintendencies and boards of public education. By tradition college presidents came from the ranks of the Christian ministry, so much so that a layman in that office was a rarity before the twentieth century. But in 1898 Yale elected its first lay president, Princeton following suit in 1902. By mid-twentieth century the clerical president, not the lay president, had become the rarity.

While religious controls over private education were weakening, religious influence in public education was disappearing. And on the college level it was to public education that Americans increasingly turned. In 1860 hardly any tax monies went to higher education, but by 1960 over 60 per cent of all college students were enrolled in public institutions. On the elementary and high school levels the percentage of students enrolled in private schools increased, but the preponderance of a growing school population remained in public hands. Of 35 million elementary school children in America in 1965 about 30 million were enrolled in public schools. On the high school level the proportion was even higher: 11 out of 12 million pupils received public education.

Confronted by the secular revolution in education, the churches' counterrevolution, or "containing action," took several forms. An educational instrument developed by an earlier generation was retained: the Sunday School. Still one of the largest religious education efforts in the world, America's Sunday Schools enrolled over 40 million scholars in 1960. The highest percentage of pupils were between three and twelve years of age, but the next highest group were adults (twenty-four and older). Despite impressive figures and ambitious programs few leaders expressed great satisfaction about what could be achieved or even hoped for in a weekly session of one hour or less. Attendance was spotty, trained personnel scarce, and pupil preparation virtually nil.

Thus many recognized the need for something more, but what? Some abandoned the public school system altogether, setting up a church weekday school that offered a total curriculum. Certain groups conducted classes supplemental to the public schools, either in early morning or late afternoon or during the summer months. Others sought an accommodation between public and religious education by dividing the pupil's time between two schools or two teaching groups. Still others experimented, with uneven success, in programs designed to insert or retain religion in public instruction. And finally, some limited their efforts to the church-related or church-operated college.

1. Papago girls leave for St. Anthony School, Arizona

2. School for Papago Children in Arizona

3. St. Mary School, Second Grade, Simsbury, Connecticut

4. *St. Adalbert School, Sixth Grade, Staten Island, New York*

5. *Roman Catholic High School Dedicated, White Plains, New York, 1948*

PAROCHIAL SCHOOLS

America's Roman Catholics developed the nation's most ambitious parochial school system. With the strong urging of the Third Plenary Council,
meeting in Baltimore in 1884, church schools increased rapidly, so that
about four thousand existed by the beginning of the present century. Sixty
years later that number had more than tripled. In 1960 twice as many
Catholic elementary pupils were in parochial schools as were in public
schools, but on the secondary level the scales tipped the other way. Many
Catholic authorities, confronted with escalating costs and diminishing quality, acknowledged that even the largest of parochial school systems had
many unsolved, perhaps insoluble, problems. Thus the whole question of
the place of that system in the religious life of the nation was sharply
debated: some sought relief from public school taxes; some sought relief
from parish financial demands; some sought accommodations or solutions
not yet tested in courts of public opinion or law; some abandoned the
parochial idea.

In *Catholic Viewpoint on Education* (1962) Neil G. McCluskey, S. J.,
comments on the basic distinctions of Catholic education, from the primary
through the graduate levels.

> Probably the most distinctive, certainly the most important, benefit of
> education within a Catholic school is the ordering of knowledge in an
> atmosphere wherein the spiritual and the supernatural are properly ordered
> in the hierarchy of values. The Catholic philosophy of education is based
> on the reality of the supernatural and its primacy in the total scheme of
> things. The values, goals, and ideals of the natural order—important and
> worthy of pursuit as these may be—are subordinate in Catholic eyes to
> those of the supernatural order. For in reality, the order created by God
> was never a purely natural order, but from its inception was elevated to the
> supernatural. . . .
>
> The Catholic school shares with the home and Church the responsibility
> of teaching the child that "his chief significance comes from the fact that
> he is created by God and is destined for life with God in eternity." In order
> to live in a modern society where "social, moral, intellectual and spiritual
> values are everywhere disintegrating," the child needs the integrating force
> of religion—a force that will arm him with a complete and rational mean-
> ing for his existence.

Protestants and Jews also operated parochial schools, but all their efforts
together amounted in 1960 to a mere fraction of the Catholic effort. In that
year about 3½ million Catholics attended elementary church schools, but
only about one-quarter million Protestants did so. Jewish pupils numbered
only twenty-two thousand. On the elementary level Lutherans conducted

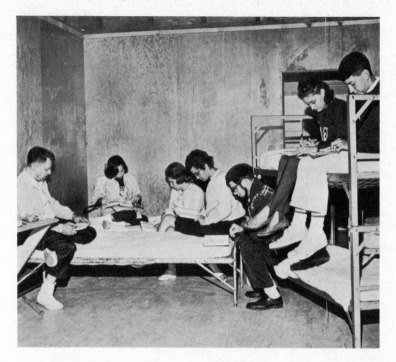

6. *National Hillel Summer Institute, Starlight, Pennsylvania, 1963*

the largest Protestant school system, followed by the far smaller denomination of Seventh-day Adventists. On the secondary level Episcopalians led the Protestant forces, followed again by the Adventists. Yet all religious groups recognized that as long as four out of every five American school children received their education under public auspices, the task of relating religion to education remained unsolved.

SUPPLEMENTAL CLASSES

Finding the time allotted for Sunday School instruction wholly inadequate, some tried other hours and other days. The Church of Jesus Christ of the Latter-day Saints, for example, conducted "seminary" classes, often in the early morning before public school instruction began. Classes held in Mormon-owned buildings were taught by Mormon-paid teachers. Jews in New York and elsewhere held afternoon classes on weekdays, again strictly as a supplement to the public school program—in no way tied to or infringing on that program. Whereas in 1960 only about 8 per cent of Jewish children attended a full-time synagogue school, almost 50 per cent of those receiving any religious instruction obtained it from the weekday afternoon school.

Others placed their emphasis and to some degree their hopes on summer camps, conferences, and "vacation church schools." In the latter activity alone about 8 million young people were enrolled in 1960. Young Men's and Young Women's Christian Association camps, Hillel or B'nai B'rith conferences, Roman Catholic retreats and novenas—all sought a concentrated time and a controlled environment for effective, enduring instruction in religious faith and practice. But again the total percentage of American youth exposed to such experiences remained modest.

SHARED, RELEASED, AND DISMISSED TIME

In recent years parochial and public school authorities cooperated in a plan known as "shared time" or dual enrollment. Under this experiment parochial students take certain courses (normally the "value" courses such as literature, history, and religion) in the church school, while other courses (generally the "neutral" courses such as foreign language, mathematics, and science) are taken in the public school. Such a plan avoided immediate controversy over the purchase of textbooks for parochial schools, for in "shared time" public funds were expended only for public texts. On the other hand, separating subjects that have religious implications from those that do not struck at the heart of the parochial school ideal: that all learning, like all living, is for the greater glory of God.

In the Champaign, Illinois, case of *McCollum* v. *Board of Education* (1948), Justice Hugo Black delivered the majority opinion of the Court. In a lengthy concurring opinion Justice Felix Frankfurter wrote as follows:

Separation means separation, not something less. Jefferson's metaphor in describing the relation between Church and State speaks of a "wall of separation," not of a fine line easily overstepped. The public school is at once the symbol of our democracy and the most pervasive means for promoting our common destiny. In no activity of the State is it more vital to keep out divisive forces than in its schools, to avoid confusing, not to say fusing, what the Constitution sought to keep strictly apart. "The great American principle of eternal separation"—Elihu Root's phrase bears repetition—is one of the vital reliances of our Constitutional system for assuring unities among our people stronger than our diversities. It is the Court's duty to enforce this principle in its full integrity.

While shared time has not received any court test, two other plans which divide instruction between lay and religious leaders have reached the Su-

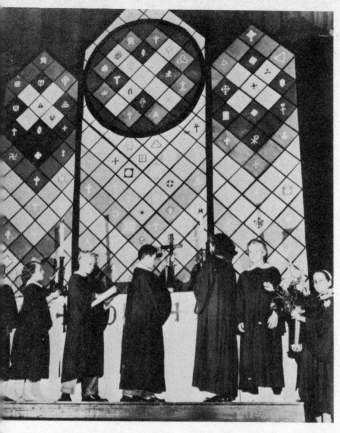

7. *"Released Time" Graduation, Minneapolis Auditorium, 1946*

8. *"Dismissed Time" Religious Education, Fort Wayne, Indiana, 1949*

preme Court. One, often called "released time," provided for public school students to be released from secular studies for an hour a week (more or less) in order to pursue sectarian studies under sectarian teachers for that period of time. Normally the religious leaders, coming into the public school buildings, conducted a class for those pupils who chose instruction in a particular ecclesiastical persuasion. In Champaign, Illinois, for example, religious instruction was offered in grades four to nine by Protestant, Catholic, and Jewish leaders for thirty- or forty-five-minute periods. Students electing to receive no religious instruction stayed in school, pursuing their regular studies. In 1940 the program was challenged on its constitutionality, and it reached the Supreme Court in 1948. Because of the use of school facilities, school time, and school personnel (to keep attendance records), the Court found with only a single dissent Champaign's "released time" program to be unconstitutional. Across the country similar programs tended to wither away or collapse at the start.

In New York City's case of "dismissed time," *Zorach* v. *Clauson* (1952), Justice William O. Douglas delivered the opinion of the Court, a portion of which follows.

> We are a religious people whose institutions presuppose a Supreme Being. We guarantee the freedom to worship as one chooses. We make room for as wide a variety of beliefs and creeds as the spiritual needs of man deem necessary. We sponsor an attitude on the part of government that shows no partiality to any one group and that lets each flourish according to the zeal of its adherents and the appeal of its dogma. When the state encourages religious instruction or cooperates with religious authorities by adjusting the schedule of public events to sectarians needs, it follows the best of our traditions. For it then respects the religious nature of our people and accommodates the public service to their spiritual needs. To hold that it may not would be to find in the Constitution a requirement that the government show a callous indifference to religious groups. That would be preferring those who believe in no religion over those who do believe. . . . But we find no constitutional requirement which makes it necessary for government to be hostile to religion and to throw its weight against efforts to widen the effective scope of religious influence.

In other communities the solution to growing secularization in education took the form of "dismissed time." The major distinction between this and "released time" was that public school facilities and classrooms were not used. Rather students were "dismissed" to their respective churches, synagogues, or religious education centers to take instruction there. School authorities might still be involved, however, to the extent of keeping records of attendance or maintaining some activity for those pupils who did not choose sectarian instruction. A case involving such a plan in New York

City reached the Supreme Court in 1952, where by a five-to-four decision it was found to be constitutional. Yet so vigorous were the dissenting opinions that confidence in this solution to secularized education was severely shaken.

WORSHIP OR STUDY

Another approach calls for the public school staff itself to accept the responsibility for religion in education. This approach took two sharply differing tacks and destinations; moreover, the feasibility and constitutionality of the two differed with equal sharpness. One tack concerned religion as *worship*, the other regarded religion as *study*.

(1) In the nineteenth century, religious exercises such as prayer and Bible reading were part of the Protestant flavor that permeated American education. Vigorous protests by Roman Catholics (e.g., in New York City) or by Jews (e.g., in Cincinnati) led to minor modifications, but traditional practices generally prevailed throughout the century. In the twentieth century, as religious pluralism advanced across the country, all religious exercises came increasingly under sectarian or secular attack. Minorities sought redress from what seemed like an indoctrinating "tyranny of the majority," while others believed the First Amendment to the Constitution to be seriously compromised by these practices. In 1962 and again in 1963 the Supreme Court agreed that religious worship in a daily program of compulsory public education was unconstitutional. Justice Hugo Black, delivering the opinion of the court in the 1962 "Regents' Prayer Case" (*Engel* v. *Vitale*), declared: ". . . We think that the constitutional prohibition against laws respecting an establishment of religion must at least mean that in this country it is no part of the business of government to compose official prayers for any group of the American people to recite as a part of a religious program carried on by government." The 1963 decision, treating prayer and Bible reading in Maryland and Pennsylvania

---

In *Engel* v. *Vitale* (1962), better known as the "Regents' Prayer Case" of the State of New York, the Court's six to one decision read in part as follows:

It has been argued that to apply the Constitution in such a way as to prohibit state laws respecting an establishment of religious services in public schools is to indicate a hostility toward religion or toward prayer. Nothing, of course, could be more wrong. The history of man is inseparable from the history of religion. And perhaps it is not too much to say that since the beginning of that history many people have devoutly believed that "More things are wrought by prayer than this world dreams of." It was doubtless largely due to men who believed this that there grew up a sentiment that caused men to leave the cross-currents of officially established

9. *Aerial View, Georgetown University*

10. *Memorial Church, Harvard University*

11. *The Duke University Chapel*

12. *Sterling Divinity Quadrangle, Yale University*

13. *Aerial View, Notre Dame University*

14. *Aerial View, Brandeis University*

state religions and religious persecution in Europe and come to this country filled with the hope that they could find a place in which they could pray when they pleased to the God of their faith in the language they chose. And there were men of this same faith in the power of prayer who led the fight for adoption of our Constitution and also for our Bill of Rights with the very guarantees of religious freedom that forbid the sort of governmental activity which New York has attempted here. These men knew that the First Amendment, which tried to put an end to governmental control of religion and of prayer, was not written to destroy either.

---

public schools, likewise found religious worship to be constitutionally excluded from public education.

(2) Justice Tom Clark, who spoke for the court in the 1963 cases, pointed out, however, the legitimacy of that second tack referred to above. In this approach religion was declared a legitimate discipline for objective investigation. Distinguishing carefully between the practice of religion and the study of religion, the Court found the latter to be not only permissible legally but highly desireable culturally. For to understand the world in which we live—its literature, its art, its past achievements, its future aspirations—a study of religion is essential. One might similarly argue that a full understanding of America is impossible without a study of the Judeo-Christian forces that fashioned and sustained the nation.

In 1963 the United States Supreme Court noted in the case of *Abington* v. *Schempp* (Bible reading in Pennsylvania public schools) the importance and the legality of the study of religion within public education.

> . . . It might well be said that one's education is not complete without a study of comparative religion or the history of religion and its relationship to the advancement of civilization. It certainly may be said that the Bible is worthy of study for its literary and historic qualities. Nothing we have said here indicates that such study of the Bible or of religion, when presented objectively as part of a secular program of education, may not be effected consistent with the First Amendment.

HIGHER EDUCATION

Finally, some saw a counterbalance to secular public education as possible only at the college level. There denominations and traditions might mold the youthful leaders of tomorrow. Beginning with Harvard in 1636, Protestantism demonstrated its commitment to a higher education unmistakably liberal but also unmistakably religious. With Georgetown University, founded in 1789, Roman Catholicism began its heavy investment in higher education. Yeshiva (1886) and Brandeis (1948) Universities exemplify

Judaism's commitment to a similar cause. In every corner of the continent, at every stage of the nation's history religion revealed its firm allegiance to higher education.

That allegiance expressed itself not only in the church colleges but also through church ministries maintained in municipal and state universities. University chaplains, denominational houses, and occasionally academic courses helped spiritual growth match the pace of a corresponding secular development. Hillel and Wesley Foundations, Newman and Canterbury Clubs, Inter Varsity Christian Fellowship, and a score of other official efforts reminded the college student of a dual loyalty: to things of the spirit no less than of the mind.

In every approach, every experiment, every strategem or design, most Americans shared a common motivation. And that was to find ways in which two great areas of national and personal life, religion and education, could constructively interact. In the absence of such fruitful encounter, the future looked fearfully bleak: a society technically proficient but spiritually vacant, or a nation with abundant knowledge about means but little wisdom regarding ends.

24 ❖ Democracy

WHILE RELIGION AND DEMOCRACY can never be identified, the relationship between them can never be ignored. To identify the two is to confuse ultimate with immediate loyalties. In America to segregate the two, each to its own high-walled preserve, is to impoverish a people and subvert the social whole.

Democracy, unlike tyranny, neither demands ultimate loyalty nor assumes absolute control. The liberty of the soul is respected, the sanctity of conscience is honored. By insisting that absolute control is God's and that ultimate loyalties are heaven-bent, religion keeps a limited democracy from becoming a prideful tyranny.

Also by reserving worship to God alone Judaism and Christianity resist the danger of a deified democracy. No state can endure godlike devotion without degenerating into demonlike corruption. Neither the Judaic nor the Christian way of life, therefore, can be made synonymous with the American way of life. Civil liberty is best preserved where spiritual integrity is truly kept.

John Courtney Murray, S. J., speaking of the shared truths embodied in the Declaration of Independence, comments on Christianity's contribution in *Religion in America* (1958).

The truths we hold were well enough stated. Three are immediate: the limitation of government by law—by a higher law not of government's making, whereby an order of inviolable rights is constituted; the principle of consent; and the right of resistance to unjust rule. These are the heritage of classical and medieval constitutionalism; they center on the idea of law. One truth is remote and metapolitical—that man is not the creature of the City but of God; that the dignity of man is equal in all men; that there are human purposes which transcend the order of politics; that the ultimate function of the political order is to support man in the pursuit of these purposes; that it is within the power of man to alter his own history in pursuit of his own good. You will not find this pregnant truth elsewhere than in the Western and Christian heritage.

Yet it is deceptive to speak of spiritual and temporal realms as though between them a great gulf was fixed. In any society, totalitarian or democratic, man's ultimate concerns are related to his immediate ones; and commitment to eternal values may direct or be directed by the worldly tasks at hand. In a free society, however, religious vision is at liberty to ennoble and enhance the social order. Believing in a God of rational order and discernible purpose, Americans also believe that the Spirit of God works in and through the people. Not some appointed representative nor some authorized faction but the voice of the people—on the whole and in the long run—best represent the voice and will of God.

For a great many Americans the dignity, indeed the sanctity of human personality, came from a conviction about man's nature and man's destiny: "You are called to be sons of God." And while a man was a citizen, he was never merely or wholly a citizen to be disposed of or manipulated as the state demanded. The state, like the Sabbath, was made for man; not man for the state. Democracy affirmed that people are ends valuable in themselves, not means to be subordinated, exploited or destroyed. Such mutual regard has been expressed in other words: "And whatsoever you would that men do unto you, do you also unto them."

History offers ample evidence of religion impeding or opposing the growth of democracy. Because this is so, none can claim that ecclesiastical authority faithfully fosters a free and open society. On the other hand, that democracy can long endure or brightly flourish apart from moral responsibility and spiritual sensitivity is far from clear. Whatever the theoretical relationship between democracy and religion, certainly in America each draws from the other. Settled by a Protestantism suspicious of the autocratic state, enriched by a Catholicism loyal to a tradition of English liberties, and strengthened by a Judaism dedicated to worship free from political meddling, these United States framed a constitution and charted a course that became a pattern for democracy around the world.

Yet, even in America religion may impede or oppose the democratic processes. Free to criticize all others, the churches and synagogues may neglect to criticize themselves. Believing a particular pattern of behavior to be right for their own following, they may attempt to cast all others into that mold. Some religious institutions may presume that only bad faith or treachery prevents the political attainment of theological goals. Still others, confusing fanaticism with faith, may resist discussion, condemn toleration, and subvert freedom. But religion that is self-critical, humble, informed, and earnest can contribute much to the maintenance of democracy. This it does not by subordinating the spiritual to the political but by being true to itself, its insights, its ends, its ultimate loyalty.

1. *Dwight D. Eisenhower at Service of Prayer and Communion, 1959 • The annual service of prayer and communion marking t h e opening of Congress was held in National Presbyterian Church, Washington, D. C. President Eisenhower is here accompanied by the moderator of the United Presbyterian Church in the U. S. A., Dr. T. M. Taylor.*

2. *John F. Kennedy takes the Oath of Office, 1961 • Chief Justice Earl Warren administers the oath to President Kennedy who uses a revered family bible, the first use of the Douai Version in a presidential inauguration.*

3. *Lyndon B. Johnson bows at Inauguration, 1965 • Archbishop Iakovos, head of the Greek Orthodox Archdiocese of North and South America, offers the benediction which concludes the inaugural ceremonies for President Johnson.*

H. Richard Niebuhr, brother of Reinhold and long-time professor of Christian ethics at Yale University, describes the Protestant's relationship to the "democratic faith" in *The Shaping of American Religion* (1961).

Protestantism in all its original forms has been concerned to emphasize the direct and absolute dependence of all men and their societies on God, and only in that setting has it affirmed independence from finite powers. Its protests against churches and states have been directed less against invasions of the rights of men than against usurpations of the absolute sovereignty of God. . . . The right to freedom of worship for such Protestants has been based on the duty to worship God; the right to freedom in speech on the duty to speak the truth as the truth is known; the rights of conscience have been derivative, for them, from the human duty to obey God rather than men. . . . [Protestantism] must protest against the assumption by any human authority—whether priest, preacher, magistrate, people, or popular majority—of the right to speak in the name of the absolute. . . . If Protestantism in America has lost sight of these points and accepted instead the dogmas of democratic faith, then indeed it has lost its independence; then it no longer challenges the social faith but is a passive representative of the culture.

In America the forces of religion, despite their plurality and diversity, contribute to a sense of community. A society proceeds on basic assumptions whose truth cannot be proved in the courts of reason nor demonstrated in the records of experience. Out of the wellspring of religious faith come the assumptions worthy of a commitment of "our lives, our fortunes, our sacred honor." When confidence in the common premises falters or fails, the community's bond is broken. Vision dims, enthusiasm wanes, resistance to strange and foreign gods is lost. "The ultimate foundation of a free society," wrote Justice Felix Frankfurter in 1940, "is the binding tie of cohesive sentiment."

Out of their long and crowded histories Judaism and Christianity bring a storehouse of wisdom that society can ill afford to discard. Wisdom about virtue, wisdom about the past, wisdom about man's capacities and, no less, wisdom about his limitations. Psychological and sociological insights as keen or keener than anything the modern world slickly sells may be found in the parables of ancient rabbis and the homilies of early church fathers. From the prospect of this religious heritage the achievements of man are too rich to permit a sterile cynicism; yet the depravity of man is too evident to justify a soft sentimentalism.

In a 1962 interview Louis Finkelstein, chancellor of the Jewish Theological Seminary (New York City) since 1951, spoke of an incidental but not insignificant contribution of Jews to the American spirit.

> There is another point to be made about the contribution that Jews can make to political and social mores in this country. There is an important role which a small minority can play in this land that no one else can play, and precisely because the minority tends to be sensitive to any act of disparagement to the stranger. The members of the majority often will, without malice but thoughtlessly, and without really entering into the spirit of members of a minority, do things that will hurt the stranger. Because the Jewish community is articulate and extremely sensitive, it has been able to help the American people understand this situation; and in that way it has been able to help all minorities, and above all, the American spirit.

Where nation vies against nation, race against race, and even creed against creed, such ancient wisdom is at least relevant to good order; it is just possibly essential for survival. Principles are strengthened when men appeal beyond the passions of the moment, the fevers of the fight, to that which exists from everlasting to everlasting, to that which knows no East or West. Psychiatrists and pastors, jurists and moralists, columnists and essayists, politicians and presidents comment at length on the rootlessness of modern man and the aimlessness of modern culture. Roots will again be established and aims again made clear as modern man recovers the faith by which free and civilized people must live.

In American society religion brings a sense of community and a fund of wisdom. But it also brings judgment. When in the Revolutionary period religion fought for its freedom, it fought for and won the right of correction and reproof. Religion that is weakly conformist, politely proper, and supremely content loses in power what it gains in number. And while religion finds much in society to conserve, it also beholds a world to transform. In one regard conservative but in another radical, the ministry of faith brings both criticism and comfort. Either alone is but half enough.

The noted historian of religion in America, Sidney E. Mead, comments on the religious foundations of democracy in *The Lively Experiment* (1963).

> These, then, are fundamental beliefs on which the democracy rests: belief in God, belief in "the people," belief in the voice of the people as the surest clue to the voice of God, belief that truth emerges out of the conflict of opinions. . . .
> Since both the ideal of destiny under God and the way of democracy were based upon a dynamic or experimental conception of human life under God, the primarily important thing is . . . the sureness of the people's

sense of direction—the firmness of their belief in the essential rightness of the general tendency or movement. So long as there is widespread confidence among the people that the direction and way are basically right, the system is sound and can function even in adversity. And this is essentially a matter of faith—faith in the guidance of God—faith that the democratic way with all its tortuous ambiguities and disappointments is nevertheless the best way yet devised.

Too readily and too frequently churches and synagogues become defenders of the status quo, proclaiming with all of the obtuse optimism of Alexander Pope, "Whatever is, is right." Denominations serve as pointers to social status; congregations, like clubs, sanctify their own interests, biases, amusements, and morality. In contemporary America hardly a political, social, or economic passion is pronounced without the mantle of religion being wrapped about it. However poisoned by bitterness, however corrupted by greed, however flooded with hate, somehow and somewhere a pulpit can be found to declare the cause biblically based and spiritually sound. The conqueror is conquered, the transformer is transformed.

From the fifteenth century to the present, the exploration, the colonization, and the expansion of America were all conceived as a noble adventure, a great experiment, a grand mission. Most who dreamed the American dream felt sure of success, not because of the courage and strength of men, though there was plenty of that, but because of the favor and grace of God, for there was more of that. On any terms the venture was bold, even audacious; and by any standards the results were huge, even prodigious. But on religious terms and by religious standards the fulfillment of that dream was occasion for gratitude, not pride. Failures, on the other hand, were occasions not for surrender and despair but for repentance and renewal. So long as faith endured, the adventure beckoned, the experiment continued, the mission grew.

"By faith Abraham obeyed when he was called to go out . . . and he went out, not knowing where he was to go." So Columbus sailed, Las Casas preached, Brébeuf died, Hakluyt wrote; so Rolfe and White, Williams and Penn, Bradford and Winthrop sowed "in a land so fruitful . . . the seeds of religion and piety." And so a nation was conceived in liberty and dedicated to the proposition that all men are created equal. And so a people, at worship and at work, go out, not knowing where they go. But by faith they do go, confident that their destiny is guided by God.

Chronology

1659   Two Quakers hanged in Boston
1663   John Eliot's Indian Bible printed in Cambridge, Massachusetts
1671   George Fox visits America
1673   Marquette and Joliet explore upper Mississippi River
1682   William Penn establishes his Quaker colony in America
1683   Francis Makemie founds Presbyterian Church in Rehoboth, Maryland
1685   Louis XIV revokes Edict of Nantes
1687   French Reformed (Huguenot) Church organized in Charleston, South Carolina
1689   Royal Sovereigns William and Mary approve Act of Toleration; King's Chapel (Anglican) opened in Boston
1690   Texas receives first permanent mission: San Francisco de los Texas
1697   Eusebio Kiño establishes Arizona's San Xavier del Bac Mission
1699   Society for the Promotion of Christian Knowledge formed in England
1701   Society for the Propagation of the Gospel in Foreign Parts organized by Thomas Bray; Yale College founded
1706   First presbytery formed in America
1708   Palatinate refugees begin to settle Hudson River Valley
1718   Jesuit mission started in New Orleans
1720   Theodore Frelinghuysen begins ministry in New Jersey
1727   Ursuline nuns open school in Louisiana
1734   Salzburg Lutherans arrive in Savannah; "surprising conversions" in Northampton, Massachusetts
1735   John Wesley preaches in Georgia
1740   George Whitefield's Charity School (progenitor of University of Pennsylvania) begun in Philadelphia; Whitefield promotes Great Awakening
1742   Heinrich Mühlenberg debarks at Charleston, South Carolina
1746   College of New Jersey (Princeton) chartered; publication of Jonathan Edwards' *Treatise Concerning Religious Affections*
1747   Death of David Brainerd
1748   Evangelical Lutheran Ministerium of Pennsylvania formed
1754   King's College (Columbia) founded in New York City
1757   John Woolman journeys through the South
1763   Fall of "New France" in America; Newport's Touro Synagogue dedicated
1764   College of Rhode Island (Brown) founded at Warren
1766   Queen's College (Rutgers) chartered in New Jersey; Methodism introduced into Maryland; Moravians establish Salem, North Carolina
1768   John Witherspoon arrives from Scotland to become president of Princeton
1769   First of California's Franciscan missions established in San Diego

1770   Francis Asbury arrives in America to direct affairs of Methodism

1773   Papal suppression of the Society of Jesus

1777   Continental Congress proclaims day of National Thanksgiving (November 1)

1779   Virginia Assembly passes Jefferson's "Bill for Establishing Religious Freedom"

1784   Methodist Episcopal Church organized; Samuel Seabury elevated to the episcopacy; Junípero Serra dies in California

1787   German Reformed and German Lutherans found Franklin College in Carlisle, Pennsylvania

1789   Protestant Episcopal Church in the United States of America organized; Reformed Dutch Church of North America formed; John Carroll named bishop of the Diocese of Baltimore; Georgetown University founded; United States Constitution ratified by 12 states

1791   First ten amendments added to the Constitution

1793   Formation of the diocese of Louisiana and the two Floridas

1801   Plan of Union (Congregational and Presbyterian) for western missions

1804   Philadelphia Quakers petition United States Congress regarding evils of slavery

1805   German Reformed permit English in service of worship

1806   Shakers establish community in Union Village, Ohio

1808   Baltimore made Roman Catholic metropolitan see

1809   Thomas and Alexander Campbell issue "Declaration and Address"

1810   American Board of Commissioners for Foreign Missions organized

1815   William DuBourg made bishop of Louisiana and the Floridas; American Education Society formed

1816   American Bible Society founded; formation of the African Methodist Episcopal Church in Philadelphia

1817   John Mason Peck sent as missionary to the opening West; American Colonization Society organized

1818   Congregationalism disestablished in Connecticut

1819   New England missionaries leave for Hawaii

1822   Formation in Lyons, France, of the Society for the Propagation of the Faith

1823   Trinity College founded in Hartford

1824   American Sunday School Union formed; Kenyon College established in Ohio

1825   American Tract Society organized; formation of American Unitarian Association

1826   American Home Mission Society created

1829   First Provincial Council (Roman Catholic) meets in Baltimore

1830   Organization in Fayette, New York, of the Church of Jesus Christ of Latter Day Saints

1831   Denison College (Ohio) founded

1832 St. Louis University chartered

1833 Secularization of the California missions; American Anti-Slavery Society formed; Congregationalism disestablished in Massachusetts

1834 Jason Lee begins mission in Willamette Valley; Ursuline convent burned in Charlestown, Massachusetts

1835 Charles G. Finney publishes *Lectures on Revivals of Religion*

1836 Joseph Smith dedicates temple in Kirtland, Ohio; publication of *Awful Disclosures of Maria Monk*; Transcendental Club meets in Boston

1837 Elijah P. Lovejoy murdered in Alton, Illinois; Knox College founded in Galesburg, Illinois

1838 "Address at Harvard Divinity School" delivered by Ralph Waldo Emerson

1839 Publication of Theodore Weld's *American Slavery as It Is*

1840 Pierre Jean DeSmet begins mission among the Flatheads

1843 William Miller announces world to end within one year

1844 Seventh-day Adventist congregation formed in New Hampshire; Orestes Brownson becomes Roman Catholic; organization of the Methodist Episcopal Church, South; Joseph Smith assassinated in Carthage, Illinois; Isaac Hecker converts to Catholicism

1845 Southern Baptist Convention formed in Augusta, Georgia

1846 Peter Cartwright defeated in congressional race by Abraham Lincoln

1847 Horace Bushnell's *Christian Nurture* published; the Whitmans martyred in Oregon Territory; Mormons migrate to Utah Territory; collapse of Brook Farm in Massachusetts

1848 John Humphrey Noyes leads group to Oneida, New York

1850 Butler University (Indiana) and Heidelberg College (Ohio) founded

1851 Young Men's Christian Association introduced into America

1852 Harriet Beecher Stowe's *Uncle Tom's Cabin* published

1853 Rabbi Isaac Lesser publishes *The Twenty-Four Books of Holy Scriptures* in English translation

1857 United States Army moves against Mormons in Utah

1863 Abraham Lincoln signs the Emancipation Proclamation

1865 Southern churchmen organize the Presbyterian Church in the United States

1866 Young Women's Christian Association begins in Boston

1868 Japanese are imported into Hawaii; Hampton Institute founded in Virginia

1870 Southern Negroes form Christian (Colored) Methodist Episcopal Church

1872 Russian Orthodox bishopric moved from Sitka, Alaska, to San Francisco, California

1873   Union of America Hebrew Congregations formed

1874   Women's Christian Temperance Union established

1875   First publication of Mary Baker Eddy's *Science and Health, with Key to the Scriptures*; Moody-Sankey revival in Brooklyn; Catholic Young Men's National Union formed

1876   First Protestant church established in Alaska

1878   Salvation Army formed in England (previously The Christian Mission)

1879   Christian Science begun in Boston

1880   Negroes organize the National Baptist Convention

1881   Mass immigration of East European Jews begins

1882   Knights of Columbus formed

1886   Yeshiva University founded; Washington Gladden's *Applied Christianity* published; formation of Student Volunteer Movement for Foreign Missions

1887   American Protective Association founded in Clinton, Iowa

1889   Catholic University of America opened; Central Conference of American Rabbis founded

1891   *Life of Father Hecker* published; papal encyclical *Rerum novarum* speaks to social and economic issues

1892   Lyman Abbott's *The Evolution of Christianity* appears; heresy trials of Charles A. Briggs and Henry P. Smith

1893   Publication of Josiah Strong's *The New Era*; Cardinal Satolli appointed Apostolic Delegate to the United States

1894   Immigration Restriction League formed in New England

1895   Creation of the Anti-Saloon League of America

1896   Charles M. Sheldon's *In His Steps* published

1899   Papal letter from Leo XIII condemning "Americanism"

1900   John R. Mott writes *The Evangelization of the World in This Generation*

1904   National Catholic Education Association formed

1906   John A. Ryan writes *A Living Wage*

1907   Publication of *Christianity and the Social Crisis* by Walter Rauschenbusch

1908   Creation of the Federal Council of Churches; Social Creed of the Churches issued

1909   Rufus Jones publishes *Studies in Mystical Religion*

1911   Catholic Foreign Missionary Society of America (Maryknoll) founded

1913   Solomon Schechter organizes the United Synagogue of America

1914   Assemblies of God form denomination at Hot Springs, Arkansas

1917   Jewish Publication Society of America issues first official translation of the Holy Scriptures; American Friends Service Committee constituted

1918   Central Conference of American Rabbis adopts program for social justice

1919   Roman Catholic Bishops promote "Program of Social Reconstruction"; Eighteenth Amendment added to the Constitution; National Catholic Welfare Conference founded

1922   Formation of the Greek Catholic archdiocese of North and South America

1923   J. Gresham Machen's *Christianity and Liberalism* appears

1924   National Origins Act adopted

1925   Scopes Trial in Dayton, Tennessee; Supreme Court defends parental choice of parochial school (*Pierce* v. *Society of Sisters*)

1926   International Eucharistic Congress held in Chicago

1928   Formation of the National Conference of Christians and Jews

1931   Catholics, Protestants and Jews hold Conference on the Permanent Preventives of Unemployment

1932   Harry Emerson Fosdick writes *As I See Religion*

1933   Eighteenth Amendment repealed; persecution and emigration of German Jews begins

1939   Reunion of northern and southern branches of Methodism

1941   Confraternity edition of the New Testament completed

1943   Federal Council issues handbook *Wartime Services of the Churches*

1945   G. Bromley Oxnam writes *Labor and Tomorrow's World*

1946   Nobel Peace Prize awarded to John R. Mott

1947   Cardinal Ritter abolishes segregation in St. Louis parochial school; Nobel Peace Prize awarded to American Friends Service Committee

1948   World Council of Churches meets in Amsterdam; Brandeis University founded in Massachusetts; Supreme Court finds "released time" unconstitutional in Illinois (*McCollum* v. *Board of Education*)

1950   Formation of the National Council of Churches of Christ in the United States of America

1952   Publication of the Revised Standard Version of the Bible; Norman Vincent Peale writes *The Power of Positive Thinking*; Supreme Court finds "dismissed time" constitutional in New York (*Zorach* v. *Clauson*)

1956   Mormon Temple dedicated in Los Angeles

1957   Congregationalists join with Evangelical and Reformed to create the United Church of Christ

1958   Martin Luther King writes *Stride Toward Freedom*

1960   First Roman Catholic elected president of the United States; Eugene C. Blake and James A. Pike propose merger of Methodists, Presbyterians, Episcopalians, and United Church of Christ

1962   Vatican II opens in Rome; Supreme Court finds Regents' Prayer in New York unconstitutional (*Engel* v. *Vitale*)

1963   Pope John XXIII issues encyclical *Pacem in Terris*; Supreme Court rules Bible reading and use of Lord's Prayer in public schools unconstitutional (*Abington* v. *Schempp*; *Murray* v. *Curlett*)

1964 Nobel Peace Prize awarded to Martin Luther King

1965 Fourth and final session of Vatican II; Paul VI celebrates mass in Yankee Stadium

1966 "God is dead" theology yields to a theology of hope

1967 Mobilization meeting in Washington of Clergy and Laity Concerned about Vietnam

1968 Assassination of Martin Luther King, Memphis, Tennessee

1969 Black Manifesto seeks $500 million from "White Christian Churches and the Jewish Synagogues in the United States of America and All Other Racist Institutions"; Father Theodore M. Hesburgh, Notre Dame University, named chairman of the U.S. Civil Rights Commission

1970 Billy Graham rally, Knoxville, Tennessee, addressed by President Nixon; theology of ecology develops; FBI arrests Reverend Daniel Berrigan, S.J.

1971 Nationwide "Jesus People" movement among the younger generation

1972 Continuing commercial success of *Jesus Christ Superstar* and *Godspell*

1973 "Key 73" evangelistic campaign launched by 140 of the nation's denominations; U.S. Supreme Court strikes down state laws permitting financial aid to sectarian schools

Suggestions for Further Reading

THIS BRIEF SECTION cannot offer, even in outline, the scholarly apparatus for a full examination of the religious history of America. Rather, emphasis has been given to those volumes that are generally readable and widely available. An asterisk (*) indicates a paperbound edition.

Those interested in more extensive aid than that provided here are encouraged to consult two excellent and authoritative bibliographical guides: Oscar Handlin, *et al., Harvard Guide to American History* (Cambridge [Mass.], 1954); and Nelson R. Burr, *A Critical Bibliography of Religion in America* (Princeton, 1961).

The number of general treatments of America's religious history has sharply increased since 1950. The University of Chicago's History of American Civilization Series includes three brief, well-written volumes on religion: John Tracy Ellis, *American Catholicism,* revised edition, 1969*; Nathan Glazer, *American Judaism,* revised edition, 1972*; and Winthrop S. Hudson, *American Protestantism,* 1961*. Important and pivotal documents of that history may be found in H. Shelton Smith, *et al., American Christianity: An Historical Interpretation with Representative Documents,* 2 vols. (New York, 1960, 1962). Reliable surveys include Winthrop S. Hudson's authoritative *Religion in America* (New York, revised edition, 1973*); William A. Clebsch's interpretive *From Sacred to Profane America* (New York, 1968); and Sydney E. Ahlstrom's remarkably comprehensive *A Religious History of the American People* (New Haven, 1972). For documentation of the pluralistic element in American religion, see Robert T. Handy, *Religion in the American Experience* (Columbia, S.C., 1972*); and for the intellectual dimension, see William A. Clebsch, *American Religious Thought: A History* (Chicago, 1973).

PART I   THE AGE OF EXPLORATION

(CHAPTERS: 1-4)

Of the treatments of Columbus, none is more engaging than Samuel Eliot Morison's *Admiral of the Ocean Sea* (Boston, 1942)—recommended especially for those who have a love for the sea. John Edwin Bakeless, *The*

Eyes of Discovery (Philadelphia, 1950; New York, 1961*), describes the virginal continent with special reference to botanical and zoological detail. While first published a generation ago, John B. Brebner's *The Explorers of North America 1492–1806* (London, 1933; Cleveland, 1964*) is well worth the reprinting it has received. In *Conquistadors in North American History* (New York, 1963, 1965*), Paul Horgan tells the story of Spanish sallies with suspenseful drama. The older works of Herbert E. Bolton continue to be indispensable; the University of New Mexico Press reissued his *Coronado: Knight of Pueblos and Plains* in 1964*. Francis Parkman's *The Jesuits in North America* (1963*) is as gripping today as when it was first published a century ago. English exploration and its relationship to religion is convincingly presented in Louis B. Wright's *Religion and Empire: The Alliance between Piety and Commerce in English Expansion* (Chapel Hill [N.C.], 1943). Hakluyt's voluminous writing has been edited by Irwin R. Blacker for a single volume: *Hakluyt's Voyages* (New York, 1965). Finally, one should not deny himself the graceful prose of either Bernard DeVoto or Howard Mumford Jones; the first is most relevant to the age of exploration in *The Course of Empire* (Boston, 1952); the latter in *O Strange New World* (New York, 1964).

PART II   THE AGE OF COLONIZATION

(CHAPTERS 5-10)

Wallace Notestein's *The English People on the Eve of Colonization* (New York, 1954, 1962*) provides essential background for this entire period. For the Southern Colonies good general orientation is available in Wesley F. Craven, *The Southern Colonies in the Seventeenth Century, 1607–1689* (New York, 1949). Anglicanism in Virginia is thoroughly described in G. MacLaren Brydon's *Virginia's Mother Church* (Richmond, 1947, 1952), while an angry itinerant from South Carolina (Charles Woodmason) gives his impressions of religion in the Revolutionary period in Richard J. Hooker (ed.), *The Carolina Backcountry on the Eve of the Revolution* (Chapel Hill [N.C.], 1953). Edmund S. Morgan delightfully re-creates the family life of the eighteenth century in *Virginians at Home* (New York, 1952; Charlottesville, 1963*), while urban life in Charleston and elsewhere is presented in Carl Bridenbaugh, *Cities in the Wilderness: The First Century of Urban Life in America, 1625–1742* (New York, 1938, 1964*). Roman Catholic beginnings in Maryland receive detailed and scholarly examination in Thomas O. Hanley, S.J., *Their Rights and Liberties* (Westminster [Md.], 1959).

For New England, the number of excellent histories, both general and religious, is abundant. Perhaps there is no better place to begin than in one of the editions of William Bradford's *Plymouth Plantation;* Samuel Eliot

Morison's edition (New York, 1952) is particularly readable. The many works of Perry Miller are altogether indispensable, and his collected essays, *Errand into the Wilderness* (Cambridge, 1956; New York, 1964*), provide a firm point of departure. From there one may move on to his major effort: *The New England Mind: The Seventeenth Century* (New York, 1939; Boston, 1961*); and *The New England Mind: From Colony to Province* (Cambridge, 1953; Boston, 1961*). If one should desire to follow New England's religious history by way of biographies, the possibilities are many. For reliability and readability Edmund S. Morgan's *The Puritan Dilemma: The Story of John Winthrop* (Boston, 1958*) and his *The Gentle Puritan: A Life of Ezra Stiles* (New Haven, 1962) are beyond compare. The many works of Ola Elizabeth Winslow also deserve to be cited, among them these biographical treatments: *Jonathan Edwards* (New York, 1940, 1961*); *Master Roger Williams* (New York, 1957); and *Judge Samuel Sewall* (New York, 1964).

For the Middle Colonies, a reliable general treatment is Thomas J. Wertenbaker's *The Founding of American Civilization: The Middle Colonies* (New York, 1938). Daniel J. Boorstin in *The Lost World of Thomas Jefferson* (New York, 1948; Boston, 1960*) revives the eighteenth-century climate of opinion, a climate for which such Middle Colony men as Benjamin Franklin, Benjamin Rush, David Rittenhouse, Joseph Priestley, Benjamin Smith Barton, Charles Willson Peale and Thomas Paine were largely responsible. Rufus Jones's classic work, *Quakers in the American Colonies* (New York, 1911, 1962), should be supplemented by Frederick B. Tolles' *Quakers and the Atlantic Culture* (New York, 1960). And for contrasting eighteenth-century views of Middle Colony life, see the *Autobiography of Benjamin Franklin* and the *Journal of John Woolman*. Both are available in many editions, the best of Franklin having been edited by Leonard W. Labaree *et al.* (New Haven, 1964*).

On the witchcraft episode, see M. L. Starkey, *The Devil in Massachusetts* (New York, 1949). For colonial revivalism, see Wesley Gewehr, *The Great Awakening in Virginia* (Durham, 1930); C. H. Maxson, *The Great Awakening in the Middle Colonies* (Chicago, 1920); E. S. Gaustad, *The Great Awakening in New England* (New York, 1957); Stuart C. Henry, *George Whitefield: Wayfaring Witness* (New York, 1957); and Alan Heimert (with Perry Miller) for documents on *The Great Awakening* (Indianapolis, 1966*). For a general cultural history of this period, see Louis B. Wright, *The Cultural Life of the American Colonies* (New York, 1957, 1962*).

PART III AGE OF EXPANSION

(Chapter 11.) In the Revolutionary period, the enduring problems of church and state are intensified and molded; the basic work in this field,

Anson Phelps Stokes's *Church and State in the United States,* 3 vols. (New York, 1950), has been brought up to date and condensed into a single volume by Leo Pfeffer (New York, 1964). Carl Bridenbaugh in *Mitre and Sceptre* (New York, 1962) carefully re-examines the role of religion, and particularly the fear of an Anglican episcopate in America in the pre-Revolutionary years. For the first three presidents, their own voluminous writings constitute, of course, the indispensable source. Comprehensive editorial labors now in progress—Julian Boyd, *The Papers of Thomas Jefferson* (Princeton), and Lyman Butterfield, *The Adams Family Papers* (Cambridge)—demonstrate the highest standards of scholarship. The engaging, illuminating correspondence of our second and third presidents is found in Lester J. Cappon, *The Adams-Jefferson Letters,* 2 vols. (Chapel Hill [N.C.], 1959). Jefferson's "Bible" is available in many editions, the latest being by I. A. O. Roche, *The Jefferson Bible* (New York, 1963); Adrienne Koch, *The Philosophy of Thomas Jefferson* (New York, 1943, 1964*), contains an excellent discussion on religion and morals. Paul F. Boller, Jr., in *George Washington and Religion* (Dallas, 1963) presents a picture of the first president that is, happily, not in the myth-making class. Also see Marcus Cunliffe's brief, intelligent treatment of *George Washington: Man and Monument* (New York, 1958, 1960*). Finally, pertinent excerpts of the founding fathers are available in Norman Cousins, *In God We Trust* (New York, 1957).

(Chapter 12.) The literature of Utopianism makes exciting reading, from the older Charles Nordhoff, *The Communistic Societies of the United States* (New York, 1875, 1960), to the latest journalistic exposé of sect or cult. On the Shakers, see Edward Andrews, *The People Called Shakers* (New York, 1953). On the Mormons, some of the more recent and dependable studies are Thomas F. O'Dea, *The Mormons* (Chicago, 1957, 1964*); Ray West, *Kingdom of the Saints* (New York, 1957); L. J. Arrington, *The Great Basin Kingdom* (Cambridge, 1958); and Wallace Stegner, *Gathering of Zion* (New York, 1964). Transcendentalism is so well represented by its own literate membership that secondary treatises are usually redundant. Most conspicuously, Emerson and Thoreau are widely available and thoroughly readable; see especially the former's *Nature* and the latter's *Walden.* On Brownson, see A. M. Schlesinger, Jr., *Orestes A. Brownson: A Pilgrim's Progress* (Boston, 1939). The excitement and variety of Methodism is transmitted in Charles A. Johnson, *The Frontier Camp Meeting* (Dallas, 1955), but even more in Peter Cartwright's *Autobiography* (Nashville, 1856, 1956). Revivalism in this period is ably presented in Timothy Smith, *Revivalism and Social Reform* (New York, 1957); Bernard A. Weisberger, *They Gathered at the River* (Boston, 1958); and William G. McLoughlin, Jr., *Modern Revivalism* (New York, 1959).

(Chapter 13.) For religion's conquest of the great American continent, see Colin B. Goodykoontz, *Home Missions on the American Frontier* (Caldwell [Idaho], 1939); Robert T. Handy, *We Witness Together* (New York, 1956); and Charles I. Foster, *An Errand of Mercy* (Chapel Hill [N.C.], 1960). The student should know of Reuben Gold Thwaites's thirty-two volume edition of *Early Western Travels 1748–1846* (Cleveland, 1904–1907), Vol. 29 of which is devoted largely to Pierre Jean DeSmet's missions. The complex relationships of missions and Indians are explored in R. P. Beaver, *Church, State and the American Indian* (New York, 1963). The extensive works of Kenneth Scott Latourette should be consulted where relevant (e.g., on Hawaii and Alaska): *A History of the Expansion of Christianity*, 7 vols. (New York, 1937–1945), and *Christianity in a Revolutionary Age*, 5 vols. (1958–1962). And certainly one ought not miss the delights of Alexis de Tocqueville's *Democracy in America* (1835, 1840), available in several paperbound editions.

(Chapter 14.) For slavery before the Civil War and Reconstruction after, see Kenneth M. Stampp, *The Peculiar Institution* (New York, 1956; 1964*); and, by the same author, *The Era of Reconstruction* (New York, 1965). The best one-volume biography of Lincoln, Benjamin P. Thomas' *Abraham Lincoln* (New York, 1952), may be supplemented by a look at his religious views in William J. Wolf, *The Almost Chosen People* (New York, 1959). Abolition is most clearly seen through the lives of its participants. See especially the autobiography, *Narrative of the Life of Frederick Douglass* (1845), attractively edited by Benjamin Quarles (Cambridge, 1960); Irving H. Bartlett, *Wendell Phillips: Brahmin Radical* (Boston, 1961); Benjamin P. Thomas, *Theodore Weld: Crusader for Freedom* (New Brunswick, 1950); and Edward Wagenknecht, *Harriet Beecher Stowe: The Known and The Unknown* (New York, 1965). Southern (and other) defenses of slavery are authoritatively described in William Stanton, *The Leopard's Spots* (Chicago, 1959).

(Chapter 15.) This country's saga of immigration is finely told in Marcus Lee Hansen, *The Immigrant in American History* (Cambridge, 1940; New York, 1964*); in Oscar Handlin, *The Uprooted* (Boston, 1951; New York, 1964*); and in M. A. Jones, *American Immigration* (Chicago, 1960*). Ray A. Billington delineates nativist reactions in *The Protestant Crusade* (New York, 1938, 1964*), and Donald L. Kinzer concentrates on one particular manifestation of this sentiment in *The American Protective Association* (Seattle, 1964). Also see John Higham's excellent *Strangers in the Land* (New Brunswick, 1955; New York, 1963*). Jewish aspects of Americanization are dealt with in Oscar Handlin's *Adventure in Freedom* (New York, 1954), while Roman Catholic stresses and adjustments are evident in John Tracy Ellis' indispensable *Life of James Cardinal Gibbons,* 2 vols. (Milwaukee, 1952). Also see H. Richard Niebuhr's *The Social Sources of Denominationalism* (New York, 1929, 1957*).

(Chapter 16.) Andrew Sinclair's *Prohibition: The Era of Excess* (Boston, 1962; New York, 1964*) is a broad and sophisticated history of this fascinating movement. Robert Peel, *Christian Science, Its Encounter with American Culture* (New York, 1958), and P. W. Wilson, *General Evangeline Booth of the Salvation Army* (New York, 1948), describe specific responses to the challenges of urban life. In the larger arena of social action, see Henry F. May, *Protestant Churches and Industrial America* (New York, 1949); Aaron I. Abell, *The Urban Impact on American Protestantism 1865–1900* (Cambridge, 1943); also by Abell, *American Catholicism and Social Action* (New York, 1960; South Bend [Ind.], 1963*); C. H. Hopkins, *History of the Y. M. C. A.* (New York, 1951); Albert Vorspan and E. J. Lipman, *Justice and Judaism: The Work of Social Action* (New York, 1959); and Oscar Handlin, *A Continuing Task* (New York, 1965). Two of Walter Rauschenbusch's works are readily available: *Christianity and the Social Crisis* (New York, 1907; 1964*), and, *A Theology for the Social Gospel* (New York, 1922; Nashville, 1960*).

PART IV   THIS NATION UNDER GOD:
AT WORSHIP

(Chapter 17.) Biblical motifs in America's development are perceptively discussed in H. Richard Niebuhr's *The Kingdom of God in America* (New York, 1937, 1959*). L. E. Nelson's popularly written *Our Roving Bible* (Nashville, 1945, 1959*) unearths biblical influences and impacts in unlikely places. On the fundamentalist-modernist controversy, read Shailer Mathews' *The Faith of Modernism* (New York, 1924) along with J. Gresham Machen's *Christianity and Liberalism* (New York, 1930). The Scopes Trial has enjoyed extensive coverage, perhaps none so pungent as H. L. Mencken's whose widely circulated essays and journalistic reports are now available in many forms. For the relationships of religion and literature, see Amos Wilder, *Theology and Modern Literature* (Cambridge, 1958); Nathan A. Scott, Jr., *Modern Literature and the Religious Frontier* (New York, 1958); and S. R. Hopper (ed.), *Spiritual Problems in Contemporary Literature* (New York, 1952, 1957*).

(Chapter 18.) The best survey of theology in America is Sydney E. Ahlstrom's in *The Shaping of American Religion* volume noted in the introductory paragraphs above. Regarding Heschel, Niebuhr and Weigel themselves, their writings are neither abstruse nor esoteric; thus, these eloquent theologians should be permitted to speak for themselves. Heschel's principal works include *Man Is Not Alone* (New York, 1952); *God in Search of Man* (New York, 1955; Cleveland, 1959*); and *The Prophets* (New York, 1962). Of Niebuhr's numerous works, some of the more seminal and readable are these: his most autobiographical venture, *Leaves from the Notebooks of a Tamed Cynic* (New York, 1929, 1957*); his most political work, *The Children of Light and the Children of Darkness* (New York, 1944, 1960*); and his most suggestive collection of smaller "pieces," *Essays in Applied Christianity* (New York, 1959*). Gustave Weigel's writings include these readable volumes: *Faith and Understanding in America* (New York, 1959, 1962*); *Catholic Theology in Dialogue* (New York, 1961, 1964*); and *The Modern God: Faith in a Secular Culture* (New York, 1963).

(Chapter 19.) The revived interest in liturgy is evident in the abundance of recent and excellent books on this subject. Two parallel studies of notable merit are E. B. Koenker, *The Liturgical Renaissance in the Roman Catholic Church* (Chicago, 1954); and M. J. Taylor, S. J., *The Protestant Liturgical Renewal: A Catholic Viewpoint* (Westminster [Md.], 1963). For simplicity and clarity it would be difficult to surpass H. A. Reinhold's *Bringing the Mass to the People* (Baltimore, 1960). And for graceful writing coupled with impeccable scholarship, few can compete with Massey H. Shepherd, Jr.; note especially his *Worship in Scripture and Tradition* (New York, 1963). Something of the liturgy of Orthodox Judaism is described in Herman Wouk, *This Is My God* (New York, 1959, reissued in a paperbound edition).

(Chapter 20.) Books on architecture have the advantage of being magnificently illustrated, the disadvantage of rarely being available in inexpensive editions. Most larger libraries, however, will have such recent volumes as the following: Albert Christ-Janer and Mary Mix Foley, *Modern Church Architecture* (New York, 1962); John Knox Shear, *Religious Buildings for Today* (New York, 1957); Peter Hammond, *Liturgy and Architecture,* (New York, 1961); and Rachel Wischnitzer, *Synagogue Architecture in the United States* (Philadelphia, 1955). Closely related subjects are ably discussed in Finley Eversole, *Christian Faith and the Contemporary Arts* (Nashville, 1962); and in William C. Rice, *A Concise History of Church Music* (Nashville, 1964).

PART V   THIS NATION UNDER GOD:
AT WORK

(Chapter 21.) On war and peace, see Rufus Jones (ed.), *The Church, the Gospel and War* (New York, 1948); Reinhold Niebuhr, *Christianity and Power Politics* (New York, 1940); and Donald Keys (ed.), *God and the H-Bomb* (New York, 1961). These and other critical issues of the interwar period are discussed in Robert M. Miller, *American Protestantism and Social Issues* (Chapel Hill [N.C.], 1958). The economic depression can perhaps be best approached through John Steinbeck's classic, *The Grapes of Wrath* (New York, 1939, available in several recent editions). Another kind of economic struggle is described in Abraham Cahan's *Rise of David Levinsky* (New York, 1917, 1960*). See also John A. Ryan,

Social Doctrine in Action (New York, 1941). Within the abundant litera-
ture on the racial revolution, the writings of some of the principal participants deserve first attention. See for example, Martin Luther King's *Stride
Toward Freedom* (New York, 1958, 1964*) as well as his *Why We Can't
Wait* (New York, 1964*). Also James Baldwin's less hopeful *The Fire
Next Time* (New York, 1963*) should be read along with Louis Lomax's
The Negro Revolt (New York, 1962, 1963*). On all the social and political issues, including race, that confront contemporary America, thoughtful
and up-to-date analyses are available from such organizations as the Na-
tional Council of Churches of Christ (New York City), the National Cath-
olic Welfare Conference (Washington, D.C.), and B'nai B'rith (Washington, D.C.) or its Anti-Defamation League (New York City). On the successful and fast-selling aspects of American religion, see Martin E. Marty,
The New Shape of American Religion (New York, 1959); Peter L.
Berger, *The Noise of Solemn Assemblies* (New York, 1961*); Walter J.
Ong, S.J., *American Catholic Crossroads* (New York, 1958, 1962*); and
Will Herberg, *Protestant-Catholic-Jew* (New York, [rev. ed.] 1960*).

(Chapter 22.) The mission abroad is extensively discussed in the multivolume works of Kenneth Scott Latourette noted above (and see the bib-
liographies therein); two of his briefer works are *Missions Tomorrow*
(New York, 1936) and *Toward a World Christian Fellowship* (New York,
1938). See also Henry P. Van Dusen, *For the Healing of the Nations*
(New York, 1940); Robert B. Considine, *The Maryknoll Story* (New
York, 1950); and an up-to-date world view by Stephen Neill in *A History
of Christian Missions* (Baltimore, 1964*). The involvement of American
Jews in rescue and relief is illustrated in Albert Vorspan's biographical
treatment, *Giants of Justice* (New York, 1960). The deliberations of the
World Council of Churches in its First Assembly in Amsterdam are covered in *Man's Disorder and God's Design* (New York, 1949). The full
history of Vatican II is yet to come, but engaging interim reports are
Xavier Rynne (pseud.), *Letters from Vatican City* (New York, 1963,
1964*); and Robert McAfee Brown, *Observer in Rome* (New York,
1964).

(Chapter 23.) So intense have the discussions about religion and educa-
tion recently become that any listing of sources will quickly be out of date.
Good background is available, however, in Neil G. McCluskey, S.J., *Cath-
olic Viewpoint on Education* (New York, [rev. ed.] 1962*); in Robert
Gordis *et al., Religion and the Schools* (Santa Barbara, 1959*); and in
Will Herberg's essay printed in *Religious Perspectives in American Culture*
(noted in the introductory section above). In *The Church and the Four-
Year College* (New York, 1955), Guy E. Snavely provides a useful review
of the founding of many of the nation's schools. Lewis Bliss Whittemore in
The Church and Secular Education (Greenwich [Conn.], 1960) argues
for a more prominent role of religion in education. More specialized but

not difficult are the essays in A. L. Sebaly (ed.), *Teacher Education and Religion* (Oneonta [N. Y.], 1959). Some of the dialogue within the Catholic community is evident in Mary Perkins Ryan, *Are Parochial Schools the Answer?* (New York, 1964*). And certainly one should read the full text of recent Supreme Court decisions in the area of religion and education; as a starter, see Joseph Tussman, *The Supreme Court on Church and State* (New York, 1962*).

(Chapter 24.) Most of the better writing on religion and democracy is to be found in pamphlets and articles rather than in book-length treatments. The Center for the Study of Democratic Institutions in Santa Barbara, California, has issued three relevant and provocative pamphlets: *Religion and the Free Society* (1958*), *The Churches and the Public* (1960*), and *Religion and American Society* (1961*). In Princeton's *The Shaping of American Religion* volume (already cited) Richard Niebuhr's essay, "The Protestant Movement and Democracy in the United States," is of high order. And in Sidney Mead's *The Lively Experiment* (already cited), the chapter on Abraham Lincoln—"The American Dream of Destiny and Democracy"—is indispensable. A broad spectrum of views—by quite able people—is available in John Cogley (ed.), *Religion in America* (New York, 1958*).

In recent years there have been several efforts to describe the prevailing consensus of the civil religion in America. Note particularly these works: Elwyn A. Smith, ed., *The Religion of the Republic* (Philadelphia, 1971); Conrad Cherry, ed., *God's New Israel: Religious Interpretations of American Destiny* (Englewood Cliffs, 1971*); Winthrop S. Hudson, ed., *Nationalism and Religion in America: Concepts of American Identity and Mission* (New York, 1970*); and Robert T. Handy, *A Christian America: Protestant Hopes and Historical Realities* (New York, 1971).

Index

(Italicized page numbers refer to a quotation, while boldface numerals indicate an illustration.)

418 – INDEX

Methodists, origin and development, 144, **147**; in the West, 168; attitudes toward slavery, 188, *188-189, 197;* social action, **250**; mission abroad, **351, 362, 365**; colleges, **75, 382**

Michaëlius, Jonas, 80-81

Middle Colonies, diversity in, 80; settlement of, 80-99. *See* individual colonies

Millennialism, 151-152

Miller, Arthur, *266*

Miller, Perry, 141

Miller, Samuel H., *322*

Miller, William, 151, *152*

Minuit, Peter, 80, 83

Missions, to America, 13, 14, 15, 18-22, 24, *28,* 29-31, 33-34; in America, 165, 167, 168-169, 324-328, 333-334, 334-335; from America, 172-173, 175, 177, 333, 349-350, **351, 352**, 353, **354**, 355-356, **359**, 360, **361, 362, 363, 367**

Missions, Spanish, **16**, *163*, **164**; Buddhist, *174*

Monk, Maria, 209

Moody, Dwight L., early career, 228; Sunday School, **229**; as revivalist, 230; reformer, *228, 230,* 230-231

Morais, Sabato, 224

Morality, 257-258

Moravians, in Pennsylvania, *96;* in Georgia, 107; in North Carolina, 107, **109**, 110; weekly worship, **287**

Mormons, origin and migration, 136, 138; **137**; colonization efforts, 171

Mott, John R., *350, 352*

Mott, Lucretia, 79

Mühlenberg, Heinrich, 94-95, *94 f.*

Murray, John Courtney, 334, *388*

Naismith, James, 234, 236

Narváez, Pánfilo de, 11

National Catholic Welfare Conference, 251, 252, *253 f.*, 334, 356

National Council of Churches, 333

National Origins Act, 217

Nativism, rise of, 208; against the Catholic, *208 f.*, 209, **210**, 211-213, 214; against the Oriental, 214; against the Jew, 214, 216; and World War I, 217

Negro, revolt in Haiti, 182; and slavery, 191; education of, 198, **199**, 200; and civil rights, 340-346, **342, 343**

New Amsterdam, *81, 87*

New Jersey, Dutch in, 87; Presbyterians in, 88; Great Awakening, 88-89, *89;* Rutgers established, 89-91; Quakers in, 91; synagogue in, **315**

New Sweden, 83-84

New York, Anglicanism in, 84-85; Columbia University established, *85;* Ger-

man migration to, 86; Jews enter, 86-87; immigration in nineteenth century, **203, 204, 205, 222, 223**; social action in, 241, 247; Jewish Centers, **250, 310**

Nicholson, Francis, 76

Niebuhr, Reinhold, idealism and realism of, 277; warns against self-deception, *277 f.;* on man's nature, 278, 279; on democracy and religion, *278-279,* 280, **281;** on Protestant architecture, *306 f.*

Niebuhr, H. Richard, *391*

Noyes, John Humphrey, 134

Nuclear Test Ban Treaty, 334

Oberlin College, 183, *183 f.*

O'Connor, Edwin, 270

Oglethorpe, James, 104, 105, 107

Oneida Community, 134 f.

Order of the Star-Spangled Banner, *213*

Oregon, 157, 158, 160

Oxnam, G. Bromley, **250**

Pacifism, *326 f.*, 327, 328

Padilla, Juan de, 12-13

Paine, Thomas, 120, 122, 123

Palmer, B. M., 188

Parkhurst, C. H., **247**, 251

Parks, Rosa, 341, 345

Passover, **291**, *295, 299*, 301

Pastorius, Francis Daniel, 95

Paton, Alan, *371*

Peabody Education Fund, 198

Peace movements, 324

Peale, Norman Vincent, *347*

Peck, John Mason, *165, 167, 189 f.*

Penn, William, in England, 91; in Pennsylvania, *92;* toleration 92-93; vision thwarted, 94

Pennsylvania, Quakers in, 92-94; German migration to, 94, 95, 96; Scotch-Irish in, 96-97; Westward move, *97;* Jews in Philadelphia, 98; diversity, 99; Russian Orthodox, **215;** Summer Institute, *375*

Perfectionism, 149

Perez, Juan, 5

Philanthropy, 232, 234

Phillips, Wendell, *183,* 191

Phips, William, 58

Pietism, 145

Pilgrims, 47-49, **48**

Plymouth Company, 37

Pocahontas, 38, **39**, *40*

Polish National Catholic Church, 218

Polk, James K., 160, 161

Pope, Alexander VI, *8;* Paul III, *12;* Leo XIII, 244, 261, *261 f.*, 262; Pius XI, 144, 334, *335;* Pius XII, *262;* John XXIII, *328,* 370; Paul VI, *370 f.*, 401

Popery, fear of, 112, 117, *118,* 210